Foundation Flash MX

Kristian Besley
Sham Bhangal
Amanda Farr

friendsof

DESIGNER TO DESIGNER™

Foundation Flash MX

© 2002 friends of ED

First printed April 2002
Reprinted June 2002

Trademark Acknowledgements

Published by **friends of ED**
30 – 32 Lincoln Road, Olton, Birmingham,
B27 6PA, UK.

Printed in USA.

ISBN 1-903450-10-1

Foundation Flash MX

Credits

Authors
Kristian Besley
Sham Bhangal
Amanda Farr

Technical Reviewers
Chris Andrade
Sally Cruikshank
Hoss Gifford
Steve McCormick
Mike Pearce
Jake Smith

Proof Readers
Jon Bounds
Andy Corsham
Jason Cuthbert
Vicky Idiens

Managing Editor
Mel Orgee

Commissioning Editor
Andy Corsham

Technical Editors
Dan Britton
James Robinson
Gavin Wray

Author Agent
Gaynor Riopedre

Project Manager
Vicky Idiens

Graphic Editors
Matt Clark
Chantal Hepworth
Will Fallon

Indexer
Simon Collins

Cover Design
Katy Freer

Kristian Besley   **www.graphci.com**

Kristian was born in Wales, grew up in the same street as Catherine Zeta Jones, and read Media Arts following interests in film and design. To this day his love of all things lo-fi is extended to the graphci web site. In his lack of spare time, you'll most likely find him pushing Flash's duplicateMovieClip command to the limit, playing the guitar like a bass, or reminiscing about how nothing will ever be as good as the Spectrum 48k. One day he vows to reform the Sigmund Freud Quartet musical combo.

Hands in the air for Lou, Bink, Cof, Pete "3D" and the editorial massive.

Blow your whistle for Mam, Dad and Karl.

Keep it real.

Sham Bhangal

Sham Bhangal originally started his career as an engineer specializing in industrial computer-based display and control systems. In his spare time he took up freelance web design, a hobby that grew slowly until it became his main career. He now writes extensively for friends of ED and is engaged in all aspects of web design. Sham lives in rural Somerset with his partner Karen.

Amanda Farr

I have been doing professional web development since 1995 and using Flash since Flash 3 when I began Virtual-FX.net Flash Developer's Resource. I've also spoken at Flashforward2001 and have had great opportunities to enjoy the Flash community very much.

Thanks to Seth & Ellen putting up with me stressin' while working full time, developing our shopping cart at home, doing freelance work, writing the book and still trying to have some fun in my spare 20 minutes.

06   Motion Tweening   203

07   Shape Tweening   231

08   Masks and Masking   253

13 Publishing 431

14 Intermediate ActionScript, Part 1 461

Appendicies

A Sound Sampling   569

B HTML and Flash   575

C Glossary   583

Index   589

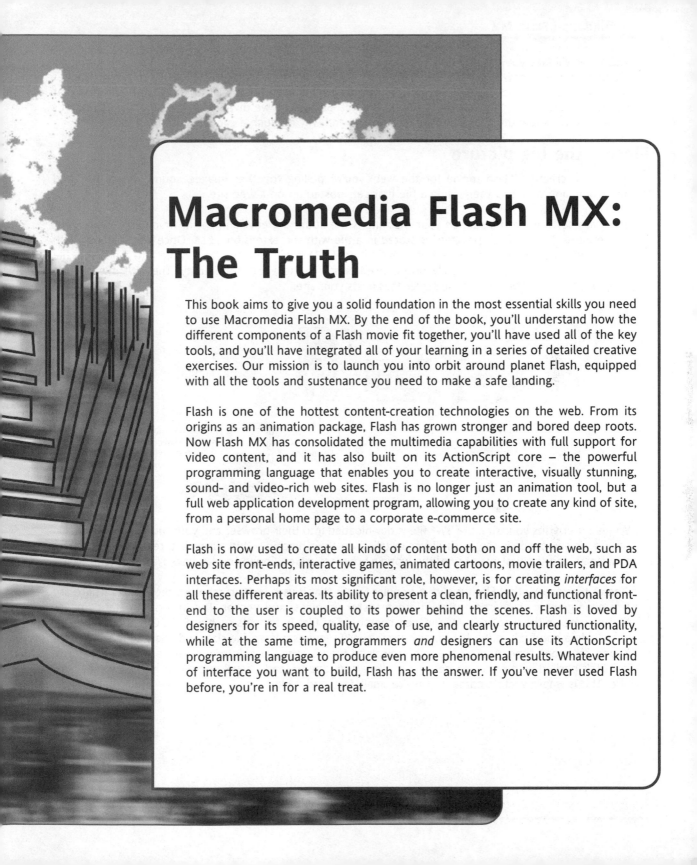

Macromedia Flash MX: The Truth

This book aims to give you a solid foundation in the most essential skills you need to use Macromedia Flash MX. By the end of the book, you'll understand how the different components of a Flash movie fit together, you'll have used all of the key tools, and you'll have integrated all of your learning in a series of detailed creative exercises. Our mission is to launch you into orbit around planet Flash, equipped with all the tools and sustenance you need to make a safe landing.

Flash is one of the hottest content-creation technologies on the web. From its origins as an animation package, Flash has grown stronger and bored deep roots. Now Flash MX has consolidated the multimedia capabilities with full support for video content, and it has also built on its ActionScript core – the powerful programming language that enables you to create interactive, visually stunning, sound- and video-rich web sites. Flash is no longer just an animation tool, but a full web application development program, allowing you to create any kind of site, from a personal home page to a corporate e-commerce site.

Flash is now used to create all kinds of content both on and off the web, such as web site front-ends, interactive games, animated cartoons, movie trailers, and PDA interfaces. Perhaps its most significant role, however, is for creating *interfaces* for all these different areas. Its ability to present a clean, friendly, and functional front-end to the user is coupled to its power behind the scenes. Flash is loved by designers for its speed, quality, ease of use, and clearly structured functionality, while at the same time, programmers *and* designers can use its ActionScript programming language to produce even more phenomenal results. Whatever kind of interface you want to build, Flash has the answer. If you've never used Flash before, you're in for a real treat.

This book will take you, step by step, through every aspect of designing your own Flash interface, gradually building up your knowledge and skills with each chapter. We'll also look at the pitfalls and practicalities that every web designer faces and teach you how to make your designs 'web friendly', also ensuring that you know how to get your hard work up on the net. But before we dive into these complex issues, let's make sure we know the basics of how Flash works, and why it's such a capable authoring tool.

Flash – the big picture

When you create a Flash movie for the web, you're pulling together images, sound, video, text and animation, and bundling them up in a file that gets posted up on a web site.

The Flash software you install on your machine is the authoring environment in which you create your masterpiece. The 'work in progress' is stored in a file with the extension `.fla`. Once you're happy with your movie and you want to publish it to the Internet, Flash will convert the FLA file into a playable file with the extension `.swf` – usually pronounced 'swiff' in the Flash community. The SWF file is then embedded in an HTML file on the server that hosts your site:

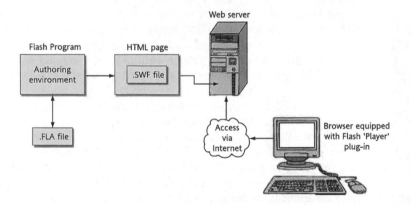

When a user visits your site, the SWF file is downloaded into their browser and your movie is played back. All the viewer needs is the Flash Player installed on their machine: this player is a reasonably compact download, and the vast majority of the world's browsers are equipped to play back Flash content.

One of the reasons that Flash is such a popular tool is that it uses **vector graphics** technology. There are two main graphic standards on the Internet: **raster** (bitmaps) and **vector**. The majority of static images that you see on the web are raster images, composed of files in formats such as BMP, GIF, and JPG. Raster images do a good job, but a big raster image usually requires a large file size, and a large file size means a long download time. And on the web, download time is *everything*. Internet users are fickle creatures: if a site's packed with raster images and is taking too long to load, they'll just skip it and go somewhere else. This is where vectors come in. They're small, fast, and funky.

> *Vector images describe the image in terms of coordinates and mathematical transformations, which sounds complicated, but really is as simple as saying, 'put a dot here, put a dot there, and draw a line between them'. This compares with the raster technique of describing the color and position of every single pixel in the image.*

Vector graphic files are much more compact and efficient compared to rasters, and Flash is the main tool for delivering vector graphics and vector-based animations on the web. The files that Flash creates are therefore comparatively small, which is one of the factors behind Flash's success. A well-constructed Flash file will also **stream** onto the user's computer: this means that it will load the first part of the animation and start playing it back while the rest of the animation loads in the background. Streaming a file correctly is an important technique for a Flash designer, as it means that a visitor to their site is presented with something visual and enticing as soon as they enter it – removing the danger that they'll get bored and go elsewhere as they wait for the site to download.

Another disadvantage of raster images is that they're *display dependent*, meaning that if you create them to look just right on one particular display, your image could come out significantly altered if someone is using a display resolution that's different to yours. Another factor is that if you *zoom in* on a raster image, the pixels just get bigger and bigger until you end up with a screen full of squares of color that are completely unrecognizable as the source image. Vector images, in contrast, can work independently of the display because they just say 'I want a line from this point on the screen to that point on the screen' and the line will always be the same relative length and clarity, no matter what resolution you view the picture at. Also, no matter how far you zoom into a vector, the image will still stay crisp and at full resolution.

So why would you ever want to use a raster? Well, raster formats are good for images with thousands of different colors. Can you imagine trying to describe a photograph in terms of vectors? It would be horribly complicated, and have a far bigger file size than the raster equivalent. Luckily, Flash makes the most of both worlds: the vast majority of its drawings and animations are vector-based, but when that extra richness that you can only get with a raster is needed, Flash will allow you to import a bitmap and use it in conjunction with the dominant vectors.

What's significant about Macromedia Flash MX?

If you've used a previous version of Flash, the first thing that you'll notice when you open up the program is that the basic interface has changed. Macromedia has implemented a more familiar interface and work environment to make learning a new application that little bit easier. The main addition is the Property inspector, a context-sensitive panel that acts as a central information resource and tool options area, and which is context-sensitive to any selected object on the stage. In conjunction with collapsible panels, timeline layer folders, and a fully customizable interface, this much-improved authoring environment means that Flash MX is more user-friendly and accessible for beginners learning the program, and it also increases the workflow and productivity of more experienced designers.

One of the most significant new enhancements for designers is the ability to import any standard video file format into your Flash movie and manipulate it just as you would any other shape or image. You can apply Flash's drawing tools and ActionScript to this video content, allowing you to create truly interactive multimedia web sites – entirely in Flash.

Flash MX has also built upon its core scripting capability that came of age with Flash 5 – a hugely powerful but easy to use programming language called **ActionScript**. Flash ActionScript is a deep and professional tool that allows you to add mind-blowing effects to your sites but keep that minimal file size. You can use ActionScript to program flexibility and complexity into your Flash web sites and to pass information backwards and forwards between the movie and the web server with greater ease.

You can now use ActionScript to dynamically load MP3 and JPG files directly into the Flash Player, meaning that you can incorporate rich media content into your web site and still keep the user's download time to a minimum as the large video and sound files are not included in the final SWF.

This may sound quite complicated for the novice user but there's no reason to be intimidated by it. Although you're taking your first tentative Flash steps, by the end of this book you'll have used ActionScript to produce an interactive web site with content that's rich and dynamic. While ActionScript is far too big a topic for us to cover definitively in a book of this size and scope, you'll learn the essentials of using ActionScript in four dedicated chapters which will allow you to build your knowledge as you explore Flash further. As ever, we're aiming to give you an accessible, secure foundation.

Our aims and philosophy in this book

As its title suggests, the aim of this book is to give you a solid, extensible foundation in Flash design, implementation, and programming. We believe that Flash is too complex a tool to cover definitively from scratch in 1000 pages, let alone 700. We're aiming to provide a rock-steady foundation: not a trivial overview of each and every feature of the interface and the package, but an in-depth treatment of the core aspects of using Flash MX.

We believe in creating a reliable foundation, enabling you to understand Flash more fully and absorb and internalize the material we cover. We're not going to list every menu option and cover every single ActionScript command in immense detail: we're going to concentrate on the real core of learning Flash successfully, taking you from a zero knowledge of Flash through to being able to put up a web site you can be proud of.

Everyone knows that the best way to learn is to play and practice. It's no good someone just *telling* you what to do – to master Flash, you have to *use* it. This book follows that philosophy by providing examples and tutorials in every chapter, and on every topic we cover. It's another well-known fact that although small examples are fun and they do help you learn, it's difficult to go away and apply those examples in the real world when you've finished the book. So, at the end of each chapter you'll be able to apply the things you've just learned to the **case study project**. Each case study is a distilled vial of information that, chapter by chapter, will build into a complete and fully functional web site that you can use as your online portfolio (opposite):

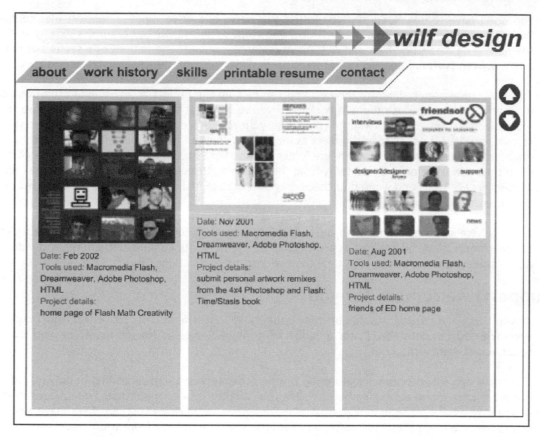

The web site you'll create has a full navigation menu, animated content, and will dynamically load in images and text files using ActionScript. As it's gradually created, this real world example will reinforce the core skills you learn in this book.

We believe that by learning the Flash skills you need, in context, you'll build the knowledge and mental adaptability to fit your expanding knowledge and specialization into a structured and reliable framework.

How to use this book

To use this book, all you'll need is a copy of Macromedia Flash MX and a computer to run it on. If you want to publish your Flash movies onto the Internet, you'll also need a connection and some web space to publish them to. Your Internet Service Provider (ISP) will be able to sort this out for you if you have any problems.

The case study you'll create contains an animated introduction, interactive buttons, examples of dynamic masking using ActionScript, and will be fully optimized for publishing to the web. Its modular nature means that you can easily go back and find the specific functionality that you're looking for and modify it or replace it with something completely different. If you want to use the buttons in a different web site, for example, or any of the animated effects, you can easily flip to the relevant chapter for a recap on how to do it, and then just pull the desired part out of the one movie and incorporate it in the other.

You don't have to download anything to use this book, but we've supplied support files containing the sounds and images that we've used to allow you to recreate the worked examples exactly as they are in the book. The case study files, and all support material, can be found in the **Code** section of our web site at **www.friendsofed.com**. We'll point you at the relevant files in the chapters as necessary.

The case study project files are there so you can pick up the project at any stage in the book and work through it, or you can use them as backups if you've lost your files and don't want to have to recreate them all again. You may just want to check that your results are the same as ours. The files are arranged so that you have a pre-prepared project as input for a chapter: for example, if you wanted to start from Chapter 5, you'd go into the appropriate folder and use the `for chapter5.fla` file, which would contain all of the work done on the case study from the beginning through to Chapter 4. If you'd just finished the Chapter 5 case study and wanted to check it against ours to make sure it looked right, you would use the `for chapter6.fla`.

We also have some optional sound and video files that can be downloaded if you want to try your hand at the compression material we cover in Chapter 11. These (uncompressed) sound and video files are quite large, and could take a long time to download on some connections.

Support: we're here for you

If you have any questions about the book or about friends of ED, check out our web site **www.friendsofed.com**: there are a range of contact e-mail addresses there, or you can just use **feedback@friendsofed.com**.

There are also a host of other features up on the site: interviews with renowned designers, samples from our other books, and a message board where you can post your own questions, discussions, and answers, or just take a back seat and look at what other designers are talking about. So, if you have any comments or problems, write us, it's what we're here for and we'd love to hear from you.

Layout conventions used in this book

We've tried to keep this book as clear and easy to follow as possible, so we've only used a few layout styles:

- When you first come across an important word it will be in **bold** type, then in normal type thereafter.

- We'll use a different font to emphasize `code` and `file names`. We'll also use this font when we want you to type in `some text`.

- Menu commands are written in the form **Menu > Sub-menu > Sub-menu**.

- When there's some information we think is really important, we'll highlight it like this:

> *This is very important stuff – don't skip it!*

- Worked exercises are laid out like this:

    1. Open up Flash.

    2. Start a new movie file, and save it as `TestMovie.fla`.

    3. Etc...

PCs and Macs

To keep the book as easy to read as possible, we've used PC commands as a default, so that every time you come across a mouse command you don't have to read something long-winded like, 'right-click on the PC or CTRL-click on the Mac'.

We've only written *both* instructions where there is a difference between the standard Mac substitute command, and the actual command required.

When we just say 'click' we mean *left*-click on the PC or simply *click* on the Mac. The common substitute commands are:

PC	Mac
- Right-click	- CTRL-click
- CTRL-click	- Apple-click
- CTRL-Z (to undo)	- Apple-Z
- CTRL-ENTER	- Apple-ENTER

OK, that's the preliminaries over: it's time to get down to work.

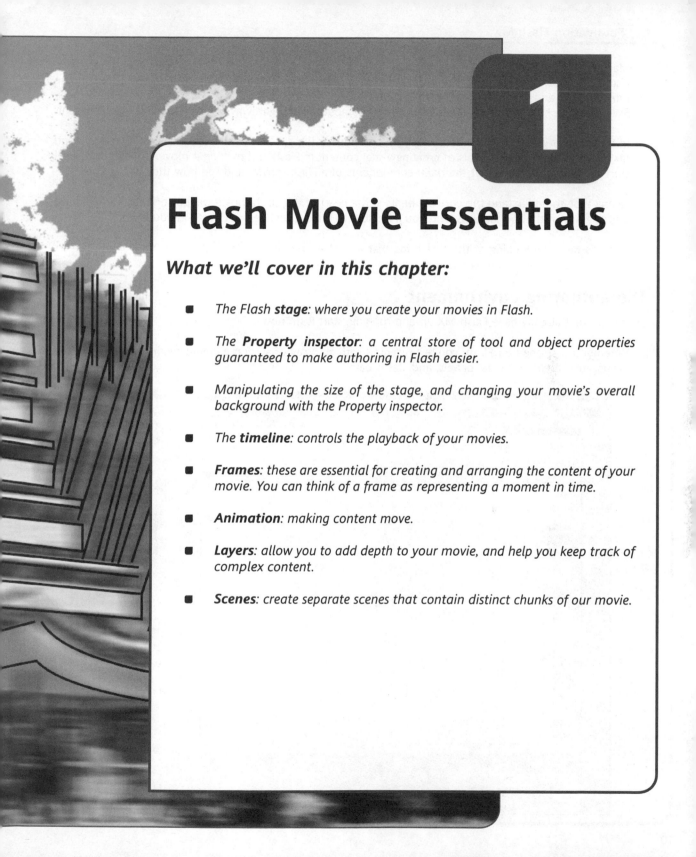

Flash Movie Essentials

What we'll cover in this chapter:

- The Flash **stage**: where you create your movies in Flash.

- The **Property inspector**: a central store of tool and object properties guaranteed to make authoring in Flash easier.

- Manipulating the size of the stage, and changing your movie's overall background with the Property inspector.

- The **timeline**: controls the playback of your movies.

- **Frames**: these are essential for creating and arranging the content of your movie. You can think of a frame as representing a moment in time.

- **Animation**: making content move.

- **Layers**: allow you to add depth to your movie, and help you keep track of complex content.

- **Scenes**: create separate scenes that contain distinct chunks of our movie.

Macromedia Flash MX is really two things; firstly, it's the standard file format for delivering interactive, visually-rich content and animation on the web – this is the SWF file format we talked about in the Introduction; and secondly, it's the actual authoring environment that lets you create and publish those SWF files. The Flash program you install on your computer is the gateway to state-of-the-art web content.

In this chapter we're going to introduce you to the authoring environment – the Flash MX interface – and take you through the essentials of creating visual content in Flash and making it move. In doing this, we'll start building up a picture of the main components of a Flash movie, and see how they fit together.

Taking time to understand the core elements at the heart of the Flash movie will pay off later – you'll have a firm grasp of the foundations, and you'll be able to build effectively on these as you learn.

So...let's begin by looking at the first thing that almost everybody wants to do when they open up their copy of Flash – create a movie and make interesting things happen on the screen.

The authoring environment

If you don't already have Flash MX up and running, start it up now.

When you first open up Flash, you're presented with an array of screen elements: icons, menus, content preparation areas, toolbars, panels, and status bars:

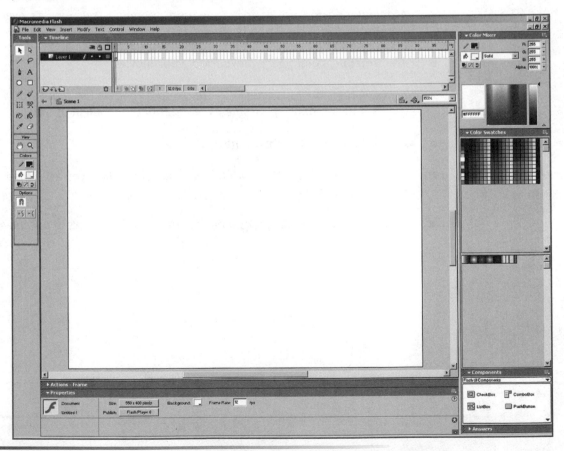

> *Don't worry if your screen doesn't look exactly like ours when you start up Flash: if you've already opened Flash up before and played around with it you'll doubtless have altered the setup in some way.*

This is the feature-rich authoring environment that lets you create your Flash movies and export them so that they can be published on the web and accessed by the adoring multitude. It's Flash's studio, workshop and test track combined.

If you've never used a Macromedia product before, you might be intimidated by the unfamiliar interface the first time you open Flash – don't be: before long you'll be navigating the interface with ease. And there's an added bonus to learning the Flash MX interface: Macromedia have a common interface across their software, so once you're familiar with Flash, you'll have no trouble finding your way around other Macromedia programs such as Fireworks or Dreamweaver.

There's a tremendous amount of detail and power tucked away in the Flash MX interface, and at first it can seem a little daunting if you're new to the software. To avoid the sense of clutter, and in order to 'turn down the volume' a little, let's clear some of the elements out of the way: that way, we can concentrate on the bare essentials for a moment (but don't worry, you won't be missing a thing – we'll be explaining all of the core features during the course of this book).

Configuring the authoring environment

1. First, let's minimize any palettes on screen. Minimize all of the palettes – called **panels** – on the right-hand side of the previous screenshot. You can do this by clicking your mouse on the white text at the top of each panel until all the panels are stacked up:

 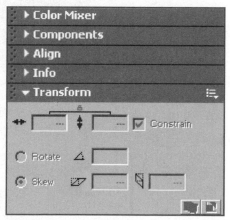

Floating panels are used to help you modify and manipulate the content of your Flash movie once you've created that content. This content could be graphic images, pieces of animation, text or any number of things – but you can use the panels (and menu options) to alter their characteristics and the way that they behave. All the panels are dockable; you can drag them around the screen and dock them to other panels if you choose. This lets you customize the authoring environment. Flash also provides some default layouts for the interface with the panels set up for a specific designer/developer interface (**Window > Panel Sets**) and you can even save your own layout (**Window > Save Panel Layout...**).

Draggable handle ⟶

You can think of any element you create in your movie (such as pictures or text) as a discrete object: each of these objects has its own attributes, such as color, transparency and size, and you can use the panels to change these attributes. Additionally, changing panel settings can also alter the way that an object behaves. We'll be looking at all of these aspects as we progress through the book. At the moment though, we don't actually have any content to work with, so let's move these panels out of the way for reasons of clarity:

2. Click on each of the panels' 'close' boxes, or choose the **Window > Close All Panels** menu option. Alternatively, pressing F4 will also close all panels, including the Tools panel. We'll come back to these panels later. Individual panels can be closed by right-clicking on the gray bar and choosing the **Close Panel** option, or choosing this option from the drop-down menu when the panel is maximized:

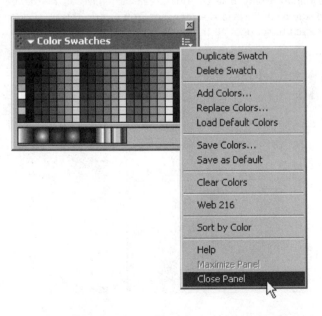

Next, we want to make sure that we can see all of the area where we're going to create the visual content in our Flash movie:

3. Click on the **Magnification** drop-down list box near the top right of the screen below the timeline...

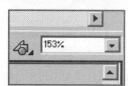

4. ...and choose the **Show Frame** option:

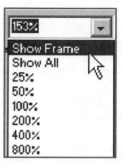

Notice that the white area in the center of the screen is now visible in its entirety:

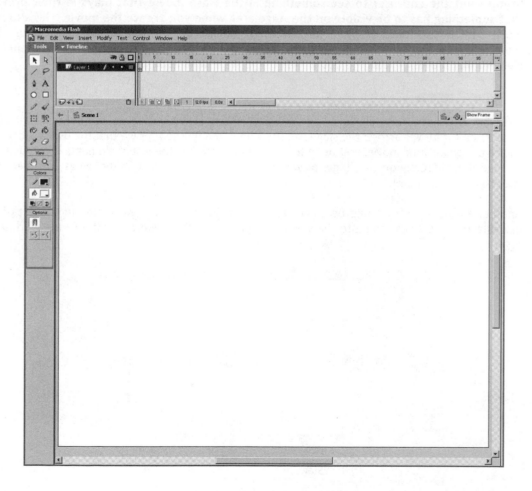

This white area is called the **stage**, and it's where all the action in your movie takes place. The gray area around the stage is called the **work area**. Let's talk about these different areas a little.

The stage

The stage can be likened to what a movie director can see in the viewfinder of a movie camera: what you see in the viewfinder is what will appear in the movie that the viewer watches in the theater. In the motion picture world, you can have action taking place on the film set (stage), and you can have actors waiting off stage, ready to make their entry and come into shot.

At different times in the movie, different people and objects will be visible on the stage and, consequently, 'in shot'. The stage in Flash works on the same principle: at any given point in your Flash movie, the things that are on the stage are what the viewer will see when the movie is rendered in their browser. Another thing to consider is that the movie set can be much larger than the camera's field of view, and the camera can move around and seek out previously hidden corners.

If you want the end user to see something in the Flash movie that plays in their browser, then that something has to be visible on the stage area when you create the movie. This also means that movie content can move onto the stage from the 'wings': for example, an animated actor could enter stage left, walk across the stage, and exit stage right. In the Flash authoring environment, any visual element that moves beyond the boundaries of the stage winds up in the **work area**.

The work area

The work area surrounds the stage. You can place content in the work area, but only content that actually appears on (or moves across) the stage will show up in the finished movie that the user watches. So, when you're designing your movie, you need to think about whether the visual elements it contains will spring into existence directly on the stage, or whether they're going to wait in the wings and then move onto the stage at some point.

Another example of this would be a car that starts its journey in the work area to the left of the stage, moves across the stage (and into the viewer's sight), and then accelerates off into the work area on the right:

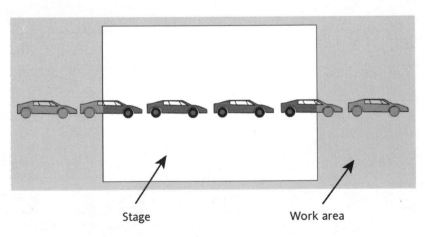

Stage   Work area

While the content is on the stage, the viewer sees it in the browser. When it's 'in the wings', it's invisible to the viewer.

What we've done so far is use the Magnification box to change our view of the stage **in the authoring environment**. Any changes we make by zooming in and out and making the stage look bigger or smaller in the authoring environment will **not** be applied to the finished movie seen by the end user. These magnification changes are just to help us see things more clearly when we're creating and modifying our movie.

To alter the size and proportions of our finished movie once it's displayed in the user's browser, we need to change the **properties** of the stage itself. Flash MX has a new resource that will enable us to do that easily. It's called the **Property inspector** and we'll take a quick look at that now.

The Property inspector

The Property inspector is a new feature in Flash MX and was introduced to make using Flash a whole lot easier. With the Property inspector, we can easily manipulate all of our movie's contents from one place. We'll be using it frequently throughout this book and it'll come to be your best friend when creating movies in Flash MX.

By default, the Property inspector is positioned at the bottom-center of the screen, although you might have closed it just now if you chose to close all panels with the **Window > Close All Panels** menu option or if you pressed F4. If you don't already have it open, you can access it with the **Window > Properties** menu option, or by right-clicking on the stage and selecting **Properties** from the context-sensitive menu. Alternatively, you can press CTRL+F3.

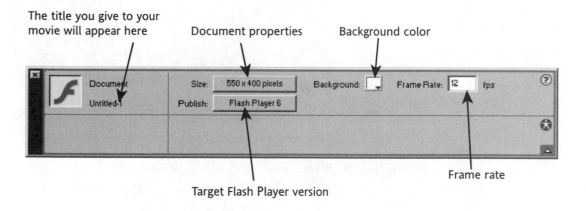

The title you give to your movie will appear here   Document properties   Background color

Target Flash Player version   Frame rate

We don't have any content on our stage yet, so this is how you'll first see the Property inspector.

The Property inspector is split into two parts: upper and lower sections. We'll see in the next chapter that when using items from the Tools panel, the upper section has properties related specifically to that tool, while the lower section is related to an actual item you have selected in your work area. The lower section can be opened and closed using the arrow in the bottom-right corner.

Let's move on to see how we can use the Property inspector even though we have no content on our stage yet.

Changing the size of the stage

When you're planning your Flash movie, you should consider how much browser real estate you want the finished movie to take up – you'll need to decide what size you want the movie's window to be, based on factors such as what kind of content you're displaying, what else will appear alongside the movie in the host page, and so on. When you've made that size decision, you can alter the size of the stage to match your plan.

You can view the stage's current dimensions and global characteristics by clicking on the **Size** button in the Property inspector. This opens up the **Document Properties** dialog box, from where you make global changes to the **properties** (or *characteristics*) that affect the whole movie:

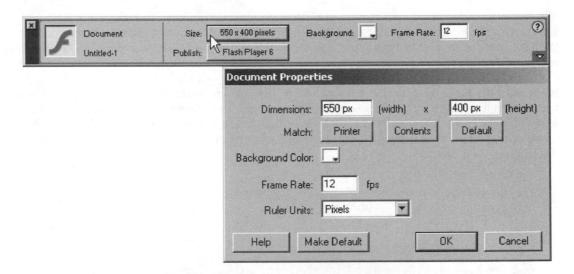

> *You can also bring up the* **Document Properties** *dialog box using the* **Modify > Document** *menu option or by right-clicking on the stage and selecting* **Document Properties...** *from the context-sensitive menu.*

You can see here that the default dimensions of the stage are 550 pixels wide by 400 pixels high. When you change the dimensions of your stage, Flash will always measure them from the top left-hand corner. For example, if you change the width of your movie to be 600 pixels and the height to be 450 pixels, Flash will simply add another 50 pixels to the right-hand side of the stage, and 50 to the bottom:

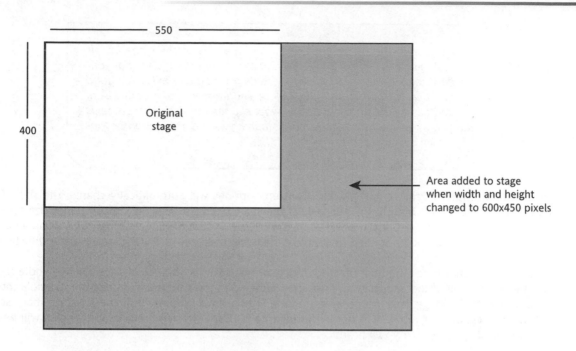

550

400

Original
stage

Area added to stage
when width and height
changed to 600x450 pixels

If your brain doesn't translate pixel-speak too easily, you can always change the units of measurement that Flash uses throughout the entire movie by picking a different option from the **Ruler Units** drop-down box:

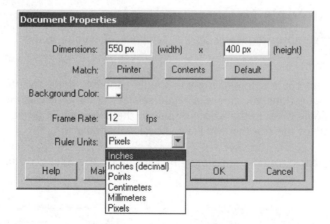

Whichever option you choose here will be applied across this whole movie until you change it to be something different.

*Remember that when you set the **Dimensions** of the stage in this dialog box, you are directly affecting the size of the window that your Flash movie will be displayed in inside the user's browser. It's good practice to think about this before you start creating your visual content on the stage. You can always change the size of the stage as and when you like, but the more planning you do, the smoother your movie creation process is likely to be!*

Note that the **Match: Printer** and **Match: Contents** options will automatically change the size of the stage if you select them: **Match: Printer** will set the stage size to reflect the default paper size for your default printer, and **Match: Contents** will change the stage so that it's large enough to contain all of the content elements that you've created (even those that spill over into the work area outside the stage).

As you can see, there are a number of other global properties that you can change for the whole movie: we'll be covering all of the important ones as they come up in the course of building our example movies in this book. At this stage, let's just observe that the **Frame Rate** property influences the playback speed and smoothness of your movie. The default frame rate is 12 fps (**frames per second**), which will be fine for most of the movies that you'll produce.

The next movie property we want to concentrate on here is the **Background Color** option. This is the option that you use to change the overall background color your movie has when it's rendered in the user's browser.

Changing the movie's background color

Probably one of the most frequently asked beginner questions in Flash is: 'how do I change the background color?'

Again, the background color is something you should probably think about when you're *planning* your movie. The kind of questions you might ask yourself are: What size will the display window be in the browser? Will the movie take up the whole display in the browser? Do I need to stick to a color scheme that matches the rest of the site that my Flash movie will appear in?

You can change the background color simply by clicking on the **Background Color** box in the Property inspector...

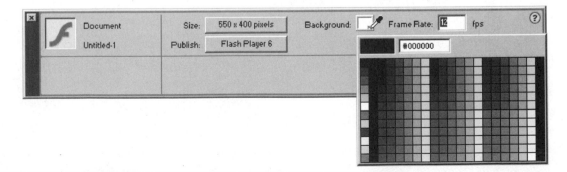

...and selecting a color of your choice. The only drawback is that the movie has to be the same color **throughout the entire movie**. You can't change the color in different parts of the movie.

Another thing you need to think about in this context is the background color of the web page that your movie will appear in. If your finished movie is embedded in an HTML page, the choice you make for the background color of the movie is important. By default, Flash will take the background movie color you specify here and use it as the background color of the HTML page that your movie appears in.

> *There are a number of different options that you can use when you're exporting your finished movie for publishing on the web. We'll talk about the built-in publishing features of Flash in more depth later in this book.*

For now, let's start on a little movie project that we'll be working on over the next couple of chapters: this will be a simple movie that'll get you practicing your Flash skills – and it'll also give you the chance to start expressing your creativity in the Flash authoring environment.

The movie background at midnight

Our test movie is set at night. The cicadas are doing their thing, there's a cool breeze, the moon is up, and there's the faint aroma of fresh mushrooms rising from our garden mushroom patch. We're going to start creating that scene inside of Flash.

The background for our little movie scenario is going to be the night sky, so we need to choose a suitable background color to reflect that.

1. If you don't already have it open, go into the Property inspector (Window > Properties or press CTRL+F3). Knowing that mushrooms only grow while we're asleep, select a deep midnight blue from the Color box in the Property inspector:

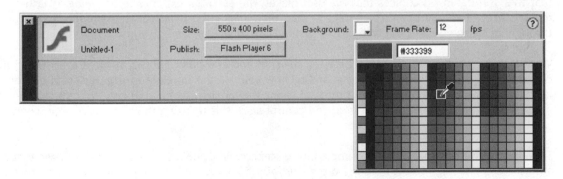

2.   Clicking on your chosen color will adjust the color of the stage accordingly. You'll notice that when you move the cursor over each color, its identity is displayed using a '**#**' followed by a **hexadecimal** value (made up of numbers and letters). These hexadecimal (hex) values are the same ones that people use when writing HTML web pages, and each combination of numbers and letters represent a unique, universally recognized color. This makes it very easy for you to match your background and host web page colors if you want to.

Saving global movie settings

The values you set for this particular movie in the Property inspector are saved automatically. If you want these settings to be applied to **all** of your Flash movies, go to the **Document Properties** box (**Modify > Document** or press CTRL+J) and click on the **Make Default** button: Flash will then assume that you want to use these settings whenever you subsequently create a new movie. You can obviously change these default settings as and when you need to.

Having set the global properties for our movie, the next step is to start creating some content. We're going to do that here by walking through a basic creation/modification/animation scenario in the context of our night time movie: this will familiarize you with some essential techniques and give you the chance to stretch those creative muscles.

In introducing you to the creation/modification/animation process, we need to talk about two absolutely critical features of the Flash authoring environment: the **timeline**, and **frames**.

The timeline

The **timeline** is one of the most important parts of the Flash interface, and one of the most important things to understand as you learn Flash.

When a web surfer visits your site and your movie starts to play, Flash 'interrogates' the timeline encoded in the SWF file and 'reads off' what should be displayed in the user's browser. The relationship between your movie's content and the timeline is absolutely vital in coordinating the end effect that the viewer sees.

You've already seen that the Flash stage has height and width: the Flash movie also has another critical dimension – **time**. Although Flash movies can have a high degree of user interaction and change the way that they run based on choices that the user makes, the essential experience of seeing a Flash movie is that it **starts** when you open a web page or click on a link, and it **finishes** when the movie has run right through, or when you exit the web page that the Flash movie lives in.

What the user sees in their browser between the start and end points of the movie is determined by the **content** that you create in your movie, and by how you use the timeline to **organize** that content. The length of your movie's timeline will control how long the movie runs for, and how content changes in the movie over time. As the movie's author, you control all of this by using the Flash timeline in conjunction with the content you create.

To help you visualize this, picture a simple movie scenario: imagine a time-lapse nature movie that shows a mushroom growing in slow motion. At the *start* of the movie, you'd have the tiny head of a mushroom poking up from the soil, and at the *end* of the movie, you'd see a full-grown mushroom, standing tall above the grass:

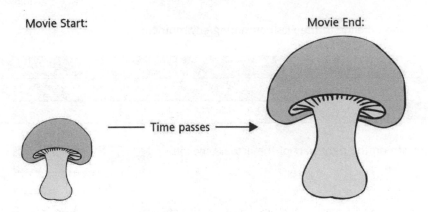

Movie Start:

Movie End:

Time passes

Clearly, your movie won't just consist of those two images, and your movie won't just jump from 'tiny stalk' to 'fully grown' instantaneously: in between the two points, time passes, and your mushroom moves through the intermediate stages of growth until it attains its full-grown state. In between the start and end-points of the time-lapse movie will be a whole series of images that represent the mushroom at the different stages of its development:

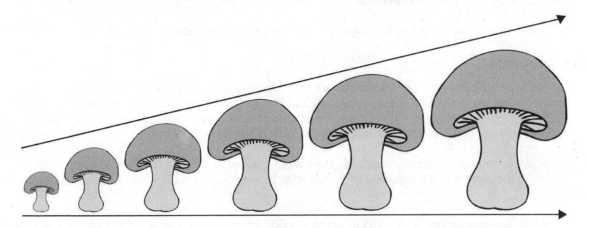

In the real world, mushrooms have a natural growth rate, which is determined by mushroom DNA or by divine guidance (depending on who you ask). In a Flash movie, you have to *imitate* the effect of time passing – and that's where the timeline comes in: to create the effect of time passing, you need a start point, an end point, and some space in between that represents the passage of time. The timeline lets you do this, and gives you complete control over the length of your movie, the speed that it plays at, and what you see on the screen at each point in time. How? By using **frames**.

Frames

Take a look at the timeline in the Flash authoring environment:

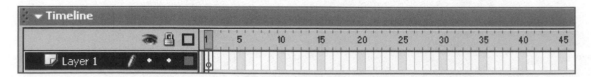

Now concentrate on the right part of the actual timeline:

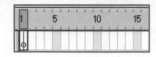

You can see that the top part of the timeline (the all-gray part) is divided up into numbered segments, and that there are corresponding divisions in the next line down, consisting of groups of four white rectangles separated by single gray rectangles.

Each of these little boxes on the second line down represents a **frame**, and the numbers on the top line give us a frame number reference: frame 1 on the left, through to frame 45 (and beyond) on the right. Your movie can be 1 frame long, or it can be thousands of frames long. The length of your movie is determined by the highest number frame you create content for.

The (red) rectangle with the line coming out of it on the timeline is called the **playhead**.

The playhead

The playhead indicates where you currently are in your movie. You can click on the playhead and drag it back and forth along the timeline and the stage will change to show the contents in the selected frame. At the moment, of course, we don't have any images or objects on the stage, but as we start to add content you'll see how you can spool through your movie using the playhead.

The playhead lets us anticipate what'll be seen when the movie plays back in the browser: when we position the playhead over a frame, we see what'll be displayed on the screen at that point during playback.

Our movie begins in frame 1. By default, when it loads into the user's browser, our movie will start at frame 1 and play through the rest of the frames in sequence until the end point. Each successive frame on the timeline represents a moment in time, a moment that'll be played back when our movie runs.

At the moment, all of the frames in the timeline shown here are empty – that's because we haven't created any content yet. If we were to play back our night time movie now (by pressing CTRL+F12), we'd just see a block of color displayed in the browser window. This is Flash displaying the background color of the movie that we set using the Property inspector. To make our movie more interesting, we have to add content at various points along the timeline so that they can play back in the browser. This is where frames come in.

By placing content in frames at different points along the timeline, we imitate the passing of time, make animations, and generally make things happen in our movie: just like that time-lapsed mushroom movie we mentioned earlier, we can create start and end points and show all of the intermediate stages in between. When the movie plays, it looks at each frame on the timeline and renders what it finds there in the user's browser. To achieve the effect of content appearing and disappearing, animating and morphing, Flash provides us with different types of frames that we can use.

To see the nature and effects of the different types of frame that Flash gives us, we first have to get some content onto the stage. So without further ado, it's time to start drawing.

Making mushrooms

What we're going to do here is create a mushroom that will live out its life under the midnight sky that we created as our background earlier.

1.   First of all, click on the **Snap to Objects** button on the Tools panel:

> *On the Mac, you'll need to use the* **View > Snap to Objects** *menu option.*

> *If you don't see the Tools panel on your PC, use the* **Window > Tools** *menu option to display it. Alternatively, you can display the* **Snap to Objects** *button in your main toolbar at the top of the screen by selecting the* **Window > Toolbars > Main** *menu option. You can dock the toolbars in Flash MX the same as you can in other packages.*

The button will appear to be 'depressed' when you've turned the option on.

Turning on **Snap to Objects** invokes Flash's ability to help us make our drawings more precise: this option will automatically 'snap' the drawing cursor to certain points as Flash anticipates what you're trying to do. For example, when you turn snapping on and draw with the Oval tool, Flash will jump to a perfect circle when you get close to it, but with snapping off, it will let you draw the oval to whatever dimensions you want. Whether you use this snapping feature or not is entirely dependent on personal preference and what you're trying to achieve: if you're drawing perfect circles it makes sense to leave it on, but for most freehand drawings it's easier to leave it off. Experiment and see what works best for you in different circumstances.

Next, we need to select the drawing tool that we'll use to draw our initial mushroom. All the drawing tools are accessed in the Flash **Tools panel**. We'll be detailing more aspects of the Tools panel and its contents in the next chapter, but we'll start making use of some of its features as we work through this example.

2. The Tools panel is located (by default) on the left-hand side of the authoring environment. If you hold the mouse cursor over any of the tool buttons in the Tools panel, a tool tip will pop up with a description of the tool that the button represents:

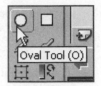

The letter in brackets next to the tool's name is the shortcut key for that particular tool. In this case, pressing O will select the Oval tool.

3. Click on the Oval tool. Each of the tools will be covered fully in the next chapter, but we'll dip into them now as we set about creating some content.

Now we need to select a color for the outline of the shape that we're going to draw.

4. If you're not already displaying it, bring up your Property inspector by pressing CTRL+F3. You'll notice that some aspects have changed from what we've previously seen inside the Property inspector. The Property inspector now reflects that we have the Oval tool selected:

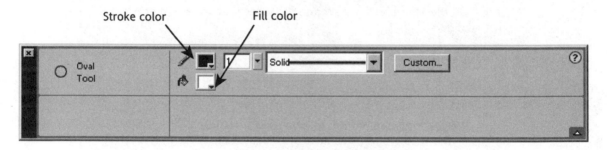

From here, you can pick a color for the outline (**Stroke color**) of the object that you're drawing. Similarly, the **Fill color** box allows you to select the color that you want to use to fill the area **inside** the outline. By default, many of the objects that you draw using tools from the Tools panel have an outline and a filled interior. You can control and modify these outlines and fills to a very fine degree, as you'll see as we progress through this book.

5. Set the stroke color to a dark brown.

6. Next, click on the Fill color box and set the fill color to a lighter, mushroom-like brown.

7. Now for the actual drawing. At the bottom of the stage, about half way along, click and drag with the Oval tool to make a small stalk for your mushroom:

8. Now, using the same click and drag action, draw a flatter, larger oval just above the stalk. Make sure that there's a gap – a small one – between the two ovals:

This larger oval will be the cap of your baby mushroom.

9. If you look at the timeline now, you'll notice that the first frame has changed:

If you look closely at the second line down, you'll see that this frame is now shaded a darker gray, and that it contains a little black circle. Why is that?

Well, in a new movie like ours, Flash always assumes that we want the action to start in frame 1. So, when we started drawing on the stage, Flash thought:

'Aha, they're drawing an oval. This is the first piece of content that they're creating for this movie, so I'll put this drawing in frame 1 – that's where the movie will start, after all.'

So Flash has created the starting point for our movie, based on the drawing that we've made. This is the first fixed point in time for our movie – the first image in a sequence of images that we want to display changing over time. If you like, this is the first snapshot in a sequence that we want to show to the user.

Flash uses a particular type of frame to store fixed points in time that hold visual (or other) content: this type of frame is called a **keyframe**.

Keyframes

A keyframe indicates that something important happens at the point in the timeline where the keyframe is located: for example, we display some content, or we make something disappear, or we make a transition from one piece of content to another. Keyframes are markers in time, indicating start and end points for different pieces of action.

Essentially, a keyframe says to Flash, 'there's something significant here'. Your Flash movies will consist of a series of keyframes spaced out along the timeline, with each keyframe flagging up the start and end points of distinct pieces of content that are to be displayed in the user's browser.

Think back to the time-lapsed nature movie that we discussed earlier. Remember how we said that the start and end points of that movie would be the baby mushroom and the full-grown mushroom?

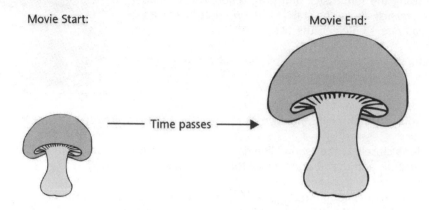

In Flash, those start and end points are defined by keyframes. We'd need a keyframe in frame 1 that contained the baby mushroom image, and a keyframe in a later frame (say frame 15) containing the image of the fully developed mushroom:

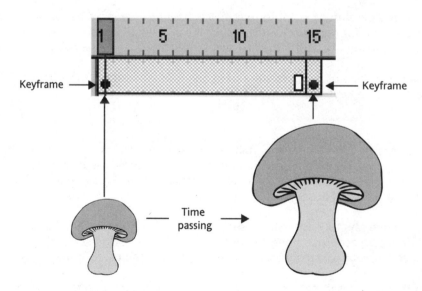

These two keyframes will tell Flash that we have images of our mushroom in two different states: 'starting to grow', and 'finished growing'. Once we have these two keyframes in place, we can get Flash to help us create and animate the intermediate growth states for the mushroom that should exist between the start and end images. We'll be looking at how to do that in more detail very shortly. For the moment, remember this:

> *If something significant changes on screen in your movie, there'll probably be a keyframe involved. Keyframes are the 'key' to making things happen.*

Much more on frames in a moment. First, a bit of housekeeping...

Saving your movie

It's good practice to save your work often – just in case your dog eats it or the computer crashes and burns. The way to save your embryonic Flash movie is the same way that you would in most other programs:

1. Click on **File > Save** in the main menu.

    You'll be prompted with a dialog box asking where you want to save the movie, and what name you would like to give it.

2. Choose (or create) a suitably named folder to save your work into, and then type Mushroom into the **File name** box and click **Save**:

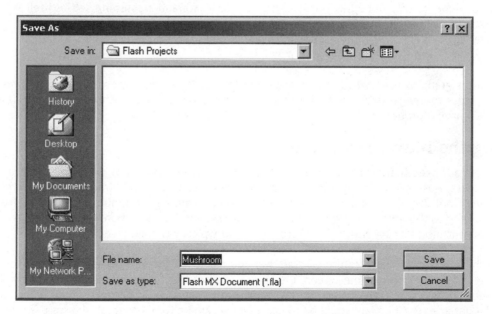

Flash will automatically save the movie that you're working on as an FLA file, which is the extension used for Flash authoring files.

> *Remember that there's a distinction between the file that you work on in the authoring environment (the FLA file) and the file that's loaded and played when a surfer visits your site (the SWF file): as an author, you create and modify your content inside the FLA, and the SWF is created when you publish your movie. The publishing process takes all of the drawings and other content that you created in your FLA file and compresses and encodes them into the SWF format. The SWF file is much smaller and more compact than its parent FLA file, and is thus much quicker and efficient to download for the end user.*

Now that we've got our example movie safely saved away, we can continue our exploration of frames.

We've already drawn a couple of ovals in frame 1: these represent our baby mushroom – the starting point for our movie. If we were to play the movie now, we'd see a static image of our baby mushroom in the browser (you can try this by pressing CTRL+F12. This will open up your default browser and render your movie – you'll need to close the browser or click back into your Flash MX window once you've finished viewing your masterpiece).

The reason that we see this static image is that we've only created a single frame with any content in – the movie has nowhere else to go except this single keyframe. When Flash plays back the movie and looks at the timeline, it only finds this single keyframe. Flash's default publishing settings tell it to **loop the playback** of our movie, so what we're seeing in the browser is the same single frame, being shown over and over again as Flash repeatedly loops through the timeline. Flash will continue to do this until we close the browser or move onto another web page.

Next, we're going to see how to add an *end* point for our 'mushroom growth' movie, and how to create the sequence of images that imitate the passage of time and show the mushroom growing. This will mean that we'll have a proper movie to play rather than a single-frame loop.

Making the movie really move

We've already seen that keyframes mark the beginning and end points of pieces of action in our movie. In this sense, Flash can be compared to traditional animated cartoons. In traditional 'toons, the animator would plan out the action sequence that they wanted to create – for example, a car driving from one side of the screen to the other. They would create the background for the action – maybe a desert setting with some distant mountains – and this background would typically remain static.

Next, the animator would create their start and end images of the car: the car on the left of the screen, and the car on the right of the screen. Clearly, you'd also need to have a series of intermediate images that showed the car in progress across the desert. Each image would be drawn onto a separate sheet of transparent acetate. The plan would be to use a movie camera to photograph the start, intermediate, and end images against the static background to create a number of different frames of film. Running the frames in sequence would show the car in motion against the static background.

This was a time-consuming business, and cartoon production companies didn't want to tie up their star animators in slaving over frame after frame of minutely-changing action. The solution was to get the lead animators to create the key images – start and end points, and important transitional images – and then use specialized 'in-betweeners' to sit down and draw up the images that came in between the keyframes that the expert animator had created. These in-between frames were critical to ensuring that the cartoon action was smooth and convincing.

In Flash, we do things similarly. We can create keyframes that define significant stages in the action that we want to show, and then get Flash to generate the in-between frames that link the keyframes together. This saves us a lot of time and effort in creating the transitional frames, and is an important factor in making Flash the successful animation package that it has become. (Note that you *can* mimic the traditional animation method in Flash if you wish, by hand-drawing each frame individually. This can be a powerful way to express yourself and create great animation, but it's really too big a subject to tackle. Maybe in another book...)

Let's get back to our mushroom movie. Currently, we have that single starting keyframe containing the baby mushroom. Next, we want to create a keyframe holding the fully-grown version, and then get Flash to create all the in-between frames that show the mushroom growing over time – let's work through that in an exercise now.

Working with frames

As we've said already, a keyframe marks a significant change in your movie. In order to create the image showing our mushroom when it's fully grown, we need to add a keyframe to the timeline. This will tell Flash that we have some important new content that it needs to be aware of.

To insert a new keyframe to the timeline, you simply click in the timeline at the position where you want to add your keyframe. Once you've selected the frame position, you can then choose the **Insert > Keyframe** menu option, or use the keyboard shortcut F6, and a new keyframe will appear.

It might occur to you to ask, 'how far along the timeline should I put my second keyframe?' The answer to this depends on how long you want your piece of action to last. The thing to remember here is the frame rate setting that we saw in the Property inspector. Remember we said that the 12 frames per second default rate was about right for most basic movies? This frame rate setting means that **for every 12 frames our movie takes up on the timeline, there will be one second of action when the movie plays back**. So, the math is fairly simple: estimate how long you want the action to last in seconds, and multiply the number of seconds by the frame rate. You can always change the position of the keyframes later on if you need to tweak the timing of different pieces of action.

Let's make that mushroom grow.

1. Click on frame 14 of your mushroom movie and press F6 to insert a keyframe.

   You'll see immediately that the timeline has changed:

   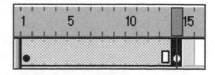

Frame 14 now has a black circle in it and a black border (note that the circle is white and the frame black in the image above because the frame is selected), and all the frames between frames 1 and 14 have turned gray. Additionally, there's a small white rectangle in frame 13, and the playhead has jumped to frame 14. Let's take a look at what this all means:

- The black border around frame 14 indicates that this is a keyframe. We're going to use this keyframe to hold some content that's different from the frames that precede it.

- The white rectangle in frame 13 tells us that this is the last frame before a new keyframe, and that all of the frames to the left of this rectangle contain the same content as the **previous** keyframe – in this case, frame 1. The frames are grayed to show you that they contain the same content as frame 1 – every frame in the black-bordered box running from frame 1 through frame 13 contains the same image of the baby mushroom that we created in frame 1.

- The black circle in the keyframe at frame 14 indicates that this frame contains some content. But how come? We didn't add any content to this frame yet, did we? What's happened is that Flash has carried over the content from the previous keyframe (frame 1). This is the default behavior when you add a new keyframe. This feature can be very useful, as you'll see in a moment.

- There's one other thing to note here: when you move the playhead backwards and forwards through your movie, the current frame number is also indicated in the area just underneath the timeline:

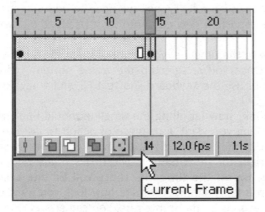

So far, then, we've got an opening keyframe (frame 1), followed by some intermediate frames (frames 2 – 13), and a new keyframe (frame 14) that will soon contain the image of our fully-grown mushroom.

All of the frames from 2 to 13 now 'belong' to the keyframe in frame 1, and reflect what is in it. If you changed the image in frame 1, the following 'slave' frames (2 – 13) would change to reflect the new picture. Frame 14 would remain as it is, however, as we've told Flash that we want this frame to be self-contained so that it can contain new content.

2. Double-click anywhere on the timeline between the two keyframes. You'll see that frames 1 through 13 turn black:

This shows you that these frames all hold the same content – they're all dependent on the content in the keyframe at frame 1. You can't alter the content of frames 2 through 13 by editing them directly – you can only change their contents *indirectly* by amending what's in frame 1. **You can only directly edit content that's in a keyframe.**

3. Deselect the black-highlighted frames by clicking away from them. Next, click anywhere between the keyframes. This time only the frame that you clicked on is selected:

4. Use the **Insert > Frame** menu option or press the F5 key twice to insert two new frames into the timeline at the position where you just clicked with the mouse. This will add two frames to the timeline, and these new frames will inherit the contents from the preceding keyframe (frame 1).

    Using the playhead to move through your movie, you can see that it is now 16 frames long, and each of the frames contains the same picture of a mushroom. We promise that your mushroom will grow soon, but first there are a few more tricks we can perform with frames.

5. Click between the keyframes again to select a single frame.

    This time, rather than inserting 'slave' frames, we're going to insert a **blank keyframe**. A blank keyframe is just what its name suggests, a keyframe that has no content in it. It is, however, independent of the content of the keyframe that precedes it.

6. Use the **Insert > Blank Keyframe** menu option or press the F7 key to convert one of the normal frames in your timeline into a blank keyframe: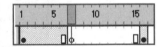

    A blank keyframe is represented in a similar way to a keyframe, except that it shows an unfilled circle in the timeline – this is because it doesn't yet have any content. The remaining white frames are all dependent on the blank keyframe that we just inserted.

7. If you now scroll through your movie using the playhead, you'll see that all of the dependent frames after the blank keyframe are also blank, reflecting the fact that the keyframe before them was empty. Blank keyframes are useful for stopping animations or dividing different pieces of content that exist on the same layer (stay tuned, there's more on layers later).

    You'll also see that the keyframe at frame 16 still has the baby mushroom image in it. That's because it inherited the content of frame 1 when we created it. However, there is no link between the inherited image and the current (possibly amended) content of frame 1 – frame 16's keyframe is completely independent.

    We don't actually want half of the frames in our movie to be blank, so somehow we'll have to get rid of that blank keyframe and its dependent frames. There are two ways to do this: you can either delete the blank keyframe or convert it into a normal frame. We're going to do the latter – the advantage of this is that the movie's length remains the same.

8. Click on the blank keyframe and use the **Insert > Clear Keyframe** menu option or press SHIFT+F6. This menu option name is a little confusing – what we're actually doing here is converting the keyframe to a normal frame – we're not actually *inserting* anything as such. The result of doing this

is that the white frames become shaded again, and if you run the movie through now, you'll see that they've all been refilled with your baby mushroom picture.

So you now have 16 frames in your movie, all filled with exactly the same mushroom image. We only wanted the movie to last for 15 frames because it's a nice round number, so you'll have to remove one of those frames now...

9.   Click to select a single frame anywhere between the two keyframes and use the **Insert > Remove Frames** menu option or press Shift+F5 to delete the highlighted frame. You should now be left with two keyframes on your timeline (in frames 1 and 15), and a set of identical normal frames between the keyframes, containing the same image of your mushroom that you created in frame 1.

The 'normal' frames that separate out the keyframes may appear to be plain and boring at the moment, but don't dismiss them: they're the Flash equivalent of pawns on a chessboard or foot soldiers in an army – not as glamorous as the other elements, but just as important.

> *In Flash there are three different methods for adding, converting, and deleting frames, each with its own advantages and disadvantages. The first, and most 'formal' method is to use the* **Insert** *menu. This menu, found on the main menu bar, contains all of the manipulation actions associated with frames. The second, and probably most commonly used method is to use the keyboard shortcuts that mimic the* **Insert** *menu options. The major problem with this is that you have to learn them first, although this is something that most people pick up quite quickly through use. The third method is to right-click on the relevant frame in the timeline to highlight it, and then to select the appropriate command from the context-sensitive menu that appears. Throughout the tutorial sections in this book, we'll use a mixture of these methods. There is no single 'best' method – whichever one you find easiest is the one that you should use.*

As promised, let's make our mushroom live and...well, breathe.

Making the mushroom grow

Frame 15 is going to be the final frame of our movie, which means that we need to populate it with the content that represents the final growth stage of our mushroom. Let's add the fully-grown mushroom image to the keyframe in frame 15. What we want to do is have our mushroom grow from the baby form in frame 1 to an adult version in frame 15.

1.   Start by clicking on frame 15 in the timeline. Notice that when you click on the frame the whole mushroom (the two ovals we drew earlier) is already selected. Remember, these ovals were inherited from the keyframe in frame 1, so they're identical in shape and position to the mushroom

in frame 1. This in turn means that we don't have to worry about positioning the image of the mushroom in frame 15 – it's in exactly the same place as it in frame 1 – this will make our animation easier to perform.

> *A related, and very useful feature in Flash is the ability to copy (or cut) and paste content into exactly the same location on the stage. This is particularly useful when you want to paste images or other components into other keyframes or onto other layers and still have them occupy the same coordinates on the stage as the original image. To achieve this, you copy (or cut) the original component, and then use the Edit > Paste in Place menu option. This way you're sure to place your object exactly where you want it. We guarantee that you'll find this feature immensely useful in your Flash career.*

2. Click on the Arrow tool in the top left corner of the Tools panel, and then click on the background of the stage to deselect the mushroom.

3. Now double-click in the middle of the cap of your mushroom: this will select both the stroke and the fill. If you had only clicked once in the middle of the cap, you would only have selected the fill.

4. Next, click on the mushroom cap and drag it up to where you want the cap of your full-grown mushroom to be. (Alternatively, holding SHIFT and using the arrow keys makes your selection move in units of 10 pixels):

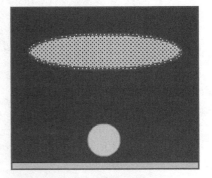

> *If you hold down the SHIFT key while you drag, Flash will help you drag the mushroom cap upwards in a straight line (provided that you've turned on the Snap to Objects option).*

5. Double-click on the stalk (the lower oval) to select it, and then press BACKSPACE. This will delete the baby version of the stalk from frame 15 (although the old, smaller stalk is still intact in frames 1 through 14).

Our next task is to create the fully-grown version of the mushroom stalk.

6. Click on the Oval tool in the Tools panel again, and draw a long thin oval from the bottom of the cap of your mushroom down to the bottom of the stage, again ensuring that there's a small gap left between the edges of the two ovals. This is your adult mushroom stalk:

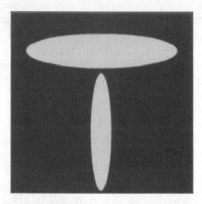

> *If you need to move your new stalk when you've drawn it, select the Arrow tool, double-click on the stalk, and drag it to the desired position. If things go wrong, you can always use the 'undo' option by selecting* **Edit > Undo** *from the menu bar, or pressing (*CTRL+Z*).*

7. OK. Press the ENTER key to preview your movie. Hmm...not particularly convincing, is it? We're getting the same picture for 14 frames, and then a sudden jump to a fully-grown fungus. What we really want is a smooth transition from 'button' mushroom to 'big mushroom', and Flash can do this for us. You're about to see how Flash can perform as an underpaid, unappreciated 'in-betweener'.

8. Double-click somewhere in between the two keyframes on the timeline to select the first keyframe and all of the normal frames that depend on it:

What we're going to do now is change the behavior of these frames. We're going to tell Flash that we want to create an animation that smoothly transforms the small mushroom in frame 1 into the fully-grown version that we've just created in frame 15. Our ability to do this is entirely dependent on the existence of our two keyframes: the keyframes define the two different states of the mushroom, and we're asking Flash to create all of the in-between frames that'll represent the growth of the mushroom. Let's do that.

9.   If you don't have your Property inspector open, right-click on the frames and select **Properties** from the context-sensitive menu. Using the Property inspector, we're going to give these frames a label, and create our growth animation:

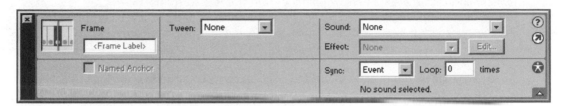

> In Flash, animation is called **tweening**. This might seem an odd name, until you realize that it's short for 'in-betweening', or the process of creating the transitional frames that go in-between the keyframes.

10.   Click inside the furthest left box (under the word **Frame**) in the Property inspector and give your frames a label that identifies them – we've called ours Mushroom Growth. This attaches the label to frame 1.

> Using labels makes it easier to identify specific bits of action inside a large and complex movie. If, as we've suggested, you keep objects on separate layers, and name those layers, then you should not need to use large amounts of labels. They'll come in useful later on when we start to deal with actions, but this will be discussed in greater detail when we come to it.

11.   Now click on the drop-down menu next to **Tween**, and select **Shape** from it:

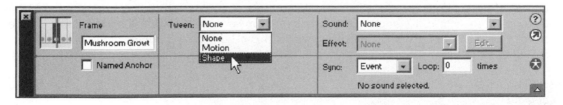

This will automatically create a **shape tween**: Flash will decide that we want the stalk in frame 1 to morph into the stalk in frame 15, and that we want the cap in frame 1 to morph into the cap in frame 15, and it'll automatically generate the in-between images in frames 2 through 14 that will produce this effect.

12. Click on the playhead and notice that the tweened frames on the timeline have now been colored green by Flash, indicating a shape tween, and that there's an arrow pointing from frame 1 to frame 15 – this indicates the length of the tween. Finally, Flash has added our label to the tweened frames, and appended a little red flag to draw our attention to it:

(For clarity, we've removed the label from subsequent screenshots.)

13. Slowly drag the playhead back to Frame 1, noticing that Flash has automatically filled in all of the animation frames between 1 and 15. Now press ENTER to preview the movie, and the mushroom will steadily grow to its full-size.

14. Save your happy-grow-lucky mushroom.

We've spent some time looking at frames in Flash, and started to see how they can help us achieve the effects that we're after in our movies. What we'll do next is introduce you to another vital element of Flash authoring files – **layers**.

Layers

Whereas the timeline and its frames help us organize and manipulate content over time, layers help us add depth to the movie, and allow us to separate out pieces of content and action that would otherwise get tangled up. If you had to place your entire movie content on a single layer, it would be horrendously difficult to achieve anything complicated. By separating out the action onto different layers, you can create much more convincing and complex movies, and make full use of the flexibility and power that Flash's timeline gives you. Multiple layers mean that your movies can have a host of different elements on the stage, all acting completely independently of each other.

A traditional animator would have a different set of sheets of acetate for each part of their cartoon. For example, the background forest would be on one set of sheets, Red Riding-Hood would be happily skipping on another set, and the Big Bad Wolf would be stalking her from yet another set. By keeping the parts separate, the animator had much greater control over the individual aspects of their cartoon. It meant that if something needed to be altered, the animator could change just one set – say, adding an evil twinkle to the Wolf's eye – without having to redraw the forest or Miss Riding-Hood as well. Another benefit of having separate animations on different sets of acetate is that they can be re-used later in the cartoon, or indeed in a completely different cartoon, so while Jack and Jill are running up the hill in cartoon two, cartoon one's Little Red Riding-Hood can be happily skipping along below them without having to be redrawn. The content on the different layers is independent and portable.

In Flash, layers are shown to the left of the timeline. Each new Flash movie comes with a single layer by default:

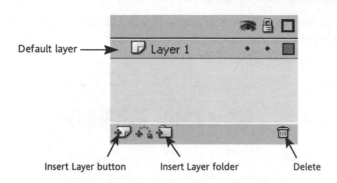

Default layer ⟶ Layer 1

Insert Layer button   Insert Layer folder   Delete

This layer – **Layer 1** – is the default layer that we've been working with in our mushroom movie so far.

In Flash, layers are the equivalent of those separate sheets of acetate containing different visual components. Layers make movies easier to alter, and allow for much greater richness of content. Let's take a look at what layers allow us to do in our sample movie.

Working with layers

It's good practice to keep each element of your movie on a separate layer for ease of editing and for neatness. We'll see how this works in this exercise.

1.   The active layer in Flash is the highlighted layer with the pencil icon next to its name: this pencil icon indicates that this is the layer that you've currently selected to work on.

2.   Click on the Insert Layer button. Flash will create a new layer above **Layer 1** and call it **Layer 2**.

3.   Notice that Flash has automatically made **Layer 2** 15 frames long to match the length of **Layer 1**. If you look at any of these frames though, they'll still all be empty:

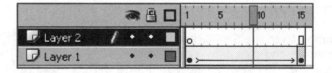

Flash always calls a new layer **Layer** *n* where *n* is the next number up from the last layer that you created. This means that even if you subsequently deleted a layer, Flash would still increment the next layer's number as if the deleted layer still existed. For example, if you deleted **Layer 2** and then added another layer, it would still be called **Layer 3** even though there was no **Layer 2**. Luckily, the good people at Macromedia understand just how confused you are at the moment, so instead of trying to work out which layer is which, they've given us the ability to uniquely name each layer – which means that we can forget about the whole numbers shebang, and work with meaningful, descriptive layer names instead. Giving names to your movie's layers is another good habit to get into, and it'll save you a lot of heartache.

4. Double-click on the name **Layer 1** in the timeline. When you double-click it, it will become editable, allowing you to change the name of the layer:

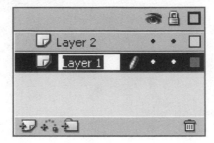

5. Type mushroom and press ENTER.

6. We want **Layer 2** to contain a picture of the moon in front of our night-sky background, so double-click where it says **Layer 2**, type moon and press ENTER. We now have our two layers meaningfully named and we can instantly infer what's on each of them.

7. Click on the Oval tool. Our moon will be a full one, so we'll use this tool to create the celestial body.

8. Click on the **Default Colors** button under the two color boxes at the bottom of the Tools panel:

Default colors

This button will reset the colors to a black stroke with a white fill.

9. Still on the **moon** layer, use the playhead to go to the final frame of the movie, and then draw a circle (remember, you can hold down the SHIFT key to help you draw a perfect circle) over the top of the right-hand side of your fully-grown mushroom cap:

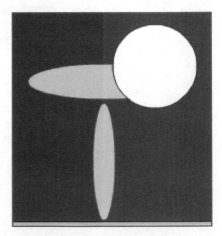

If you look at the timeline, you'll notice that Flash has automatically created a keyframe at frame 1 of the **moon** layer, and that it has also populated all of the frames on this layer with the image of the moon. This is a handy effect, as we want the moon to be visible in the sky throughout our movie. If we'd wanted the moon to appear in the movie from frame 15 onwards (and not before), we'd have needed to create a keyframe at frame 15 in the **moon** layer.

10. Press ENTER to play your movie. Flash has zipped through the timeline and displayed the content of both layers for us.

But something looks slightly wrong, doesn't it? The mushroom seems to be further away than the moon, and bigger, too. If we're going to get the perspective right, then you'll need to put the moon *behind* the mushroom. We need to get the layers' **stacking order** right.

The higher up a layer appears in the layer list on the left of the timeline, the closer the contents of that layer appear to you on the screen. So to get your mushroom in front of the moon, you just have to move its layer above the moon's layer in the layer list. Let's do that now.

11. Click on the name of the **mushroom** layer in the layer list and drag it above the **moon** layer. You'll see a shaded bar appear while you're dragging the layer:

This indicates where the layer will go when you release the mouse.

12. Now when you play your movie, the mushroom should rise in front of the moon. Perspective has been returned, and the tale of the very big mushroom and the very small moon has been consigned once more to legend.

Deleting a layer is as easy as adding a layer – it only takes the click of a button. To delete a layer, you'd just click on the layer to highlight it, and then click on the **Delete Layer** button, which is indicated by the trash can icon underneath the layer listing. You should note that Flash will not let you delete *all* the layers in a movie: there must always be at least one layer left. If you're trying to delete everything from a movie and start again, it's easier to close the current movie and start a new one.

> *As we've seen, layers are a useful way to manage and control our content. Flash MX has the added ability of using layer folders to bundle together similar layers for further ease – more on these in Chapter 4.*

Layer modes

Layer modes define how you view and alter specific layers in the authoring environment. There are three layer modes in Flash and, by default, they're all turned 'off'. The three modes are controlled by clicking on the icons in the three columns after the layer name, and the status of the modes for a particular layer is indicated by the two dots and the square next to that layer's name:

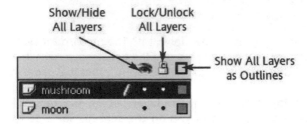

The first column controls showing and hiding a layer, the second controls locking and unlocking a layer, and the third column is used for viewing the contents of that layer as outlines. Let's take a look at how these different modes interact in the authoring environment, and see what benefits they give us.

Working with layer modes

With all three of the layer mode selector icons in the 'off' position, the authoring environment will behave exactly as it has done so far: if you were to start drawing a circle with the Oval tool right now, it would appear as normal on the currently selected (active) layer. Let's see what happens when we start switching the layer modes 'on'.

1. In the **mushroom** layer, click on the dot underneath the picture of the eye.

   Three things will happen:

   - As we've hidden the layer, its contents will disappear from the stage in the authoring environment.

   - A red cross will replace the dot in the eye column, reminding us that this layer is currently hidden.

   - The pencil icon will have a red line struck through it, indicating that the contents of the hidden layer cannot be edited. If you try to draw on the stage now, you'll find that the cursor has changed to a pencil with a warning circle next to it:

The warning circle tells us that the currently selected tool cannot be used at the moment. The logic here is that if you were able to draw on the hidden layer, you'd be able to unwittingly draw all over the content that you'd created so carefully already. Flash is protecting you from yourself.

If you were to actually click on the stage with the Oval tool, you'd get an error prompt:

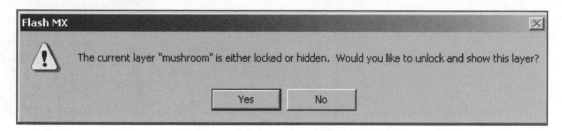

Hiding layers is very helpful when you need to concentrate on some content on a particular layer and you don't want to have the contents of other layers obstructing your view. For example, in the final frame of your mushroom movie, the mushroom covers part of the moon. If you wanted to draw a face on your moon it would be hard to see what you were doing because the mushroom would be in the way. By hiding the **mushroom** layer, you can see the whole of the moon, select the **moon** layer and draw away to your heart's content. You could then click on the cross in the eye column and the **mushroom** layer would be visible again.

2. Click on the cross in the eye column to return everything to normal. Now click on the dot in the 'lock' column. A small padlock will replace the dot, and the pencil will again have a line through it. This time, although the layer is locked and you cannot draw or select objects on it, the mushroom will still be visible.

Locking layers allows you to work with objects above or below them without accidentally selecting anything in the locked layers. This is useful when you're drawing or modifying on one layer and you want to see the contents of the other layers to keep things in context. Locking the surrounding layers means you can draw and edit confidently, secure in the knowledge that you won't mess anything up on the other layers.

The final mode allows you to display all objects on a layer as **outlines only**, rather than as filled shapes.

3. Unlock the **mushroom** layer by clicking on the small padlock across from the layer name. Now click on the colored box to the right – the mushroom will be reduced to just an outline. The outline takes its color from the color of the box that you just clicked on. Each layer will have its own dedicated outline color (automatically allocated by Flash), so you can easily make out which objects belong to which layer.

4. Click on the outline button on the **moon** layer, and (on your monitor, at least!) you'll see that the moon's outline is a different color to the mushroom's:

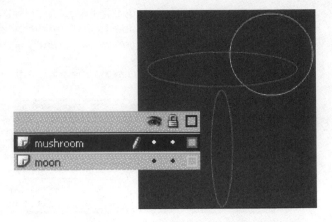

Outline mode is useful for helping you get a grip on exactly what's in your movie across all layers. Things start to get complicated when you have lots of different things on lots of layers and you can't quite see what is going on. Outline mode lets you step back from the jumble and get a clear view. Outline mode is also helpful in previewing your movie, as Flash finds animating outlines easier to render than fully filled shapes, meaning that the movie preview displays quicker.

You can easily change the layer mode for *all* of the layers by using the icons at the top of each of the columns. So, to turn outline mode *off* for both of our movie's layers, just click on the black box next to the eye and the lock: This will instantly return your mushroom and moon to their full-color glory.

If you're working with a lot of layers and want to lock every layer except the layer you're currently working on, it is easiest to click on the **Lock/Unlock All Layers** button to lock every layer, and then click on the small padlock on the layer that you want to use to just unlock that layer. The same principle applies to the show/hide feature invoked via the eye icon.

Using layer folders (see Chapter 4), it's possible to lock or hide the content of a folder with one click. Locking or hiding the folder layer also affects all of the content within the layer in the same way. This makes it easy to show/hide or lock/unlock similarly grouped elements while editing other content on the stage.

Layer modes only influence how you see the layers as you are constructing them: they have no effect on the final movie that you create, so layers that are hidden in the authoring environment will be visible in the final movie. Similarly, layers that are in outline mode will be seen in full color when they're rendered in the browser.

Now let's move on to the last Flash concept that we want to introduce into this chapter – **scenes**.

Scenes

Scenes are used to organize your movie into sections that you can view as independent pieces of the whole movie. The ability to have a multi-scene movie allows you to break up your content into logical chunks and helps you organize things efficiently.

Flash movies can be large or small, simple or complex. Small, simple movies can usually be contained in a single scene with no problem, but when you're talking about a large movie with many components, or a movie that has long animations or multiple navigation elements, then multiple scenes can be the way to go.

You can think of scenes as an extension of your timeline, giving you the facility to break up the action and continue from one scene to another. The benefit to you as an author is that your authoring files are more manageable, and the benefit to the user can be a more navigable movie. Many developers simply use separate scenes for their preloader (an element of a Flash movie that downloads movie components in advance of their being used), the introduction, and the main movie.

Some developers also use separate scenes in the same way as traditional designers use HTML pages on their sites – *one* scene is equivalent to *one* HTML page. This can be a useful model when you're designing a whole site in Flash – you can create a front page for your site, and then jump to different scenes (pages) depending on which buttons the user presses. We'll discuss this design approach in depth in a later chapter.

Each new Flash movie starts out with one default scene, named **Scene 1**. You can tell what scene you're currently in by looking at the scene name directly below your layers:

You can add and delete scenes as you wish, using the **Insert > Scene** and **Insert > Remove Scene** menu options. You can see the names of all of your scenes by opening up the **Scene** panel. You do this via the **Window > Scene** menu option or by pressing SHIFT+F2:

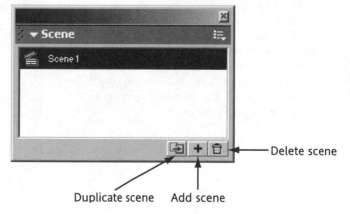

Here, you can use the buttons to manipulate scenes, and you can also drag scenes to change the order of playback. Usefully, you can also double-click on any scene in the Scene panel and give it a meaningful name. Once again, this is useful for bringing clarity to your movie authoring files.

By default, Flash will always play the scenes in the sequence in which the scenes are listed in the Scene panel, so make sure that you keep the right scenes in the right order here. However, you can also use Flash ActionScript to jump from scene to scene and play them in different sequences.

Another way to swap between scenes in the authoring environment is to click on the **Scene** button directly below the frames on the right, and click on the scene you want to edit in the drop-down list:

There's yet another way of navigating between your movie's different scenes in the authoring environment: the **Movie Explorer**.

The Movie Explorer

The Movie Explorer gives you the ability to browse your way through your whole movie at different levels of detail. You can open up the Movie Explorer by choosing the **Window > Movie Explorer** menu option or by pressing ALT+F3 (OPTION + F3 on a Mac).

The Movie Explorer window looks like this:

As you can see from this view from our mushroom movie, the Movie Explorer can reveal the contents of your movie to you in depth, in terms of its component scenes, layers, and keyframes (provided that you've chosen the relevant options from the **Show** buttons along the top). You can click on any node in this displayed hierarchy and be taken to that point in the movie. This is a really powerful way of helping you navigate through your movies – especially as your movies grow in size and scope. We'll be seeing more of the Movie Explorer as we progress through the book.

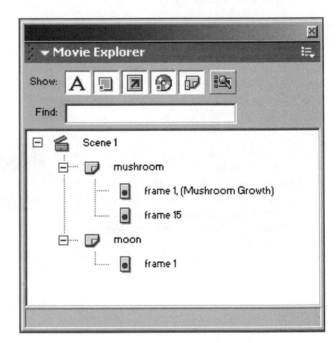

For now, though, let's just recap where we've been before we move on to the next chapter.

Summary

In this chapter, we've introduced you to the Flash authoring environment and demonstrated some of the essential elements of Flash movie creation.

We saw that:

- We create movie content on the **stage**, which has a surrounding **work area**.

- We can use the Property inspector to change the global characteristics of our movie, such as size and background color.

- The content we add to the stage is displayed in the viewer's browser when the movie plays back.

- Our movie is a series of points in time: these are played back in sequence as the **playhead** moves along the **timeline**.

- We use **keyframes** to hold new or changed content, and to indicate to Flash that something significant is happening. Keyframes are separated by 'normal' **frames** that influence how long the action between keyframes lasts.

- **Layers** add depth and manageability to your movies.

- **Scenes** allow us to separate our movies into distinct chunks.

- The **Movie Explorer** lets us navigate through our entire movie and browse through its content.

In the next chapter, we're going to look in more depth at the built-in Flash tools that let us create movie content. As we've already seen, these tools live in the Flash **Tools** panel.

The Flash MX Tools Panel

What we'll cover in this chapter:

- *The Flash **Tools Panel:** where we find Flash's integral drawing and manipulation tools, and what they're capable of.*

- *How to use these tools to create and amend movie content: images and text.*

- *Precision drawing and fine-tuning with **Bezier curves**.*

In the previous chapter, we took a look at the key structures contained in every Flash movie – the stage, the timeline, keyframes, frames, layers and layer folders. In this chapter, we're going to start exploring Flash's built-in facilities for creating and manipulating movie content.

To do this, we'll examine each of Flash's drawing and editing tools in the context of enhancing our mushroom movie: these tools are the integral means that Flash gives us for drawing pictures, creating text, and manipulating these and other visual elements on the stage.

All of these built-in content creation tools are accessed via the **Flash Tools panel**.

The Tools panel

The Tools panel is where you'll find all of Flash's drawing and editing tools. Using these tools in conjunction with Flash's Property inspector and other panels, you'll have at your disposal everything you need to design and manipulate the visual components and building blocks of your movie.

By default, the Tools panel is situated on the left-hand side of the screen when you open up Flash for the first time, but you can move it around or hide it, just like any other window. The Tools panel itself is subdivided into four sections – **Tools**, **View**, **Colors**, and **Options**:

- The **Tools** section is where all of the basic design and manipulation options are found. These tools can be used to draw pictures, create text elements, select objects, and move them around the stage – amongst other things.

- The **View** section contains tools for two main functions: zooming in and out on the stage, and changing the stage's position on the screen. These changes of view and position only apply to the screen display in the authoring environment where you're creating the movie – changes you make to the view here have no effect on the way that the finished movie itself is rendered in the user's browser. You might, for example, wish to shift the stage around on-screen so that you can see other screen elements – such as open panels – more clearly.

- The **Colors** section is used to control the color of the **stroke** (line) or **fill** of an object. For instance, if you wanted to have a blue circle with a black outline, you'd choose those options in the Colors section. The topmost tool in the Colors section determines the stroke color, and the tool below it (the one with the paint bucket icon) controls the object's fill color. Reading from left to right, the three remaining tools in the Colors section are responsible for: setting the stroke and fill colors to black and white; switching off the stroke or fill (depending on which of them is selected); and swapping back and forth between black stroke/white fill and white stroke/black fill. You can actually assign your own colors to stroke and fill – more on that later.

- The **Options** section is where you can change some of the properties of the currently selected tool. For example, you can change the size and shape of the **Brush tool** to make different kinds of brush marks. Note that not every tool in the Tools panel has options that modify their characteristics, so don't worry if this section appears blank for some tools.

If you're working in Windows, you'll see that the modifiers in the Options section of the Arrow tool are duplicated in the main toolbar at the top of the screen:

These options become visible on the main toolbar once you've selected an object on the screen using the Arrow tool. We'll be looking at how to use these modifiers as we progress through the book.

> *Remember that you'll need to have the main toolbar activated – otherwise, you won't see these options. To activate the main toolbar, choose the* **Window > Toolbars > Main** *menu option.*

You've already used a couple of tools to help create your prototype mushroom in the previous chapter, and in this section you'll be amending and expanding your movie to incorporate the effects of all the other tools. By the end of this chapter, you'll have a working knowledge of all of the basic tools, and have a sense of how to apply them to achieve the results you want.

Let's start with the Arrow tool, which is used for manipulating visual elements of the movie.

The Arrow tool

The Arrow tool is maybe the most important tool in Flash, and probably the one that you'll use most often when creating and amending visual content on the stage. Essentially, the Arrow tool is used to select objects on the stage for editing, and to move and place those selected objects just where we want them. The Arrow tool has a few little quirks that are important to understand. Let's take a look at them now.

Using the Arrow tool for selection and manipulation

Here, we're just going to examine the basics of using the Arrow tool. To do this, we'll need something drawn on our stage.

1.   First, open up a new movie, click on the Oval tool in the Tools panel...

2.   ...and select a black stroke, and a fill color of your choice from the Property inspector. To choose a color for strokes and fills, simply click on the relevant color selector box to bring up the color palette and make your choice:

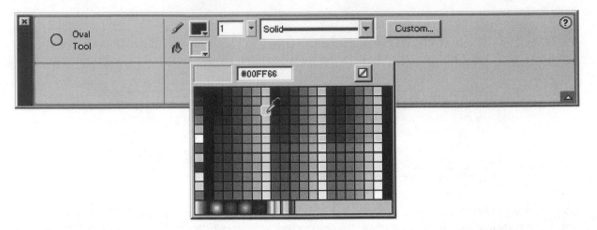

3.   Next, click on the stage and hold down the mouse button, dragging the mouse so that you draw a nice big circle on the stage:

   (Remember that holding down the SHIFT key while you drag will result in a perfect circle.)

4.   Now select the Arrow tool by clicking on its icon in the Tools panel:

   When we select the Arrow tool, its three associated modifiers appear in the Options section of the Tools panel:

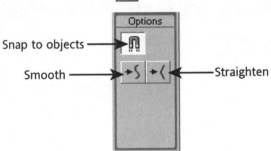

   These modifiers can be applied to the objects that we select with the Arrow tool – we'll be seeing how to use each of these later.

5. Now that you've selected the Arrow tool, the next thing to do is point at the center of the big circle you've drawn:

Note that when you move the Arrow tool over the center of the circle, a cross with arrows on each of its arms appears next to the cursor. This indicates that you're hovering over an object that can be selected and moved simply by clicking and dragging.

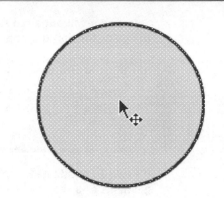

6. Click on the colored part of the circle (it'll be highlighted as soon as you click on it) and drag it off to the side. Then release the mouse button:

You'll see that what's happened here is that we've separated the fill part of the shape from its enclosing line (stroke) – the circle has become two separate objects.

Note that, by default, the enclosed shapes you draw using the tools in the Tools panel will consist of an outline and a fill. You can choose to have 'no outline' or 'no fill' by selecting the Stroke Color or Fill Color box in the Property inspector and then clicking on the **No Color** selector.

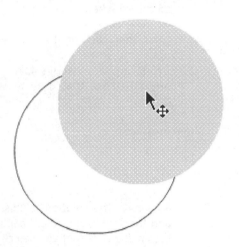

7. Select the Oval tool from the Tools panel and click on the Fill Color box. Above the palette of colors is a white box containing a red diagonal line. This is the No Color selector:

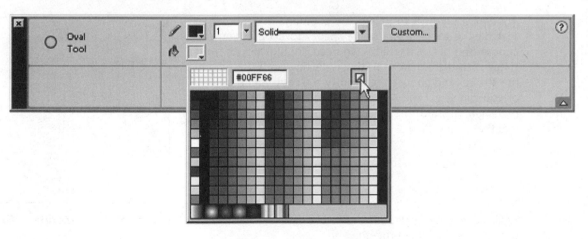

Selecting it will put a red slash through the Fill Color box in the Property inspector, indicating that the color for that drawing element (stroke or fill) is switched 'off':

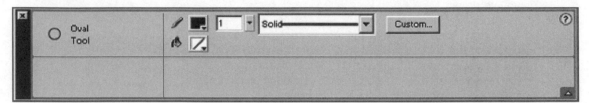

It's easy to accidentally separate the stroke and fill elements of a shape when using the Arrow tool as a selection device, and it illustrates the need to take care when selecting objects. Furthermore, if we now click away from the highlighted disk of color, then click on it and drag it again...

...you can see that it's taken a bite out of the original stroke that used to surround the circle. Dang.

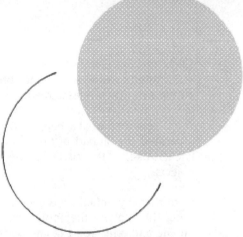

So, what's the solution to this? Well, we can always undo the change we just made using CTRL-Z, and then try again. A less haphazard way to avoid separating an object into its component pieces is to make sure that you select both the colored fill and the surrounding stroke before moving the object. The way to achieve this is to double-click on the object that you want to move – this will select its stroke and its fill. By double-clicking on a shape like this, you ensure that you can drag it around as a single entity.

Another solution is to **group** the components together so that they're treated as a single shape. To do this, you can choose one of two methods: you can double-click on your shape with the Arrow tool (thus selecting both the fill and the stroke) and choose the **Modify > Group** menu option; or you can select the Arrow Tool and then use it to draw a rectangle around the shapes that you want to group together:

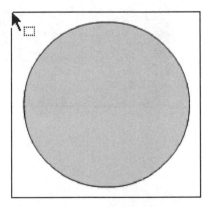

Again, this will select both the stroke and the fill, and you can use the same **Modify > Group** option to group them together.

Whichever of these two methods you use, the result will be the same: your objects will be grouped together – in this case, the two objects being the circle's surrounding stroke and color fill.

Grouped objects, when selected, will be highlighted by a colored line that indicates that they're a group. (The color of this line is determined by the global **Highlight Color** setting that you choose via the **General** tab of the **Edit > Preferences** menu.)

To separate grouped items back into their component parts, select the group, and then choose the **Modify > Ungroup** menu option.

And there's another common mishap that can befall us when we're using the Arrow tool to select and move objects. Take a look at this:

Yes, it's that familiar circle, drawn once again using the Oval tool – this time with a green fill (honest) and a black stroke.

Now, let's suppose we want to use the Arrow tool to select the circle so we can move it. I remember that I need to select both the fill and the stroke, so I decide to use the Arrow tool to draw a selection box. I click and drag the mouse to draw the box...

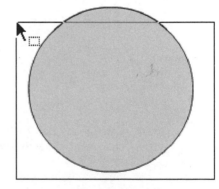

...but, sadly, I've misjudged the starting position for my drag, and I've accidentally missed the top of the circle. However, I decide to persevere. At the end of the drag, I release the mouse button, then click on the center of the circle and try to drag it away to the right...

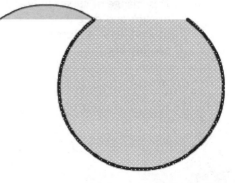

Hmm...not quite what I wanted. Flash thinks that I want to carve up my circle rather than move it as a single entity. Again, this problem can be avoided by grouping the stroke and fill segments. Take care – those selection boxes can be sharp!

We've looked at the selection and moving of objects, both here, and in the last chapter when we constructed our first mushroom-oriented Flash movie. The Arrow tool has one other important use, though – it can help us change the shape of objects by dragging their outlines. Let's take a look at this functionality next.

Extending your mushroom's cap

What we're going to do here is modify the mushroom-based movie that we started work on in the previous chapter.

1. Open Mushroom.fla from the end of the last chapter.

2. Click on your keyframe in frame 15 of the **mushroom** layer.

3. Choose the Arrow tool from the Tools panel once more.

4. Click on the stage, away from the drawn shapes, to ensure that you've got nothing selected.

5. Now position the point of the arrow cursor on the edge of the mushroom cap – that is, touching the line around the filled shape:

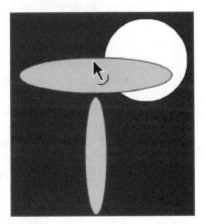

You'll notice that when the arrow point touches the line, the cursor changes to an arrow with a curved line underneath it:

This change of cursor indicates that you are now in a position to click and drag a point on a line, thus changing the shape of that line. A cursor with a right angle underneath the pointer, like this...

...means that you're in a position where you can drag a corner.

6. Now click on the line and drag it upwards to create a domed, more 'natural-looking' cap to our mushroom. Notice that when you release the mouse button, the fill expands to flood the modified shape with color:

    OK, our little bit of genetic modification is complete.

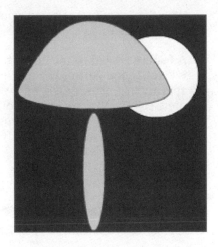

7. Play the movie. You'll see that Flash has automatically modified all the frames in-between the keyframes so that the animation shows the smooth growth of our newly amended mushroom cap. Flash is great at making life easy for us in this respect: if we change the start or end points of our animation – the keyframes – then Flash will recalculate all of the in-between images, without even asking us.

Next, let's take a look at a tool that lets us really close in on the objects in our movie and see them in fine detail – the **Zoom tool**.

 # The Zoom tool

Here's the Zoom tool in the Tools panel, along with its related modifiers in the Options section:

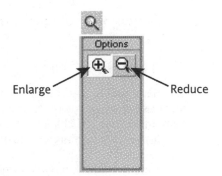

The Zoom tool is very easy to use: clicking on the screen with the **Enlarge** option selected will zoom in on the screen, and clicking with the **Reduce** option selected will zoom out. Simple.

Once you've selected your zoom in or out mode, you can temporarily switch from one state to the other by holding down the ALT key in Windows or the OPTION key on the Mac. When you click on the screen with this key depressed, the zoom will operate in the opposite direction from what's selected in the Options section: this saves you having to keep changing the mode in the Options box whenever you want to zoom in and out.

With the Zoom tool selected, you can also drag a box around an area, and Flash will enlarge that area to fill the screen.

A feature related to the Zoom tool that's new in Flash MX is **Pixel Zoom**. When you zoom in beyond 400%, a pixel grid appears that allows you to draw shapes and objects more precisely. For this feature to work, you need to select the **View > Snap to Pixels** menu option. You can see the pixel grid here when we zoom in to 1600% at the bottom of our mushroom movie:

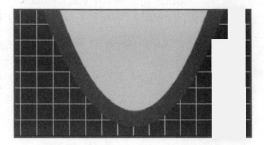

Zooming in and out on the moon

1. Still in your `Mushroom.fla` file, hide the **mushroom** layer by clicking on the dot in the eye column next to its name:

2. Use the Zoom tool to enlarge the moon until it fills the screen. Look at the edge of the moon and notice that the quality of the image doesn't degrade as you zoom in, however much you increase the magnification. This is one of the wonders of working with vector graphics – you never lose any detail.

    Also, note that any changes in magnification you make inside of the FLA file won't affect the finished movie: the zoom features are just there to help you when you're creating your movie.

The next tool we're going to look at is also a relatively simple one – the **Hand tool**.

 ## The Hand tool

The Hand tool is used for moving around the segment of the stage that's displayed on your screen. It's most useful when you're zoomed right in and you're not able to see the entire movie all at once. Remember that any changes in view you make in the authoring environment won't have any effect on the display of your finished movie.

Using the Hand tool, move around your zoomed-in movie, making sure that you finish up with the moon in the middle again. You can achieve the same effect using the scroll bars below and to the right of the stage, but the Hand tool feels somehow more controlled and intuitive.
Now let's zoom in on our next Tools panel component – **the Oval tool.**

 ## The Oval tool

You've already used the Oval tool a couple of times. When drawing the moon in Chapter 1, we saw the option of pressing the SHIFT key when you're dragging to automatically 'snap' the oval so that it becomes a perfect circle. We'll use the **Oval tool** again here to enhance our moonscape.

Making craters with the Oval tool

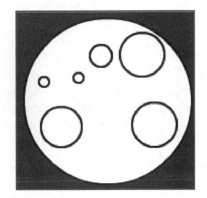

1. With the moon filling the screen to ensure precision, ensure you have the **moon** layer selected and then use the Oval tool to draw a number of craters on the surface of the moon. You can draw them as ovals or as perfect circles – it's your call:

2. Now zoom back out to 100% to view the current state of the picture – the night, the moonlight, and a groovy mushroom.

OK, that's enough admiration of our handiwork for the moment – let's move on to the next tool.

 ## The Rectangle tool

The Rectangle tool, as the name suggests, is used for drawing squares and rectangles.

It operates virtually identically to the Oval tool in the way that selecting the tool, then clicking on the stage and dragging the shape to an appropriate size can create shapes. Similarly, pressing the Sʜɪꜰᴛ key while drawing will snap the rectangle to a perfect square.

As you can see in the screenshot, the Rectangle tool has a modifier in the Options section of the Tools panel – the grandly named **Round Rectangle Radius** modifier. Translated into simpler terms, this modifier controls the extent to which the corners of the rectangle you're drawing are rounded off.

Let's put the Rectangle tool to work in our mushroom movie.

Making a rectangular signpost

We're going to create a sign that'll stand at the edge of the mushroom patch.

1. Create a new layer on top of the other two layers in your Mushroom.fla movie and name it signpost:

2. Next, click on the Rectangle tool, then on the Round Rectangle Radius modifier, and enter the figure **15** into the **Rectangle Settings** dialog box that pops up:

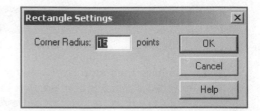

You can also bring up the Rectangle Settings box by double-clicking on the Rectangle tool in the Tools panel.

3. Click on **OK**.

By entering the number 15, we're telling Flash that we want to round off the corners of the rectangle by a factor of 15 points.

4. Draw a rectangle on the left-hand side of the picture, a little higher than the moon. This will be your sign board in the movie foreground:

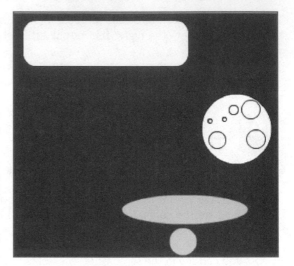

We'll be enhancing our sign soon. In fact, almost immediately, using the **Line tool**.

 # The Line tool

The Line tool is used for drawing lines: yup, it really is as easy as it sounds. To use the Line tool, you select it, and then just click (and hold) on the start point of your line, then drag the mouse and release on the end point. To work with the Line tool really effectively though, the Property inspector will enable us to closely control the characteristics of the line that we draw. Let's look at that in a short exercise.

Making a Post with the Line tool

1. Make sure that the Property inspector is open (open it with **Window > Properties**).

2. Now choose the Line tool from the Tools panel. The Property inspector will be updated to show the current properties for the Line tool, showing line color, height (size), and style, as well as a button that allows you to further customize your line:

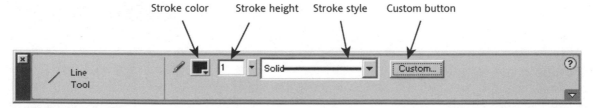

These modifiers will also work in conjunction with the other drawing tools: this means that you can alter the characteristics of the outlines of your ovals and rectangles after you've drawn them.

Next, you're going to use the Line tool to draw a post to support your signboard.

3. Click on the downward-pointing arrow to the right of the **Stroke Height** box:

A slider will pop up – this controls the height of our line. (You can also type a precise height into the box if you prefer – the maximum size being 10.)

4. Choose the thickest stroke you can by moving the slider to the top of its range – this will result in a size 10 line.

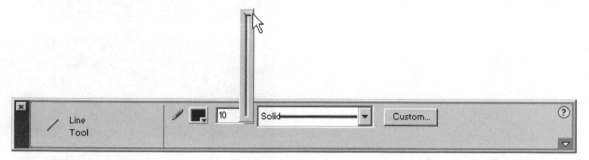

5. Fix your size choice by releasing the mouse button.

6. Now click on the **Stroke Color** box to bring up the Property inspector's standard color palette, and select a dark woody brown for the post. To preview the line, click on the **Custom** button. In the **Stroke Style** window that appears, a simple preview is displayed on the left:

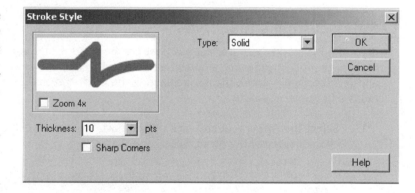

Don't pay too much attention to the rest of this window, as we'll take another look at it shortly.

7. Choose the **View > Snap to Objects** menu option.

This will ensure that when your line gets close to a perfect vertical or horizontal orientation, the line will automatically 'snap' to the vertical or horizontal. When you draw your line, you'll see that there's a small circle at the end of the line while you're dragging the mouse, and that when the line snaps this circle grows bolder to signal to you that you've reached the desired angle. When you're in **Snap to Objects** mode, you can also hold down the SHIFT key while you're dragging: this will snap your line in increments of 45 degree angles.

8. OK, back to our example. Click and drag a line from the bottom of your sign to the edge of the stage (which is where the ground is on our mushroom patch), snap the line to the vertical, and release the mouse to fix the line. Don't worry if the end of the line sticks out over the edge of the stage. Remember, only things that appear on the stage will be seen in the final movie.

Here's our movie content so far:

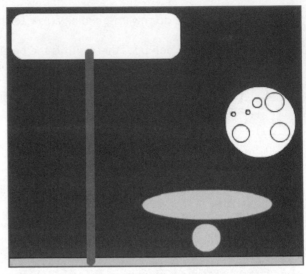

Earlier on we sneaked a look at the Custom Stroke Style window when we used it to preview the height and color of our line. Let's take a closer look at it now.

Creating custom stroke styles

If you find it hard to believe that our post can be so straight and perfect, there's an easy way to make it more authentic – by creating a **custom stroke style**. Flash allows us to easily change contents of the stage and replace them – more than just changing the color and size of our stroke. Let's change our post so it looks a little more realistic:

1. Select the Arrow tool and click on the post. When the post is selected, the Property inspector will change to show the properties of the stroke.

2. Click on the **Custom** button in the Property inspector. A new window will open with some stroke options visible:

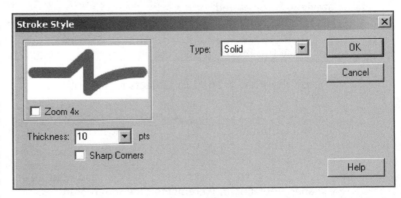

The preview on the left shows potentially every possible use of the line – from a perfectly straight line to a variety of curves and edges. This is meant to show us how our line will cope in almost any situation.

We're going to make the post rickety and old from many years of wear by creating a customized stroke style that is textured and rough.

3. Click on the **Type** drop-down menu and select **Ragged**. When you do this, a number of other drop-down menus appear to make the line more customizable and the preview pane reflects these selections:

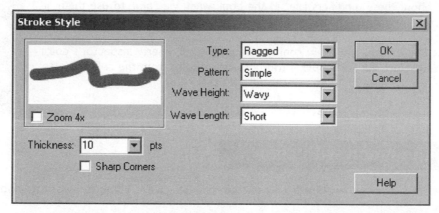

We won't go through all of the menu options here, as there are different options for each Type style – and one of these has seven different options to change! Have some fun and experiment with the other options later on.

Let's change the line a little so we get the effect we're looking for.

4. Select **Solid** from the **Pattern** drop-down menu, **Very Wavy** from the **Wave Height** drop-down menu, and **Short** from **Wave Length**. The line in the preview pane of the **Stroke Style** window will look like this:

5. Now click **OK** and take a look at our post, which looks more like a twig right now:

Of course, if you aren't happy with this post, you can change it by creating a new custom style or by reverting to our original. Some of the options will give you some pretty wacky results, but others help you to quickly achieve some decent effects, such as the creation of a dotted line.

Let's make some more modifications to our scene, this time using the Paint Bucket tool.

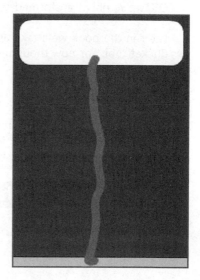

The Paint Bucket tool

The Paint Bucket, also commonly known as the 'Fill' tool, is used for filling in empty shapes or for changing the fill color of existing shapes.

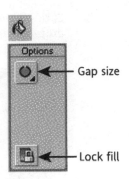

Gap size

Lock fill

We'll talk about these modifiers later in the book when we come to use them 'in anger'. For the moment, let's stick with the core functionality of the Paint Bucket tool.

The Paint Bucket tool is used in conjunction with the Property inspector's color palette. You select the Paint Bucket tool and pick a color from the color palette, then click on the area that you want to fill with that color.

Let's do that now in the context of our mushroom world.

Filling the moon with color

1. Select a pale yellow color from the color palette – we're going to paint the moon.

2. Click on the Paint Bucket tool, then click once on the main section of the moon: it will instantly be filled with the pale yellow that you selected.

    Every cursor has a point, called a **hotspot**, that tells the computer exactly where you're clicking on the screen. The hotspot for the Paint Bucket tool is the end of the paint spilling out of the can.

3. Select a slightly darker yellow and fill the craters in the same way that you re-colored the lunar surface. If you find it hard to click exactly on a small crater, try zooming in so that you have a larger area to hit with your Paint Bucket's hotspot.

OK, we've now transformed the surface of the moon – not bad going for just a few minutes work.

Later in the book we'll take a closer look at the Fill Transform tool, which is closely related to the Paint Bucket tool. For now though, we're going to move on and look at the **Ink Bottle tool**.

The Ink Bottle tool

The Ink Bottle tool works hand in hand with the Paint Bucket. Where the Paint Bucket changes fills, the Ink Bottle does the same for lines. The hotspot for the Ink Bottle is at the tip of the spilled ink. Let's use it to alter the nature of our signboard's supporting post.

Changing lines with the Ink Bottle

Here, we're going to transmute our signpost from a wooden to a metal version.

1. Select the Ink Bottle tool, and then choose a gray hue from the color palette in the Property inspector.

2. Click on your post if it's not selected already, and it will instantly change to the gray that you just chose. A gnarled wooden stick to a mangled metal bar in one click – superb. If only those medieval alchemists had known about Flash – their lives would have been so much easier.

Having seen a couple of ways of applying changes to different objects on our stage, let's now look at how we can 'copy' characteristics from one object to another. We use the **Dropper tool** to do this.

 ## The Dropper tool

This tool is used to 'suck up' the colors and styles of fills (or lines) from objects that you've already created. When you use the Dropper to pick up an object's attributes, Flash will then automatically switch over to the tool that you'll use to apply these attributes to another object. That is, if you pick up a fill style, Flash will flip over to the Paint Bucket tool, and if you pick up a line/stroke style, Flash will take you to the Ink Bottle tool.

The Dropper tool can also be used to pick up bitmaps and gradients, and we'll cover these uses in more detail later.

Let's now apply the Dropper tool to our example movie.

Picking colors from lines and fills

What we want to do here is change our signpost so that it mirrors the attributes of our yellowish moon. This will give us a nice tonal continuity.

1. Click on the Dropper tool and move it over the yellow-filled surface of the moon. Notice that a little picture of a paintbrush appears next to the cursor: this indicates that if we were to click here, we'd be picking up a fill style. When the cursor is held over a stroke rather than a fill, a little pencil icon is shown:

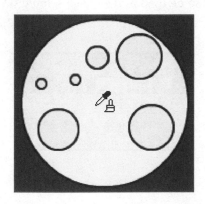 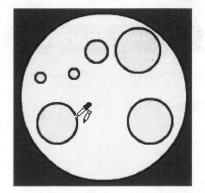

2. Click on the pale yellow moon. The Dropper will immediately swap over to the Paint Bucket tool. Notice that the fill color in the Tools panel has now changed to the color you've just selected.

3. Now click on the middle of your signboard and fill it with the same pale yellow as the moon.

4. Select the Dropper tool again, but this time click on the gray line that you drew for your signpost's supporting strut. Look in the Property inspector and you'll notice that it has selected all the properties that we assigned to our post. If you were to click on the line around the sign now, it would become the same thickness as your signpost.

5. Instead, though, change the line thickness in the Property inspector to **3**, and revert back to the **Solid** option from the **Stroke Style** drop-down menu:

    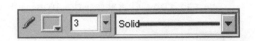

6. Click on the sign's outline and it'll immediately become a medium-height line the same color as your signpost:

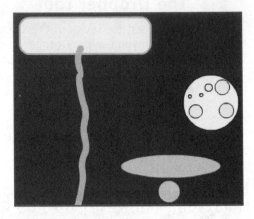

OK, we've now got a nicely proportioned sign at the edge of our mushroom patch. What's next? Well, the sign should probably communicate something. How about some text to tell people that we don't want their big boots all over our precious mushrooms? For that, we need the **Text tool**.

The Text tool

The Text tool is used in conjunction with the Property inspector. Together, they allow text entry and editing in your Flash movie. In Flash, text fields can also be used as hyperlinks – more on this later.

Giving your sign character

First, we'll define how our text should look.

1. Create a new layer and call it `text`:

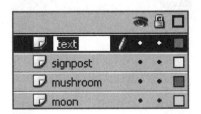

2. Click on the Text tool in the Tools panel. This will open the Text tool properties in the Property inspector. Make sure that the drop-down menu on the far left is set to **Static Text**.

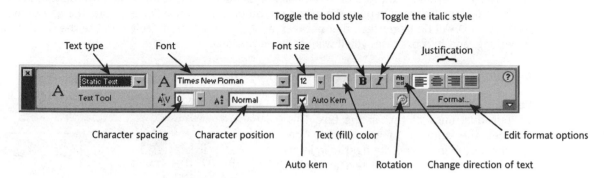

The options displayed are similar to those in a word processing program, and many of them will probably be familiar to you. For now, let's concentrate on the top section of the Property inspector – if the lower section is visible, close it using the arrow at the bottom right of the Property inspector. Just for the record, the options that you have here are:

Text Type – The type of text box we're creating (more about this later in the book).

Font – The name of the font you want to use. Note that Flash previews the fonts when you open the font list:

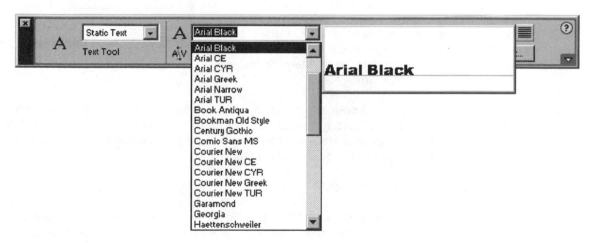

Font Size – This is the size, in points, that you want your font to be.

Direction of Text – This allows the text box to flow in three different directions: horizontal, vertical left to right, or vertical right to left.

Justification – The alignment control for your text. This can be set to left, right, centered, and full.

Character Spacing – This inserts a uniform gap of your chosen size between each of the characters.

Character Position – This is where you can choose to display the font as subscript or superscript.

Auto Kern – Kerning is the gap between pairs of characters. Most fonts will have built-in kerning so that the gaps between certain characters will be different sizes. For example, the gap between an **A** and a **D** will be larger than that between an **A** and a **V**. The default is to use the font's built-in kerning, and in most cases you'll want to leave this on.

Rotation – The amount of rotation applied to your text.

Format – Increased control over the format of individual lines of text in the box. This includes the amount of the indent, line spacing, left margin, and the right margin of each line. Individual lines of text are given their own settings:

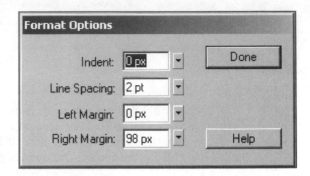

The **Bold** and **Italic** modifiers will make the text either bold or italic, and the **Color** button will open up the standard Flash color palette so that you can choose the text color.

3. Select the Text tool and click on the pale yellow fill of the signboard:

   A small text box appears with a blinking cursor at the text insertion point. Don't worry if your insertion point is not in exactly the right place – we'll be able to position the text precisely later by selecting the text box and relocating it with the Arrow tool.

   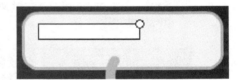

4. In the Property inspector, choose a font that you like the look of (we've used Arial Black), and choose a font size that will fit nicely on your sign. Notice that as you move the Font Size slider up and down, the text box on your stage is automatically resized: this guide will help you to choose how large a text size you should select to fit on your sign.

5. Set the color of your font to black.

6. Finally, you can type some text into your text box. To maintain the sanctity of our mushroom, we chose to write `Keep Out` on the sign, but you can write whatever you like (provided that it fits).

7. Click on the Arrow tool.

   The white box around the text will disappear to be replaced by a thin, colored highlight (this will be the color that you have set as your default **Highlight Color** on the **General** tab of the **Edit > Preferences** menu). You can now pick up this text with the Arrow tool's cursor and move it around until you're happy with its position on the sign:

8. To go back and edit the text again, just click on the text with the Text tool.

Also note that in Flash, there's no text modifier that will underline text. If you want to have underlined text in Flash, you'll have to manually draw a line underneath it.

We've now got a number of elements that we created using straight lines, ovals, rectangles, and text. Next, let's live on the edge a little and try some freehand drawing. For that, we can start with a pencil.

The Pencil tool

The **Pencil tool** is used to draw freeform lines. This tool uses the Property inspector to set its different characteristics, such as stroke height, style and color. The Pencil tool also has one modifier in the Options section of the Tools panel – the **Pencil Mode** modifier. This sole modifier is an important one, though – it controls how the line behaves when we draw by clicking and dragging with the mouse.

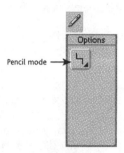

Clicking on this modifier reveals that there are three Pencil Modes to choose from:

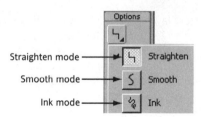

Let's see how these work, in the context of adding some foliage to our mushroom patch.

Penciling in some grass

Here, we're going to add a little local color to our mushroom movie.

1. Save away your Mushroom.fla movie and create a new movie by choosing the **File > New** menu option or by pressing CTRL-N. This will open a fresh, blank white movie in Flash.

   Don't worry about not being able to see your Mushroom movie any more – it's still there, as you can see by choosing the **Window** menu option. At the bottom of the resulting pop-up window, you'll see a list of currently open movie files. Alternatively, you can toggle through the movies you have open by pressing CTRL-TAB.

2. Using the Pencil tool, draw a series of similar lines with the different Pencil modes and notice the results.

- **Straighten** mode will flatten out some of the curves in your line. Another feature of this tool is that it will automatically complete simple shapes that you draw. For example, if you draw a rough circle with Straighten mode on, Flash will snap it to a perfect circle:

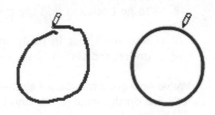

- **Smooth** mode will refine the curves in your hand-drawn shapes, rounding out kinks and generally softening awkward shapes. It's a good mode to use if your freehand drawing is a little shaky, as it will neaten the lines and make them look more professional.

- **Ink** mode is the basic Pencil Mode. If you want to draw something on the screen and have it come out exactly the way that it was drawn, this is the mode to use. In this mode, you'll notice that Flash does seem to smooth the lines a little bit: this is just a result of the process of converting the line from the raster line that it uses while you're drawing to the vector version that it will actually store and render.

3. Close the movie that you've been using to experiment with the Pencil modes: choose not to save it (unless you really did like it), and you'll be returned to your original mushroom movie.

4. Create a new layer, and call it `grass`. By now, the layers on your timeline are getting a bit cramped. You can increase and decrease the size of your timeline area by holding your cursor between the timeline area and the border that surrounds the stage. You can then adjust the size of your timeline according to the movie you are working with:

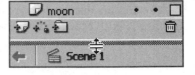

5. With the Pencil tool selected, choose a nice grassy green from the color palette in the Property inspector, and then click on the Ink mode modifier so that you can draw truly freehand.

6. Scribble some rough lines around the base of your sign. Don't worry if they look a bit messy, as these will be tufts of grass at the bottom of your signpost:

7. Save your movie again.

Now we'll take a look at the **Brush tool**.

The Brush tool

The Brush tool is very similar to the Pencil tool, but instead of drawing lines, you're painting fills. Every time you use the Brush tool on your movie, you're simply painting a fill with no enclosing border line.

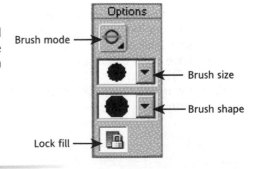

The Brush tool has four options:

- **Brush Mode** controls the way that your brush strokes are painted. This option has five additional modifiers:

- **Paint Normal** will paint over anything else that's on the screen (provided it's on the same layer as the one you're drawing on, of course).

- **Paint Fills** will only paint fills, and leave lines as they are – in place, and visible through the fill that you just painted.
- **Paint Behind** will only paint on blank areas of the current layer – any objects on that layer won't be painted over.

- **Paint Selection** will only paint on selected areas of the screen – those are areas that have been highlighted with the Arrow tool.

- **Paint Inside** is the tool you always needed when you had those coloring in books as a kid. When you start painting, Flash will ignore any marks you paint when your brush crosses a line:

- The **Brush Size** option changes the width and spread of the brush strokes.

- The **Brush Shape** button opens a menu containing a selection of different shapes to paint with – round, flat, and so on.

- The **Lock Fill** button works in the same way as the button of the same name under the Paint Bucket tool, and its use will be covered in a later section.

Having seen how to paint, let's see how to erase our mistakes...

The Eraser tool

The **Eraser tool** is similar in operation to the Brush tool – it just erases rather than paints. It has three modifiers:

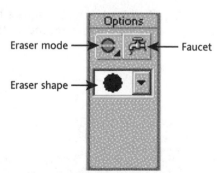

Eraser mode —— —— Faucet

Eraser shape ——

- The **Eraser Mode** button has five modifiers. These are the same as those for the Brush Mode button on the Brush tool, and they behave in the same way.

- The **Eraser Shape** button lets you change the shape of the eraser brush.

- The **Faucet** button changes the Eraser tool so that it will erase an entire fill or line at once. In this mode, you just touch the Eraser tool hotspot to the target line or fill, and the whole thing is erased.

Next, let's take a look at the **Free Transform tool**.

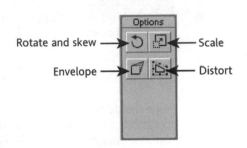 The Free Transform tool

The Free Transform tool is used to manipulate different properties of our content. It can be used to resize, rotate, and perform some pretty impressive tasks on elements on our stage.

Clicking on this tool reveals four different options in the Tools panel:

- **Rotate and Skew** – this limits the function of the Free Transform tool exclusively to rotating and skewing objects.

- **Scale** – this allows the Free Transform tool to only scale our objects.

- **Distort** – this allows scaling from each point giving maximum flexibility and as the name suggests, distortion.

- **Envelope** – this uses Bezier curves (more on these later) to manipulate simple shapes. Like the Distort option, this cannot be used on grouped objects.

By default, none of the options are selected and the tool allows us to rotate, scale, and skew. Let's try this:

1. Open up a new movie in Flash with the **File > New** menu option. Don't close the mushroom.fla file yet as we'll be returning to it a little later.

2. Draw a square using the Rectangle tool with a red fill and a black stroke. Give it a stroke height of 5. If you still have rounded corners set from earlier on and want a straighter looking rectangle, click on the Round Rectangle Radius modifier button in the Options section of the Tools panel. This brings up the Rectangle Settings window – to draw a rectangle with no rounded corners, enter 0 in the Corner Radius box.

3. Double-click on the square to select its fill and stroke, and select the Free Transform tool in the Tools panel:

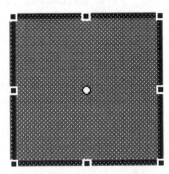

4. A number of anchor points will appear around the shape. These points can be moved to manipulate the scale of the shape in different directions. Let's make our square a rectangle.

5. Place your cursor over the top-center point. As you do this you'll notice that the cursor changes to a double-ended arrow, showing us that we can resize our selection.

6. While the cursor is a double-ended arrow, click and begin to drag upwards. You'll notice that Flash is showing us a ghostly outline of our future shape. This affects none of the other sides; only the side we're pulling is changed.

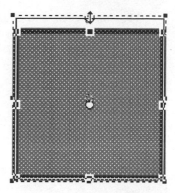

If you release the mouse, the shape will be updated and you'll now have a rectangle. We've resized the square in one direction only – if we had chosen any of the corner anchor points, the square would be resized in both height and width. Let's give that a try.

7. Move your mouse cursor over the top-right corner anchor point. You'll notice that it changes into a diagonal double-ended arrow pointing north-east and south-west. Click and drag to manipulate the shape in width and height.

If you take a look at the square on the stage, you'll probably notice that it isn't centered. You can center it by putting your cursor over the square so that it turns into the familiar arrow with which we can drag the shape:

One of the other default actions of the Free Transform tool is rotation. Let's experiment a little with it.

8. It would help if our square had an identifier for our rotations. Choose the Text tool and place a large N at the top-center – we'll use this as our north indicator:

At this point we'll need to **group** our objects so that they act as a unit – otherwise our north will remain north while our square goes south.

9. Click on the Arrow tool and select all the objects on the stage by drawing a box around them. Choose the **Modify > Group** menu option or press CTRL-G to bundle them together as one unit. Now that our objects are grouped, we can manipulate them all at once.

10. Select the grouped objects with the Arrow tool and then click on the Free Transform tool. The familiar anchor points should appear, so place your mouse cursor just outside any of the corner points and you'll notice that it's been replaced with a circular cursor:

11. Now click and drag right to rotate the square 90 degrees. Again, if you hold down the SHIFT key Flash gives you a helping hand and snaps in increments of 45 degrees:

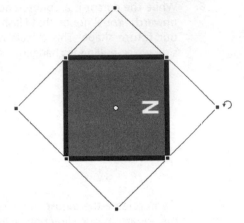

A new feature in Flash MX is the ability to adjust the center pivot of your rotation. When the square is selected, you'll see a small white circle in the center – that's the pivot for the rotation. We can move that white circle anywhere we wish and the shape will still rotate around it – even if the pivot is off the stage.

Let's now take a look at the final basic function of the Free Transform tool – the **skew**.

12. Make sure the group is selected and place the cursor over the perimeter of the square between any of the points.

You'll notice that the cursor turns into a peculiar shape that on closer inspection is two arrows pointing in different directions:

13. Click and drag to see the skew in action:

Let's now take a look at the **Distort modifier** option. This can only be applied to simple elements and not grouped objects.

14. Return your skewed square back to its original square shape by pressing CTRL-Z. Select the square using the Arrow tool. In order to ungroup the object so that we can try out the Distort option choose the **Modify > Ungroup** menu option.

15. Select the square again, click on the Free Transform tool and then select the **Distort** modifier from the Options section at the bottom of the Tools panel:

16. When your square is selected, you'll see those familiar anchor points again. Placing the cursor over the anchor points will make it change to a small white chevron. Select the top-left corner anchor point and drag it towards the center of the square:

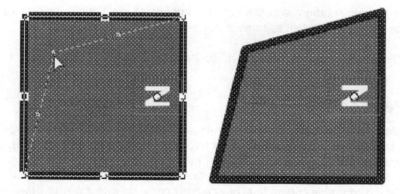

The shape is adjusted to where you just dragged the anchor point.

To conclude our look at the Free Transform tool, we'll now quickly use the **Envelope** modifier option. Like the Distort option, this cannot be used on grouped objects.

17. Return your shape to its original square state by pressing CTRL-Z to undo the distortions.

18. Select the square and, ensuring that you have the Free Transform tool selected in the Tools panel, click on the **Envelope** modifier option:

You'll notice that when you select the square with the Envelope modifier option, there are many more anchor points around the entire perimeter of the shape.

19. Drag as many anchor points as you like in whatever directions you wish.

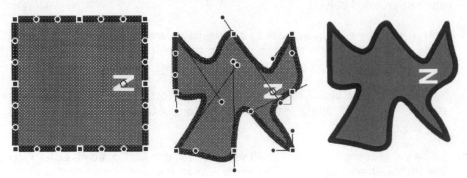

Some experimentation with the last two options of the Free Transform tool will enable you to create some wild, as well as some subtle shapes.

Now onto the next tool in the Tools panel, the **Pen tool**.

The Pen tool

The principles embodied in the Pen tool are an example of how high science and math can have unforeseen spin-offs. The space race gave us microprocessors and non-stick pans, but a less well-known spin-off comes from the automobile industry of the 1970s: designers had just started using CAD/CAM packages to design cars, but there was a problem – the computers couldn't draw squiggly lines. They could do straight lines and simple curves, but they couldn't come up with a way to draw squiggles. Squiggly lines are difficult because the equations that define them – unlike those for straight lines or regular curves – are extremely complex.

Bezier Curves

The solution to this problem was a special kind of curve called a **Bezier**, named after a mathematician by the name of Pierre Bezier. Monsieur Bezier's curve is used in all sorts of computer applications today, from designing curved cars to displaying postscript fonts.

The difference between a Bezier and a normal curve is that a normal curve is made up of points. A Bezier curve, on the other hand, is made up of points that include two additional pieces of data that we'll call direction and speed.

Bezier curves are drawn using the Pen tool – let's see how the Pen tool works in practice.

Working with Bezier curves

1. Open up a fresh Flash movie to experiment inside.

2. Select the Pen tool, making sure you have a fill color and line color of your choice selected. The cursor will change into a pen nib with a little cross next to it:

3. Next, click and while holding the mouse, drag away in the general direction
    you want the curve to go:

You'll see a line start to appear as you drag. This line consists of three points; one at the center and one on each end, so there's a kind of bow tie look to the line. The center point of this line is where our finished curve will start.

4. Don't let the bow tie get too big, and once you're happy with it, release the mouse. You've now created the starting point of the curve.

5. Now position the mouse pointer at another point on the screen
    that you want your curve to pass through. In the same way as you
    did before, drag out another bow tie, keeping the mouse button
    down as you position the bow tie:

Notice that as you drag the second bow tie around, the curve between the two center points of the bow ties changes in real-time. The way it changes is pretty difficult to describe in words, but once you have seen it, it somehow looks totally natural: the direction of the bow tie defines what direction the curve goes in, and the length of the bow tie affects its curvature.

A good way to think of it is that the bow ties represent the position (via the center point of the bow tie) and the speed (via the length of the bow tie) of a car trying to move in a straight line between the two points. As it gets faster (bow ties get bigger) the car travels in a curved path. Some of you may recognize the bow tie as the car's velocity vector, but the rest of us will just be having fun making the squiggle dance about to care too much about the math. In fact, practicing drawing the curves using the bow ties is the best way to get the feel of what's happening – sometimes words are just too much!

6. Keep adding bow ties to form a roughly puddle-shaped squiggle
    as shown here:

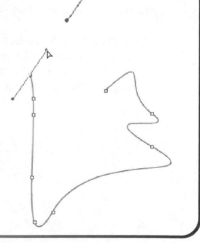

As you put the pen near the original starting point of the first bow tie (or near any point on a line that would make a closed area), the Pen tool changes to show an '**O**' where it was previously an '**X**':

This is Flash's way of saying that the next point you add will create a closed shape. This sounds a little complicated, but just try it. As with mostly everything associated with Beziers, it's actually easier to do than to explain!

Sometimes, when you're constructing shapes with the Pen tool, you don't want a shape composed completely of curves, but rather a mixture of curves and sharp corners. If you want to create a corner rather than another curve, you simply click on the stage with the Pen tool rather than clicking and dragging. This will give you a mix of curves and straight lines:

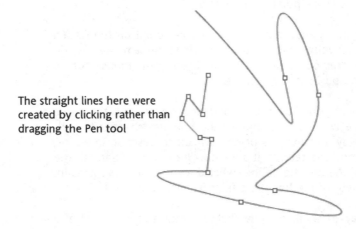

The straight lines here were created by clicking rather than dragging the Pen tool

Once you've used the Pen tool to create your basic Bezier shape, you can edit it with the **Subselect tool**.

The Subselect tool

This tool is certainly worth getting to know: it allows you to select and alter specific points on a curve, which means that you can have far greater control over modifying the curves that you've created.

If you choose the Subselect tool from the Tools panel and click the mouse on one of your pre-drawn Beziers, you'll see that a skeleton-like structure is shown inside your shape. This shows you the start and end points of the curves, and the shape of the curves that underlie the displayed drawing:

You might have to zoom right in to see this clearly – it's easier to see this if you have a big fat line like the one in this screenshot.

And there's more: if you click on one of the little 'nodes' on the skeleton, the Bezier bow ties will appear...

...allowing you to modify the curves with precision and confidence.

There's another application of the Subselect tool that's extremely useful – you can use it to modify shapes that weren't drawn with the Pen tool, too.

Go into your Mushroom movie, choose the Subselect tool, and then click on the outline stroke of the moon image.

Although it's difficult to see outside of the authoring environment, the same skeleton and node structure appears. Click on a node, and those familiar bow ties spring into view again:

This reveals that all the shapes you've drawn using Flash's drawing tools are implicitly composed of Beziers that you can modify. Once again, this shows that these integral tools can be used precisely and powerfully. By dragging the bow ties, you can rework shapes:

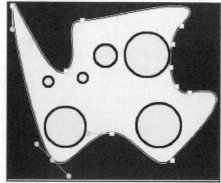

This facility is useful, way beyond converting the moon to an ectoplasmic form.

Beziers and animation

One thing about Beziers that doesn't become apparent until you play around with them is that they're not just a fancy drawing tool: they can be used to simulate real world movements much better than standard curves. For example, imagine a tennis ball hitting a net. When the ball makes contact with the net, the ball's weight and momentum will drag the net with it, changing the net's shape. If you draw your net with Beziers, the fine control we have with the bow ties lets us regulate a significant parameter – the tension of the net:

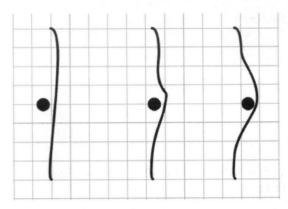

As you'll learn in detail later, these images could be animated with a shape tween. The Bezier curve bow ties can be used to 'set the tension' of the net, and therefore show its acceleration. Acceleration is a fundamental attribute of good animation, since it's the direct result of forces acting on the shape – which is what animation should try and express. With Beziers we can animate the effects of these forces more easily.

The use of Beziers used for animation rather than just for shape creation opens up a whole new facet to expressive animation. If you stop thinking 'tennis net' and start thinking 'eyebrows and mouths' for example, you can begin to see how these curves could help you animate a face as its expression changes. Why not have a play and give it a try?

In this chapter we've taken a long look at some of the more important aspects of Flash's integral tools. We haven't covered every single option, but we'll be looking at some of the other tool uses as we progress through the book.

Case study

In this exercise we're going to set up the layout and begin to create the basic interface for our portfolio web site. We'll be using this throughout the book to implement the things we discuss in each chapter, and this will help us see the Flash components we're learning about in context.

Let's start by creating the background to our movie. First, we'll set up our movie's global properties.

Background and base elements

1. Create a new Flash movie. Open the **Document Properties** dialog box using **Modify > Document** and change the dimensions of the movie's stage to 500 (width) x 400 (height) pixels.

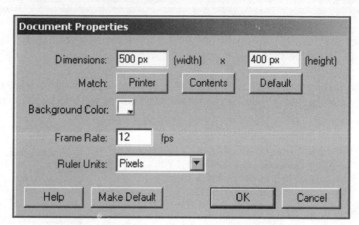

2. Change the name of the movie's default single layer to Background lines.

3. Save your movie with a suitable name.

4. Using the Rectangle tool, draw a thin rectangle (a height of 6 pixels is fine) with **no stroke** and a simple gray fill all the way across the top of your stage:

5. Using the Arrow tool, click on the gray rectangle shape to select it and copy it using the **Edit > Copy** menu option. To duplicate your shape use **Edit > Paste in Place**. Don't click on anything else yet – your new rectangle is actually selected and copied right over your original shape. Holding down the SHIFT key, press your DOWN arrow once:

6. Repeat this process until you have four lines in total. Feel free to move them around so they fit nicely together:

These lines will rest at the top of our background layout in our web site. We now need to start creating the interface that the viewer of our web site will use.

7. Add a new layer and call it `Buttons`. This is where we're going to add several shapes and words that we'll develop into a fully-fledged navigation bar as we build up our movie in later chapters.

8. Use the Text tool to create the following five separate pieces of text underneath your gray lines (making sure in the far left of the Property inspector that your Text type is set to **Static Text** in the drop-down menu):

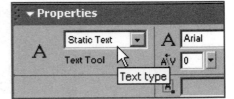

- about

- work history

- skills

- printable resume

- contact

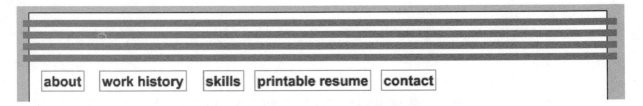

You can move the text around a bit but don't worry if they're not perfectly lined up together for now.

9. Use the Arrow tool to drag a box around all five text fields and, in the Property inspector, set the text fields' font to Arial, the font size to 12pt, and make them bold. We've chosen a dark gray color here for our text:

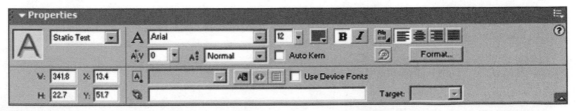

We have one more component left to draw in order to finish off our initial design: a folder-shaped window that will display our content.

10. Insert a new layer and call it content.

11. Check that **Snap to Objects** is still on (remember you can check this using **View > Snap to Objects**) and then select the Line tool. In frame 1 of the **content** layer, draw a large folder shape.

Always hold the SHIFT key while you're doing this to ensure your horizontal and vertical lines are straight. Also, make sure that the angle at the top of the folder is a perfect 45 degrees – holding the SHIFT key will constrain any angles to 45-degree increments as shown below:

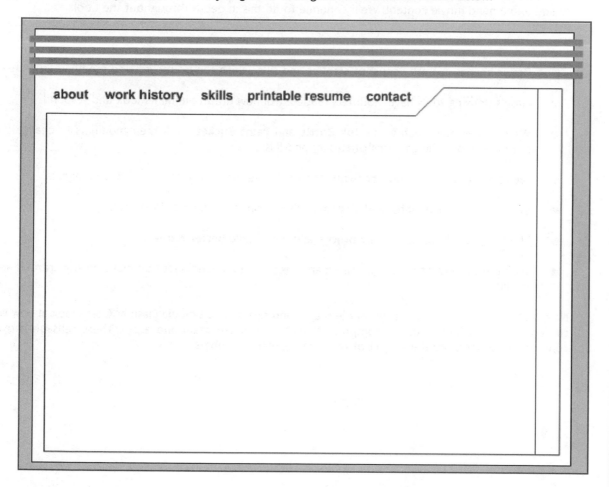

We've made the angle 45 degrees so that when we work on our button interface later it will match up perfectly with the folder shape for a nice clean look.

12. Delete any unwanted extra lines you may have made by selecting them with the Arrow tool and pressing DELETE or using the Eraser tool.

13. Save your file and close it.

That's all for the case study in this chapter. This might seem simple so far, but as you work through the case study exercises at the end of each chapter you'll see the concepts and content build bit by bit. This is the way any Flash movie is built: first you have an idea, then you create the building blocks that you need for your movie, and then you splice them all together.

Summary

In this chapter, we walked through some of the main features of the Tools panel, using the different tools to add and amend movie content. We'll continue to do this in depth throughout the book.

We saw that:

- Drawn shapes in Flash consist of **strokes** and **fills**, which can be moved and modified separately.

- Flash's drawing tools have modifiers that control how drawn elements look and respond.

- We can use tools (such as the **Ink Bottle** and **Paint Bucket**) with their modifiers to change the attributes (color, height, etc.) of strokes and fills.

- We can also use the **Property inspector** to change the characteristics of drawn objects.

- We can create **text fields** and customize them using the Property inspector.

- The Pen tool allows us to draw precise and amendable **Bezier curves**.

- With the Subselect tool, we can select and alter the curves and lines that make up any drawn shape in Flash.

Now that we've seen how to create simple shapes and text in Macromedia Flash MX, let's look at how we can convert them into re-usable components that we can use again and again. These reusable movie content components are the subject of our next chapter – **Symbols**.

Flash Symbols and Libraries

What we'll cover in this chapter:

- **Symbols** – what they are, why they're useful, how to create them, and how to store and re-use movie content elements in the **Library**.

- The different kinds of symbol:

    - **Graphic symbols:** contain simple moving content – the cornerstone of cartoon animation in Flash.

    - **Button symbols:** the easiest method to achieving interactivity.

    - **Movie Clip symbols:** independent, self-contained movie components that free you from the linear tyranny of your movie's main timeline. They can contain as much interactivity as buttons and are the most powerful of Flash's symbols.

In Macromedia Flash MX, a **symbol** is a particular kind of movie *content* component – a piece of self-contained content that you can save away and re-use time and time again. Symbols add life and richness to your movies by loosening up the rigidity of everything having to happen along the movie's main timeline. Now that you know how to get around the stage and main timeline, and you have a working knowledge of the Tools panel, you can begin to really make Flash come to life. **Symbols are a vital part of making great Flash movies.**

Typically, you create symbols when you know that you're going to have particular elements that you'll use repeatedly in a movie or in a number of movies, or when you want to encapsulate a little piece of action or animation and use it independently of what's going on in the rest of the movie – and you can *share* the saved symbols from one movie with your other movies, too.

Using stored symbols rather than uniquely-created content for every element in your movie has at least three advantages: firstly, symbols allow you to create far more interesting, flexible, and extensible movies; secondly, it gives you the benefits of mass production and re-usable components; and thirdly, it helps you keep your movie file size small and the end user happy and attentive to your site.

In this chapter you'll learn about the three types of symbol that Flash employs, and create and use an example of each. The more complicated aspects of critical symbols will also be covered in more detail when we come to use them later in the book. Here, we'll give you a solid grounding in the basics of symbols that will stand you in good stead.

Symbol essentials

A **symbol** at its most basic level is a 'thing' in Flash that you can use time and time again. That 'thing' could be a simple picture, an interactive button, or even an entire mini-movie that runs within your main movie. You can convert your existing movie content into symbols, or you can create symbols from scratch – either way, you'll be saving the completed symbol away so that you can use it again later in your movies:

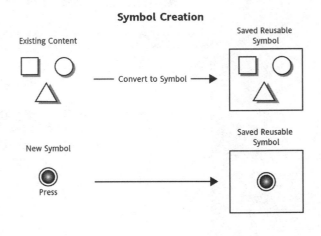

Every time you create a new symbol in Flash, it's added to a **Library** that's attached to your FLA authoring file. The Library is where all of the re-usable symbols are stored for the movie that you're working on:

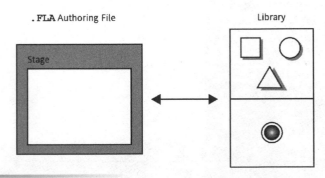

Whenever you use one of these saved symbols in your movie, you open up the Library, select the symbol that you want to add, and drag it onto your stage. The original symbol remains in the Library, however – Flash creates a 'copy' of the stored symbol and renders it on the stage for you. The stored symbol kept in the Library is like a *template* that Flash uses to create a brand new copy of the saved symbol. When you create a new, individual copy of a stored symbol on your stage, it's known as an **instance** of that stored symbol.

Each new instance is a unique object – an exact copy of the stored symbol that the instance is based on. There's also a default link between the symbol and its instances: if you amend the underlying symbol, these amendments ripple through to the instances too. However, you can change the properties (tint, size, and so on) of individual instances without affecting the underlying symbol.

One way of picturing the relationship between the stored symbol and the copy (or copies) of it that you create on the stage is to think about that familiar kitchen tool – the cookie cutter. A cookie cutter is designed to turn out multiple copies of cookies that are the same size and shape. The cookie cutter is a template for mass production of identical objects:

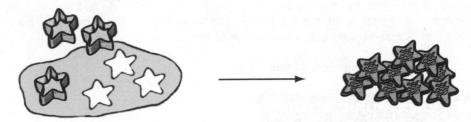

You apply the cookie cutter to the cookie dough and produce identical cookies every time. In Flash, the stored symbol is the cookie cutter, and the instance copied onto the stage is the identical individual cookie derived from the cookie cutter. With cookies, you can add toppings to specific cookies, and in Flash you can change the characteristics of individual instances via the Property inspector.

One of the beauties of creating instances of symbols is that you can then customize each instance on the stage individually. For example, suppose you need a series of buttons in your movie that the user can click on to navigate through your web site. Rather than create the same button 15 separate times, you can just create one button symbol in your Library, and then customize each instance of the button on your main movie stage.

Let's start creating some symbols and see how to implement them in practice.

Symbol types

When we create symbols in Flash, we have three basic types to choose from:

- **Graphic symbols**

- **Button symbols**

- **Movie Clip symbols**

Each type of symbol has different capabilities and levels of complexity, and the type of symbol we decide to create will be based on our judgment of what we want that symbol to do – how we want it to *behave*. For example, if we just want to re-use a static graphic that's essentially inanimate, the graphic symbol is the best fit. For a symbol that embodied some animation and maybe some sound, we'd choose to create a movie clip symbol. Each of the different symbol types has its own *range* of possible behaviors – from the simple graphic symbol, up to the potentially very complex movie clip symbol.

All three types of symbol are created by two alternative methods: either by converting an *existing* drawing or other object (such as a text field) into a symbol, or by creating a *new* symbol from scratch. You'll use both of these methods to construct symbols of all three types in the following examples.

Let's begin with the simplest kind of symbol – the graphic symbol.

Graphic symbols

Although graphic symbols are not as feature-rich as button or movie clip symbols, they're no less important. They're used for static images throughout your movie, so if you know that you're going to use an object over and over again, but don't need it to be interactive or animated, then a graphic symbol is your best bet. A graphic symbol is a symbol whose content remains static.

Let's create a simple graphic symbol now.

Creating a graphic symbol

Here, we're going to create a new symbol.

1. Open Flash and create a new movie by clicking on the **File > New** menu option.

2. Select the Text tool from the Tools panel (ensuring that you have **Static Text** selected in the left-hand side of the Property inspector) and click on the stage. In the text field that appears, write the words `Graphic Symbol`. Click on the Arrow tool so that you can select the text that you've just placed on the stage and then choose the **Insert > Convert to Symbol** menu option. The **Convert to Symbol** dialog box will appear:

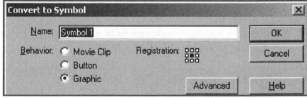

This is where we choose the *type* of symbol that we want to create. Notice that Flash labels the different categories of symbol using the term **Behavior** – as we've seen, this is because each type of symbol has its own repertoire of behaviors.

3. If it's not selected already, change the behavior of the symbol to a graphic by clicking on the bottom-most radio button – next to the word **Graphic**.

4. Next, change the name from Symbol 1 to Graphic Symbol by deleting the existing text in the **Name** field and typing your own.

5. Also in this dialog box, you'll see a square that's composed of nine small squares, one of them black. This is the **Registration** matrix and you can click on any of the squares to define where Flash will consider the center of your symbol to be. If it's not already selected, click on the center square because we want the **registration point** to be in the very center of our symbol. Finally, click **OK**.

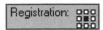

After clicking **OK**, you'll see that your text field now has a registration point – a small cross – in the center, like we wanted:

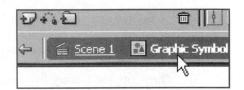

So far we've created a new graphic symbol, assigned it a registration point and given it a symbol name. This is the name that the symbol will be stored under in the Library.

6. Double-click on the **Graphic Symbol** text field. When we do this, Flash whisks us away to a separate editing window. We're no longer looking at the main stage – instead, we're in the **Edit Symbols** window for our graphic symbol. Flash indicates this to us by highlighting the name of our symbol below the timeline, next to the name of our movie's default first scene:

> *The blue arrow on the left is Flash's equivalent of the ubiquitous back button, giving us a shortcut to step back a level from wherever we are. In our current scene, the back button will take us back to the main timeline in Scene 1*

Our symbol was created by converting content using the **Insert > Convert to Symbol** menu option. However, you can also create a symbol from scratch by choosing the **Insert > New Symbol** menu option.

When you choose to create a symbol from scratch, rather than converting existing content, Flash automatically puts you into Edit Symbols mode. This is because when you create a new symbol, or convert existing content to a symbol, you don't modify it on the main stage – you can only alter the symbol's content in Edit Symbols mode.

You'll see that even in Edit Symbols mode, the timeline and layer list are displayed. This is very important: it shows you that each symbol has its own internal layers and timeline. So, if you added extra layers while inside Edit Symbols mode, this would only affect that one symbol, not the entire movie.

> *It can sometimes be a bit confusing to see whether you're in Edit Symbols mode or normal editing mode, and the only way to really be sure is by checking below your timeline to see if the symbol name appears there: if it does, you're definitely in Edit Symbols mode, and if it doesn't, you're not. Additionally, creating symbols from scratch in Edit Symbols mode denies you seeing the rest of your movie. You're more likely to achieve the continuity you want by designing your symbol on the main stage and converting it once you're happy that it fits well with the rest of your movie.*

7. Click on the back button or **Scene 1** button to return to the main timeline (these are to the left of our graphic symbol name, just below the main timeline).

    We're now back in normal edit mode, and we're looking at the stage and the main timeline.

8. Select the text field with the Arrow tool and delete it. Our symbol has disappeared and to see it again we need to open up the Library. Flash has automatically created a place to store our new symbol in the Library that's associated with this authoring file.

9. Open up the Library by using the **Window > Library** menu option, and take a look at the window that pops up:

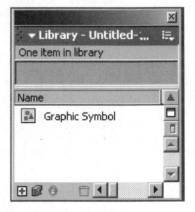

10. There's the entry for our new graphic symbol – in the white box at the bottom. The small icon with the circle, square, and triangle on it next to the name is the visual identifier for a graphic symbol.

11. Double-click on the icon next to our new symbol's name in the Library window. This will take us back into Edit Symbols mode, where we can work on the actual content of our symbol.

12. Back in Edit Symbols mode (you'll have a blank screen containing your Graphic Symbol with the registration point in the center), select the Text tool from the Tools panel.

13. Using the text properties in the Property inspector, change your font's color. Finally, click on the blue back arrow or the **Scene 1** button to return to the timeline and normal editing mode.

Although there's no text anywhere on the stage because we deleted it earlier, if you look in the Library and click once on your Graphic Symbol, you'll see the changes you made to your symbol in the Preview pane of the Library. To put the symbol back on the stage, we can simply do so by clicking and dragging it out to the main stage.

The Library works like a mini file browser. You can use it to find symbols and use them, or to create new symbols, or delete symbols you no longer need.

Preview Window ──→

Symbol in Library ──→

New Symbol   New Folder   Properties   Delete

An alternative way to convert an object to a symbol is to use the Library as a shortcut, simply by dragging an object into it from the stage. Let's give this a try.

14. On the main timeline, use the Rectangle tool to draw a square anywhere on the stage.

15. Using the Arrow tool, double-click on the square to select its fill and stroke.

16. Drag the square into the bottom of the Library and you'll see a small rectangle appear at the bottom of your cursor (or a plus sign, depending on your system), suggesting that we want to add something to the Library:

When you release the mouse button to confirm, a familiar window appears:

Yes – it's the **Convert to Symbol** dialog box again.

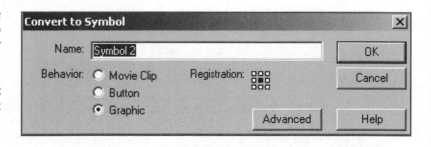

95

17. Name your symbol `Square Symbol`, click on the center-left square of the Registration matrix, and give the symbol a **Graphic Behavior**.

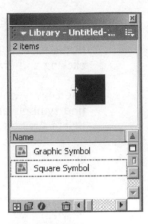

Notice that your new symbol has been added to the Library, and that you're getting a preview of the symbol in the Preview pane. The preview also shows the square to the right of the registration point.

> *Dragging an object into the Library to convert it into a symbol is just another one of Flash's shortcuts. There is no standard way to create a symbol, just use what suits your way of working. The useful thing about this particular approach is that you can choose where in the Library you want to put the new symbol by dropping it over a specific folder. We'll look at how to create folders in the Library in a moment.*

Before we move on to the next part of this chapter, let's take a quick look at *manually* adjusting the registration point of a symbol.

18. Double-click on your new **Square Symbol** so that Flash takes you to Edit Symbols mode.

19. Choose the **Window > Info** menu option to bring up the **Info** panel:

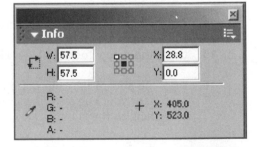

The **X** and **Y** boxes on the right are the coordinates that determine the position of the registration point:

20. Enter a value of 14 in the **Y** box and press ENTER. You'll notice that the registration point is now closer to the top left corner of the square:

The Info panel affords you greater flexibility when positioning your registration point.

You might be wondering why we have these various options for positioning the registration points of our symbols. Well, if we wanted to make a preloader bar, we would use the center left point, or if we were animating a flower growing from the ground, we would set the registration point to the bottom center of the flower symbol.

Registration points other than the center point are more commonly used (but not exclusive to) ActionScript scenarios – such as building a preloader bar. We'll see how it can have a beneficial effect when animating a little later in the book.

Let's now go back to the Library window and see what else we can do with it.

Working with the Library

The **New Folder** button allows you to create folders in your Library as a means of organizing your symbols.

1. In the Library window, click on the **New Folder** button (second from the left at the bottom of the window); a new folder will appear in your Library with its (so far generic) name highlighted:

    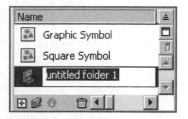

2. For the new folder's name, type `Circle Folder`, and press ENTER. Flash automatically sorts the contents of the Library into alphabetical order, so your new folder will suddenly jump above the **Graphic Symbol**.

3. Now click on your **Graphic Symbol** in the Library and drag and drop it onto the **Circle Folder** icon. As you'd expect from a file browser program, the **Graphic Symbol** is now located inside the new folder:

    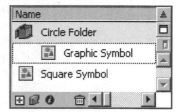

    You can tell it's inside the folder by the level of indentation.

4. Double-click on the **Circle Folder** icon: it will change to a 'closed' folder and your circle will disappear. Double-click on it again and it will reopen. Double-clicking on the name of the folder now will allow you to rename it – if you do this by mistake, just press ENTER to leave it as it is.

5. With the folder open, click on the **Graphic Symbol** to highlight it and then click on the **Properties** button in the Library:

    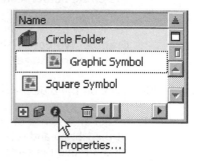

This will open the **Symbol Properties** dialog box, from which you can rename your symbol or change its behavior – that is, its *type*:

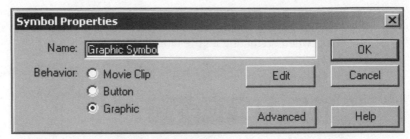

6. Click **Cancel** to exit the dialog box without making any changes.

7. Now click on the **Square Symbol** to select it. Next, click on the **Delete** button in the Library. You'll be prompted with a dialog box asking whether you *really* want to delete the **Square Symbol**:

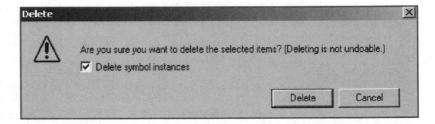

Flash always gives you this prompt, as you cannot undo deleting something from the Library: once it's gone, it's gone, and the only way to get it back is to load a previously saved version of the file, or just bite the bullet and draw it again.

The checkbox entitled **Delete symbol instances** is an option that allows you to choose whether or not to delete any instances of that symbol that reside in your movie. If the checkbox is ticked and you delete a symbol, all instances of that symbol in your corresponding movie will be deleted also.

8. Click **Delete** to get rid of the **Square Symbol**.

9. Select the **Graphic Symbol** and drag it out of the folder so that the **Graphic Symbol** icon is at the same level of indentation as the **Circle Folder** icon, then delete the folder:

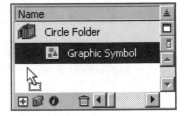

You'll now be back where you started with just the single original **Graphic Symbol** in the Library. Let's put an **instance** of this symbol on our stage.

10. Click on the blue arrow to get you back to the main stage if you're not there already.

11. To get an instance of your symbol onto the stage, just click and drag the name of your symbol out of the Library and release it on the stage. Don't worry about placing things too precisely – you can always move the symbol around again later.

You'll now have a single instance of your symbol on the stage.

12. To illustrate how easy it is to re-use symbols, drag out another couple of instances of the **Graphic Symbol** and put them anywhere you like on the stage:

> **Graphic⊕Symbol**
>
> **Graphic⊕Symbol**
>
> **Graphic⊕Symbol**

That's a lot easier than making each component separately every time, isn't it? Notice that we've selected all three instances on the stage, and that they're all displaying a little cross, indicating that they're symbols.

Perhaps the best thing of all here is that even though we now have *three* images on the stage, they still only take up the space of *one* picture in the final SWF file: this is because the *instances* of the symbol on the stage are really just 'coordinates' telling Flash where to put a copy of the content of the *master* symbol stored in the Library.

OK, we've got our instances of the symbol on the stage – what if we decide that we want to change the symbol in the Library that they're based on?

Modifying symbols

When you change the symbol defined and stored in your Library, all of the *instances* of that symbol on your stage will change as well.

Modifying a symbol in the Library

1. Select the **Graphic Symbol** in the Library, and then double-click on its picture in the Preview pane. This will take you into Edit Symbols mode.

2. Select the symbol on the (Edit Symbols) stage and then select the Text tool from the Tools panel. In the Property inspector choose a text color that's obviously different from the original color.

3. Now when you click on the **Scene 1** tab below the timeline to return to the main stage, you'll notice that *all* of the instances of your graphic symbol have changed to the same color as the master in the Library.

This is clearly a very powerful feature, meaning that you can redesign and amend significant parts of your movie without having to edit each and every symbol throughout the movie – you can just change the symbol in the Library that the individual instances are based on.

Let's now experiment with the second, and slightly more complex type of symbol – the **button symbol**.

Button symbols

Buttons are essential features of any interactive web site, and they're the key to any good menu or site navigation interface. Why? Because we're all tuned-in to clicking on buttons and having them do things for us – it's almost an unconscious action – using buttons is such an obvious thing that we're often unaware that we're doing it when we're interacting with a web site or software application. However, if you ever go to a site whose navigation architecture doesn't provide you with buttons, you'll quickly become aware just how vital they are.

It's amazingly easy to create buttons in Flash and include them in our movies, and they're one of the components that take Flash from being a great animation package to being a web application development tool. Flash buttons are irresistibly important because they let you into the world of true interactivity, where your site visitor can control their experience. Whether it's jumping from movie to movie or kicking off a series of complex actions, buttons can be the way in. In Flash, button symbols embody the behaviors that open up the interactive world.

To get us started, we'll build a simple button and take you through its basic features and capabilities. Later in the book we'll be doing some extremely interesting and important things with buttons.

Creating a button symbol

Let's create that button symbol. First, we need a shape to convert to a symbol.

1. In the same movie where you created your graphic symbol, select the Oval tool and draw a circle with a stroke and fill of your choice. (Delete the instances of **Graphic Symbol** from your main stage to give you a clean space to work in.) To adjust the properties of the circle, select it with the Arrow tool and go to the Property inspector – you'll see the circle's dimensions in the **W** and **H** boxes in the bottom half of the Property inspector. We've made our circle 120 pixels across to create a big hefty button.

2. Select the circle and change it into a symbol, either by using the **Insert > Convert to Symbol** menu option or by pressing the F8 shortcut. (Incidentally, why this 'convert' option comes under the **Insert** rather than the **Modify** menu is one of the many mysteries of Flash, and something that just has to be learnt and accepted. Suggestions on a postcard please...)

3. In the **Convert to Symbol** dialog box, choose the **Button** behavior type. Name your button Button Symbol, give it a central registration point and press **OK**:

You should notice three things: your circle on the stage will now have a bounding box around it, indicating that it's now a symbol; the new symbol will appear in your Library; and, if you bring up the Property inspector, you'll see the symbol's name displayed next to a 'pointy finger over a rectangle' icon – this is the icon for a button symbol:

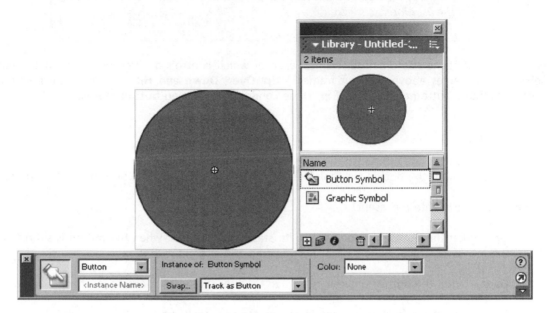

4. The circle that you drew on the stage has now become an instance of the new symbol in the Library.

5. Double-click on the instance of your **Button Symbol** on the stage, and you'll be taken into Edit Symbols mode again.

> *Editing a symbol by double-clicking on its instance on the stage sends Flash into* **Edit In Place** *mode. This mode is particularly useful for changing a symbol when you need to view it in relation to other symbols on the stage.*

6. You may have noticed that your timeline has changed:

    Whenever you create or edit a button symbol you'll see this button-specific style of timeline. This timeline is only visible in Edit Symbols mode, and every button symbol has this same kind of special internal timeline: it's this timeline that controls how the button will behave when we interact with it.

> *A button symbol's internal timeline is 'nested' inside the symbol. When Flash comes across an instance (copy) of the symbol on the stage, it is aware of the button's timeline, but the button only does anything when the user interacts with it.*

Every button timeline has only four frames, each of which controls a different aspect of the button's behavior. The names above the four frames – **Up**, **Over**, **Down** and **Hit** – refer to the four possible conditions that a button can find itself in. These conditions are called **button states**.

Button states

The states of a button are defined in the four frames of the button's timeline, as mentioned above. Each frame describes what the button will look like and what it will *do* when the button is in that state.

So what does each state represent?

- **Up** – What the button will look like in its 'static' state: that is, when the button is sitting there in the movie interface, waiting for a user to come and interact with it.

- **Over** – What the button will look like when the user runs their mouse over it.

- **Down** – What the button will look like when the user clicks on it.

- **Hit** – This is a special state that you can't see in your finished movie: the Hit state defines the part of the button that is actually clickable. Think of it as a target for the mouse to hit: hitting this target will make the button work. Make sure that whatever part of the button you want people to be able to click is defined in the Hit state. It doesn't have to be pretty, but it's important to clearly define the Hit state.

OK, let's see how these states work by defining them for our circular button symbol.

Making your button work

At the moment, your button is just a single-state, lifeless circle that might as well be a static graphic symbol. What your button needs is that extra something that makes a button a button – interactivity. We define this interactivity in the four frames of the button's timeline.

Notice that only one of the frames on the button's timeline is actually a **keyframe** – the first frame, which represents the button's Up state – the other three frames are currently blank:

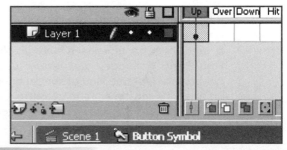

This is because Flash automatically populated the button's Up state when we created the button symbol: Flash assumed that we wanted to display the circle we'd drawn when the button is in its Up state. We can edit this keyframe and change the image that's displayed if we want to.

To create the other three states for the button, we first need to convert the three blank frames in the timeline into keyframes: remember, a keyframe is what defines a significant change to a piece of Flash content. By defining these keyframes and their content, we're telling Flash how we want our button to behave.

1. Click individually on each of the three blank frames in the button timeline and press F6 to insert a keyframe. You should now have a full timeline:

2. Click on the Over state in the timeline. Your button will automatically be selected.

3. Select a color from the Property inspector that's different to the original button symbol color. The color of your button will automatically change to reflect your new choice.

4. Now select the Down state keyframe in the timeline and change it to another color in the same way. Leave the Hit state as it is for now.

5. Test your movie by using the **Control > Test Movie** menu option, or by pressing CTRL-ENTER. This will open a new window showing what your finished movie will look like when it's rendered in the web browser.

6. Move your mouse over the button...

    ...and it changes color. This color is the color you defined for the Over state.

    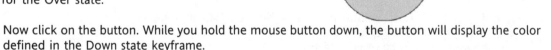

7. Now click on the button. While you hold the mouse button down, the button will display the color defined in the Down state keyframe.

8. You have just created your first button and taken your first steps towards interactivity. It was pretty easy, wasn't it? But remember, what you're learning here about button states is the basic foundation on which you can build an infinitely complex universe of interactivity.

9. Close the Test Movie window and you'll be returned to the Edit In Place mode where you left it.

    At the moment, we haven't explicitly defined a different Hit state for our button: Flash is currently using the image from the preceding keyframe to define the Hit state. Let's be more explicit...

10. Click on the Hit state keyframe on the timeline and use the Rectangle tool to draw a big rectangle (any color you like) around your button:

    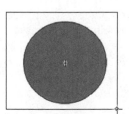

11. Now go into the **Test Movie** window again.

This time, even though everything looks the same, when you run the mouse over your button you'll see it change color before you get to the actual button itself:

This is because you defined the Hit state (invisible to the user) as a larger area than the (visible) button. You may be wondering why you would ever want to do this – normally you wouldn't, but there is one case where this technique is incredibly useful: when you want to use a piece of text as a button.

Making buttons from text

1. Click on the **Scene 1** tab below the timeline to get back to the main stage.

2. Using the Text tool, find a clear part of your stage and type `Hello` in any font and color.

3. Click on the Arrow tool, select your text, and then convert it to a button symbol (F8), naming it `Hello`. As normal, give it a central registration point.

4. Insert a keyframe into each of the button states as you did before, and test your movie.

This time when you move your mouse over the text, it seems to flicker on and off. This is because the Hit state of the button is defined, by default, as the actual text itself – the gaps between the letters and the 'holes' in the letters don't respond to the mouse. If all text buttons were like this, nobody would be able to use them, and this is where the Hit state comes in.

Go back to Edit Symbols mode and click on the Hit state keyframe. Using the Rectangle tool, drag out a rectangle (make sure it has a fill) that just covers all of your text:

Don't worry about not being able to see your text any more in the authoring environment. As you saw before, the Hit state image is invisible in the displayed movie.

5. Test your movie again. As your mouse moves over the text it stays highlighted: this is because there is now a (invisible) border around the text, which means that the whole of the text is now defined as the Hit area.

6. Close the **Test Movie** window, and then click on the **Scene 1** tab to return to the main stage.

There's an easy way to see, and edit, all of the symbols in your movie. There are two buttons below the timeline on the right:

Edit Scene

Edit Symbols

If you click on the **Edit Symbols** button, a drop-down menu will appear with a list of all of the symbols available to you in your movie's Library:

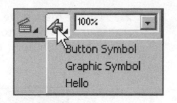

When you click on one of the named symbols, you'll instantly be taken to the editing mode for that symbol. Try it with your three symbols and see. You can go back to the main stage by either clicking on the **Scene 1** tab as you've done before, or by clicking on the **Edit Scene** button and then selecting **Scene 1** from the menu that pops up.

If you look at the Property inspector when you're in Edit Symbols mode, you'll see on the right that there are options to add sound and script to our creations. We'll be looking at this later in the book. Next though, let's take an initial look at the third type of symbol in Flash – the **movie clip symbol**. We'll be using movie clips more and more as we progress through the book.

Movie clip symbols

The **movie clip symbol** is the third and final member of the Flash symbols set. Movie clip symbols – usually referred to as **movie clips** – are vitally important components in Flash movies. The simplest explanation of movie clips is that they are 'a movie within a movie': you can use them to create entirely self-contained pieces of action that you want to run independently of the rest of the things on the main timeline. Movie clips can have multiple layers, just like the main timeline, and contain many graphic, animation, and sound components. An example of a typical movie clip would be a clip that encapsulated a logo and some background music: you can have the music playing and the logo fading in and out repeatedly throughout your whole main movie while other action changes around it.

> *Like the button symbol, a movie clip symbol has its own internal timeline. However, a movie clip's timeline isn't just limited to the four standard frames. As we progress through this book, you'll find that movie clips are truly flexible and multi-talented members of the Flash team.*

Movie clips can be very complicated things, containing all manner of actions and animations. In this section we'll just introduce the basics of what movie clips are and how to use them.

Creating a movie clip symbol

1. We'll need an uncluttered stage, so close the current movie and create a fresh new one.

2. On the main stage, use the Rectangle tool and draw a square – any color you like. Select the square and convert it to a symbol. Make sure the symbol's behavior is set to **Movie Clip** and its registration point to the center. Name the new symbol `Square Clip`:

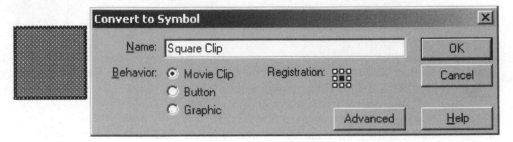

3. Now double-click on the square with the Arrow tool to get into Edit Symbols mode.

Notice the timeline inside your new movie clip. This timeline works just like your normal one above the stage in the main movie. The difference is that your movie clip symbol's timeline only applies to what happens inside the symbol itself: any action and animation that you create using this timeline will be encapsulated inside this movie clip. You can do anything that you would normally do in your main movie inside a movie clip, letting you create completely self-contained units of movie content that you can then add to your main movie by dragging the movie clip symbol onto the main stage.

Let's make a quick shape tween as an example.

4. Still inside your new movie clip, click on frame 20 and press F6 to insert a keyframe.

5. Now click outside the square in frame 20 to deselect it, and use the Arrow tool to pull out the sides and make an irregular shape to your taste:

Now that we've got two keyframes with distinct content in them, let's animate the shape tween.

6. Click on frame 1 and go to the Property inspector. Select **Shape** from the **Tween** drop-down menu to create a shape tween between the two keyframes (just as we did with our mushroom movie in Chapter 1).

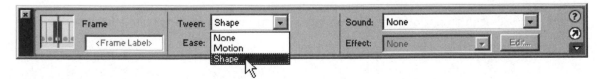

7.   Now click on the **Scene** tab below the timeline to get back to the main stage.

8.   Open your Library if it's not already displayed: there'll be one thing in it – your **Square Clip**:

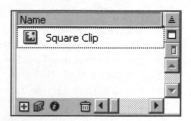

   The strange blue sunburst next to the symbol's name is the icon that identifies movie clip symbols.

9.   Click on the icon for the **Square Clip**.

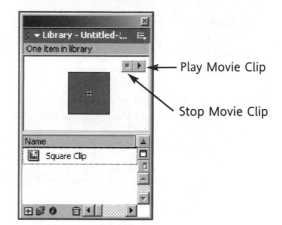

Play Movie Clip

Stop Movie Clip

   You'll see that there are two interesting features in the top right of the Preview pane:

10. These two VCR-type controls are used to preview your movie clip inside the Library window (these controls are also available when you select a button symbol in the Library). If you click on the 'play' button, your movie clip will start playing in the Preview pane. You can use the 'stop' control to halt playback if it's a long movie clip.

11. Drag a couple of copies of your **Square Clip** from the Library onto the stage.

12. Press ENTER to preview your movie – nothing will happen. This is because movie clips aren't rendered in preview mode.

   If you want to see your movie clips play, you have to use the **Control > Test Movie** (CTRL-ENTER) menu option. Alternatively, you can publish your movie by pressing CTRL-F12. If you do this you'll see your animations happily, er, animating. Movie clips can do so much more than this though, but you'll have to wait until the later chapters before you can find out just how powerful they really are.

13. Save your movie as Movie Clip.fla.

14. Close down the Movie Clip.fla movie.

It's probably worth mentioning here that graphic symbols have similar functionality to movie clips. The main difference is that movie clips can be scripted, whereas graphic symbols cannot. Graphic symbol file sizes are slightly smaller than a movie clip, so if you just want a symbol with a simple tween, it's probably worth using a graphic symbol.

Movie clips and the main timeline

When you drag an instance of a movie clip symbol on to your stage, you bring with it all of the action that you've added to the movie clip's timeline. When Flash finds the instance of the symbol in a keyframe on the main timeline, it digs down into the symbol and plays the content that it finds encapsulated in the symbol's internal timeline. Simultaneously, Flash continues along the main movie's timeline, rendering any content that it finds there. In this context, you can think of movie clips as separate 'loops' that get started off and are then left to run their course while the main movie's playhead continues along the main timeline. Your movie clip is still integrated with the main movie, though – it shares the host movie's frame rate and background color, for example.

Another way of thinking about movie clips is that they're the 'children' of the main movie. The main 'parent' timeline plays in sequence, and periodically in its life – when it comes across a movie clip symbol in a keyframe – it'll spawn a movie clip. Once Flash has given life to the movie clip, that movie clip enjoys an independent life of its own while the main timeline continues separately.

Imagine a movie where we create a static background layer (a gradient) that lasts for fifty frames:

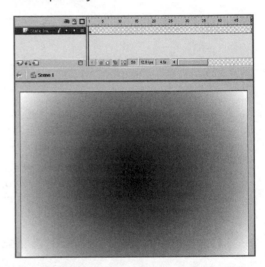

When we test our movie, we see the static image displayed for fifty frames, and then the movie loops and starts again. Now suppose that we create a keyframe at frame 10 and drag a 'morphing square' movie clip from our Library into it. Next, we could add a 'morphing circle' movie clip in a new keyframe at frame 25:

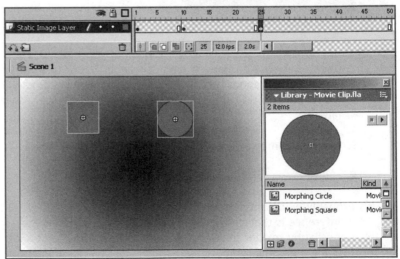

When we test our movie now, we'll find that the static background will display for a few frames and then, when the playhead hits the keyframe at frame 10, the morphing square movie clip will be triggered. The main movie playhead will continue along the main timeline until it encounters the morphing circle at frame 25, whereupon it will kick off that movie clip before continuing to display the static background until frame 50 – the end of the movie. It's very important to remember that launching these movie clips doesn't pause or stop the playback of the main timeline: all three playback elements (the main timeline, plus the two internal movie clip timelines) play back simultaneously:

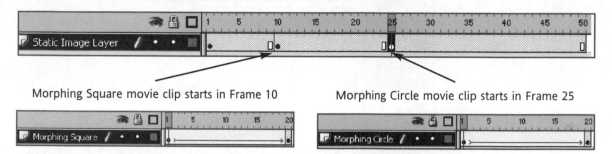

Morphing Square movie clip starts in Frame 10   Morphing Circle movie clip starts in Frame 25

A movie clip has a mind of its own: its behavior is embedded in its internal timeline. However, the parent timeline can still have the authority to tell the child movie clip what to do: it can use ActionScript commands to tell the movie clip to stop, start, and change position and so on. We'll see this in practice once we've learned some ActionScript.

So far, we've dealt exclusively with symbols in the Library that are attached to the specific movie that we've been working on. But, Flash also gives us the facility to re-use symbols from other movies' Libraries.

Sharing symbols

Let's take a quick peek at this facility.

Using symbols from other movies

1. Create a new movie file.

2. Now open up the new movie's Library window. As you might expect, it's currently an empty Library:

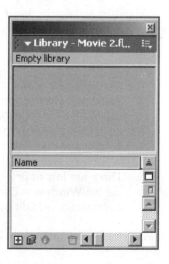

3. Go to the **File** menu and choose the **Open as Library** option.

4. In the resulting dialog box, navigate to the folder where you stored your Movie Clip.fla file and select it:

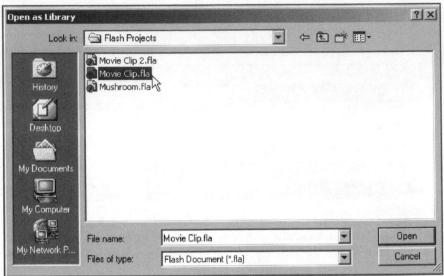

5. Once you've clicked on the **Open** button, take another look at your Library window:

You now have the symbol from that movie available to use in your new movie. This means that you can build up a collection of common symbols and share them between different movies – another laborsaving device from Flash! Flash also implements a feature whereby people can share Libraries across networks and even over the web, but this is a little beyond the scope of this present book.

There are lots of pre-built buttons and other symbols already stored in Flash. You can access them via the **Window > Common Libraries** menu option. Open up some examples and check out their construction in Edit Symbols mode.

Finally in this chapter, let's implement some of the things that we've just discussed in our case study project.

Case study

Creating symbols

1. Open up the case study movie that you were working on at the end of the previous chapter.

    At this point you should have your basic button interface, content window (the folder shape), and the background lines all sitting on their separate layers. In order to give them life we need to convert some of our objects into symbols.

2. Open up your Library by going to **Window > Library**.

3. Select your **about** text box and convert it to a button symbol by dragging it into the bottom half of the Library window. Name this button symbol about button and give it a central registration point:

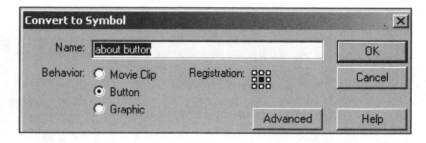

4. Repeat this process to convert the remaining text fields into button symbols, naming each one according to the individual text. When you're finished you should have five button symbols in your Library:

    At the moment our buttons don't really look like buttons do they? They're just text. Let's make them look more realistic.

5. Double-click on your **about button** to enter Edit Symbols mode. With the Rectangle tool, draw a rectangle with no stroke and a light gray fill around your **about** text. It doesn't matter what the width is, but ensure that the rectangle's height is **30** pixels.

6. Double-click on the gray rectangle with the Arrow tool and enter the height of 30 pixels in the bottom half of the Property inspector.

7. With the gray fill still selected, go to **Window > Transform** to open the Transform panel and enter 45 in the **Skew horizontally** field:

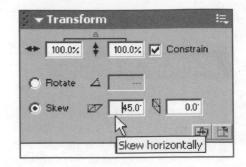

8. Move your gray skewed shape so that the **about** text is in the center.

Now we've drawn our button shape let's make it work.

9. Enter a keyframe in its Over state (F6). With the Line tool, draw a dark gray outline around the shape and make the text a lighter shade of gray. (Remember that holding SHIFT when using the Line tool enables you to draw perfectly straight horizontal, vertical or 45 degree diagonal lines.)

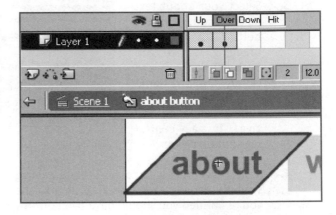

10. Enter a keyframe in the Down state and use the Free Transform tool to make your button very slightly smaller.

11. Finally, enter a keyframe in the Hit state. Copy the Up state keyframe and paste it here in the Hit state using the **Edit > Paste in Place** menu option.

All the button states have now been set. All that remains now is for you to repeat steps 5 through 11 for the other four buttons in your Library – so go ahead and do just that. (Remember to click on **Scene 1** or the blue arrow to return you to the stage after working with each button.)

12. Once you've finished editing all five of your buttons, click on the **New Folder** button and name the resulting folder Buttons:

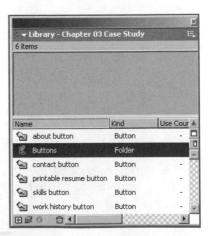

13. Now select all five of your button symbols and drag them into the **Buttons** folder:

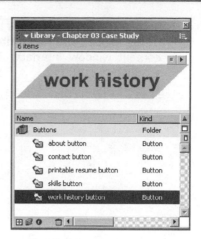

Now you can go back to your main movie stage and delete the text symbols from the stage. This doesn't actually delete them from your movie as we have them safely stored away in the Library. We'll be retrieving them from the Library later as we enhance our case study web site.

Now we've finished converting our buttons, let's move on to the folder shape where the content is eventually going to be placed.

14. Select the whole of the lower content window and convert it into a movie clip called `content`:

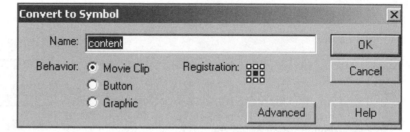

15. Double-click on your **content** movie clip to go into Edit Symbols mode. Insert a new layer called `scroll buttons` and rename layer 1 `interface`:

16. Go to **Window > Common Libraries > Buttons** to open the pre-built buttons Library. Open up the **Circle Buttons** folder:

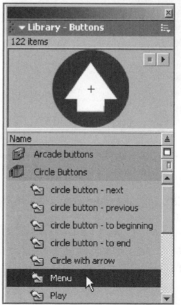

17. Back on the **scroll buttons** layer, drag an instance of the **Menu** button out onto the right side of the content window interface. This will become our scroll area:

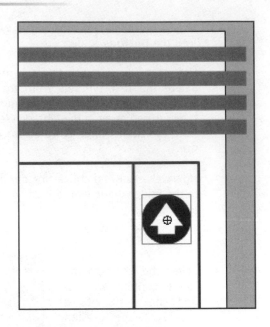

18. Copy the **Menu** button instance you just dragged onto the stage. Then go to **Edit > Paste in Place**. While holding down the SHIFT key, press your DOWN arrow key several times to move your button straight down. With the button still selected, go to **Modify > Transform > Flip Vertical**. Now you should have a pair of buttons that, later in the book, we'll activate to scroll the content up and down:

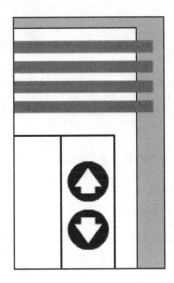

19. To help keep things organized, select the **Menu** button in your Library and drag it into the **Buttons** folder.

20. Finally, save your case study movie and close it.

Summary

In this chapter, we've taken a preliminary look at the nature, creation, and storage of symbols in Macromedia Flash MX.

We saw that:

- **Symbols** are self-contained pieces of movie content that we can create once and then use many times in our movies.

- When we create a copy of a symbol on the stage, it's called an **instance**.

- Symbols are stored in a **Library**, and we can organize the Library and use it to share symbols between different movies.

- Symbols have their own '**internal timeline**', which allows them to work independently from the main movie's timeline:

    - **Graphic symbols** can contain multiple frames and moving images in their timeline.

    - **Button symbols** have a standard four-frame internal timeline. This timeline encodes the different button **states**.

    - **Movie clip symbols** are the multi-talented superstars of the symbols world. Their internal timelines are infinitely customizable. You can embed the same kind of multi-layered graphics and sound content in movie clip symbols that you can on the movie's main timeline. It's also possible to have graphic and button symbols as well as other movie clips within a movie clip symbol.

We'll be seeing much more of symbols and their use later in this book. In the next chapter, we're going to examine the features that Flash gives us to help us manage and arrange multiple pieces of content on the stage.

Managing Content

What we'll cover in this chapter:

- *Precision content assembly and placement on the (three-dimensional) Flash stage.*

- ***Grouping objects*** *for consistency and convenience.*

- *Using **grids**, **rulers**, **guides** and **alignment tools** to place objects exactly where you want them.*

- ***Transforming objects*** *with control and confidence.*

- ***Stacking*** *multiple objects inside a layer.*

- *Splitting content with **Distribute to Layers**.*

- *Layer management with **folders**.*

In this chapter we're going to examine the tools and facilities that Macromedia Flash MX gives us for aligning and arranging objects on the stage. In doing so, we'll be working on the stage in **three dimensions**: width, height, and depth.

When you're creating movies that only have a couple of visual components, arrangement and alignment isn't so much of an issue, but if you're building larger-scale movies, or if you want to make your movies look more elegant and effective, you need to ensure that the components in your movie are efficiently and harmoniously set out. Additionally, when your movies are growing in size and complexity, you need ways of grouping content elements together so that they're easier to maintain and amend. Flash provides us with plenty of tools in these respects, and getting a grip on these tools will save you a lot of pain and frustration.

Let's begin by seeing how Flash can ease the burden of moving things around and editing them while maintaining proportions and relative positions.

Grouping objects and editing groups

You've already seen how useful grouping can be when you're manipulating single objects, preventing you from cutting objects in half or picking up just the fill. Here, we'll look more closely at grouping and the benefits that it brings. You can think of grouping as an easy way to organize and manipulate multiple objects.

Grouping multiple objects

1. Open a new movie.

2. Using the Rectangle tool, draw a square type shape anywhere on your stage. Now draw a smaller circle on a nearby part of the stage with the Oval tool.

3. Use the Arrow tool to drag a box around both objects to select them, and then group them using the **Modify > Group** menu option (or CTRL + G). Now when you move one of the objects, the other will move with it, staying in exactly the same position relative to the other object:

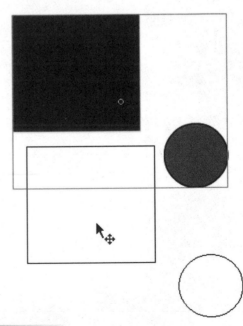

This is clearly a useful feature when you're dealing with large numbers of objects and you don't want to move them around individually by hand, and it'll help you maintain the design and look of your movie when you're maintaining it.

You can group lines, fills, buttons, graphics, movie clips and text – in fact pretty much anything that you can put on the movie stage. A sure sign to tell whether an object is part of a group or not is the thin colored highlighting line that appears around the outer edges of grouped objects. You can change your default highlight color by choosing the **Edit > Preferences** menu option and amending the **Highlight Color** option on the **General** tab:

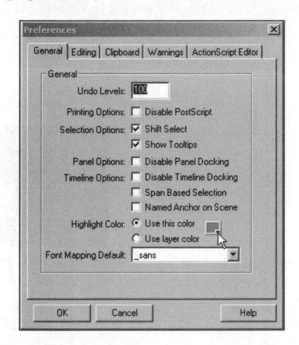

It's also extremely easy to ungroup objects in Flash and have them go back to their original individual states.

4. Click on your grouped shapes with the Arrow tool to select them and use the **Modify > Ungroup** menu option. They'll now be returned to two distinct objects with their own separate lines and fills.

5. Use the Line tool to draw a triangle on your stage and fill it with color.

6. Now drag a box around all three of your objects with the Arrow tool and group them all together.

It would be a laborious process if, every time you wanted to edit a specific line or fill within a group, you had to ungroup it, edit it, and then group it again. Flash gets around this by having an **Edit Group** mode. This mode is used to add, subtract, or change elements in groups.

Editing a group of objects

1. To enter Edit Group mode, simply double-click on your group, or select the group on the stage, and use the **Edit > Edit Selected** menu option.

2. Once you're in Edit Group mode you'll notice something has changed below your timeline. In the same place where the symbol name was displayed in Edit Symbols mode, it now says **Group** with an icon next to it similar to that of a graphic symbol:

   This is Flash's visual cue to let you know that you're currently editing a group of objects. Another visual cue is that when you're in Edit Group mode, as with Edit in Place when editing symbols, all of the objects on the stage apart from the group you're editing will be 'dimmed down' and inaccessible.

3. In Edit Group mode, deform your triangle using the Arrow tool and move it to somewhere else on the stage:

   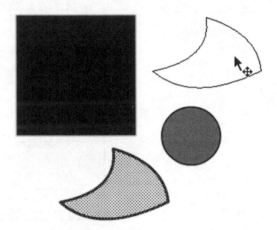

4. Return to the main stage using the same method as you would from Edit Symbols mode – clicking on the **Scene 1** button or the back button to the left of the Scene icon.

   Back on the main stage, everything is still grouped together and moves as one object, but your 'once-was-a-triangle' shape is now happily sitting in its new position in the group.

5. Save your file as group.fla and then close it. We'll be using it later on in this chapter.

   There's no limit to the amount of groups you can have in Flash. In fact, you can have symbols within groups, groups within groups, and even groups within symbols within groups – the possibilities are endless.

Symbols within symbols

'Nested' symbols are easily manageable from within the Flash interface.

A hierarchy of nested symbols

1. Open a new Flash movie with **File > New**. Select the Line tool and give it a stroke width of 4 in the Property inspector. Draw a rough car body on the stage:

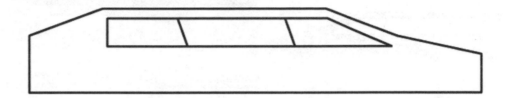

2. Fill the body of your car using the Paint Bucket tool, selecting your favorite color from the Color palette in the Property inspector.

3. Draw a box around the car with the Arrow tool and select **Insert > Convert to Symbol**, or press F8, to make the car graphic a symbol. Name the new symbol car, select **Movie Clip** as its behavior, and give it a central registration point:

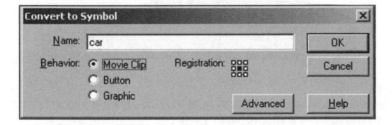

4. Double-click on the **car** symbol in the Library to enter Edit Symbol mode.

   By looking at our beautiful automobile, you might notice something key missing from it, something vital to making that baby move...our car has no wheels! Time to put that right.

5. Rename the current existing layer car and lock it from editing. This will prevent our car becoming scratched while we do other things to it:

6. Create a new layer by clicking on the Insert Layer button:

7. Double-click on the new layer name and rename it `wheels`, because that's what our car needs more than a flame paint job right now.

8. On the **wheels** layer, use the Circle tool to draw a circle at the rear of the car – holding down the SHIFT key to keep it in proportion. When you're happy with your circle, select it and make it into a symbol with the **Insert > Convert to Symbol** menu option.

9. Make it a graphic symbol with the name `static wheel` and a central registration point:

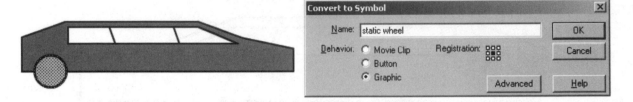

At this point our car is a little more able, but is more suited to being towed to an auto shop than speeding down the highway. Let's give this baby a much needed helping hand.

10. Go to your Library (if it's not still open, open it using **Window > Library**) and drag an instance of the **static wheel** symbol onto the stage. Use the Arrow tool to select the new wheel and position it at the front of the car, finally making it stable:

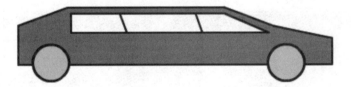

Now, if we were to animate our wheels, we'd have no idea if they were rotating or not. Let's give them something to show a little rotation.

11. Double-click on either of the wheels to edit the **static wheel** symbol:

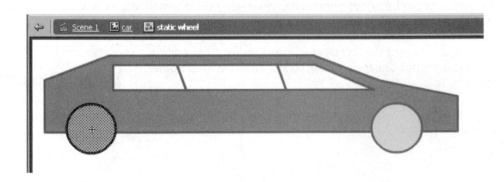

When you double-click on any symbol within another symbol, you're taken to the Edit Symbols mode – inside the previous symbol. You can tell you've gone one level deeper by looking at the icons below the timeline:

To return to the previous symbol you were working in, just click on the symbol name to the left of the one you are currently in, or use the back button. This can all be a bit confusing at times, but as long as you keep an eye on the icons below the timeline, you should be able to work out where you are. If in doubt, return to the main stage and work your way back through your nested symbols to reach the one you wanted.

12. In the **static wheel** edit mode, create a new layer and select it so you can work on it. Use the Line tool to draw a black horizontal line across the center of the wheel:

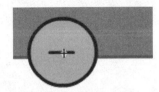

This line will be used to show the wheels of the car in motion. The next bit may seem a little tricky at first, but it'll be explained fully in a later chapter – so bear with it.

13. Click on the back button to return to the **car** editing mode:

14. Select the rear wheel and use the **Insert > Convert to Symbol** menu option. Name it `animated wheel`, with a movie clip behavior and a central registration point.

This will place our wheel, already a graphic symbol, within the timeline of a movie clip called **animated wheel**. We have nested the **static wheel** graphic symbol within the **animated wheel** movie clip symbol. Within this movie clip we'll animate the wheel a little.

15. Double-click on the animated wheel on the stage to edit it. The bar below the timeline will look like this:

Finally – let's animate our wheel.

16. Click on frame 20 of the timeline and press F6 to insert a keyframe.

This time we'll use motion tweening to make the wheel rotate a little – there'll be more on motion tweening in Chapter 6.

17. Click on frame 1 and make sure that the Property inspector is visible (use the **Window > Properties** menu option if it is hidden). In the Property inspector, select **Motion** from the **Tween** drop-down menu and **CW** from the **Rotate** drop-down menu (if you can't see the **Rotate** drop-down, click on the white triangle in the bottom right-hand corner of the Property inspector).

The frames in the timeline should have turned a blue color and there should be an arrow from frame 1 to 20:

18. In the box to the right of the **Rotate** drop-down, type in 3:

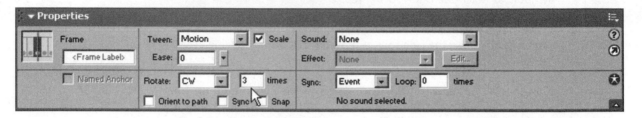

This will set the wheel to rotate three times in a clockwise direction over the designated 20 frames. Remember, we'll explain motion tweens in detail a little later on in the book.

19. Test the movie with the **Control > Test Movie** menu option.

If all went well, the rear wheel should be turning – the car is almost moving! To make the other wheel move we need to replace the **static wheel** graphic symbol with the **animated wheel** movie clip.

20. Click on the back button to enter the **car** movie clip's editing mode.

21. Click on the front wheel and delete it with the backspace key. Now drag a copy of **animated wheel** from the Library and place it on the stage at the front of the car.

If you now test the movie with **Control > Test Movie**, you'll see that both wheels are turning in the same direction, at the same speed. Your car is driving on a treadmill and isn't going anywhere fast.

22. Save the movie as car.fla and close it for now. We'll give our car traveling independence in Chapter 6.

Now that you know how to create and manage groups and symbols, how can you get them lined up neatly and evenly on the stage? You could always do it by eye of course, but Flash gives you a couple of quicker and more precise methods. Let's start out with the most basic way – using the built in **grid** and **rulers**.

The grid

By default, the grid in Flash gives you a background of fine-lined squares that you can use to guide the placement and alignment of objects.

Using the grid

1. Open the file `group.fla` you were working on earlier. To access the grid in Flash, use the **View > Grid > Show Grid** menu option. The stage will now have a series of grid lines across it:

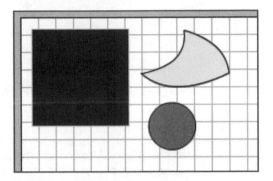

2. Turn on Flash's **grid snapping** feature by clicking on **View > Grid > Snap to Grid**.

3. Select your square, making sure you select both the fill and the stroke. Carefully click on the center of your square and drag it – it will 'snap' to a grid line when it gets near one:

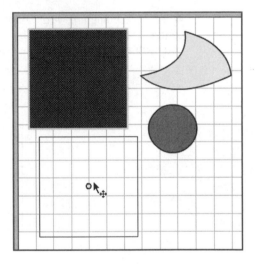

If you miss the middle of the square when you click and drag, the square won't snap to the grid and you'll be able to move it around freely. It can be deceptively difficult to find the middle of an object, and the only solution to this is to try and try again. When you click in the center of an object and drag it, a small black ring appears next to the cursor: this is called the **snapping ring**.

When you drag an object close to a grid line, the ring will jump to the grid line and become larger and darker:

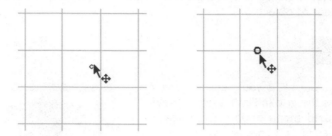

The snapping ring snaps to any gridline, but is easiest to snap to the grid at an intersection – where vertical and horizontal grid lines meet.

Experiment by moving your square around the stage with snapping turned on and off, and see the different effects. Also, try zooming in and moving the object again: notice that it gets easier to position things precisely the more 'zoomed in' you are. The trade off for this is that you won't be able to see your whole image. The best solution here is to experiment until you find a happy medium – this will, of course, be different for each movie you work on.

When you're aligning your shapes, you won't always want to do so by dragging the shape at the center. Flash caters for this by allowing you to drag the shapes by their corners as well. When you're dragging shapes by the corners, a similar snapping ring appears:

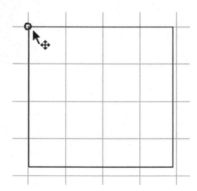

These are the default behaviors of the grid. Flash also gives you the ability to customize the grid and its settings to suit your every need.

Changing the grid settings

1. Open the Grid dialog box by using the **View > Grid > Edit Grid** menu option:

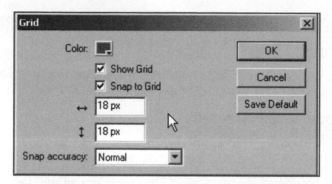

From here, you can change the spacing and the color of your grid lines.

It can be useful to change the grid color if the current grid lines are merging into the color of your movie background, or even if you just prefer another color aesthetically. The units of measurement will be the same movie-wide values that we saw how to set in the Property inspector and Document Properties dialog box.

The **Snap accuracy** option allows you to alter how close the snapping ring has to be to something before it will snap to it. So, if you find those lines are just too 'sticky', you can set it to **Must be close**. On the other hand, if you want to be seriously snap-happy (sorry) you can set it to **Always Snap** and never be left with those 'middle of nowhere' blues. Again, you can experiment with these settings at different levels of zoom.

The option to **Save Default** is the same as **Make Default** in the Document Properties box – using this will apply these values to all of the Flash movies that you create.

2. When you're finished, close the dialog box by clicking **OK**. To turn off the grid, go to the **View > Grid** menu option again – there'll be a check next to the **Show Grid** option, indicating that it is currently turned on:

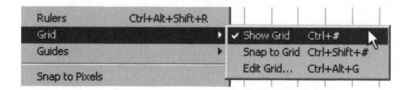

3. Click on the **Show Grid** option and the check mark will disappear along with the grid lines. Try moving your square around: you'll find that even though the grid is no longer visible, your square will still snap to it if the **Snap to Grid** option is on. To stop this you have to go into the **View > Grid** menu again and click on the **Snap to Grid** option.

As you might expect, the grid isn't shown in your final movie. If you wanted to see a grid effect in your finished movie, you'd have to draw one yourself: this could be easily accomplished by drawing over the grid in the authoring environment on the farthest back layer using the Line tool with snapping turned on for precision.

Flash has yet more ways of making drawing and alignment easier. Among these are **rulers** and **guides**.

Rulers and guides

Guides are an extremely useful feature of Flash and, in conjunction with Flash's rulers, they give you a powerful, customizable, and easy-to-use set of alignment tools. Let's see these in action.

Using rulers and guides

1. Use the **View > Rulers** menu option to display Flash's rulers. As soon as you do this, a pair of vertically and horizontally-oriented rulers will appear around the stage:

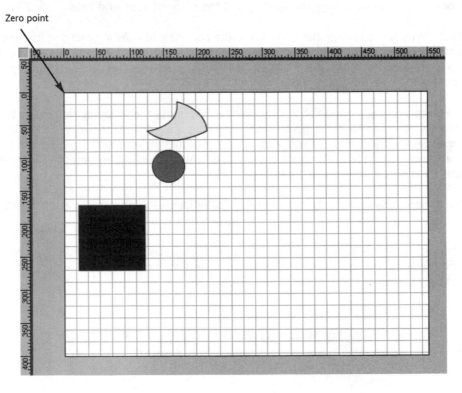

These rulers are marked out in the units currently defined in the Document Properties dialog box. The **zero point** for your rulers (where everything is measured from) is always at the top left-hand corner of your stage.

2. Using the Hand tool, move the stage around and notice how the zero point moves with it.

Rulers aren't just handy for alignment: they're also useful for seeing how big your object is and how all of the changes that you're making are affecting it.

3. Grab hold of your square with the Arrow tool and move it around the stage, taking a look at your rulers as you do so. You'll see two black lines on each ruler that shift position as your shape moves. These lines indicate the dimensions and position of your shape on the stage:

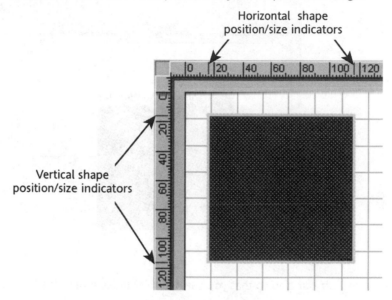

These lines mark the shape at its widest point, so if you have a big irregular weird shape, Flash will put an invisible bounding box around it at its very edges and use these for reference:

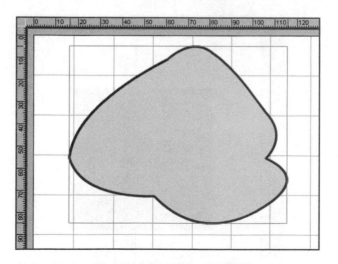

Another feature of rulers that you might have seen in other packages is the ability to drag **guides** out of them. Guides are basically reference lines to help you with shape alignment, and the great thing about them is that – unlike grids and rulers, which are in a fixed position – you can put guides wherever you like, and add as many as you like. This means that no matter where an object is or what shape it is, you can always use a guide to help you line it up precisely with another shape.

4.   Click anywhere on the ruler at the top of the stage and, still holding the mouse, drag a horizontal guide down onto the stage:

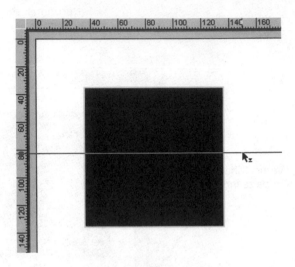

(We've turned off our grid so that you can see the guides more clearly in the screenshot.)

5.   Release the mouse anywhere on the stage to fix the guide at that point. The color of the guide defaults to a rather lurid green, but it can be altered via the **View > Guides > Edit Guides** menu option. To get a vertical guide, just drag out a line from the left-hand ruler in the same way:

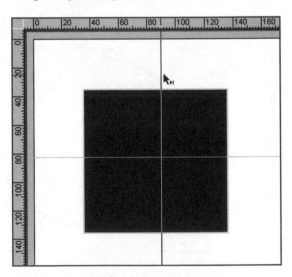

A guide's position is never set in stone. Whenever you move your mouse over a guide, the cursor will change:

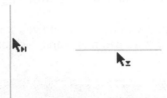

When the cursor looks like this, you can pick up your guide and move it elsewhere, and you can even drag it right off the stage to get rid of it altogether.

6. Click on your horizontal guide to pick it up, drag it to the bottom of your square, and release it to anchor it there:

In the same way that we can get shapes to snap to the grid, we can snap objects to guides, too.

7. Make sure that this snapping functionality is active by going to the **View > Guides** menu and ensuring that the **Snap to Guides** option is turned on.

8. Now click in the center of your circle and drag it until it snaps to the guide. Your circle will now be perfectly lined up with the bottom of your square:

One more circle and we've got us a wagon...

To get rid of your guideline, just click on it the same way you did to move it, and drag it all the way back onto the top ruler and release it. Dropping it anywhere on the ruler will do.

If you've a number of guides on the stage and you want to get rid of them all at once, you can use the **View > Guides > Edit Guides** menu and click on the **Clear All** button in the **Guides** dialog box:

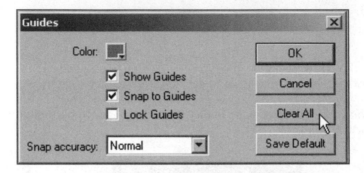

The **Lock Guides** option here will fix all current guides in place, meaning that you won't be able to move them after dropping them in place. This is useful when you're working with a lot of guides for precise placement purposes, and you don't want to pick them up by accident when you're moving other objects around. This may seem a little awkward at first, but with more practice you'll find these guides to be very useful in arranging your work on the stage.

As your movies become more complex, multi-layered and sophisticated, you'll find guides increasingly useful, particularly as they are visible through all the layers of a movie. But, as with a lot of things, Flash offers more than one way to align objects.

Alignment

There's a place in Flash that acts as a hub for a number of alignment features: the **Align** panel.

The Align panel

With the Align panel you can fine-tune the position of multiple objects on the stage by aligning them, spacing them evenly, and even sizing them to ensure that they all have exactly the same dimensions.

You access these features via the **Window > Align** menu option, or (in Windows), by clicking on the **Align** button on the main toolbar:

This will open up the Align panel:

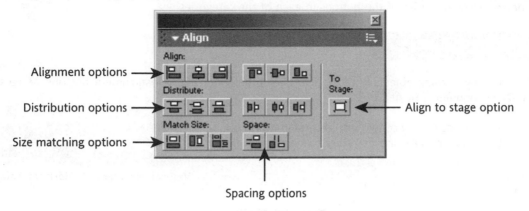

Alignment options ⟶

Distribution options ⟶

Size matching options ⟶

Align to stage option

Spacing options

In this panel you can see all the different alignment options that you have. The seventeen options that take up the bulk of the panel work, by default, on the objects that you have selected on the stage, aligning them in relation to each other. If you turn the **To Stage** modifier on and then use the alignment buttons, the selected objects will be aligned relative to the stage:

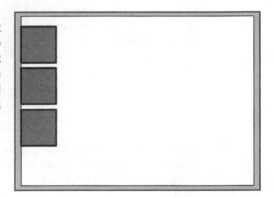

The key to using each of the options is to look at the thin black line on each button and its positions relative to the objects shown on the button. This line dictates how the objects will be aligned. For example, look at the first group of alignment buttons at the top left of the panel:

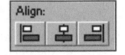

In the first button, the black line is to the left of the objects, meaning that the objects will all be aligned along their left-hand edges. The next button along will align your objects by their centers, and the third button will align them along their right-hand edges.

As you'd expect, if you hold the mouse cursor over any of the buttons, a tool tip will appear to help you check out the basic function of the button:

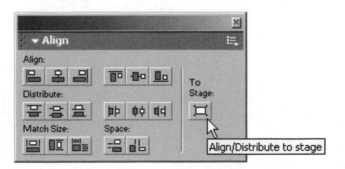

The best way to get a grip on using the Align panel is through practice and application. We'll look at representative examples of the buttons in each of the categories.

Aligning objects

Let's start by aligning objects in relation to each other with the basic alignment buttons. Make sure the **To Stage** modifier is turned off.

The Align options consist of two sets of three buttons: one set for aligning horizontally, and the other for vertical alignment:

Vertical alignment   Horizontal alignment

1. In a new movie, draw three new objects: a square, a circle, and a triangle. Make the objects different sizes, similar to these shown here:

2. Select the line and fill of the square and group them. Repeat this step for both the circle and the triangle so that you now have three separately grouped objects (this will make them easier to move around and manipulate).

   When aligning objects, Flash puts a box around the object or group of objects marking its boundaries, and then uses this to align by. You see this highlighted box for a grouped object or a symbol when you select it. Flash uses the center of this highlighting box as the notional center of the object or group. This can be a bit confusing at first, because we humans tend to credit two-dimensionally drawn objects with real-world characteristics – giving them weight and volume, for example. In contrast, your cold-hearted computer sees these objects as just a collection of pixels on the screen.

   For example, the center of this (grouped) shape is marked by the cross...

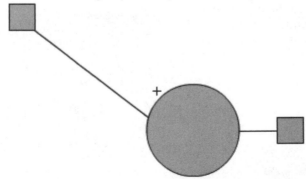

...which is probably not where you expected it to be. To show why Flash put the center-point there, look at the same object with the bounding box around it:

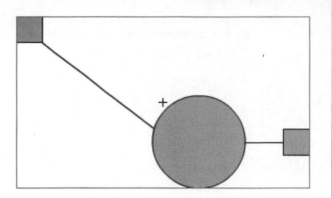

You can clearly see now that the cross is in the center of the box, which Flash treats as the center of the whole object.

3. Arrange all three of your grouped objects on the stage on a rough, unevenly spaced diagonal:

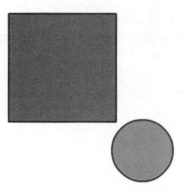

4. Select all of your objects together by dragging a box around them with the Arrow tool (or CTRL + A).

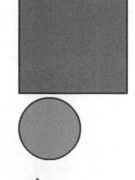

5. Now click on the **Align left edge** button (the one at the top left of the Align panel) and your objects will immediately reposition themselves by aligning with the left-hand edge of the left-most object – in this case, the square:

    If you'd selected the **Align right edge** button they'd all have lined up along the right-hand edge of the triangle.

    The **Distribute** options will ensure that there's an equal distance between the respective edges of the objects.

6.   For example, with all three of your objects still selected, click on the **Distribute left edge** button. Your objects will now rearrange themselves like so:

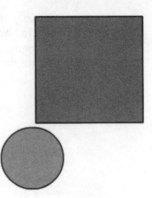

7.   To see the effect that this has had, make sure that rulers are turned on, and then drag guides out to each of the left-hand edges of the objects:

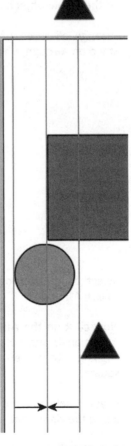

Now, you can clearly see that Flash has spaced the objects with equal distances between each of their left-hand edges.

8.   Remove your guides either by dragging them individually off the stage, or by choosing the **View > Guides > Edit Guides** menu and clicking on the **Clear All** button.

9. Now turn your attention back to the Align panel and click on the **Match width** button (bottom-left in the Align panel). Your circle and triangle will suddenly grow in size:

The **Match Size** options work by making all of your selected objects the size of the largest one in the selection. So by clicking on the **Match Width** button, you have made all of your objects the same width as your square. To ensure all objects on your stage are exactly the same dimensions, just click on the **Match width and height** button, and in the blink of an eye Flash will do the job for you. An example of when this comes in very handy is when you're drawing buttons and you want each button a different shape, but the same size in relation to the others.

The two **Space** options at the bottom right of the Align panel will ensure that the gaps between the objects are the same size. This means, for example, that you can precisely arrange a set of buttons so that they look 'just right'. Compare the left-hand set of buttons with the evenly spaced selection on the right:

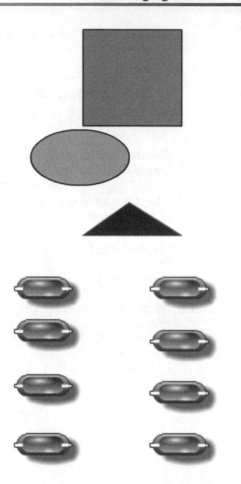

Although the differences in spacing are subtle in isolation, an accumulation of unevenly spaced objects in your movies can quickly make things look rough and sketchy.

10. Back in your movie, click on the **Space evenly vertically** button. This is another option where using guides can help to clarify exactly what Flash has done:

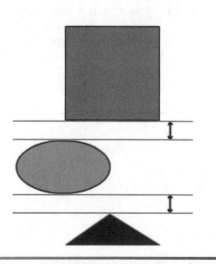

You can clearly see from the previous image that the space between each of the objects is now the same.

The final option remaining on the Align panel is the **To Stage** button on the right-hand side:

This is a global switch that will affect all of the other options on the Align panel. As you have already seen, so far Flash has used one of the other objects to align the others to, for example the largest object for matching size, the left-most object for aligning to the left and so on. When **To Stage** is turned on, Flash uses the stage to align the objects to instead, so aligning to the left will align the objects to the left of the stage, and matching size will match the objects to the full size of the stage. You could use this latter option to size an imported graphic image to match the dimensions of the stage – for example, if you wanted to use the image as a background layer.

11. Clear all of your guides away, then click on the **To Stage** button to highlight it.

12. With all of your shapes still selected, click on the **Match width** button: all of your objects will be resized horizontally to mirror the width of the stage:

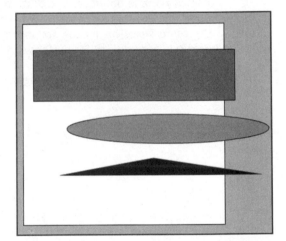

13. You can see that they're all exactly the same width as the stage by clicking on the **Align horizontal center** button. This will align your three shapes perfectly to the horizontal center of the stage:

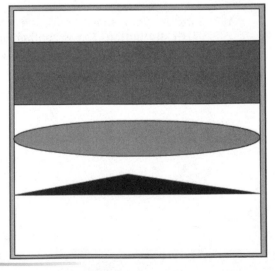

As you've seen from this series of examples, the different alignment buttons can drastically affect the way that your objects appear on the stage. You can also see how much easier it can be to use these tools to do the job rather than attempting to align and match everything by eye.

Now let's take a look at how to control objects in Flash in another dimension through depth arrangement and layers.

Stacking order

In Chapter 1 you were introduced to **layers** and how they function in a background/foreground relationship. For example, when your mushroom was growing behind the moon, you simply pulled the moon layer underneath the mushroom layer, and hey presto, the mushroom grew in correct perspective. There's a similar effect within individual layers, too: Flash's default behavior is to give objects that are on the same layer a 'front to back' order – this is called the **stacking order**.

Only symbols or grouped objects can be stacked in Flash: all other objects – such as hand-drawn shapes – will 'fall down' to the lowest possible level of the layer: they'll be stuck right at the back. You can see this effect when you hand-draw two or more shapes on the stage. If, for example, you draw a rectangle and a circle on the stage...

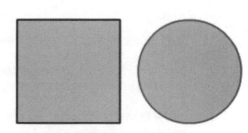

...they'll both be occupying the same plane.

If you drag the circle onto the rectangle and then click away somewhere on the stage, Flash will assume that you want to merge these shapes on this plane:

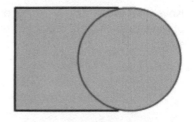

The overlapping areas of these shapes now share the same piece of stage real estate. If you click on the arc of the circle inside the shape...

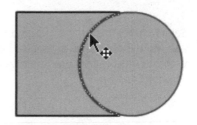

...and delete it, the two shapes will now become a single, fused entity, with all the lines and fills on the 'floor' of the layer:

This is why drawn shapes 'eat each other' when they overlay each other and are then shifted around – their component lines and fills are all trying to occupy the same space at the back of the layer.

However, in contrast to this 'hand-drawn object' behavior, Flash assumes that we want to be able to move symbols and groups backwards and forwards in relation to the base of the layer. To facilitate this, Flash assigns each new group or symbol that's added to the stage on a particular layer a 'stack position' that determines how far up from the floor it sits. Flash assigns these positions based on the order in which the symbols or groups are added to the stage: this means that every time you create a new symbol or group, it's placed on top of the ones that were already there.

Let's look at this principle in action.

Shuffling a deck of cards

1.   Start a new movie, and set the movie background color to a warm, casino-style, baize green.

2.   Double-click on the Rectangle tool and set the **Corner Radius** modifier to 15: we want to create round-edged rectangles that'll represent playing cards.

3.   In the Property inspector set the stroke width to 2, the stroke color to black, and the fill color to white.

4.   Now that everything is ready, draw a playing card-shaped rectangle on the stage:

5.   Select the whole shape (fill and stroke) and convert it into a graphic symbol with a central registration point. Call the symbol Card Base:

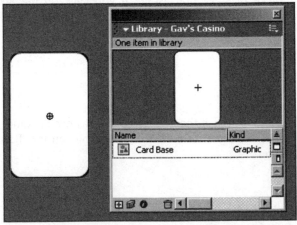

We now have a blank card symbol that we can use for all of the cards that we'll show on the stage.

What we need to do next is create four cards on the stage – the Jack, Queen, King and Ace. Each card will use the same **Card Base** symbol as its background, but will have a different letter on top of that background to indicate its seniority – J, Q, K, or A. We can easily do this by adding separate text boxes that we'll place on top of each instance of the card base.

6. Select the Text tool and choose an appropriate font and color from the Property inspector.

7. Next, click in the middle of your card – this will help you judge what size the font should be:

    (Make sure you don't actually go into Edit Symbols mode on the **Card Base** instance: all we want to do is create a text box that'll float above the symbol instance.)

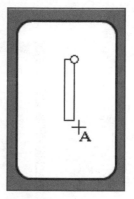

8. In the Property inspector, use the font size slider to set the font size to something that will look good on your card:

9. Type a capital 'J' for 'Jack' and use the Align panel to center your text in the card:

The simplest way to achieve this centering is to select the symbol instance and the text box by dragging a box round them with the Arrow tool, and then click on both the **Align vertical center** and **Align horizontal center** buttons on the Align panel.

10. Finally, make sure you have both the card and the text selected and convert them into a symbol using the **Insert > Convert to Symbol** menu option. Give it the name Jack, a graphic symbol behavior and a center registration point. Your card and its unique text identifier are now tied together in one symbol.

11. Now use the same process to drag out three more instances of the Card Base symbol onto your stage. Add the letters 'Q', 'K', and 'A' to these other three cards, **in that order**. Align the text over each card and then convert all the cards into graphic symbols as you did with the Jack card.

    When you've finished, you should have four cards on your stage looking like this:

12. Now drag each of your cards to the left so they overlap each other:

    Notice that the Jack, which you created first, is at the bottom of the stack, and the Ace, which you created last, is at the top. The Queen and King are in the correct sequence, too, so the stacking order is currently J, Q, K, A. Flash has faithfully created a stacking order for the cards based on the sequence that we created them in.

You can change the stacking order of these cards by using the options brought up by using the **Modify > Arrange** menu option:

13. Click on your King card to select it, and use the **Bring to Front** option from the **Modify > Arrange** menu. Your King will now jump to the top of the stack, so that the stacking order (from back to front) is changed to J, Q, A, K:

14. Now click on the Jack and use the **Modify > Arrange > Bring Forward** menu option.

   The **Bring Forward** option pulls the selected object up one level in the stacking order, so the Jack will immediately be brought forward one space, and jump in front of the Queen.

15. To test the Jack's position in relation to the other cards, pick it up and drag it between the King and the Queen:

OK – that shows us that it's in front of the Queen.

16. Now drag the Jack across between the King and the Ace:

You'll notice it is behind both of them. As we expected, from bottom to top, the order is now Q, J, A, K.

17. Click on the Ace and use the **Modify > Arrange > Send Backward** menu option. The Ace will now be moved backwards one level, jumping behind the Jack:

18. Drag the Ace up next to the Jack, between the Queen and the King.

The Jack will now be in front of the Queen, but behind the King:

The order is now Q, A, J, K.

19. Finally, click on the King and use the **Modify > Arrange > Send to Back** menu option. This will send the King all the way to the bottom of the stack:

This gives us a final order of K, Q, A, J.

20. Save the file as `cards.fla` and leave it open.

This exercise illustrates that you can manipulate the stacking order of symbols or groups to a very fine degree, which can be of real help when you're putting together complicated objects and pieces of content.

There'll be times when you're building something on your stage and you'll find that one component disappears behind another one: having a grasp of stacking order means that you'll be able to understand why it disappeared, and how to get it back.

However, there is another way to make the card shuffling a little easier...

Distribute to layers

For those of you that found arranging the royal part of the deck a little too much like hard work, there is Flash's **Distribute to Layers** option. Distribute to Layers is incredibly useful for making order out of chaotic situations.

Distribute to Layers takes all of the selected objects – symbols, grouped objects, or primitives (simple graphics drawn on your stage that haven't been converted to a symbol, nor grouped with other graphics) – and calculates associations between them before creating and placing them on as many different layers as required.

Distribute to Layers works differently when it comes to the selected objects:

- If the selected items are symbols, grouped objects, or text boxes, then each individual element is placed on its own individual layer.

- If the selected items are primitives then Flash will try to make associations on the geographic location of items. If two or more primitives are within touching vicinity then they'll be treated as one object and placed together on the same layer.

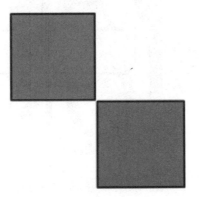

These would be distributed to two layers

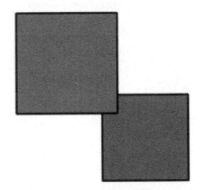

These would be distributed to one layer

So the rule is – if they are touching, they're forever hitched!

If the selected items are symbols then the layers they're distributed to are given the symbols' names. This makes Distribute to Layers very useful for cleaning up that Flash mess you've made.

Let's give it a try with our deck of cards and make their organisation a great deal easier.

Distributing our deck of cards to layers

1.   Open up your `cards.fla` file (if it isn't still open).

2.   Select all of the cards with the Arrow tool and choose the **Modify > Distribute to Layers** menu option.

      Each card has now been placed on its own layer, and each layer has been given the same name as the symbol, which resides on that layer. There's also an extra layer that has no content, just a blank keyframe – this was the layer that all our symbols were taken from. Let's remove this superfluous layer before proceeding.

3.   Select the blank layer in the timeline. Click on the **Delete Layer** icon – the trashcan – below the timeline.

      The unused layer has now been deleted, leaving us with just our card layers, and allowing us to get back to the card game.

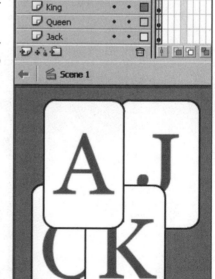

      The order we left our cards in our last exercise was K, Q, A, J. It's easy to change their order by dragging and moving the layers up and down in the timeline. Let's put them in their correct order with the Ace at the top where it belongs.

4.   Click on the **Ace** layer and drag it to the top of the layer list (above the **King** layer). This leaves the Ace as the top card – just where it wants to be.

      Our cards are now in their correct order – A, K, Q, J:

5.   Save the movie as **cards2.fla** and leave it open.

Now that we've seen how Flash can save us a few headaches by organising our content for us, let's see how it can ease the pain a little more with **layer folders**.

Layer folders

As we've seen, layers are an excellent way of controlling our content. Flash MX has the added ability to use **layer folders** to bundle together similar layers, helping us organize our content even more efficiently. A layer folder works just like any folder that you have on your hard drive, enabling you to maintain some kind of control over the chaos of your files.

Let's create a layer folder to place the King and Queen together in their honeymoon suite – away from the prying eyes of the Jack and the Ace – while maintaining the physical depths of all the cards.

Managing layers in your timeline with layer folders

1. Select the **King** layer and click on the **Insert Layer Folder** button:

   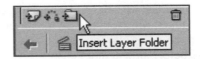

   Flash will create the layer folder above the **King** layer and will give it a generic name such as '**Folder 6**'. Flash increments layer *folders* along with layers. In this scenario, our next new layer would be '**Layer 7**' or our next layer folder would be '**Folder 7**':

   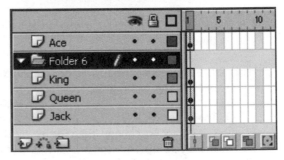

2. Double-click on the layer folder name in the timeline, type in 'Honeymoon Suite', and press ENTER.

   So far we have a new layer folder with no content in it. We can tell this because the arrow to the left of the layer folder icon is pointing down, meaning that it's in an open state. If you're a Mac user, you'll be familiar with this from the list-viewed folder on the Mac:

   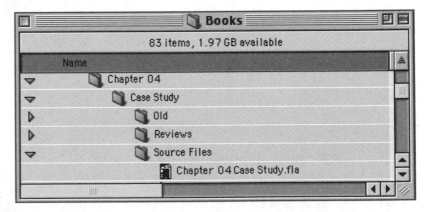

   When the arrow is pointing to the right, the folder is in a closed state. You can toggle the open and closed states by clicking on the arrow.

Now let's give our royal couple some peace and put the **King** and **Queen** layers in the **Honeymoon Suite** folder.

3. Make sure the **Honeymoon Suite** folder is open and click on the **King** layer. Now hold down the SHIFT key while clicking to select the **Queen** layer. Both layers should now be selected.

4. Drag the layers up to the **Honeymoon Suite** folder. As you do this, you'll see a shaded gray bar appear with a small notch sitting on it. Make sure this notch is indented – the folder icon will also be highlighted – and release the mouse button:

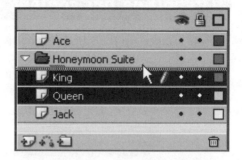

What we've just done is place the **King** and **Queen** layers within the **Honeymoon Suite** folder. If you did this correctly your list of layers should now look like this:

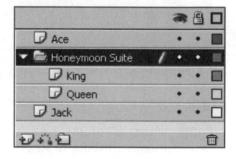

The **King** and **Queen** layers are indented and are now within the **Honeymoon Suite** layer. To further prove that they're within the folder, click on the arrow to the left to close the folder and hide them away – now they have some peace and quiet!

With the two layers inside the folder, any actions performed on the folder will also apply to whatever is inside it. This applies to locking/unlocking, showing/hiding, moving, or deleting the folder. This shows us the time bought by using layer folders.

One final point to bear in mind: Flash gives you many ways of operating in the third (depth) dimension – **layers**, the **stacking order** within layers, and **layer folders**. With experience, you'll develop your own strategies for combining these options, but one rule of thumb is that if you're going to have lots of separate overlapping objects, it's usually best to have them on different layers and keep these controlled in layer folders. The stacking order is particularly useful when you're constructing individual objects and groups of objects that'll always be kept together and can be assigned to a layer using the Distribute to Layers command.

Case study

We'll now begin to organize our content into a more manageable form, based on what we've covered so far in this chapter.

Organizing our content

1. Open up the case study movie from where you saved it last.

2. On frame 1 of the **Buttons** layer, drag an instance of each of the gray button symbols and place them just above the content window:

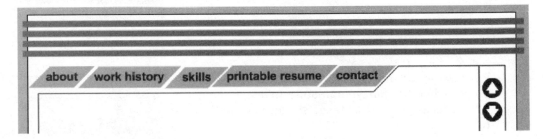

We now need to arrange these buttons into a nice neat layout for our navigation bar.

3. Select all of the buttons and open the Align panel (using **Window > Align**). With the **Align/Distribute to stage** button off, click on the **Align bottom edge** button.

4. Next, with all the buttons still selected, click on the **Match height** button.

5. Finally, hit the **Space evenly horizontally** button to perfectly distribute your buttons:

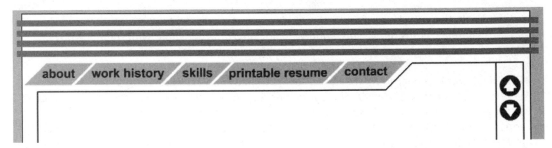

6. Now that our buttons are drawn and placed where we want them on the stage, lock the **Buttons** layer so that we can't accidentally displace them.

Before we start getting too deep into work on our case study, now is a very good time to step back and see if there's a better way we can organize our content. This is very important: if you get used to efficiently organizing layers, symbols, and other information early on, it'll save you from lots of headaches as you further develop the case study.

It's also necessary to make sure you keep your files organized for clients. Let's say you create a Flash file, find a better job, and then somebody comes along behind you and needs to update the file. Unless your file is well organized, they will have to spend needless amounts of time just trying to find out where everything is and how your file has been set up.

First, let's take a look at the layers on our main timeline and see if there's a better way that we could organize them.

Later on in the case study we're going to have more buttons, which help form our navigation interface. Let's prepare for that.

7. Insert a new layer folder called `Buttons` and move the existing **Buttons** layer inside that folder:

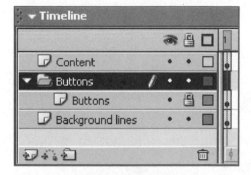

8. Create another new layer folder, call it `Background components`, and move the **Background lines** layer into this new layer folder:

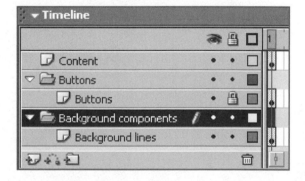

Now let's take a look at our Library (if it's not already open go to **Window > Library**). You should see quite a few buttons and one content movie clip. We've already organized our existing buttons into a **Buttons** folder, but we can go further.

Thinking ahead, let's go and create folders for each of our designated content areas that will be displayed when the appropriate button is pressed. We may or may not use all of these, but we're setting ourselves up for proper organization later in our project. This enables us to efficiently store all kinds of objects such as imported graphics, sounds, text, and other items that may be used in these sections.

9. Insert five new folders in your Library and call them about, work history, skills, printable resume, and contact:

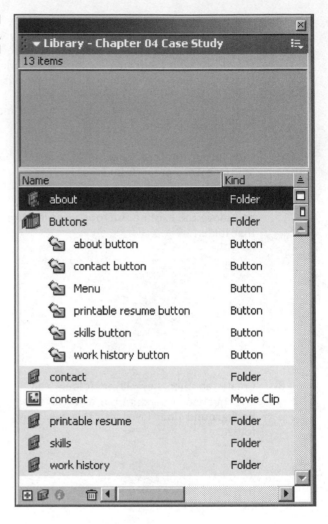

10. Save and close your case study file.

Summary

In this chapter, we've introduced ourselves to the integral Flash facilities that help us arrange, align and nest objects. These features are intimately linked with the ability to arrange content in space on the Flash stage in the three dimensions of width, height, and depth.

We saw that:

- We can **group objects** together to maintain their relative proportions and still have access to them for editing.

- We can **nest groups within groups** and **symbols within groups** and so on, giving us the ability to create hierarchies of precisely arranged, related, objects.

- Flash's **grids**, **rulers** and **guides** help us draw with a steady hand and sure eye.

- Flash's **Align** panel, and the **Transform** menu/panel allow precision placement and transformation of objects.

- Each Flash movie layer has an implicit **stacking order** for symbols and grouped objects, which we can manipulate explicitly.

- **Layer folders** give us further scope to manage and arrange our content, by enabling us to nest layers inside them.

The focus in this chapter has been on working with multiple objects and seeing how to arrange them. In the next chapter, we're going to drill down inside of some objects and see how to use color to enrich content and effects.

Enhancing your Appearance

What we'll cover in this chapter:

- *How Flash **renders color**.*

- *Creating and saving **custom colors**.*

- *How **gradients** work, and how to use them effectively as **fills** on drawn objects.*

- ***Manipulating** object fills.*

- *The essentials of importing and using **bitmaps**.*

In this chapter, we're going to see how Macromedia Flash MX allows us to customize the objects that we create by fine-tuning their colors and fill styles. We'll see how Flash handles color, and how you can ensure that the color features are working smart for you. Additionally, we'll take a quick look at how to import bitmaps and manipulate them in Flash. This is a long chapter, with a lot of worked examples, but stick with it: by the end, you'll be handling all of the color features with much greater confidence.

Colors, fills, and gradients are the extra paprika on the already tongue-tingling dish that is Flash. If you've used any of the many graphics programs that are available today, you'll be instantly at home with Flash's color creation methods. If, on the other hand, you're new to the world of swatches and radial gradients, don't worry: by the end of this chapter you'll be whistling along to '*R-G-B, as easy as 1-2-3*' while using the Alpha slider to open new windows in your movies.

It's never going to be entirely satisfactory discussing colors in a book printed in black and white, but with a little bit of imagination, and by working through the exercises with MX open in front of you, you'll get through without any problems.

Let's begin by talking about computerized color in general terms – then we'll see how MX does it.

A color background

Color on a computer monitor, as on a TV, is rendered using a mixture of three discrete components of colored **light**: some red light, some green light, and some blue light – hence **RGB**. When you're working with paint on a blank white canvas, you know that you need to add colored paint to make the painting. And you've probably also discovered that if you add red, blue, and green paint together in the right quantities and mix them up, you end up with a murky black.

When you're dealing with *light* color rather than *paint* color, however, the opposite applies: with light, if there's no color present, everything is black, and if we add all the colors of light together at the right strength, we get white light:

White light
= Red + Green + Blue

The three different color elements can be combined in an infinite variety of mixtures and strengths: just blue light on its own will give us a blue screen, whereas if we add a little green to that blue, we'll see the color change.

Each unique color that a computer monitor displays is composed of different proportions of red, green, and blue. Furthermore, these unique colors can be described *numerically* by values that specify the amount of R, G, and B that we want to display – these values determine the color that we see on the screen, and it's these numbers that tell the computer what to show. On a computer, these numbers are expressed in base 16, otherwise known as **hexadecimal** or **hex** for short.

In base 10, which we use every day for counting, our numbers fall into familiar columns: the right-most figure in a number is the number of 'units' (1s), the next column is the number of '10s', the next is '100s' and so on:

100s	10s	1s	Base 10
4	7	9	= 479

In hex, a different model applies. The right-hand figure in a number is still expressing the number of '1s', but the next column along is telling you how many *16*s there are in the number, etc.:

256s	16s	1s	Base 16 (HEX)
0	1	F	= 31

Because the second column from the right starts at 16, the units column has to go up to 15, but still be expressed as a single digit. This is achieved by using letters rather than numbers: in the units column, you count from **0** to **9** as in normal base 10, but the numbers from **10** through **15** are expressed as the letters **A** through **F**. So, **A** in hex is equal to **10** in base 10, **B** is **11**, and all the way up to **F**, which is **15**. After that, the units column goes back to 0, and the 16s column increments to 1. Thus, the figure 10 in hex means '1 lot of 16, and zero units'.

Back to our colors. Remember we said that they're expressed in hex. Each unique color is the result of combining the three base colors, and each unique color has a six-digit identifier. In this six digit number, there are two digits for each of the base colors: the first two digits describe the amount of red present, the next two the green, and the last two the level of blue light. This means that black – the absence of any color of light – is expressed as 000000. That's 00 (hex) of red, 00 of green, and 00 of blue:

	Red	Green	Blue
Black =	00	00	00

Now, the largest number that can be expressed in two digits in hex is **FF**, which means (15 x 16) + (15 x 1), a total of 255. So a color whose number was **FF0000** would be 255 parts of red, zero parts of green, and zero parts of blue – which means that some red would be displayed on the screen. The opposite of this is white, which is a mix of all the colors at full strength, so pure white in hex is FFFFFF. Play around with the hex values of each base color component in a six-digit identifier, and you're creating different colors. In fact, the different combinations possible with this hex numbering system give us access to a range of over 16 million colors. Enough, I'm sure you'll agree, for most people to find one that they like – even if you can't find a shirt that matches it.

Right now, you're probably thinking, 'this chapter said it was about color, and all I've had so far is a math lesson', and you'd be right. Hopefully though, this brief explanation will help you to understand how Flash sees color, and from there, how you can best manipulate it to get the effect you want.

Let's take this theoretical knowledge and see how it's implemented in MX. A good place to start is with custom colors: this is where MX lets us create our own mixtures of the base colors that we can use and save.

Custom colors

Bored with seeing the same colors everywhere you look? Want to make your whites whiter than white? Then you need...the **Color Mixer panel**:

This is where we can get MX to mix us up *exactly* the color that we're looking for. The Color Mixer panel is partnered by the **Color Swatches panel**, which is used for choosing default palette or custom-made colors:

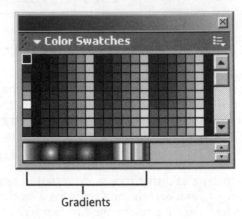

Gradients

On the Color Mixer panel, we can enter the precise RGB values that we want our strokes and fills to have, and then apply these colors to the objects in our movies. The Color Swatches panel shows us all the colors that we have available to choose. (A *swatch* is the name given to a single color, and a group of swatches together is called a *palette*.)

Here's an exercise to take us through the process of creating our own custom colors.

Creating custom colors with the Color Mixer panel

1.   Open the **Color Mixer** panel and the **Color Swatches** panel from the **Window** menu.

The colors shown in the top part of the Color Swatches panel make up the 216 **web-safe colors**, and this is the default palette used by MX. These web-safe colors are guaranteed to work on any computer using *any* browser running anywhere in the world, which means that if you always want your work to render perfectly on any old or superceded browser, exactly as you designed it, then these are the colors to use.

If you're not sure about using a particular custom color you've created, then the best thing to do is to test your movies and web pages in as many different browsers as you think is necessary: ultimately, there's a trade-off here between how certain you want to be that your page looks tip-top *everywhere*, and the time and effort that it takes to test *everything*. For most people, testing their movies and sites on up-to-date versions of Internet Explorer and Netscape is the norm.

In the Color Mixer panel you'll see the familiar Stroke and Fill Color boxes in the same layout as you find in the Property inspector and Tools panel:

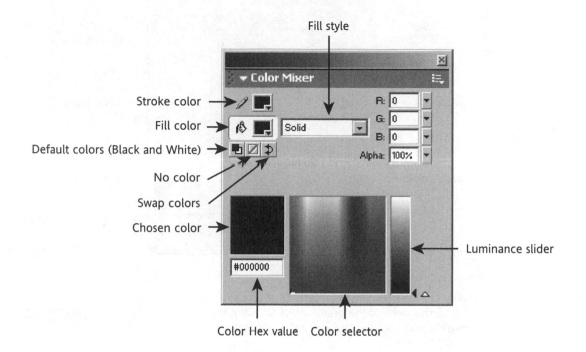

Fill style

Stroke color

Fill color

Default colors (Black and White)

No color

Swap colors

Chosen color

Luminance slider

Color Hex value   Color selector

Also, on the right-hand side, there are four input boxes: three where you can change the RGB value combinations for the current color (using a value of 1 – 255 for each base color), and one where you can set the **Alpha** value. *Alpha* is essentially another word for **transparency**: 100% Alpha is solid opaque color, 0% is fully transparent, and anything between will give an appropriately intermediate degree of transparency. Alpha is commonly used to make objects fade in and out of movies, or to create 'windows' in objects so that you can see through them. How to use alpha in your movies will be more fully explored in the next chapter, when we look at animation in more detail.

The final tools on the Color Mixer panel are the **Color selector** and **Luminance slider** bars at the bottom. The Color selector is a quick, visual way to choose a color – click anywhere on the bar, and that will automatically be selected. The Luminance Slider bar lets you fine tune that selection – drag the arrow up and down – until you get the shade that you want.

2. Click on the square next to the bucket in the Fill Color selection box – the current color palette will appear:

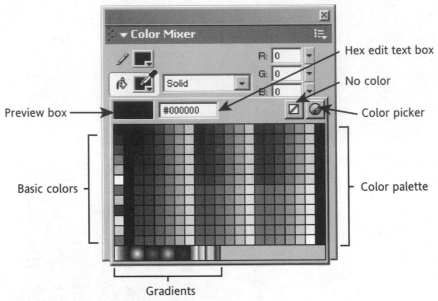

Hex edit text box

No color

Color picker

Preview box

Basic colors

Color palette

Gradients

On the very top row of this color selection box (above all the available colors, and to the right of the preview box showing the currently selected color) there's a box showing the *hex value* of that color:

It can be extremely useful to know the hex value, as it means that you can match the color of your Flash movie to that of the host web page, and vice-versa, since web page colors are also defined in hex.

3. Click on the **Color Picker** button – the circular one at the top right of the color palette, with the rainbow-hued disk on it. Doing this will open the **Color** window, where we can create a custom color:

Color window

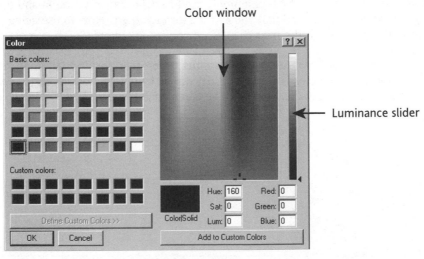

Luminance slider

This is where all of your alchemical color mixing takes place. To the left of the color window is a set of basic, solid colors, which you can use as starting points. Your attention though, was no doubt already drawn to that lush, blush-drenched window pane on the right, the one that looks like a piece of blotting paper used to mop up a spilt rainbow. This window, with the luminance slider next to it, contains all of the colors that you can use in your movies.

> *For our Mac-using audience, the preceding picture and description will have been extremely confusing. The Mac's color picker, you'll no doubt have noticed, is very different in appearance to the PC version pictured above, but it works in almost exactly the same way.*

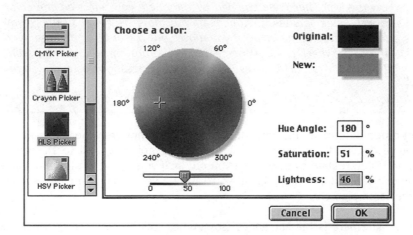

In **HLS Picker** mode, pictured above, a color picker takes the place of the blush-drenched window and the slider beneath it controls lightness rather than luminance. If you want to adjust the RGB values of your color, you simply click on the **RGB Picker** icon in the scroll menu on the left. The color picking options available to the Mac user are more sophisticated than those on the PC, and are beyond the scope of this chapter. What the Mac doesn't have, however, is the ability to create multiple custom colors in one visit to the picker – you'll have to mix your new colors one at a time.

The black cross in the Color window marks your currently selected color.

4. Click in the Color window and drag the mouse around. You'll notice that everything seems to change at once, the colors in the luminance slider shift like a tie-dyed chameleon, and the RGB values rush frantically to keep up with your waving mouse.

5. Release your mouse finger and let the chameleon take a rest.

It's time to explain some more of those numbers. To the left of the RGB values are three boxes containing the **Hue**, **Saturation**, and **Luminance** (HSL) of the current color:

These three terms are just another way to describe color. The *hue* is the actual color, and it's a relative of the RGB settings, but with a smaller range.

6. Click and drag your mouse carefully left and right, perfectly horizontally across the color window, and you'll see that only the hue setting will change.

7. If you move the mouse *vertically* up and down the window, only the saturation value will change.

> *On the Mac, hue is determined by the angle you select on the color wheel, while saturation changes as you move nearer or further away from the hub of the wheel. If you move your cursor along the radius of the color wheel, towards the center, the saturation will decrease from 100% at the rim to 0% at the hub, but the hue setting will stay the same.*

The saturation determines the *amount* of that color, so now imagine you've got a tin of white paint, and you've chosen the pigment (hue) that you're going to add to this paint. The amount of saturation is determined by how much you put in: if you only put a little in, you'll have a very pale color, and if you put the whole lot in you'll have a very deep rich color, even though you're still using the same pigment.

The final value here is the luminance (sometimes called brightness – hence HSB and called lightness on the Mac), which is the *amount of light* in the color. So far, you've chosen your original pigment (hue), and you've mixed it into your white base to get the depth of color (saturation) you wanted, and now you paint it onto a big sheet of glass. You then place a light behind the glass: this light determines the *luminance*. If you use a small, dim light, then the color will be a dark, gloomy shade, but if you position a huge arc light behind the glass, the color will become so painfully bright that there will only be a negligible difference between it and white. The luminance value is controlled from the slider bar on the right of the Color window:

It's probably worth briefly mentioning here that in MX you can use the HSB color model as your default color value display instead of RGB. If you go to the Color Mixer panel and click on the white icon on the right-hand side of its title bar, a menu will appear giving you the option to switch to HSB. For this chapter, we'll stick with RGB.

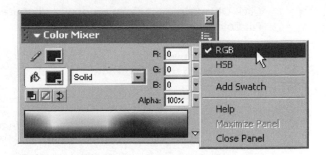

You might now be thinking 'Wait a minute! The Color window shows HS**L**, while this menu shows HS**B**. Don't worry, it's just a small discrepancy in the software and although the color option is referred to differently, it still does the same job.

8. Choose a color from the vast spectrum available to you in the Color window.

9. When you've chosen a color, look in the color preview box to ensure that you have the color you want. You may think this is obvious, but it's very easy to choose a color from the Color window and leave the luminance set to 0, which will mean that everything comes out as black!

10. Finally, when you're sure everything is right, click on the **Add to Custom Colors** button at the bottom of the window:

    On the Mac, once you have chosen the color you want press OK to return to the Color Mixer. Go on to point 13 – the next load of stuff is for PC users only.

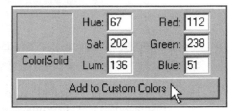

Your color will now become a swatch in one of the **Custom color** boxes on the far left. These boxes serve as a temporary storage area for your swatches: next time you want to use your swatch, you can come back to this window and it'll be there waiting for you.

> *Beware though, next time you open the Color window. If you select a color from the spectrum and add it to your custom colors, Flash will automatically overwrite the color in the top left of your Custom color boxes:*

By default, Flash will always save your color into this first box, even if it's currently filled with the perfect peach tone that you took hours to perfect. The only way to specify which box your new color goes into is to click on the specific custom color box you want to use, *then* select your color from the spectrum, and finally add the color to the box.

Click **OK** to close the Color window, and notice that your custom color is currently selected in the Fill Color box of the Color Mixer panel.

11. If you were now to use the Oval tool to draw a circle, it would be filled with your beautiful custom color. (Go on; try it...you know you want to...).

> It's important to remember one thing when creating custom colors: Flash does not automatically save them permanently for you. If you close Flash and reopen it again, all of your carefully constructed colors will be gone from the **Custom color** boxes.

So the question arises – just how the heck do I make my custom colors *persist*?

Persistent custom colors

Saving custom colors in Flash is, unfortunately, quite a long-winded process. Once you've created your color, and defined it as a swatch in a **Custom color** box, you must then add it to the main color palette, and finally save this as a color table.

Let's see how.

Saving custom colors permanently

1. Make sure the **Color Mixer** panel is open. Also make sure that the swatch that you want to add is displayed as the currently selected fill or stroke color: this means you need to ensure your chosen Custom color box is selected when you close the Color window after choosing your color from the spectrum.

2. Click on the white icon in the top right of the Color Mixer panel, and have another look at the resulting drop-down menu:

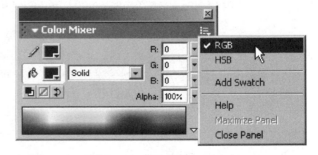

As we already know, the menu contains two options for displaying color values – RGB and HSB, and an option for adding a swatch to a palette. This is the one that we want to use here.

3. Click on the **Add Swatch** option.

4. Now, when you open up your color palette on the Color Mixer panel or in the Tools panel, you'll see your new swatch in a fresh row at the bottom of the palette:

You can now easily select your new color from this palette.

New Swatch ——▶

Once you've added all of your new swatches to the bottom of the palette, you still need to save it away so that it'll be available to you in the future.

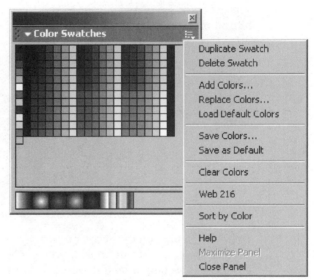

5. In the Color Swatches panel, click on the small icon in the top right corner to access the drop-down menu options:

This menu contains all of the commands for dealing with swatches and palettes. For the moment, let's just focus on a couple of these options – **Save Colors** and **Add Colors**.

6. Click on the **Save Colors** option, which will open up the **Export Color Swatch** dialog box. This dialog box will allow us to save our current colors away into a permanent file – a **color** set – that Flash can always access in the future:

Flash's default location for these files is in the **Color Sets** folder, which lives inside your **Macromedia\Flash MX** folder. The *exact* location of this folder on your machine will depend on where you installed the Flash program to – typically it's at **C:\Program Files\Macromedia\Flash MX\First Run\Color Sets** on a PC, and in your **Hard Drive>Applications > Macromedia Flash MX > First Run > Color Sets** folder on a Mac.

7. Navigate to where you'd like to keep your swatches, give your color set a name, and then click **Save**. Your swatches will now be saved in a Flash color set (**CLR**) file.

The files that are already in this folder are the ready-made palettes that come with Flash, each one designed to cater for a specific set of requirements. Note that Flash's default behavior is to open up the standard color set whenever it restarts. If you want to access your self-created color set again, just open the drop-down menu from the **Color Swatches** panel and click on the **Add Colors** command. This will open the **Import Color Swatch** dialog box, from where you can select the specific color set that you want to use to enrich your palette. Once loaded, you can use the slider button on the right edge of the Color Swatches panel to scroll through the newly available colors:

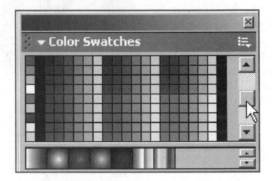

There are many different ways of creating and describing color, but a detailed analysis of them is beyond the scope of this book. If you're interested in learning more, there are plenty of resources around just waiting to be discovered, ranging from the Internet to your local library. The best thing you can do is experiment and see how the different values affect the final color. It's up to you to decide which method you prefer from RGB or HSL, but remember that your color will be rendered in Flash, and on the web, as an **RGB** value.

Our next step now is to look at color and **gradients**.

Gradient color

The ability to create custom colors is great, and the only problem with them is that no matter how much work you put in picking and choosing your color values, you still end up with a single flat color. This is where **gradients** come in. Gradients are distinct color features that we can apply to our objects' fills.

A gradient consists of a smooth change from one color to another. In Flash, gradients can be simple and 'pure', with a starting color and an end color, or they can be more complex, with up to eight different colors: in complex gradients, intermediate colors create distinct 'steps' in the gradient, giving the effect of a richer and more complicated spectrum:

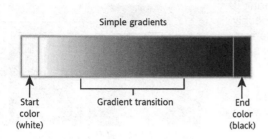

Simple gradients

Start color (white) Gradient transition End color (black)

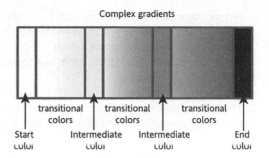

Complex gradients

transitional colors   transitional colors   transitional colors

Start color   Intermediate color   Intermediate color   End color

These different types of gradients allow for some pretty spectacular effects, especially when you tween transitions from gradient to gradient. For now though, we'll start with the basics.

This next screenshot shows a simple gradient, which runs from white to black:

This is an example of a **linear gradient**, so named because the gradient runs in a straight line from the first color (white, on the left) to the second color (black, on the right). With linear gradients, you just define the start and end colors (and any intermediate ones, if you want a more complex effect), and Flash works out the intermediate colors between those that you define. Flash has a number of pre-defined linear gradients in its palette, but we can also mix our own too, as you'll see shortly.

The other type of gradient is a **radial gradient**:

Radial gradients have their 'starting' color at the center, and their 'finishing' color at the outside. The gradient radiates out from the center to the edge. Again, Flash has some standard radial gradients but, once again, we have infinite customization features at our fingertips.

The choice about which gradient to use for a given task is entirely down to your personal taste: there's no right or wrong gradient type, just use the one that you think looks the best for what you're trying to do.

Gradients are really just smooth transitions of color between two (or more) distinct colors. If you've ever tried to create a gradient on paper with colored pencils or paint, you'll know how difficult it can be to get the effect right. Thankfully, Flash gives us a little studio and palette where we can create, preview, and amend gradients to our heart's content.

To work with gradients, you need to use the Color Mixer panel.

Creating and modifying gradients

1. If the Color Mixer panel isn't currently open, bring it up from the **Window > Panels** menu. You'll probably already have noticed some boxes at the bottom of the color palette that don't look like the other solid colors:

   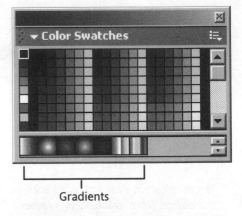

   These are Flash's predefined gradients. There are five basic (two-color) gradients and two more complicated ones.

2. Open the Color Swatches panel to open up the palette. From here, click on the black and white linear gradient, at the bottom on the far left, to select it.

   Notice that as you select the gradient, the Color Mixer panel automatically changes to reflect this choice:

   We've now chosen the gradient style that we want to use – a simple, linear, black and white gradient. We can now either use this as the fill on a new or existing object, or we can customize it as we're going to do here.

   Let's ensure that we don't *overwrite* the default linear gradient.

   Gradients

3. Select **Add Swatch** from the Color Mixer panel drop-down menu. This will add a new gradient at the right-hand end of the list:

   We now have our very own gradient to tinker with.

New Gradient

4. Click on the new gradient's box at the bottom of the Color Swatches panel to ensure that this is the one you're working on. The currently selected gradient box will have a white outline around it:

As we've selected a linear gradient to work on, we can see the gradient controls in the Color Mixer panel:

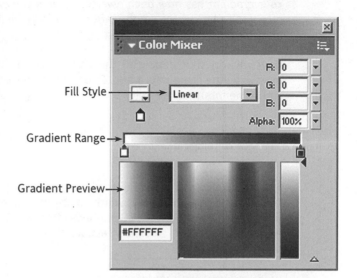

The most important of these is the long bar across the middle with the white paint pot hanging from the left-hand side, and a black paint pot hanging from the right. This bar shows the **range** of your gradient – that is, its start and end points.

Fill Style

Gradient Range

Gradient Preview

5. Click on the white paint pot and drag it along to the middle of the bar:

The gradient in the little preview window on the bottom left will now be half bleached-out, with only a smudge of black creeping in from the right-hand side:

We've effectively told Flash 'I want everything to the left of the white paint pot to be white. Start the gradient where the white paint pot is, and use the black as the end point'. Notice also that the gradient box in the Color Swatches panel has also changed to reflect your alteration.

6. Now click on the black paint pot and drag it past the white pot in the middle, all the way over to the left-hand side where the white paint pot used to be:

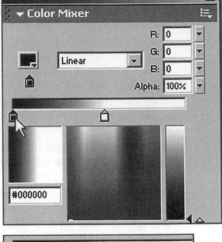

Your gradient has now been reversed: it now consists of a small black stripe on the left, with a large white mass to its right.

Now we can start adding to the basic gradient and make it a little more interesting. To do this, we have to add some intermediate color stages to the range bar.

7. Place your cursor below the gradient range bar, just to the right of your current white paint pot. When a plus sign is added to your cursor, indicating that you wish to add to the current selection, click to place another pot:

Because we clicked underneath a white part of the gradient, this new paint pot will inherit that color. If we'd clicked in a black area, we'd have got a black paint pot.

8. Click in the same way under the gray gradient between the black and the white pots:

Again, your new paint pot will be filled with the same gray as the color immediately above it in the gradient range bar. Notice that the currently selected paint pot has a black pointer at the top, and that the body of each paint pot indicates what color that pot represents. Furthermore, the color box to the right of the gradient bar shows us what color is in the current paint pot.

We can now change the color content of our paint pots and thus customize the gradient still further.

9. Click on the color box above the gradient range bar in the Color Mixer panel to open up the color palette.

10. From here, pick a color – say, a pure blue. As soon as you click on the color, the current paint pot will be filled with it and the gradient bar will change to reflect its new technicolor glory.

> *When you're mixing a gradient, it's tempting to try and use the Color Swatches panel to pick the color. Don't do it. If you do, Flash will think you want to use a solid color instead of a gradient, and it'll take you out of the gradient selection in the Color Mixer. If you do this by mistake, just click on the **Fill Style** drop-down box and reselect the gradient type you were editing, and your gradient colors should still be there, exactly as you left them.*

11. Click on the paint pot on the far right and, using the color box at the top right again, change its color to red.

12. Your gradient should now flow from black on the left to blue, with a very thin white bar in the middle, which rapidly fades into red on the right:

Now that you've created your gradient, how do you use it? Easy. It's now your selected fill for any objects that you draw, and if you click on the Paint Bucket tool you can use it to fill existing objects.

13. Draw a square with the Rectangle tool, and you should see something much like this, but in glowing color:

Radial gradients are created in exactly the same way.

14. Go back to the Color Mixer panel and select **Radial** from the **Fill style** drop-down menu:

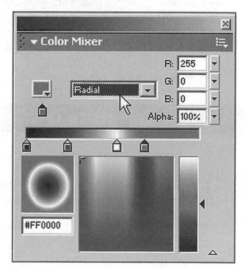

Note that Flash has retained the colors that you defined on the gradient range bar, but that they've now been mapped onto a radial gradient with what was the left-most color (black) in the center of the gradient, and the right-most color (red) on the outside.

15. Draw another square next to the last one.

From this, you can clearly see the relationship between linear and radial gradients: they're both based on a spread of colors that we define on the range bar, and the way that this range is displayed depends upon the left to right arrangement of those colors. We can alter the way that the gradients display by shifting the relative positions of the paint pots on the range bar.

16.   To save your gradient permanently, use the same technique we used in the previous exercise: bring up the menu by clicking on the white icon on the Color Mixer panel and save (or overwrite) your customized color set. **Make sure you don't overwrite any of Flash's default color sets.**

17.   If your gradients get messed up (as they sometimes can while you're experimenting), you can always revert to your saved color set (using the **Add Color** option from the Color Swatches panel menu), or reload Flash's default colors:

Now that you have an initial understanding of gradients, let's have a look at how they can be used to create light effects in your movies.

Light and shade with gradients

By combining simple gradients with drawn shapes, it's easy to create convincing light effects, simulating shadow, shade, and implicit light sources. In reality of course, we won't be building true 3D light-sourced objects (you need other packages to create those), but we *can* fabricate an adequate enough illusion to fool the eye. These effects can add real interest and depth to your movies.

Let's explore this by constructing a shaded sphere.

Using gradients to create a shaded sphere

1.   Open up a new movie.

2.   Start by selecting your Oval tool, then select the green radial gradient from the bottom of the Color Swatches panel:

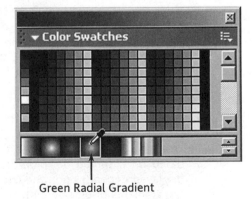

Green Radial Gradient

Because we want the sphere to look like a realistic three-dimensional object, we need to remove the stroke line from around the edge.

3. Click on the **Stroke** button in the Tools panel, and then click on the **No Color** button, either at the top of the palette, or in the Tools panel:

Now you're ready to draw your circle.

4. Use the Oval tool with the SHIFT key held down to keep it perfectly symmetrical. You should now have a black sphere with a green center:

To bring the sphere to life you need to adjust the position of the green center 'light' on your sphere. Traditionally, spheres are lit from the top left, and this has become such a widely accepted convention that if the lighting is anywhere else, it just doesn't look right.

5. Reposition the center of the fill – the point from which the gradient radiates – using your Paint Bucket tool. Imagine that the tip of the bucket is your light source, and click in the top left–hand side of your circle to re-adjust this source. You'll end up with a passable sphere like this:

6. And that's it, your very own 3D sphere, just waiting to be moved around on the stage and morphed into something else. From this basic technique, it's easy to make more complicated shapes with multiple gradients. Maybe a festive egg...

...or a metal cube made from two skewed rectangles:

> *Just like custom colors, custom gradients are not permanently saved when Flash is closed. To save them, you must go through the same process that you did for custom colors. First add the gradient to the palette by selecting* **Add Swatch** *from the Color Mixer panel drop-down menu. Then click on the* **Save Colors** *command on the drop-down menu from the Color Swatches panel.*

We've seen how to make a basic shape look three-dimensional with a standard gradient. Flash also has some features that let you finesse the gradient effects you apply to your objects.

Applying gradients to objects and modifying them

It's all well and good being able to make a perfect linear gradient for your shape, but what if your shape itself isn't perfectly linear? For example, a linear gradient looks fine on a square, but on a skewed parallelogram, the standard gradient doesn't really enhance the impression of a real object with the light falling on it:

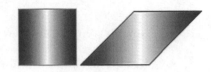

Luckily, Flash provides ways of changing your gradient to suit your shape.

The simplest and most painstaking way of applying the gradient in a non-standard way is achieved with the Paint Bucket tool.

If you draw a filled rectangle on the stage after selecting a linear gradient for the fill, you get a dandy-looking gradient:

The only problem is that all of your rectangles drawn with the basic gradient as a fill will look the same. However, you can change this. If you select the Paint Bucket tool with the standard linear gradient as the fill, and then *click and drag* the mouse to apply the fill to the shape, you can simulate light coming from a different direction:

The angle that you drag at will make the gradient flow from a different starting point. This method is one of trial and error – experiment and see the effects you can get with different types of gradient.

You'll not be surprised that Flash also has more precise methods of manipulating gradients with the **Fill Transform tool** from the Tools panel:

This tool is your key to modifying gradients professionally. In this next exercise, you'll find out how to fit a gradient to a skewed parallelogram, and see the methods you can use to alter gradients in a controlled manner once they're on the stage.

Scaling and rotating linear gradients

First of all, you have to create your parallelogram.

1. Use the Rectangle tool to draw a square with a black border, but no fill. Skew your square using the Free Transform tool from the Tools panel:

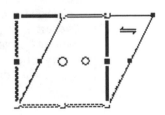

2. Now fill the new shape with a linear gradient. We've used a custom gradient consisting of two black paint pots at each end of the gradient range bar, and a white one in the middle:

The effect we're trying to achieve with this shape is to make it look like a length of metal pipe. It looks like a piece of metal, but more like a flat lozenge than a tube. Let's see if we can model it better.

3. Select the Fill Transform tool from the Tools panel.

Your cursor will change to an arrow with a gradient filled rectangle next to it. This indicates that you're in **Transform Fill** mode:

4. Click on the gradient that's filling your skewed shape. Two blue lines will appear around your shape, along with a circle in the center, and a square and a circle on the right-hand side:

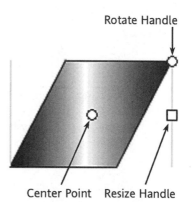

These are the handles used to move and transform your gradient, and you can think of them as the **Scale** and **Rotate** commands rolled into one. When you move your mouse over each one, it will change to a different cursor depending on its function: the Center point is a cross with arrow heads on each end; the Resize handle is a two headed arrow; and the Rotate handle is indicated by curved arrows around a circle:

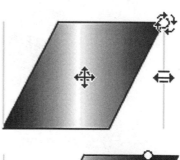

Each of these handles controls a different aspect of the gradient that's filling the parallelogram.

5. Click on the Center point and drag it to the left-hand side. When you release the mouse, the gradient will be centered around this new point. Notice also that the lines at either side of your shape moved as well. These bounding lines act as a quick guide to seeing the position, size and angle of your gradient:

6. Next, click and drag the Rotate handle down until the gradient is on a similar slant to the sides of your skewed square:

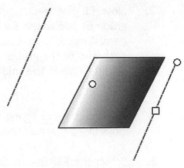

7. The gradient looks a little too big now, and to our eye it seems to be bleaching the shape a bit. We can get around this by squeezing the gradient to fit into the shape better.

8. Click on the Resize handle, and move it in until you achieve your desired effect – a strip of metal pipe in low light:

And there you have it, a gradient that you've fitted perfectly into your skewed parallelogram.

From here, the sky is the limit and it's surely only a matter of time before you start building all manner of objects, such as a metallic ice-cream cone, or maybe a cone of metallic fries...

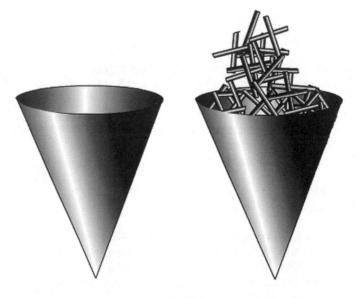

Radial gradients are also amenable to our creative sleight of hand.

Modifying a radial gradient

When dealing with a radial gradient you have four parameters to transform the fill, rather than the linear gradient's three. The majority of them are the same, but their implementation can appear very different on a radial gradient.

1. Still working on your skewed parallelogram, click on the gradient fill with the Arrow tool to select it, then select **Radial** from the drop-down menu in the **Color Mixer** panel to convert the linear gradient to a radial one:

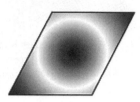

2. Now choose the Fill Transform tool, and then click on the gradient to select it:

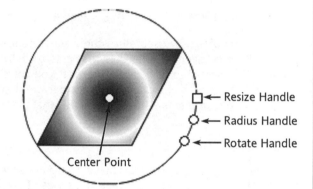

The circle around the radial gradient is the equivalent of the two bounding lines that were on either side of the linear gradient. This marks the shape and the limits of your gradient.

Click on the Rotate handle (the bottom circle) and drag it around.

Notice that nothing seems to happen when you release it. This is because you're rotating a circle, and as you know, no matter how much you spin a circle, it will always remain the same. You're probably thinking, 'So what's the point of having a Rotate handle then, if it doesn't do anything?' And if it didn't do anything, you'd be perfectly right to think such a thing, but luckily it does. The secret is to change the *shape* of your gradient first, so that it's no longer a perfect circle.

3. Click on the Resize handle and drag it in towards the center of the shape:

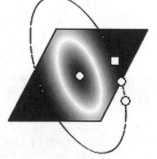

Your gradient will now be elliptical, but at a funny angle to the rest of your shape.

4. Now's the time to use the Rotate handle to spin the gradient so it fits nicely into your parallelogram:

Now for the Radius handle (we'll leave the Center point handle aside, as we want to keep our ellipse centered in our shape). The Radius handle is similar to the Resize handle, but rather than squashing or stretching the shape, it resizes the circle uniformly.

5. Click on it and drag it towards the center a little. Your gradient will shrink, but retain the same proportions:

You've now used all of the gradient tools, bar one. So far you've only been able to give gradients to individual shapes, and then modify those, but imagine what you could do if you could apply your gradient evenly to a number of different objects spread out over the entire stage? That's just what the **Lock Fill** option gives us.

Locking fills

By locking the fill, you can make a gradient span across multiple shapes. That is, you can get the effect of a series of cut out shapes that reveal a common underlying background, almost as if you were opening up little windows to reveal a big picture behind them:

Here's how to use the Lock Fill feature.

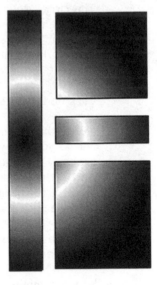

Locking a fill

1. Start off by selecting a gradient from the **Color Swatches** panel. We've used the black and white linear gradient for clarity, but feel free to experiment with something a little more adventurous.

2.   Now use the Rectangle tool from the Tools panel to draw a long, thin rectangle across the stage from left to right:

3.   Next, change the Rectangle tool's fill to **No Color** and draw six small squares underneath your original rectangle:

4.   Select the Dropper tool, and then click on your big gradient-filled rectangle. This will tell Flash to use this particular gradient (and its orientation on the page) as a fill for other objects.

Flash will automatically change the cursor to a paint bucket with a small padlock next to it, the sign for – you've guessed it – a locked fill:

5.   Finally, click on each of the squares to fill them with the gradient:

See how the gradient stretches across the six squares as if they were a continuation of the fill in the big rectangle? Flash is intelligent enough to work out the continuation of the gradient beyond the original shape and map it onto the new shapes. This can be a very powerful way to achieve symmetry across your gradients.

To unlock these fills, with the Paint Bucket tool selected, click on the **Lock Fill** icon in the Options area of the Tools panel:

Once the lock is unselected, the fill is unlocked and you can color your squares with any fill you wish.

We have spent all of our time so far talking about ways of drawing images directly in Flash, but it's also possible to create images in external programs and then import those into Flash for manipulation and use. One of the most common image types that you might want to bring into Flash is a bitmap.

Using bitmap images in Flash

A bitmap image (otherwise known as a **raster** image) is a generic name for an image that's defined in terms of thousands of individual *pixels*. Typical bitmap formats include JPGs, BMPs, GIFs, and TIFs, the difference between them being the particular ways they store the image data. Bitmaps are usually used for complicated images like photographs or paintings, where every single pixel can make a difference in the finished picture. The problem with bitmaps is that the image file has to describe each and every pixel that the image is composed of, which often results in a large file, in turn meaning long download times. (Some *lossy* bitmap formats such as JPG can compress images by describing blocks of similar color, rather than every pixel, but at the expense of picture quality).

A **vector** file, on the other hand, will describe an image in terms of mathematical expressions – such as the start and end points of a line. It's this fact that allows vector files to compress a lot of graphical information into a small space. Mathematical line description is great for simple shapes, but it's more difficult to try to describe the Mona Lisa in terms of vectors.

The first thing to remember when you're considering using bitmaps in Flash is that Flash is not designed as a bitmap program. To get the best performance in your movies, it's always preferable to create everything inside Flash using the drawing tools provided, or to use vector graphics imported from other software applications. In this way, Flash can optimize the file to ensure it is the smallest (and therefore the quickest) download possible. It's possible to create a 'flipbook' style movie by using a sequence of imported bitmaps, but this will create such a huge file, and take so long to download, that most people will have moved on to the next site before the first couple of frames of your movie have loaded!

There'll be times when you've got a nice logo that you've created in a paint program, and you're tempted to just pull it into Flash and then animate it. Although you *can* do this, in the long run you're better off doing it from scratch in Flash. It may not look exactly the same, but the benefits of smaller size and higher speed will probably outweigh the small graphical differences. So, the first rule of thumb when using bitmaps is – think carefully about the trade-off between file size and the benefit that the bitmaps will bring to your movie.

So, a couple more rules of thumb. Use bitmaps when:

- You need to have photos or lifelike images.

- You need to have screenshots.

- You need to have pictures of drawings or artwork.

For anything else, draw it inside Flash or another vector program.

> *Don't forget that the web-safe color rule that applies to the colors you use in Flash also applies to the colors of any images that you import into Flash. If you want your image to be guaranteed to display correctly on all computers, you should use the 216-color palette throughout all of the stages of your movie's creation. This means that when you find an image to import, its best to change its colors in a graphic editing program first to make sure it will display as you want it to, and then bring the image into Flash.*

OK. You've considered all the warnings, you've tried your best to draw your picture in Flash, but you've come to the decision that you're just going to have to import a bitmap image into Flash...so how do you do it?

Working with bitmaps

1. Inside a new movie, Click on the **File > Import** menu option to open the **Import** dialog box.

2. Navigate to a BMP, JPG or GIF file image on your computer (or you can download the example we've used here from this book's download section on our web site):

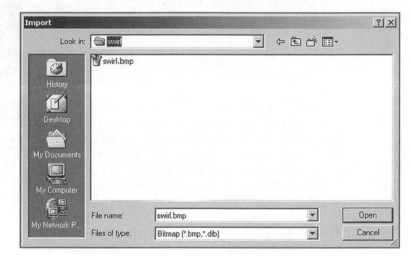

3. Open the file.

4. Your file will be imported into Flash and placed on both the stage as an object, and in the Library:

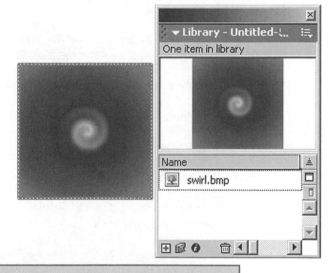

Flash uses the original image stored in the Library as a reference point, so if you delete this, it can cause problems with your Flash movie. Even if you break apart the image and convert it to a graphic symbol, it will still be inexorably linked to the original bitmap.

Once you've imported the image into Flash, there are a couple of methods that you can use to modify it.

5. Right-click (or CTRL-click on a Mac) on the bitmap symbol in the bottom pane of the Library. This will open a context-sensitive menu with a list of commands that can affect your image:

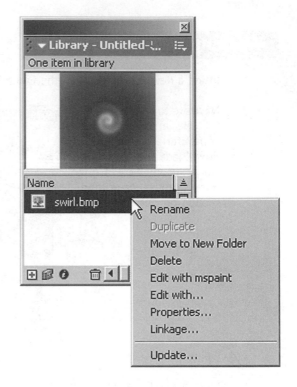

The commands that we're concerned with are the **Edit with** commands. The first of these (**Edit with mspaint** in this example) will open up the default image editing program that your computer has associated with that file type. The second **Edit with...** option will open a dialog box, and from there you can choose a program to edit your image in. Both of these commands will open the bitmap within the selected editing program. When you've finished editing the bitmap, save it and close the program to return to Flash, and you'll find that the image in the Library will have been updated to reflect any changes you've made.

The second method of altering bitmaps is to modify them *within Flash itself*. At the moment, the bitmap on the stage is an instance of the symbol in your Library.

6. Double-click on the instance on the stage: you might be expecting to be taken into an 'Edit Bitmaps mode', but instead, nothing happens.

To alter a bitmap inside Flash, you first have to *break it apart*.

7. Click on the **Modify > Break Apart** menu option.

Your bitmap image has now become a *shape*, with no outline, and filled with the image from the Library. This shape can be modified as any other shape can be in Flash: you can draw on it, cut bits out of it, and scale or rotate it.

8. Click on the **Lasso** tool, and you'll see three options for it at the bottom of the Tools panel:

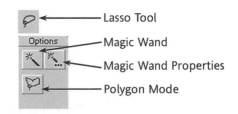

The two important options in the bitmap-editing context are the **Magic Wand** and the **Magic Wand Properties**. The **Magic Wand** is used to select a *specific color* in the image, which means that if you had a picture of a sky with clouds, and you only wanted to select the sky and *not* the clouds, you'd use the Magic Wand tool. With this tool, you could just select the blue areas and ignore the gray and white clouds.

9. Select the Magic Wand option. If you've downloaded the `swirl.bmp` from our web site that we're using in this example, then click on the far top left corner of your broken-apart image. (If you're working with one of your own images, click on an area comprised of mostly one color). A small section of the image will be selected:

    Selected Area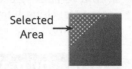

    This is because Flash has *only* selected the sections of the image whose pixels are a very close color match to the original pixel you clicked on.

10. Now click on the **Magic Wand Properties** option, and a dialog box will appear:

    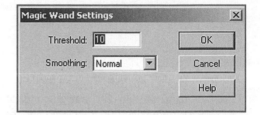

    From here, you can alter the settings for the Magic Wand tool.

    The **Threshold** box defines the amount of *deviance* Flash can make from the clicked-on color when it determines the 'matching pixels' to include in its selection. Imagine a bitmap photo image of a cloudy sky: if your sky ranged from a deep blue to lighter gray-blue, then just using the Magic Wand on its default settings would only select a small piece of the sky. A setting of **10** will only allow Flash to select 10 shades of blue different from the one that you clicked on. If you put a larger number into this box, Flash would select a greater portion of the sky.

11. Type 20 into the **Threshold** box and click **OK**.

12. Click off the stage to deselect the corner of the image, and click again with the Magic Wand in the same place on the image as last time:

    Now you can see that Flash has selected a much greater part of the image. If you were to increase the **Threshold** number again, Flash would select an even bigger portion.

    The other option in the Magic Wand Settings dialog box is **Smoothing**. This controls the amount Flash will smooth the boundaries of the selection:

    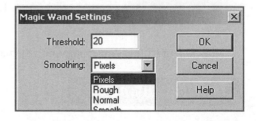

    The **Pixels** setting means Flash will not smooth the boundaries at all, and that only a very tight range of color will be selected. The other 'granularity' options range all the way up to **Smooth**, which does as its name suggests – smoothes out the differences between bordering colors.

    If you're trying to select a very specific area of color, then you should set this to **Pixels** with a low **Threshold** (1-2), and if you're trying to select a large area with variable color, then set **Smoothing** to **Smooth** and choose a high **Threshold** figure.

You've already played with solid and gradient fills in objects, but you can also fill objects using *bitmap* images. Using bitmaps to fill shapes in your movie can give some very interesting results, just so long as you always bear in mind that wherever bitmaps are involved, a larger file size is sure to follow.

Using bitmaps as fills

1. Working with the same imported bitmap image as before, use the Arrow tool to pull out and deform the sides of the shape, and increase its size:

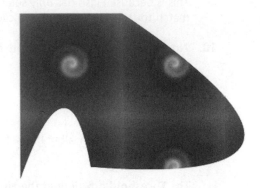

   You'll see that your image has automatically been used to 'tile' the background of the altered shape. Whenever you draw a shape that's bigger than the actual bitmap image, Flash will tile the bitmap to fill the shape's outline.

2. Click on your shape with the Dropper tool. If you now look at the fill color in the Tools panel or Property inspector, you'll see that there's a small copy of your image inside the box, which means that the current fill color is actually your bitmap image!

3. To really demonstrate the selected bitmap fill, draw a simple rectangle on the stage next to your other shape:

   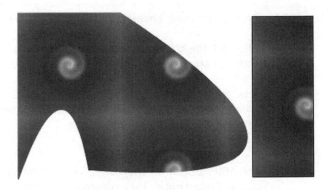

   The new shape will be filled with the bitmap, showing a continuation of the tiling that was apparent when we stretched our original shape. This is because the bitmap image is effectively acting as a locked fill on the stage, just as we saw earlier with our locked gradient fill.

Another useful way to manipulate bitmaps in Flash is to use the **Trace Bitmap** command.

Tracing bitmaps

Tracing a bitmap converts it from a bitmap image into a series of vectors. Although giving you bitmap detail with vector scalabilty sounds like a good thing, the results, in practice, *can* leave a lot to be desired. You'll need to experiment with this feature and make a judgment about the benefits it has. Let's walk through an example of bitmap tracing.

1. Delete what's on your stage at the moment, and drag another two instances of your bitmap image out from the Library and on to the clear stage.

2. Select the first bitmap instance and click on the **Modify > Trace Bitmap** command. You'll see this dialog box:

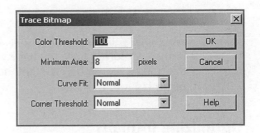

The settings are as follows:

- **Color Threshold** – This works on the same principle as the **Threshold** setting in the Magic Wand Properties box: a higher number means that Flash will include a greater number of colors as 'matching', which means that your final (traced) image will decompose into fewer vector shapes.

- **Minimum Area** – This defines the minimum size (in pixels) that an area can be, while still being considered a shape. The more detailed that you want your final image to be, the smaller you should make this number, remembering of course that more shapes means bigger file size.

- **Curve Fit** – This is similar to **Smoothing** in the Magic Wand Properties box. Setting this to **Pixels** here will ensure that the resulting traced curves will stay faithful to the original bitmap, while setting it to **Very Smooth** will let Flash round out the curves in its selection. The smoother a line is, the less vectors Flash needs to define it, and so the smaller the file size.

- **Corner Threshold** – This performs the same task as **Curve Fit**, but it deals with how far a line must bend before Flash breaks it into two lines with an angular corner. The fewer corners in the image, the smaller the file size.

3. Leave the settings as the defaults shown in the screenshot, and press **OK**. Flash will now convert the first bitmap instance into a group of vectors using the settings you provided. You'll get a result like this:

You can see that this isn't *particularly* faithful to the original bitmap. Let's try and trace an image that's a little closer to the original.

4.   Click on your second bitmap instance, and open up the Trace Bitmap dialog box again.

5.   This time, set the values to **10**, **2**, **Pixels**, and **Many Corners** respectively, then press **OK**:

We think you'll agree that this looks virtually identical to the original bitmap. Unfortunately, the price you pay for this accuracy will give you an enormous file. You'll see just how big this file is when you come to **optimize** it in a moment.

Optimizing bitmaps

Optimizing minimizes the amount of corners in an image, and smoothes out the lines to give a smaller, but less precise picture. You can optimize any shape that you've drawn, but the feature comes in particularly useful when dealing with traced bitmaps.

Optimizing the traced bitmap

1.   Select all of your first bitmap image instance with the Arrow tool and use the **Modify > Optimize** menu option to open the **Optimize Curves** dialog box:

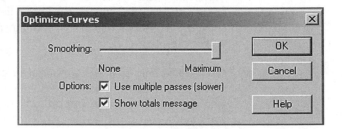

2.   Change the settings to those in the screenshot by dragging the **Smoothing** bar to the far right and checking the **Use multiple passes** box. By doing this, you're ensuring that Flash will optimize the curves as much as possible, and create the smallest file it can.

3.   Click **OK**:

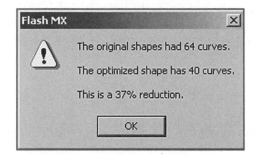

You'll see a report window, showing the amount of curves that Flash was able to optimize.

If you look at your image on the stage now, you'll see that it is a lot spikier than it was before, because Flash has converted all the pixilated smoothness into vector precision. By keeping the Smoothing slider at a lower setting, you can keep the image more faithful to the original, but at the expense of optimization.

4, Do the same thing with your second (more accurately traced) image, using the same settings as before:

Now you can see how tracing bitmaps accurately can leave you with a huge amount of curves, which all add up in the final file size. Whereas with the first image there were only 64 curves, in the second there were 5839, and even after optimization there are still 1531 curves. The final image though, is not too shabby a reproduction of the original, and at a considerably smaller size:

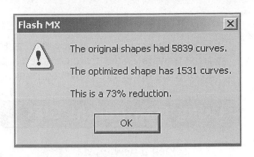

The original bitmap image is on the left, the highly optimized vector image is in the middle, and the accurately traced and optimized vector image is on the right. Again, you're on the horns of that old 'size vs. quality' dilemma – and only you can make the ultimate decision about whether those extra k are worth it.

> *The Trace Bitmap tool will not always give the best results, and can leave you with very large files. It is sometimes more useful to import the bitmap onto one layer, lock it, and then physically trace it using the Pencil tool on another layer, deleting the original when you're finished.*

We'll now focus on another type of bitmap image – the GIF file, and see how Flash treats these when it imports them.

Importing GIFs into Flash

The **GIF** (Graphic Interchange Format) file is one of the most commonly used image types on the Internet. What makes them so special is that not only can they be compressed to produce relatively small images, but they can also include animations and single color transparency. When you import a GIF into Flash, you can retain these attributes.

Let's see how, starting with the GIF transparency idea.

Transparent GIFs

GIF transparency is not as powerful as Flash's Alpha setting. Whereas with Alpha you can have a range of partial transparencies from completely opaque through to totally transparent, with a GIF, the transparency can only be on or off. However, re-using transparent GIFs in Flash can still be a useful feature to exploit.

Using transparent GIFs

1. Open a new movie.

2. In the **File > Import** menu, navigate your way to a transparent GIF that you have on your computer, or use the downloadable `transparent.gif` file from this book's support area on our web site. You should have a red square on your screen with a circular hole in the middle:

    The hole in the middle is the transparent area of the GIF.

3. Draw a line across the stage, and right across the image, using the Paintbrush tool. The line will pass behind the image, but it will still be visible through the hole:

    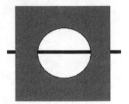

    Move the GIF around on the stage. Wherever you put it, you should still be able to see the painted line behind it through the hole.

    Remember that there's not actually a gap in the image, such as you'd get if you drew a vector rectangle with Flash's Rectangle tool and then used the Oval tool to cut a vector circle out of the middle. The hole in the GIF is more akin to a window: there's still a solid piece of image there – it's just that it's completely transparent.

4. To test this, try and click on the part of the line that you can see through the window. If there was a gap here you'd expect to be able to select the line, but instead, you'll find that the 2 is selected, even though it looks like there's nothing actually there.

The next type of GIF to look at is an animated one.

Animated GIFs

An animated GIF is basically just a collection of static images that play one after the other at a specified speed. You can import these into Flash and incorporate them into the main timeline or into a movie clip's timeline.

Using animated GIFs

1. Start a new movie, and use the **File > Import** command to locate an animated GIF and bring it into Flash. Again, we've provided a file on the web site that you can use – `animated.gif`.

2. When you bring an animated GIF into Flash, you'll notice that your timeline changes:

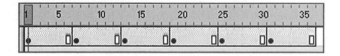

Flash creates a new keyframe for each frame in your animated GIF, and the number of normal frames between each keyframe on the timeline is dependent upon the delay specified inside the GIF. For example, our original GIF has six frames, and a delay of 1/2 a second between each frame. This gives a total running time of three seconds (6 x 1/2 = 3).

In Flash, each keyframe is followed by five 'keyframe-dependent' frames on the timeline, meaning that each of the GIF frames is displayed for six Flash frames. The movie is playing at the default twelve frames per second, so each set of six frames will take 1/2 a second to display. This is the same as it was in the GIF, as is the total time, thirty-six (frames) divided by twelve (fps) = three seconds.

3. Each of the keyframes reproduces each of the GIF frames as bitmaps within that frame. Open up your Library:

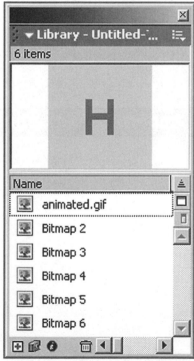

You'll see that there are six bitmap images within it, one for each frame of the GIF. The first one is named after the filename of the GIF, and the following images are just named **Bitmap** followed by a number. If you're going to be using animated GIFs in Flash, it is helpful for your reference to create a folder in your Library for the GIF and store all of its frames within that folder.

It's also possible to create a similar effect by importing a sequence of images into Flash. So, if you have a number of images named slide1.gif, slide2.gif, slide3.gif, *etc... in the same directory, and you import the first one, then Flash will ask you if you want to import the rest of these as a sequence of images.*

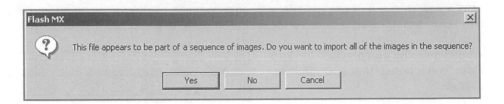

If you answer **Yes** *to this, Flash will import your sequence of images as keyframes, one after another in a straight line.*

Importing and optimizing JPGs in Flash

The **JPG** image format is best suited for photographic images. If you have a photo from say, a digital camera that you wish to bring into Flash, it will probably already be in the JPG format.

JPGs are imported in the same way as GIF images, but need to be optimized a little differently. JPG images can largely inflate the file sizes of our Flash movies if you aren't careful and if they're not used in moderation.

Let's bring a JPG into Flash and see how to deal with it.

Importing and optimizing a JPG in Flash

1.   Open a new Flash movie and choose the **File > Import** menu option.

2.   Locate a **JPG** on your hard drive, or use the downloadable spiky.jpg from our web site. Click **Open** to import it.

3. The chosen JPG image will now be placed on your stage and within your Library:

4. Test the movie with **Control > Test Movie**.

Our image looks pretty good, but the price to pay for this is that our Flash movie has a large file size, and although you might not believe it, Flash is actually compressing the image a little...but not nearly enough.

Let's see where Flash is doing this.

5. Select the **File > Publish Settings** menu and then click on the Flash tab located along the top of the window:

On this tab is the **JPEG Quality** slider bar. This is the default compression setting for JPG images in your Flash movie, usually set as 80 by default. Rather than change this setting and affect any future imported images, we'll override this default document setting and edit the quality of our JPG through the Library.

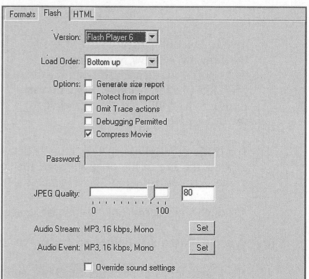

6. Double-click on the image name in the Library to bring up its properties:

You'll notice that you have a preview window for your image in the top left-hand corner.

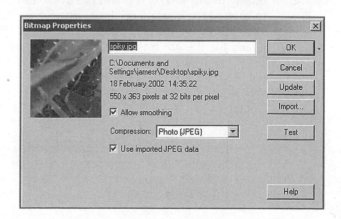

The **Allow smoothing** option gives Flash control over whether the compression is smoothed out. Sometimes JPG compression can leave harsh edges or blocky sections. Smoothing eliminates this, but adds a little to our image size. In most cases it is better to leave this on, but it is always worth checking your image with and without it to see how much difference it makes to different images.

The **Compression** option allows you to choose the type of compression that will be applied to the image. There are two options – **Photo (JPEG)** and **Lossless (PNG/GIF)**. Luckily, Flash has aided us by putting the most appropriate format following the type.

Let's take a look at the last feature and try to shave some kilobytes off our image.

7.   Uncheck the **Use imported JPEG data** box. This will bring up a box below with a compression digit in it. Type 10 into this box and click the **Test** button:

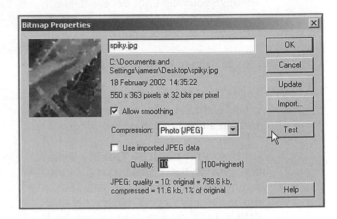

If you now look closely at the image in the preview window, you'll see that it looks pretty granular. Place your cursor over the preview window – so that it turns into a hand – and click and drag to see other parts of the image.

The **JPEG: quality** information, directly below the **Quality** field, shows the amount of compression applied, the size of the original image, the compressed image size, and the size of the compressed image as a percentage of the original.

Although the figures look healthy the image certainly doesn't.

8.   Type 30 into the **Quality** field and press **Test** again.

The image looks a lot better this time, and the file size is still pretty low. To be sure of the final quality of any image, it is always a good idea to test your movie with **Control > Test Movie** and to assess each image individually. There is no right and wrong when it comes to JPG compression. The choices you make will depend a lot on the JPG image itself, the context in which you are using it, and the file size restrictions upon the whole Flash movie.

For example, imagine a scenario where you are creating a web site for a photographer's portfolio. You would be forced to retain as much image quality as possible – a lot of compression just wouldn't show the images as the photographer intended.

> *If you import a photographic image in another format into Flash – say a TIFF or PICT, you can still apply JPG compression to it by opening the image's properties from the Library. JPG compression is not only limited to imported JPGs.*

We'll now look at importing files from other Macromedia products, and get a glimpse of the extended integration between them.

Importing files from FreeHand and Fireworks

One of the great things about Flash is its integration with other Macromedia products such as FreeHand and Fireworks. Here we will give you just a basic overview of how to import files from these programs.

Importing Fireworks files is a very simple process. Simply use the **File > Import** menu and then select **PNG file** from the menu. You'll then be prompted with a dialog box like the one here:

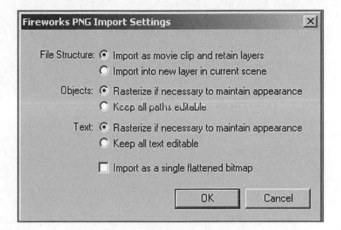

When importing your Fireworks file, it's wise to try and retain the original Fireworks file in the best possible format to allow further manipulation in Flash. Here a run-down of the options available to you:

- **File Structure** – use **Import as movie clip and retain layers** for the most efficiency. This is because Flash will place all the Fireworks content in one movie clip and retain the original layer format by making new matching layers within the movie clip.

  Flash will create a new folder in the Library called **Fireworks Objects** and will place a generically titled movie clip within it. Flash will place all Fireworks imports within this folder.

- **Objects** – use **Rasterize if necessary to maintain appearance** for an import true to the original file, but use **Keep all paths editable** to keep all objects editable within Flash.

- **Text** – again, as with the **Objects** options, use the **Rasterize...** option wherever possible. Use the **Keep all text editable** option in situations where your text is rasterized in Flash and you wish to keep it as a vector object.

If the objects and text options don't give you a satisfactory result the first time around, try using the other option. Where the situation arises, sometimes a little trial and error is required.

The same basic process also applies to importing FreeHand files. Use **File > Import** but select FreeHand from the **Files of type** drop-down menu. Once you've selected a file, you'll see a different dialog window appear:

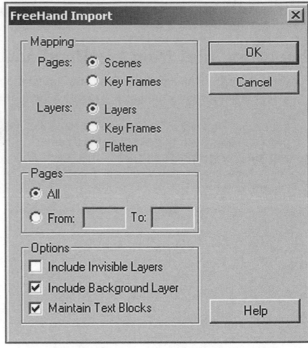

As you can see, you have many more options when importing FreeHand files. FreeHand is also a vector program, but instead of creating images for the web, it is mostly used for print design. FreeHand gives you the ability to have multiple pages. Flash will allow you to import these pages as separate scenes with one page in each scene, or it can simply import them into their own individual frames.

You can also tell Flash how you want the layers of FreeHand to import. If you want to keep everything exactly the same as you had it in FreeHand, then just keep the **Layers** radio button checked. Or, you can make Flash flatten out the FreeHand file, but the problem with this is that none of your text or artwork will then be editable, just like with Fireworks.

In the **FreeHand Import** dialog window, you can specify which pages of the FreeHand file you want to import, and you also have a few extra options to import layers that you had hidden in FreeHand, as well as your background layer. You can also make sure that any text that was in the file is imported as text, and is therefore still editable.

It's recommended that you keep the default settings here as well, as by doing this all of your artwork is editable once imported (unless it wasn't vector artwork to begin with in FreeHand) and is easy to manipulate in case a mistake is made.

Importing and using vector clipart

Clipart has had a wonderful history in print art, presentations, and web pages, so it should come as no surprise that it can be used in Flash as well. The greatest thing about clipart though is that, unlike bitmaps, most of it is already in vector format, and so can be easily imported and used in Flash.

The best type of file, and easiest for Flash to import, is a **WMF** file (Windows Metafile). These files can be easily imported into Flash through the **File > Import** menu and then, because they are already vectors, are easily manipulated once inside Flash.

WMFs are usually imported as groups, so if you want to start editing them, you can either edit each group separately, or highlight the whole image and use the **Modify > Ungroup** option to convert them all into lines and fills. There are sometimes lines and fills behind others in clipart files, which can add up to unnecessary file size. To ensure this is not the case, ungroup the whole image, and deselect the object to let Flash merge the visible objects together, then discard the hidden ones. Also, it's always a good idea to optimize clipart with **Modify > Optimize** – clipart is made for print and is not designed to be compact for the web. Optimizing it ensures a lower file size.

Don't be afraid to use clipart in your Flash movies. Some people don't like the way clipart looks, but keep in mind that you can use clipart as a building block for your own art, as you can edit it to the look and feel of your own web site.

Images are not the only visual elements that Flash can handle though: it can also use your system fonts and some modification tools to give your movies that extra personal zing.

Fonts and typefaces

It comes as a surprise to some people just how much of a difference a font can make. Fonts are so much more than just boring 'clothes' for words: they can define a web site, and a bad choice of font can easily put people off from viewing your movie or staying at your site. Building up a font collection is a relatively easy task, as the Internet holds many free font repositories, and there are hundreds of font collections on CDs that can be found lurking in computer store bargain bins.

A lot of people don't realize that fonts, like images, are usually copyrighted. If you find a font that you like and you want to use it on your site, or in your movies, it's always best to check the copyright on the font and get the permission, or buy a license, to use the font. The easiest way to get around this is to use system fonts that you know are copyright free, or just create your own, although this latter option is not as simple as it sounds!

One of the advantages of Flash is that it's not as fussy as HTML when it comes to fonts. While HTML supports the standard fonts – Arial, Times New Roman, and Courier (and a few other differing fonts on Macs and PCs) – if you use some more 'exotic' fonts in HTML, these will just be substituted for one of the standard types, robbing you of the effect that you sought after spending so long choosing the perfect typeface. It is possible to *embed* a font in an HTML document, but again, Macs and PCs differ in the fonts they use, and this also makes your files slower to completely download.

There are two ways to get over these obstacles in Flash. The first way is to convert the font to a graphic symbol, although this means that the text part of the object can no longer be edited or selected. The other method is to *embed the font within the movie*. Flash will automatically include embeddable fonts in your movies when you publish them from the FLA file.

Flash will also work with TrueType, PostScript Type 1, Bitmap fonts (Macintosh), and device fonts.

Working with device fonts

Of the four font types mentioned above, the first three are embedded into a Flash movie, bulking up its SWF file size. The fourth type, **device fonts**, will not be embedded, so the file size is much smaller. When you use a device font, Flash will search the computer that your movie is being played on for a suitable font, and then use that to display your text.

Flash comes with three device fonts, and you can identify a device font in your font list because the names start with a _ (underscore):

The standard device fonts are:

- _sans (will display as similar to Arial or Helvetica)

- _serif (will display as similar to Times New Roman)

- _typewriter (will display as similar to Courier)

Be sure to either select the font from your font list when you first use it, or have **Use Device Fonts** checked in the bottom half of the Property inspector:

Working with text

In Flash, you have many of the same commands at your disposal that you find in a word processing program. We covered most of the text options in the Property inspector earlier, but there are a few more options available for text.

You can change text to be any solid color and still remain as editable text, but to make any more complicated effects, the text must be broken apart and converted to graphics. This will increase file size, but it does mean you can give your text some pretty interesting effects:

We'll be looking at some more advanced use of text later in the book, when we learn how to use text fields for user input and interaction.

Finally in this chapter, let's work on our case study exercise.

Case study

In the last chapter, we finished setting up the navigation bar, arranging the final layout for our site's interface. Now that everything is in place, let's use what we've learnt in this chapter to spice up our site and make it look more colorful. We'll also make a start on the content, importing some example graphics of our work to display in our portfolio.

Modifying the background lines

Instead of having just dull gray lines on our header, let's jazz it up a bit by adding a gradient fill.

1. Open up your Color Mixer panel (if it's not open use the **Window > Color Mixer** option). Choose **Linear** from the drop-down menu next to your Fill bucket:

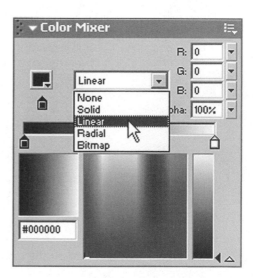

When you first set your fill to Linear, the Color Mixer displays a simple gradient fill of black on the left through to white on the right. In our layout, we want our background lines to fade from being completely transparent on the left, to a slate blue in the middle, and back to transparent again on the right-hand side.

2. Click on the black paint pot and drag it to the center of the gradient range bar:

3. Add a new paint pot on the left-hand side of the bar:

We now want to change the color and transparency of the paint pots to create the gradient fill we want.

4. Set the left paint pot to white, and change its Alpha value to 0%:

Notice that you can tell the color is transparent when the grid is visible in the color box.

5. Select the right-hand paint pot and repeat the last step, changing the color to white and the Alpha value to 0%.

6. To finish creating the gradient fill, change the middle paint pot to a nice slate blue color, but do *not* change the Alpha value as we *do* want this color to be visible:

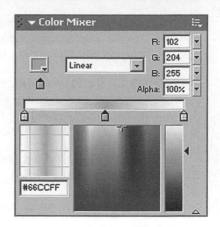

We've finished making the fill – let's go and color in...

7. Making sure our special gradient fill is still our designated fill, use the Paint Bucket tool to add the gradient fill to all the lines at the top of our stage:

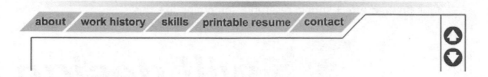

We've set up the background lines but there's something missing at the top of our web site– whose portfolio is this anyway? We want the viewer to know that this is all our own work, so let's stamp our name and identity at the top of the stage.

My portfolio

1. Above the **Background lines** layer, insert a new layer called Name. In frame 1 of this new layer, use the Text tool to name your portfolio however you like:

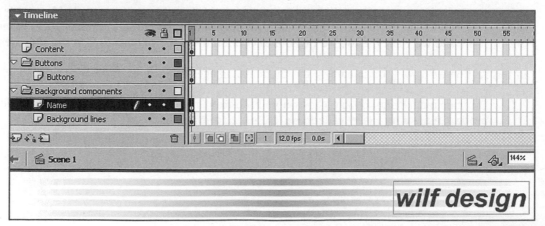

Let's make our name stand out even more, by adding three triangular arrowhead shapes pointing to it. To make things more interesting we'll vary the alpha of each triangle: darkest next to the name, and getting lighter to the left.

2.   Still on the **Name** layer, draw a triangle shape with no stroke and a dark gray fill. Copy and paste this triangle so that you have three identical triangles in a line next to your name:

3.   Select the right-hand triangle and change its Alpha value to 60% in the Color Mixer (make sure your fill style is reset to Solid).

4.   Next select the middle triangle, make it slightly smaller, and set its Alpha value to 40%.

5.   Click on the left-hand triangle, make it smaller than the middle triangle, and set its Alpha value to 20%.

6.   Finally, in the Align panel use the **Align vertical center** button to ensure your triangles are accurately lined up together, and also click on the Space evenly horizontally button.

Your finished effect should resemble something like this:

We've now completed the basic layout of our web site background. Let's go on and start work on the actual content that we want to show.

Importing content

When the user clicks on our **work history** button, we want them to see thumbnails of example web sites that we have designed in the past. The content window will display these thumbnails and other relevant information, and we want the user to be able to click on these thumbnails to visit the sites we've made.

In this section we'll work on importing the thumbnail images of these example web sites.

1.   On your main stage, double-click on your **content** movie clip, taking you into the Edit Symbols mode. Create a new layer called web site info boxes.

2.   On this layer draw three solid, filled, boxes, all with Alpha values set to 50%. Use the Align panel to arrange them evenly in your content interface:

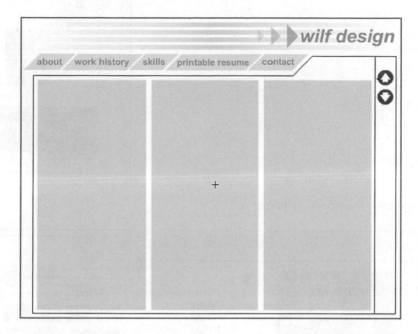

3.   Insert a layer above **web site info boxes** and call it `web site thumbnails`.

We're going to import three screenshot files now to act as examples of our work. The three GIF images used here are available in the download files for this case study but feel free to use any of your own graphics if you want.

4.   With the first frame of the **web site thumbnails** layer selected, go to **File > Import**, and in the **Import** dialog box select the three thumbnails you want to use:

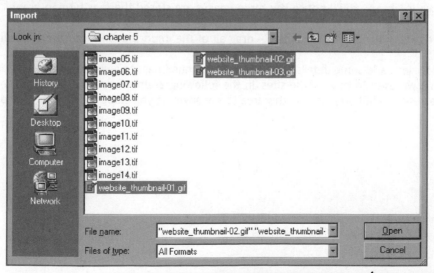

You'll see your images, now imported, stacked on top of each other on the stage:

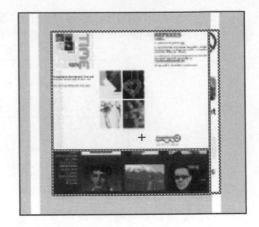

5.   Arrange each thumbnail in its own info box:

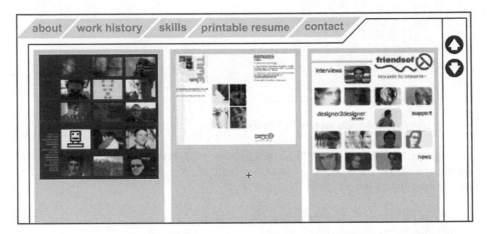

In your Library, you'll notice the three images are stored there as bitmap graphics.

6.   Let's keep our Library organized – drag all of the imported GIFs into the **work history** folder.

Lastly, let's add some details underneath these thumbnails to give the visitor some information about what we used to make these sites. In the following example, I've just listed the tools used to make these sites – but you can use this area to say anything you want about your own personal projects.

7. In frame 1 of the **web site info boxes** layer, create a static text field underneath each of your graphics, and enter in any appropriate text you want:

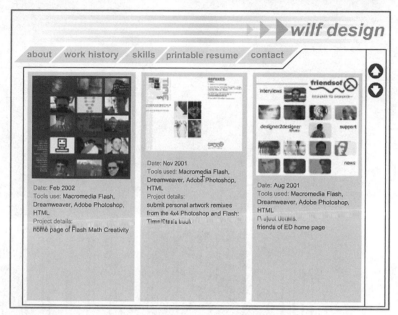

8. Save your movie and close it.

We'll be returning to this case study at the end of the next chapter.

Summary

In this chapter, we've examined some general Flash features, all of which are targeted at helping you make the objects in your movies look more effective.

We saw that:

- There's a palette of **web-safe** colors that we can always rely on to render properly in any browser in the known universe.

- We can create our own **custom colors**, and have great control over their constituent colors.

- We can use **hex** values to match and amend colors.

- **Gradients** can bring flat objects to life, and we can create, modify, and save our own customized gradients and color sets.

- We have infinite potential to manipulate **gradient fills** once we've applied them to an object.

- We can import, trace, and optimize **bitmap images** for use in our movies – even though there can be a file size penalty to be aware of.

In the next chapter, we're going to focus on **animation** and put more detail onto the sketch that we drew in the first chapter when we built that simple animated mushroom.

Motion Tweening

What we'll cover in this chapter:

- **Motion tweening**: the art of moving objects around in your movies and animating them convincingly.

- How to scale, rotate, fade and change objects' color as they move.

- Making objects appear to accelerate and decelerate using **easing**.

- Using **onion skinning** to view multiple frames simultaneously – this helps you make convincing animations.

- Creating **motion paths** for your moving objects to follow.

The five preceding chapters have immersed us in a number of different aspects of Macromedia Flash: its basic layout, its tools, how it uses symbols, and color. We're now going to start combining these different elements in some more sophisticated ways, giving you plenty of opportunity to test things out and – of course – practice, practice, practice. This is an important one – as well as learning about motion tweens, we'll apply a substantial amount of what we've learned so far in our case study exercise – you'll see the case study further take shape and begin to come to life.

The next step we're going to take is to return to the subject of animation, which we touched upon briefly in the first chapter when we encountered an animatronic mushroom.

Animation revisited

As you'll no doubt recall from the first chapter, Flash animation is based on the simple principle of representing change over time. When Flash 'tweens', it draws the frames 'in-between' two significant moments of action, which are themselves defined by the contents of keyframes. The replayed sequence of 'keyframe, in-between frames, keyframe' is the essence of a Flash animation.

There are really two different types of animation in Flash: the **shape tween** that we used to make our mushroom grow, and the **motion tween**. A *shape* tween is a *morphing* operation, where the original object is *transmogrified* into a different object, and a motion tween is the representation of an object *moving* around the stage:

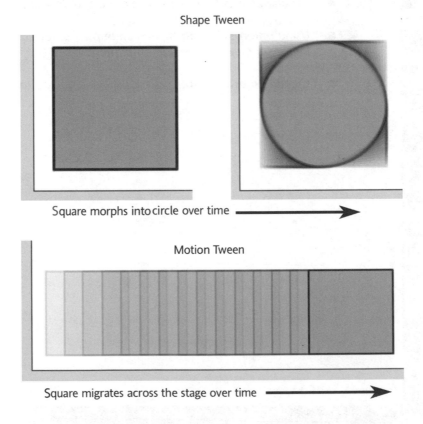

Shape Tween

Square morphs into circle over time ⟶

Motion Tween

Square migrates across the stage over time ⟶

In this chapter, we're going to focus on motion tweens, and in the next chapter we'll look at shape tweening in more detail.

Motion tweening

Motion tweening, put simply, is moving an object from Point A on the stage to Point B on the stage. Motion tweens will only work on symbols or grouped shapes.

Here's an example:

Simple movement with motion tweening

1. In a fresh movie, draw a square, select the fill and the outline together, and convert them into a symbol with the name square, a graphic behavior and a center registration point. Place the square symbol on the left-hand side of the stage.

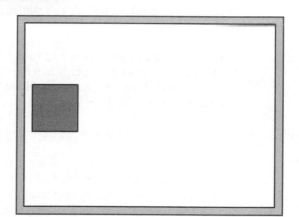

2. In the timeline, insert a keyframe at frame **30** (F6).

3. In the new keyframe (click on the frame in the timeline if it's not currently selected), move the square symbol to the far *right*-hand side of the stage:

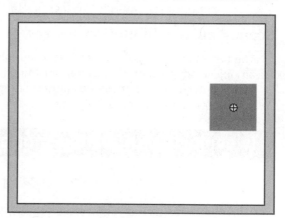

4. Now go back to the timeline and click on any frame between 1 and 29.

5. Bring up the Property inspector and select **Motion** from the **Tween** drop-down menu:

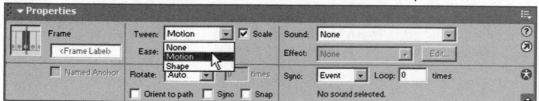

Notice that Flash has drawn an arrow-headed line from frame 1 to frame 29 and colored in the frames:

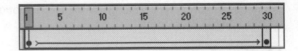

As with our shape tween in the first chapter, the arrow indicates the length of the tween from frame 1 through frame 29. Here, the tweened frames are colored blue to indicate a motion tween.

If you see a dotted line instead of the arrow-headed version, it means that there is a motion tween between the frames, but it's not executing properly:

This is an indication that there's something wrong with the events in the timeline, meaning that Flash can't construct the tween successfully.

You may, for example, be trying to motion tween ungrouped shapes, which cannot be tweened. Alternatively, make sure that you haven't added extra keyframes or objects that are disrupting the motion, and if you still can't see where you've gone wrong, don't be afraid to delete the whole layer and start over from scratch.

6. Test the movie and watch the object move from the left to the right.

You might be thinking that you want the objects in your animations to do more than just move from A to B. You might even be thinking that this plain vanilla motion tween looks kind of wooden and mechanical. Well, through using some of the more sophisticated features of motion tweening you can make your objects change size, spin round, move in complex patterns and move more convincingly. Let's look at these features now.

Scaling objects in motion tweens

The first thing we're going to do is *scale* our object – change its size – as it moves across the stage. Scaling an object using a motion tween is not the same as the shape tweening, or morphing, that we did in the first chapter when we made our mushroom grow. In a scaled shape tween, the *shape* itself remains the same: only its *size* changes.

Tweening simultaneous motion and scaling

1. In the same movie that we've just been working on, click on frame 1 on the timeline.

2. If it's not already displayed on the screen, bring up the Property inspector now.

Notice that the tween **Scale** field is already checked:

This is always checked by default and there is no real reason to uncheck it. **Tween scaling** will allow you to progressively change the size of your object over the duration of your animation. With tween scaling

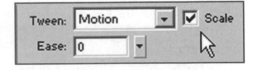

turned *off* in our current test movie, the square would remain at its original size for 29 frames, and then suddenly jump to its new size in frame 30. This will look very abrupt, and this isn't the staccato effect we want here.

We know that the tween scaling option is turned on, so let's scale our tweened square so that it'll make use of the default tween scaling feature.

3.   Go back to the stage and, still at frame 1, ensure the square is selected.

4.   Select the Free Transform tool and click on the **Scale** button in the Tools panel options (or right-click on the square and choose **Scale** from the context-sensitive menu).

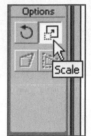

The selected object will now have a dotted box around it with eight scaling selection handles:

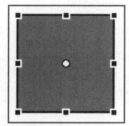

5.   Grab the lower right-hand corner handle and use it to scale the object down to about half of its original size.

6.   Now click on frame 30 on the timeline, where the motion-tweened square is located at the right side of the stage. This time scale the square *up* by about a half, using the bottom left handle to do the scaling.

7.   Test the movie, and you'll see the square gradually grow larger from frame 1 to 30 as it passes across the stage.

8.   To see exactly what the tween **Scale** option does for your animation, go back to frame 1 and turn it off in the Property inspector by unchecking the box. Now retest the movie and notice the migrating square's sudden change in size when the playhead hits frame 30. With the tween scaling option turned *on*, Flash is doing all the hard work in 'joining the dots' of the animation, creating a relatively smooth and gradual motion and growth effect.

Motion tweening also allows us to spin objects round and round as they move on their path. Again, this is fairly straightforward. Here's how...

Motion and rotation

1.   Back in frame 1, turn tween scaling back on in the Property inspector.

2.   Now click on the arrow next to the **Rotate** box and take a look at the resulting menu:

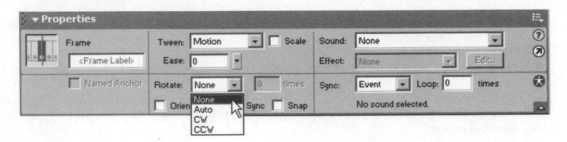

You can choose to rotate an object clockwise, counterclockwise, or not at all. The value in the (currently grayed-out) box to the right of the Rotate menu controls how many times, if any, an object will rotate in the selected direction.

You'll see that you currently have no rotation selected – let's change that.

3.   Click on frame 1 in the timeline and then select **CW** (clockwise) in the Rotate drop-down menu. Change the number of times to be rotated from 0 to 3.

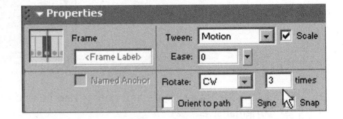

4.   Test the movie again, and now you'll see the object rotate clockwise three times during its movement across the stage.

This is OK for a start, but we can also customize the rotation to achieve a more interesting effect. For instance, we can change the center point around which the square rotates.

5.   In the keyframe at frame 1, draw a box around the grouped square shape to select it, and then choose the Free Transform tool. As usual, you'll see a white dot in the center of the square. This is the center point:

This shows you the position of the currently-defined center point of the shape. This is the point that Flash will use as the center of rotation and, by default, Flash will always position the center point slap bang in the middle of the object. This applies both to symbols and to grouped shapes.

6.   Click on the center circle and drag it to a different position on the square – we've put ours at the bottom-middle.

7.   Play the movie again, and notice the difference in the movement. This time, the square seems to have some weight that's governing the rotating motion. Experiment with the center point in different locations, and see the effect that this has on your square's style.

For further variation, you can try placing the center point *outside* the square:

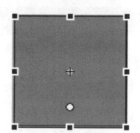

If you play your movie now, the square will rotate in bigger, weightier, arcs. This makes us think about maybe animating some amusement park rides or martial arts equipment...

Back to reality. The ability to rotate objects around different center points helps us to imbue our objects with character and individuality – essentially, with characteristics that mimic how things move in the real world. This is one of the secrets of really convincing animation. Flash has other features to help us here. One of them is **easing**.

Easing

If you need another way to add a touch of real world physics to your Flash animation, you can use the **easing** feature on motion tweens to make an object move more naturally. Easing is essentially a way of controlling the apparent **acceleration** and **deceleration** of the motion-tweened object.

If you look just above the Rotation field in the Property inspector you'll see another field called **Ease**:

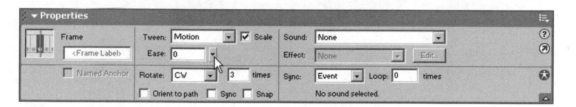

Easing is set to 0 by default. On this setting, motion-tweened objects will move at a constant speed – as they have in the motion tweens we've created so far. By entering a figure in the **Ease** box, you can make your tweened objects start slowly and *accelerate* (**easing in**), or start quickly and *decelerate* (**easing out**).

Easing runs on a scale of -100 to 0 for Easing In and from 0 to 100 for Easing Out. The number represents the amount of easing that's applied to the tween. The further away from 0 you get, the more pronounced the easing becomes:

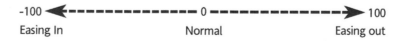

To illustrate how easing can be used effectively, we're going to create an animation of a bouncing ball.

Easing a bouncing ball

First, we need a ball...

1. Open a new movie. Rename its default layer **Standard Ball**.

2. Using the Oval tool and a suitable radial gradient fill, create a strokeless sphere on the **Standard Ball** layer, and then convert it to a graphic symbol called **Bad Ball**.

3. Place this ball at the top left of your stage:

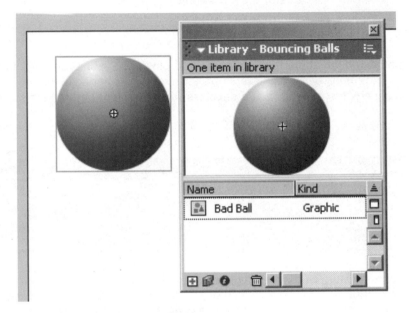

4. Now add keyframes at frames 10 and 20.

5. Next, click on keyframe 10 and move the ball to the bottom of the stage (remember that by holding SHIFT you can ensure that the ball will drop in a straight line). If you click on keyframe 20 you'll see the ball is still at the top of the stage. We now have three positions for the ball:

    ■ 'top of the drop' (frame 1)

    ■ 'bottom of the drop' (frame 10)

    ■ 'top of the bounce' (frame 20)

    The next step is to animate the bounce.

6. Add a motion tween between frames 1 to 10, and then another between frames 10 to 20. These two tweens animate the fall and the bounce of the ball respectively.

*You can select both sections by clicking on the timeline between frames 1 and 10, holding down the SHIFT key, and then clicking on the timeline between frames 10 and 20. With both sets of frames selected, you can add both motion tweens at once using the **Tween** drop-down menu in the Property inspector.*

Whichever way you add the two motion tweens, your timeline should now look like this:

7.   Test your movie.

You'll see that it kind of drops and bounces – but the movement is too uniform to *really* resemble a bouncing ball, isn't it?

Let's add another ball to our animation – and try and make it act more realistically under the influence of gravity.

8.   Add a new layer to your movie and rename it **Eased Ball**.

9.   Create a new graphic symbol on this new layer, consisting of another sphere: a different color to the last one, but about the same size. Call this symbol **Good Ball**.

10. On the new **Eased Ball** layer, repeat the steps you took with the **Bad Ball**: click on keyframe 1 and place your new ball at the top of the stage next to the original ball; create keyframes at frames 10 and 20; move the new ball to the bottom of the stage at keyframe 10, and then add two motion tweens to make it bounce.

11. Test your movie and verify that both balls drop and bounce in identical fashion:

Now we can add some easing to the second ball.

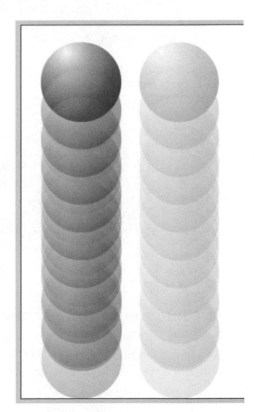

12. Making sure you're working on the **Eased Ball** layer, select keyframe 1 and use the **Ease** box on the Property inspector to set the easing to **-100** (that's 'minus' 100). You can do this with the slider or by keying the value in. This easing value will only apply to the first motion tween on the timeline.

   Remember, this is the most extreme 'easing in' value: the ball will start slowly and accelerate as it approaches frame 10 – the bottom of the stage position. This will make the ball appear to accelerate as it falls to the bottom of the stage.

13. At keyframe 10, set the easing out value to 100 – the maximum. This will make the ball *accelerate* out of the bounce, and *slow down* as it reaches the top of the bounce.

14. Test your movie.

   The **Good Ball** will now look more like a real ball – speeding up as it falls (easing in) and slowing down as it rises (easing out). This is a good way of mimicking the effects of gravity on animated objects: you just need to think how the object would behave in the real world, and add the appropriate easing to the motion tween.

> *Remember: ease in to speed up, ease out to slow down.*

It's also important to note that you can only specify easing values *once* on any single motion tween. To make an object speed up *and* slow down, as in the example above, *two* motion tweens are needed. Each motion tween has its own easing setting, so for every change of speed you want your object to have, you *must* create a separate motion tween.

> *Another thing to keep in mind when practicing your animations is that if you want two or more objects to move simultaneously, they have to be on separate layers. For example, you can't have two circles in layer 1 with one moving from top to bottom and the other moving from bottom to top: to achieve this, each circle should be in its own layer, with its own separate motion tween. Two objects can move on the same layer provided that each has its own tween at separate points on the timeline.*

Next, we're going to look at some editing options that Flash uses to help us when we're creating tweens.

Fine tuning your animations

When you want to make minor corrections to your animation, or get a sense of the flow and direction of the animated frames, it can be a great help to be able to view more than one frame at once. Flash's **Onion Skin** tool allows you to do just this – and there's also a feature that lets you *edit* more than one frame at a time.

Onion skins

Using onion skins allows you to work as if you were drawing each frame on a sheet of tracing paper and piling them on top of each other as you worked. The term 'onion skin' comes from the days when traditional cel-based animators used transparent onion paper to ensure that the frame they were drawing followed on correctly from the previous one. Being able to see the outlines of the previous drawing through the semi-transparent paper meant that they could better gauge changes of position, acceleration, and so on over time.

In Flash, onion-skinning is freed from the tyranny of shuffling paper sheets and is instead wrapped up inside a couple of buttons in the bottom left corner of your timeline:

You may never have used them before, but they'll prove to be very useful as your Flash career develops.

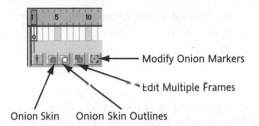

Modify Onion Markers

Edit Multiple Frames

Onion Skin   Onion Skin Outlines

So how is onion-skinning used? Well, go back to your animation of the two bouncing balls. If you click on the **Onion Skin** button, the transitional world of the motion tween will start to reveal itself:

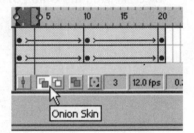

There are a couple of things to notice here.

Firstly, as the playhead is on frame 1, we see both balls in all their glory, clearly defined at the top of the drop. We can also see a ghostly presence of each of the balls at subsequent stages of the drop. Note that the appearance of each ball is slightly different in the ghosted frames: this is because one has easing and the other one doesn't.

The second important thing to notice is the change up on the timeline – two little markers have appeared, and they're spanning frames 1 to 3:

Onion Markers

The onion markers define the number of frames that will be ghosted in around the frame that the playhead is currently on.

If you click on the right-most marker and drag it off to frame 20, you'll see that you now get a preview of *all* of the movie's frames:

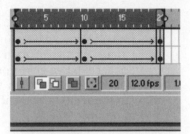

By clicking and dragging the markers, you can alter the range of onion-skinned frames.

If you find that the density of ghosted frames in the onion-skinned view is affecting the clarity of your vision, it's possible to just view the ghosted *outlines* of the animated frames. You get access to this feature by clicking on the **Onion Skin Outlines** button:

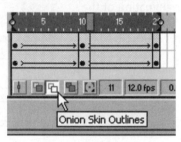

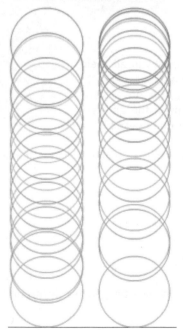

You can see here that for the eased version of the ball, there's a cluster of tightly packed frames at the top of the drop, and only a few at the bottom of the bounce. To see things even more clearly, turn off the **Onion Skin Outlines** option, and switch **Onion Skin** back on. Click on frame 20 and drag the 'finish position' version of the **Good Ball** (remember this is the ball on the **Eased Ball** layer) away to the right:

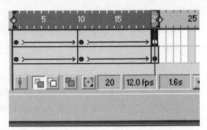

Now you can see the uninterrupted flight of the ball without the 'down' and 'up' legs being superimposed on each other. Note also that Flash has automatically recalculated and re-rendered all the in-between frames. If you test the movie now, you'll see that moving the 'final position' image has resulted in a new flight path: onion-skinning is an excellent way of seeing just what effect your amendments will have on the finished movie.

Let's just consider those clusters of frames again. The density of frames shown by the onion-skinning is greater at the start of the drop and at the top of the bounce, and smaller at the bottom of the bounce. This is because when we apply the easing option, Flash uses a tighter time-clustering of frames to simulate slow motion, and a looser clustering to represent high speed. This can be a little counter-intuitive at first, until you realize that the apparent speed of an object is determined by a combination of the number of frames *and* the frame rate. The more frames it takes for an object to move, the slower the apparent motion will be on the screen. When your brain 'sees' only a few images within a fixed timeframe, it 'fills in the blanks' and figures that the object must be moving *fast*. If your brain gets the chance to register more images (frames) in that fixed timeframe, it figures 'I'm seeing a lot of intermediate images here. This object must be moving *slow*.'

Let's get an overview of the other onion-skinning options we have.

The **Modify Onion Markers** button...

...allows you to alter the way your markers and onion skins appear on the timeline and the stage. If you want the markers to always be shown on the timeline (even when you aren't using onion skins), select **Always Show Markers** from the **Modify Onion Markers** menu:

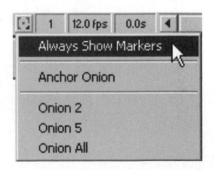

The **Anchor Onion** option, when checked, simply prevents your markers from moving as you move the playhead. This means that you only see the frames of your movie that are *within* the markers as you move the playhead. If this option is *not* checked and you move the playhead along the timeline, the markers move with the playhead to show you the onion skins in the section you are viewing.

Selecting the **Onion 2**, **Onion 5**, or **Onion All** options from the menu moves the markers to show varying numbers of onion-skinned frames. For example, **Onion 2** will show you the frame you're on, plus *two* onion-skinned frames on either side.

It's important to note that the onion skin effect does *not* export with your movie, and is never seen by the end user. If you want to create an onion skin effect for the user then you have to manually create it frame by frame (sorry about that...).

Onion-skinning allows us to *view* multiple frames simultaneously, but Flash also has a feature that lets us *edit* multiple frames.

Editing multiple frames

Being able to edit several frames all at once can be extremely useful – provided you take care!

Imagine you decide that everything on your bouncing ball animation needs to be moved to the right to accommodate another graphical element on the left of the stage. Thanks to the **Edit Multiple Frames** feature this can be done in one hit rather than having to alter every single frame.

In your bouncing balls movie, click on the **Edit Multiple Frames** button:

Now adjust your onion skin markers so that all the frames in your animation are selected:

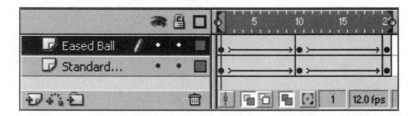

Making sure that none of the objects on the stage are currently selected, use the **Edit > Select All** menu option to select everything on the stage.

Both of the balls, at all phases of their existence, will now be selected:

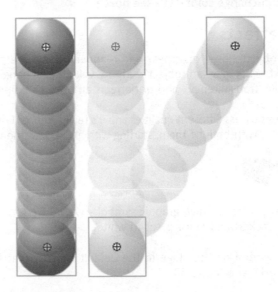

Note that if you'd chosen the **Edit > Select All** menu option *without* having first chosen the **Edit Multiple Frames** option, only the objects in the current keyframe would have been selected. Using Edit Multiple Frames, we pick up *everything* within the bounds of the onion markers.

Now you can drag *all* of the selected content across the stage to its new position:

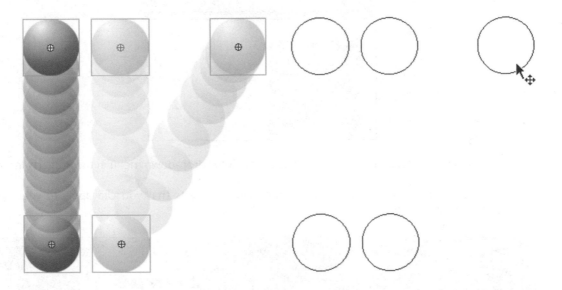

This option can save you real pain, as it means that you don't have to worry about precisely repositioning everything frame by frame. Another great example of getting Flash to do our work for us.

Motion tweening isn't just limited to controlling the movement of objects. It can also be used to make them fade in, fade out, and change color. Let's see how.

Motion tweening effects

If you want to make an object slowly disappear and reappear, there are two ways you can do it in the motion tweening context: changing an object's **alpha** value, or changing its **tint**. *Alpha*, as we've mentioned before, is really 'transparency', and *tint* affects an object's color characteristics.

Each of these two attributes possess different qualities and it's really your call on which one you use and when. Let's work through examples with both of them, starting with alpha, and then you can decide for yourself.

Fading with alpha

1.   In a shiny new movie, create a new graphic symbol – we've used a simple filled square here. Make sure your movie's background color is set to white.

2.   Place the graphic symbol on the stage in the default keyframe at frame 1, and then insert new keyframes at frame 15 and frame 30:

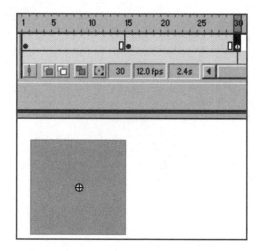

3.   Click on frame 15, select the symbol, and open the **Color** drop-down menu in the Property inspector.

Hidden away in this drop-down list are the different effects that you can apply to your symbol instance on the stage:

4. Select **Alpha** from the drop-down menu, and then set the alpha slider to **0%**. This setting will render the symbol instance totally transparent in the keyframe at frame 15:

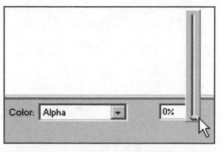

5. Now simply add two separate motion tweens from frames 1 to 15, and frames 15 to 30 as shown below:

When you test your movie you'll see the object fade in and fade out. All that's happening here is that we're gradually increasing and decreasing the square's level of transparency. When we get to frame 15, where the transparency is 100% (invisible), we're looking clean through the square and seeing the movie background. Our square doesn't actually turn white. The tween from frames 15 to 30 fades the square back up, gradually obscuring the movie background again.

Now we'll achieve the same end result again, but using the **Tint** approach.

Fading with tint

Use the same movie you created in the previous exercise, retaining the white movie background.

1. Insert a new layer.

2. Place a second instance of your graphic symbol on the stage at frame 1 in the new layer, and again insert keyframes at frame 15 and frame 30.

3. At keyframe 15 select the second symbol and open the **Color** drop-down menu in the Property inspector.

4. This time, select **Tint** from the drop-down menu.

   Unlike the Alpha effect, Tint has a percentage value *and* RGB values. With Tint, you're effectively overlaying an opaque layer of color on top of the object's existing color. The parameters of the Tint effect control the actual color used and its opacity.

5. Set the Tint's opacity value to **100%** and choose white from the Tint Color box.

   When you choose white, notice that the RGB values are all set to equal 255, indicating that all the constituent colors of (electronic) white are present at full strength. Each of the three R, G, and B boxes has its own slider, which lets you control the amount of each base color in the tint color. If you prefer to use Hex values to select your colors you can open up the palette and type in the appropriate value in the Hex field.

By setting our values to **100%** and **white**, we're saying to Flash, 'at this frame, I want an overlay of pure white that's completely opaque over the top of the symbol':

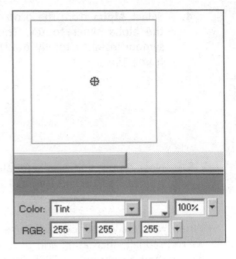

6. Now simply add motion tweens from frames 1 to 15, and frames 15 to 30.

7. Play the movie.

Again, you'll see the object fade in and out, just as before, but this time the mechanism underlying this effect is different. The *alpha* effect literally makes the object disappear by decreasing its opacity and making it transparent, while the *tint* effect changes the color of the object itself. The great thing about alpha fades is that you don't have to make sure that the color of your object changes to match the background – the background color shows through naturally. However, the trade off is that this process is more CPU intensive – it's harder for computers to process, and is a bit slower. Using tint is a little more involved because of the need to alter the color settings, especially if you have multicolored objects and backgrounds.

Alpha is the easy way out as far as fading is concerned, but tint also allows you to *change* the colors of your objects during your animation.

Animating a color change

Let's take a look at how to change the color of an object during a motion tween.

Changing object color mid-tween

In this example, we'll move an object (some text) across the stage and change its color as it moves.

1. In a new movie, start by creating some text to apply the color effect to (check in the Property inspector that you are typing **Static Text**). You can use any font, but a large blocky sans serif font (Arial Black at 48 points, here) will best illustrate the effect. Use black for the text color:

2.   Select the text on the stage and convert it into a graphic symbol. Remember, only symbols (movie clips, buttons, and graphics) and grouped objects can be motion-tweened.

3.   Place the symbol on the stage at frame 1 (if it isn't already there) and create three more keyframes at frames 10, 20, and 30.

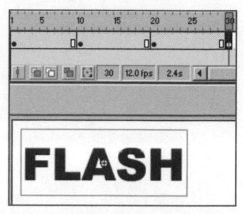

4.   At keyframe 10, select the symbol and open the **Color** drop-down menu in the Property inspector.

5.   Select **Tint** from the **Color** drop-down menu and change the tint amount to **100%.** Then, using the color selection palette, change the color to red.

6.   Repeat this procedure at keyframe 20, but selecting *green* as the tint, and at keyframe 30, this time selecting *blue* as the color. Now your text should be red at keyframe 10, green at keyframe 20, and blue at keyframe 30. If you test the movie you'll see it change color in jumps.

7.   Last but not least, add three motion tweens to the timeline between frames 1 and 10, 10 and 20, and 20 and 30:

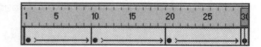

8.   Now if you test your movie you should see your text undergo a chameleon-like constant color-change.

Now you could try clicking on each of the keyframes in succession and dragging each particular instance to a different position on the stage (doing this with onion-skinning turned on will give you some groovy psychedelic effects). If you do this and then play the movie, you can see the basis for some more experimentation, and this also shows that the tint (and alpha) effects can be combined with *actual* motion around the stage.

There's something else of real significance here: although we only had a single copy of the graphic symbol containing our text on the stage, we were able to change its color in three different keyframes, using the **Tint** option on the **Color** drop-down menu of the Property inspector. What's more, we're able to drag each of the different colored versions of the text around on the stage independently. The reason that we can do this is that each different colored version of the text in the different keyframes is effectively treated as a separate *instance* of the graphic symbol: all of the instances have the original symbol as their *base*, but each instance has *properties* that we can change independently of the underlying symbol.

We've already seen how you can change an individual instance's tint and alpha, but you can also scale, skew, and rotate instances – all without affecting the underlying symbol. However, if you edit the underlying symbol in Edit Symbols mode, these changes will ripple through to *all* of the instances – although any instance *properties* you've set (tint, alpha, etc.) will be retained:

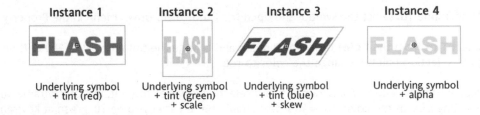

This facility gives us a tremendous amount of flexibility and power in the way that we use symbols.

So, you can now make your objects grow, shrink, spin round, speed up, slow down, disappear, and change color – but they're still all moving in straight lines. This chapter promised to get your objects moving in complex patterns like curves, loops, and zigzags. To add these features to your animation, you need to learn to use **motion guides**.

Motion guides

A motion guide is basically a path that you draw for an object to follow during a motion tween. The motion guide is invisible outside of the authoring environment, and it sits on a special layer underneath the object you're tweening. How does it work? Well, let's create a motion guide of our own and see.

Using motion guides

1. Before you start creating, make sure the 'snap' feature is on by selecting the **View > Snap to Objects** menu option and making sure that the option is checked; we want our drawn object to snap crisply to an underlying motion guide.

2. Create a simple new graphic symbol of any type – this will be the object that we motion tween. We've used a small fish:

3. Insert your symbol in the default keyframe at frame 1 and rename the default layer **Fish**.

4. Next, select frame 30 and insert a new keyframe.

5. Now make sure you've got the **Fish** layer selected, and use the **Insert > Motion Guide** menu option to create a guide layer or, alternatively, click on the **Add Motion Guide** button at the bottom of the layers window.

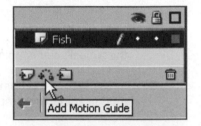

The motion guide layer will automatically appear above the current layer, and it will inherit the name of the layer that it's a guide for, prefixing this with the helpful word 'Guide' and a tiny icon of a bouncing ball – the signifier for a guide layer:

So, the motion guide has its own layer, and it's on this layer that we'll draw the **motion path** that we want our object to follow. A motion path simply consists of a drawn line.

6. Click on the guide layer to select it, and then use the Pencil tool to draw the path that you want your object to follow. Draw the path at the location on the stage where the action will take place – although you can always move it later if you want to.

The motion path itself can be any length or shape you like: up, down, side to side, zigzag, curves, loops – just so long as it's a continuous line with no gaps. You don't have to use the Pencil tool – the Line tool, Pen tool, Brush tool, and even unfilled rectangles and circles can all act as motion guide shapes. The important thing is that you have a *line* on the guide layer.

We've used a simple line to start with:

Remember that you don't need to worry about the color of the path because it will not be seen in the final exported movie. Also, you can treat the line just like any other object: you can resize it, trim it, skew it, and so forth once you've selected it on the guide layer.

Now for the exciting part: making the object travel along the motion guide. To do this, you need to snap the object to the start and end points of the motion path – that's why we've got two keyframes: one for where the guided motion tween will start, and one at the end of the action.

7. Lock the guide layer so that you don't accidentally click on the guide line.

8. In the first frame of the **Fish** layer, grab the graphic symbol instance at its center and drag it over to the left-hand side of the motion guide.

    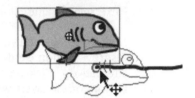

    As you'd expect with snapping turned on, the snapping ring at the symbol's center point will 'pop' when it's snapping to the line:

9. In the second keyframe at frame 30, pick up the fish and drag it to the right-hand end of the motion guide and drop it when it snaps.

    You now have the fish attached to the line in the desired start and end positions. Now all we have to do is make the movement happen!

10. Still on the **Fish** layer, select a frame between 1 and 30 and add a motion tween. Then test your movie and watch your object move along the motion path.

Although motion guides are fairly simple to create, getting the object to snap correctly to the guide takes time to get used to and not getting the object snapped properly is a common problem. So practice and don't get discouraged.

> *The motion guide must be the same length as the timeline for the object that's being guided.*

For example: if the animation is 30 frames long, the guide layer's timeline has to be 30 frames long too. In this exercise you inserted a keyframe at frame 30 on the object layer and then added the motion guide layer. Flash automatically added 30 frames to the guide layer to match the **Fish** layer that the guide layer was spawned from. Flash is intelligent enough to look at the contents of the layer and work out where to put the keyframes in the guide layer – provided that you decide how long the actual animation will take and mark its boundaries first.

Adding keyframes to the **Fish** layer *after* creating the motion guide will obviously alter the length of the animation. For example: if we created a new movie and drew an object on the stage in the default keyframe at frame 1, and then immediately added a motion guide layer, the guide layer will only be 1 frame long. If we were then to add a keyframe at frame 30 on the **object** layer, that layer would be 30 frames long, but the motion guide would remain at a measly 1 frame long. The resulting problem is that the motion guide itself will not exist in frame 30!

You can get around this problem by adding frames to the guide layer, but it's much easier to plan things out, create the animation layer, and then let Flash create an appropriate guide layer when you ask it to.

Motion path effects can produce some really wild results, especially when combined with the other effects we discussed earlier in the chapter. Once you've got the basic idea nailed down, experiment with different color combinations, timeline lengths, and different shaped motion paths. The possibilities are endless.

Case study

Now that we've designed our whole interface, let's add some motion to our project. We want things to move very quickly so that the user doesn't have to wait too long – but we also want to add a little jazz to it. In this case study we'll animate our main button navigation bar, making it slide in from the left of the movie very quickly. At the same time we'll make each individual button slow down as it approaches its final resting position.

We'll also animate our content area, scaling it up to its normal size and position, and fading it in. You don't have to overburden your Flash pieces with too many animations: simple and straightforward can sometimes be better *and* it makes for lower file sizes.

Animating the interface

On your main timeline, you should have a layer folder called **Buttons**. Our first step is to break each button out onto its own layer under that folder. We need to do this because in order to motion tween each button separately, each button must live on its own unique layer.

1. Re-open your case study movie and click on frame 1 of your **Buttons** layer, inside the **Buttons** layer folder. All of your button symbols in the navigation bar will be selected.

2. With all buttons still selected, choose the **Modify > Distribute to Layers** menu option.

Within your **Buttons** layer folder, you should now see that five new layers have been created, with each name corresponding to its associated button. Each of our five buttons are now resting on frame 1 of their own individual layer:

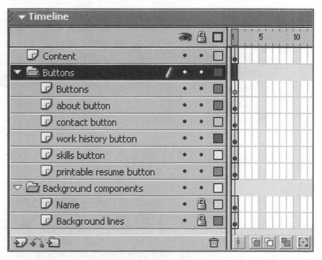

Now that all instances of the button symbols have been moved to their own layers, notice that the original normal **Buttons** layer now has no content on it.

3. Go ahead and delete the old empty **Buttons** layer.

4. Before we proceed with the motion tweening, make sure that the new button layers are ordered the same from the top downwards as they appear from left to right on the stage. If they're not in the correct order, drag each layer up or down as required.

   Before we go further, your layers should now be arranged like this:

5. On the **about button** layer select frame 10 and insert a new keyframe.

6. Go back and select frame 1 and add a motion tween between frames 1 and 10. Set the **Ease** value to **100** to make the button slow down as it nears its final position.

7. In frame 1, move the **about button** just off of the left-hand edge of the stage:

   If you press ENTER you'll see the **about button** move in from left to right, decelerating as it moves.

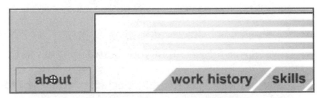

8. Repeat this same process for the other four buttons, adding motion tweens between frames 1 and 10, setting the Ease value to 100, and not forgetting to move each button just off stage in frame 1:

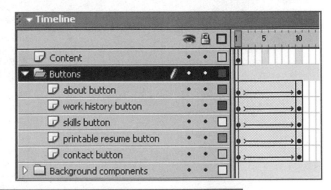

> Tip: After inserting keyframes for all buttons in frame 10, hold down SHIFT and select all of the buttons' keyframes in frame 1 of each layer. You can then assign motion tweens and set the **Ease** value for all buttons at the same time.

We want the buttons to slide in from the left of the stage, slow down, and finally stop in their final position to form the navigation bar. We now need to stagger the time at which each of the buttons begins their motion tween, so that they don't all slide in at once.

9. Select frames 1 to 10 on the **printable resume button** layer. Click and drag the frames so they're now resting on frames 10 to 19:

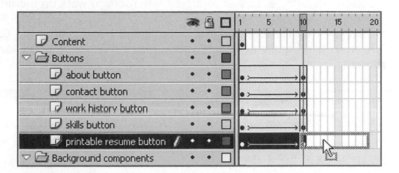

10. Repeat this for the **skills button, work history button**, and **about button** layers, staggering the start of each motion tween by 9 frames each time:

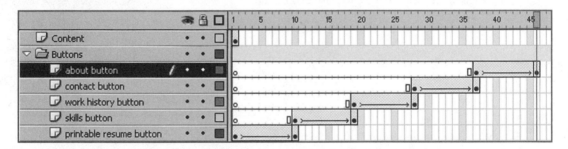

11. Click on frame 46 in the **work history button** layer, and holding SHIFT, select frame 46 on *all* of the other button layers beneath. Then press F5 to insert blank frames on all these layers:

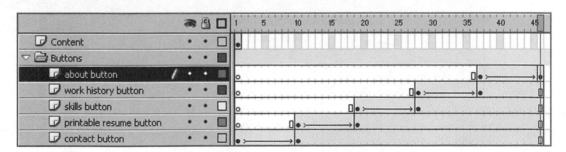

That's our button animation. The individual buttons will now animate in from the left and slow down to a stop, finally forming our navigation bar.

Animating the content movie clip

Moving on, we want to animate the content movie clip section. We're going to make it fade in, and also scale up from being very small to its normal size.

1. Close your **Buttons** layer folder so that we have more room to work on the timeline.

2. On the **Content** layer on the main timeline select frame 1 and choose the **Edit > Cut Frames** menu option. Next, select frame 46 (where your navigation bar animation ended) and go to **Edit > Paste Frames**.

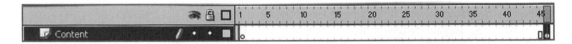

3. Insert a new keyframe at frame 56.

4. Go back to frame 46 and select the **content** movie clip on the stage. In the Transform panel (**Window > Transform**) scale the movie clip down to **20%**:

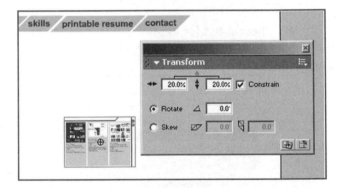

5. With the movie clip in frame 46 still selected, click on the **Color** drop-down menu in the Property inspector. Change the Alpha amount to **0%**. This will make the content movie clip totally transparent:

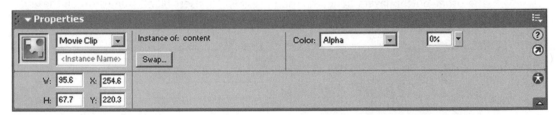

6. With frame 46 selected, use the Property inspector to insert a motion tween and set the **Ease** value to **100.**

7. Reopen your **Buttons** layer folder (and the **Background components** layer folder if it's currently closed) so that all of your layers are visible. Insert a blank frame (F5) in frame 56 of all the layers except the **Content** layer that you've just been editing.

By doing this your graphics won't disappear once they reach the end of their animations. Your timeline should now look like this:

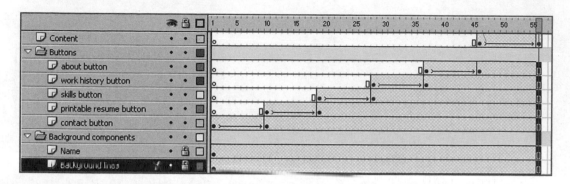

8. Test your movie. You should see your buttons slide in, then your content movie clip fade in to view, increasing in size as it does so.

9. Save your case study movie and close it.

Summary

We've traveled quite a distance in this chapter, passing through the varied landscape of motion tweening, that's taken us to a country where multi-layer motion tweens containing movie clips embedded in symbols happen simultaneously. These case study exercises were important because they started to weld together all the elements that we've seen in the book so far. And they were great practice, too.

In this chapter, we saw that:

-   **Motion tweening** can move objects around the stage, and we can use **motion paths** to guide the objects and **onion skins** to see multiple frames in the animation.

-   We can alter objects as they move: we can **fade** them into the background, change their **tint**, and **scale** and **rotate** them.

-   Using **easing**, we can simulate **acceleration** and **deceleration** for more convincing animation.

In the next chapter, we're going to have some fun with motion tweening's sibling: **shape tweening**.

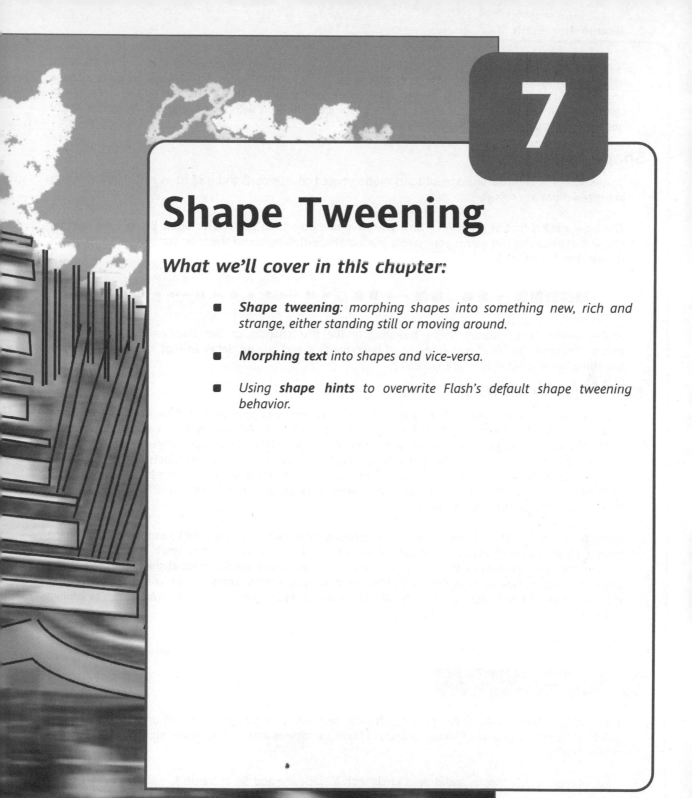

Shape Tweening

What we'll cover in this chapter:

- **Shape tweening**: morphing shapes into something new, rich and strange, either standing still or moving around.

- **Morphing text** into shapes and vice-versa.

- Using **shape hints** to overwrite Flash's default shape tweening behavior.

Now that you've seen what motion tweening can do and experienced the power of Macromedia Flash MX as an animation workhorse, it's time to climb the next rung on the ladder. So far, you can move a shape around the stage, but it will still be the *same* shape at the end of the animation. By the close of this chapter, you'll be able to start the race with a tortoise and finish it with a hare, though Darwinians might not be too happy with what happens in between.

Shape tweens

Shape tweening is similar in concept to its motion tween counterpart, and it's just as easy, but the results are often more impressive.

The basic idea is that at point A in time you have one object, and at a later point B you have another object: between the two points you have a gradual shape-shifting transformation from object A to object B. Like this, for example:

You've already encountered shape tweening in the first chapter of the book, where you made a mushroom grow, and in this chapter you'll be expanding and adding detail to that knowledge, fleshing out the whys and hows of shape tweening.

How shape tweens work

Shape tweens work just like motion tweens, in the sense that you provide a start point in one keyframe and a finish point in another, and Flash fills the intervening frames. And like motion tweens, it's advisable to only have one shape tween going on at any time on a layer – this way, you get more predictable results and less mayhem on the stage. Of course, if you want to shape tween multiple objects into one object at the same time, the objects will have to be on the same layer. It's really a question of necessity: if you need your tweens to interact with each other, they'll need to be on the same layer, but if they don't interact, then keep them on separate layers.

The most important thing to remember when creating shape tweens is that, unlike motion tweens, shape tweens must involve **shapes** and *not* groups or symbols. For a shape tween to work, it must be able to change the basic attributes – the stroke and fill – so that it can morph the original shape into something else. The simplest way to ensure that all of the elements you want to shape tween are 'shape tweenable' is to select all of the objects and use the **Modify > Break Apart** menu option to ensure they're broken down into their constituent elements.

Let's play.

Squaring the circle

We'll set up a basic shape tween to start off with, and then play around with it to understand the finer points of tweening. The two simplest objects in Flash are squares and circles, so we might as well use these in our first example.

1.   Create a new movie, and draw a circle with a black line and fill in frame 1.

2. Click on frame 15, and press F6 to insert a keyframe. You'll now have 15 frames full of nothing but a circle.

3. In the keyframe at frame 15, draw a large, filled square (again with a black line and fill) over the top of the circle:

4. If you want to position the square more...*squarely* over the circle once you've drawn it and released the mouse, don't forget that you can always turn on the **View layer as outlines** option in the **Layer Properties** window. You can bring up the Layer Properties window by right-clicking on the layer name in the timeline and selecting **Properties** from the context-sensitive menu.

You've now got your beginning and end keyframes, and all you need to do is tell Flash to morph from one shape to the other over time by putting a shape tween between the two keyframes.

5. Click on the timeline anywhere between the two keyframes, then open the **Property inspector** and select **Shape** from the **Tween** drop-down menu:

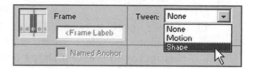

6. Select the Arrow tool, and then click on a blank part of the timeline to deselect your other frames. You can now see that the frames are colored *pale green* and have a solid arrow on them:

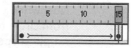

If you click on the **Onion Skin Outlines** button just below the timeline and arrange the onion skin markers to encompass all 15 frames, you'll see a rather beautiful rendering of the shape tween:

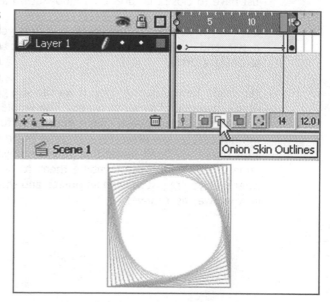

All of this indicates that you've got a functional shape tween on your hands.

7. Select **Control > Test Movie** to preview the movie. You'll see the circle smoothly transforming into a square. It's as easy as that.

    At the moment, the animation loops back to the beginning when the playhead hits frame 15, meaning that your smoothly morphed square suddenly jumps back to being a circle again in a fraction of a second. Ugly. To correct this, you need to create some extra frames that will facilitate the smooth return of the square back to the circular starting image – this will make the animation loop much smoother.

8. Close the movie preview window and deselect the **Onion Skin Outlines** button for now.

9. Click on frame 1: your circle should automatically be selected for you. Now choose **Edit > Copy** (CTRL-C), and click on frame 30.

10. Next, press F7 to insert a *blank* keyframe. It's important that it's blank because we don't want this frame to inherit the image of the square from the previous keyframe.

11. Now use **Edit > Paste in Place** to put the copied circle in exactly the same place in frame 30 as it was in frame 1.

12. Finally, click between frames 15 and 30 on the timeline to select them, and use the **Property inspector** to create a **shape** tween:

    Now when you select **Control > Test Movie** to preview your movie, you'll see a smooth transition from circle to square and back to a circle again. It's strangely mesmerizing to just sit and watch this simple shape beating out its regular morphing rhythm, but if we're going to get any further you'll just have to close that preview window down and return to the MX interface.

13. Click in the keyframe in frame 15, and drag your square a little way off to the side. Preview your movie, and you'll see the circle will move as it tweens into the square, then move back as it returns to being a circle.

    You might be wondering: 'Hey! If we can still get motion effects on a shape using a *shape* tween, what's the point of a *motion* tween?' The simple answer is 'computing power' – it takes more power to perform a shape tween than it does to perform a motion tween. Running a lot of shape tweens will noticeably slow down the computer but running the same amount of motion tweens will run a lot smoother. Don't forget that you can only have one type of tween in the same frame on the same layer, so you can't combine them. It's a question of judgment really – use motion tweens whenever you're just *moving* an object, and shape tweens whenever you want an object to change in some way as it moves.

Here's a simple chart, comparing when you would want to use each type of tween:

Shape Tweens	**Motion Tweens**
Tweening shapes into different shapes	Moving groups or symbols without altering them
Changing the color of objects	Changing the transparency of objects as they animate
Moving objects while altering them	When you need to use a motion guide

Now we have the basics of shape tweening under our belt, let's get a little more sophisticated, and introduce some text-based tweens.

Common tweening text effects

In the following exercises we'll be tweening pieces of text so that they transform themselves into different pieces of text, and we'll also morph shapes into text.

The main thing to bear in mind when working with text is that to be able to tween it, you must first break it apart to convert it into a graphic. This means that you can no longer edit it as if it were a text field, so ensure that the text is *exactly* how you want it to be before you break it apart.

The first tween that we'll practice is the text-to-text tween.

Text to text tweening

This animation starts off with one word and uses shape tweening to change it into a different word.

1. Create a new movie, and in frame 1, use the Text tool in conjunction with the Property inspector to write a big chunky `This is my first`, on the left side of the stage:

We've used Arial Black at 35 point.

2. Now select frame 30 and create a new keyframe.

3. Highlight the text with the Text tool, delete it, and then type `text 2 text tween...` into the text field and move it to the right-hand side of the stage:

text 2 text tween...

4. Use the Arrow tool to select the text field that that you just created (you *don't* want to be inside of the box and selecting the text by dragging), and use the **Modify > Break Apart** menu option to first break the text into separate letters:

Flash has broken the original text field into loads of smaller text fields – not exactly how you need it to be. It's worth remembering that Flash does this because it can be very useful for creating interesting text effects. Each letter is contained in its own text field, so each letter can be changed or moved individually. A simple example:

Text is the only thing that needs to be broken apart twice; symbols are broken up with one command.

5. Make sure you have each text box and letter selected and select **Modify > Break Apart** again to break them into graphics.

6. Do the same thing to the text in frame 1, remembering to break the text apart twice.

7. Click between the two keyframes on the timeline, and use the Property inspector to create a shape tween.

8. Now if you preview your movie you'll see the first words morph into the second while moving across the stage...

We said earlier that shape tweens would only work on 'raw' shapes that have been reduced to their constituent lines and fills. If you've already created a *symbol* to use in your movie, and you want to animate it, you can, providing that you first *break it apart*. Let's see how this works.

Shape to text tweening

In this example, we'll work through reproducing the shape to text tween we showed right at the start of the chapter – where five squares morphed into the word 'Flash'.

1. Open a new movie and draw a *strokeless* black square on the stage – make the square about three quarters of an inch (2 cm/60 pixels) across.

2. Convert your square to a graphic symbol called Square.

3. Drag another four instances of your square out from the Library to make a total of five — one for each letter in the name of the world's greatest piece of software.

4. Use the **Align** panel to align your squares and space them evenly across the stage:

5. Now use the **Modify > Break Apart** menu option to convert your squares back into their component fills.

6. Insert a keyframe in frame 20. This keyframe will inherit the broken-apart squares from the first keyframe.

Now we want to create the letters that spell out the word Flash — one letter to fit in each square.

There are two ways to fit the letters over the squares. The longest, but most precise way, would be to type the word as it is, break the one text field apart into five smaller text fields and position each individual text field correctly, before breaking them all apart again. Phew. The second method is to write the word as one piece of text, then modify its size and spacing to fit over the squares. Because we're using a simple tween, we can get away with using the second of these options. If you were designing a more complicated tween, it would probably be better to treat each letter individually.

7. Use the Text tool to write FLASH on the stage. Choose a text color that contrasts nicely with black.

8. Select the text field with the Arrow tool and move it so that it's over the top of the squares, at the left-hand side:

9. Use the Arrow tool to select the text field again, and then use the **Character Spacing** slider in the Property inspector to adjust the text spacing so that the letters are positioned over the black boxes. The Character Spacing slider is directly below the Font menu (the one with **45** in it in the screenshot below):

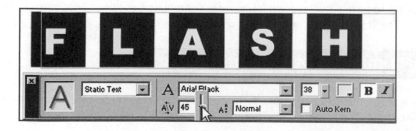

Don't worry about getting things *too* precise: just so long as the letters are roughly in the right place, things will be OK.

10. Click away from the text field to deselect it.

11. Now double-click on each of the black boxes behind the letters and delete them:

    This will leave you with just the word '**FLASH**' on the stage.

12. Now that the boxes are out of the way and we can see clearly, highlight the text and change its color to black.

    We've finished working with the text *as text* now, and it's time to break it up.

13. Select the text with the Arrow tool and use the **Modify > Break Apart** menu option twice to convert it to a graphic. If you don't perform this action twice, your text will still be in text fields.

14. Everything is now ready for tweening, so click between the keyframes on the timeline and use the Property inspector to add a shape tween. Your tween should now work perfectly when you preview your movie.

    If some of the animations look a little odd to you – like the way that the 'A' square transforms into the A – don't worry: we'll be looking at ways to tweak these little gremlins later in the chapter.

First though, we'll look at ways of making your shape tweened animations more enjoyable for your viewers. For the most control here, you really need to use some of the ActionScript that we'll be encountering later in the book, but here are a few simple methods you can use right away...

Making your tweens look more natural

Whether you move a morphing object across the stage or keep it stationary as it changes from shape to shape, there's one slight drawback about using only two keyframes: the object starts immediately into its tween from frame 1. This can be a problem. For instance, with a text tween, the user usually needs to see what the text says before it starts to change into the next word, or shape.

In our previous example, the text was only whole in the final keyframe, which means that it was only perfectly readable for 1/12 of a second – not really long enough for the average person to read. The way to change this is to add a 'buffer zone' of frames, containing the tween-free text, to the beginning or end of the tween. The static images in these frames will mean that Flash appears to pause over the static text.

Creating a more subtle shape tween

We'll carry on using the same example as in the previous exercise, but we'll make one small change to it before adding the buffer zone – we'll make it go backwards.

1. Click on the layer name in the timeline to highlight everything that's on that layer:

2. Now use the **Modify > Frames > Reverse** menu option to reverse the order of the selected frames. You'll now find that your movie starts off with the word '**FLASH**', and then tweens into the five squares. We've done this to make the changes that you're about to apply stand out more clearly.

3. Select all of the frames again, but this time click and drag them across the timeline until the last frame is in frame 30, and then release them:

Notice that as you click and drag, a little rectangle is added to the cursor, showing that a selection of frames is being dealt with. You'll be left with ten empty frames at the beginning of your movie. Your animation will start at frame 11 and run normally through to frame 30:

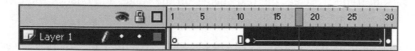

4. Click on the first keyframe of your movie (now in frame 11), to automatically select all of the text that's in it.

5. Next, copy this text to your computer's clipboard by using **Edit > Copy** (CTRL-C).

6. Lastly, click in frame 1, and use the **Edit > Paste in Place** menu option to paste your text into the frame in the exact position as it was in frame 11.

7. Now preview your movie. The text will stay on screen for about a second, and then tween into the five squares. It's now easier to read the text before it starts to change into the shapes. Obviously, if you had more text, you'd want to have a longer buffer zone to allow people more time to read it.

Now that we've covered different shape tweens, let's spice things up a bit by looking at **changing color** while tweening.

Adding color to the mix

Just like the Tint feature does in motion tweens, you can also add color to your shape tweens. In the previous chapter, you made text fade through different colors by using the Tint effect, and in the following example you'll be expanding your '**FLASH**' text animation to include color.

Coloring your shape tweens

1. Still using the movie from the last example, click on the layer name again to select *all* of the movie's frames.

2. Click and drag them, as you did before, so that the final frame is now at frame 50.

3. Click on your first keyframe (now in frame 21) to select all of the text, and **Edit > Copy** it to the clipboard.

4. Now click on frame 1 of your movie, and use **Edit > Paste in Place** to put the copied text on the stage:

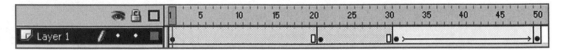

5. Next, move the playhead to frame 10 and use F7 to insert a blank keyframe. Then paste your text in place on *this* keyframe in the same way as you did for frame 1.

    You now have your basic structure set up and are ready to tween. The only thing left to add now is color.

6. Click back in frame 1, select the text shapes on the stage, and change the color in your fill color box to red. The text on your stage will change to reflect this.

7. Now do the same for the keyframes in frames 10 and 21, but using the colors green and blue respectively.

8. The last thing to do is to create shape tweens between all of the keyframes to make your timeline a lean green tweening machine:

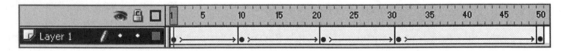

9. Now if you preview your movie, you'll see your text waltz through the spectrum before settling for black and tweening into the five squares.

10. As an added touch to show the power of Flash, click in frame 50 to select your squares and change the fill color to yellow. When you preview your movie you'll now see the final animation changing shape *and* color at the same time.

So how do we get even closer control? With **shape tween modifiers**, of course!

Shape tween modifiers

As with many other elements in Flash's expansive toolkit, shape morphing has modifiers and helpers that you can use to tweak your tween. The place to look, as always, is the Property inspector, in the **Ease** and **Blend fields**.

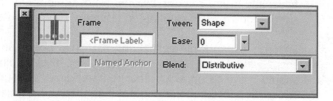

In shape tweens, **easing** acts in exactly the same way as it does with motion tweens – it controls Flash's ability to speed up and slow down the action at the beginning or end of our animations. Here's a quick reminder on the effects of easing:

- **Easing In** to a value of **-100%** will make the shape tween start slowly and **accelerate** as it progresses towards the end of the tween.

- **Easing Out** to a value of **100%** will make the shape tween start quickly and **slow down** as it progresses to the end of the tween.

Unlike motion tweens, shape tweens also offer the option of playing around with the *sharpness* of lines in your tween – the values for this are set in the **Blend** drop-down menu.

- A **Distributive** shape tween will create an animation where the intermediate stages of the tween are smooth and irregular, with no straight lines.

- An **Angular** shape tween will create an animation where the intermediate stages of the tween *preserve* corners and straight lines.

An **Angular** blend is used to shape tween shapes that have straight lines and corners, but if the shape has no corners Flash will revert to a **Distributive** blend.

Now that you know how to create and work with basic shape tweens, we'll turn to those promised tweaking methods that'll bring them that little bit closer to perfection.

One of the best enhancers available to us is the **shape hints** feature.

Shape hints

Shape hints are used with shape tweening to give a higher degree of control in the morphing process. To apply shape hints you must select a frame that has shape tweening already set on it. If it doesn't have shape tweening attached, Flash won't allow you to add hints.

Usually when you shape tween, Flash will automatically take the easiest route to turn one shape into another, but this route won't always give the precise visual effect you're after. This is where shape hints come in: you can step in and override Flash's default 'as intelligent as it can get' tweening and finesse things to your taste. Shape hints can be a little complicated to implement in a complex movie, and they can give some spectacularly strange results when they go wrong, but with practice you can get a beautiful tween every time.

There's one other factor to note: shape hints demand a lot more processing power than straightforward tweening. If you can get away with not using them, it's best to avoid them rather than risk your movie slowing down when running on less powerful computers.

Shape hints work by highlighting particular points on a shape, and telling Flash explicitly where those points should move to on a subsequent frame after a motion tween. Suppose you created a movie that had a square in frame 1 and a triangle in the same location in frame 15, and you wanted to shape tween one into the other:

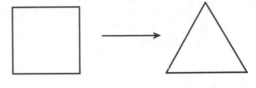

Frame 1   Frame 15

If you get Flash to make the tween, it'll do something slightly counter-intuitive: instead of pulling the top left and top right-hand corners of the square into the middle to form the point of the triangle, it'll twist the square through some weird contortions to perform the tween – as shown by the transformation lines in this ghosted tween:

Using shape hints, we can force Flash to pull the two top corners of the square into the center, giving us a slightly more intuitive tween:

You mark the specific points that you want to 'steer' in your *initial* shape, and you mark where you want them to end up in your *final* shape:

A different letter represents each hint so that you know which matches up with which. The only drawback to this is that you can only have a maximum of 26 shape hints, but this should be plenty. If you need any more, you should consider splitting your animation up onto different layers, as it is probably too complicated anyway. Let's see this in action.

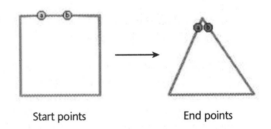

Start points   End points

Using shape hints to control your tween

1. Start a new movie, and draw a big yellow rectangle with a black outline on the stage. Use similar proportions to our rectangle here:

2. Use the Line tool to draw two lines forming a triangle on one side of the image, and fill it with the same yellow color:

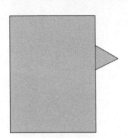

3. Now select the part of the line that acts as the base of the triangle where it meets the rectangle, and delete it, leaving a shape like this:

4. Now draw a small blue circle inside the rectangle on the right-hand side, just above the triangle:

    This is the eye of your (admittedly basic) face.

5. Now click in frame 30 and press F6 to insert a keyframe.

    We're going to make an animation of the face turning from 'looking to our right' to 'looking to our left', with the face looking straight at us in the middle of the tween. The first thing we need to do is make the image in the final frame look in the opposite direction.

6. In the new keyframe at frame 30, use the **Modify > Transform > Flip Horizontal** menu option to turn it around.

7. Next, insert a shape tween between the two keyframes. You're now ready to preview your movie in all its glory...

    ...but seeing as this exercise is about fixing tweens that go wrong, you probably guessed something like this was going to happen. So now we have to go about fixing the tween.

8. Click on the first keyframe, and use the **Modify > Shape > Add Shape Hint** menu option. A little red circle with an 'a' in it will appear like a beauty spot in the middle of the face:

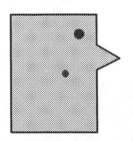

This is the first of your shape hints. Note that it's red at the moment.

Shape hints will appear by default in the center of the shape that you're tweening. Remember that the 'center' of the shape is defined by the invisible 'bounding box' around it, and isn't always where you might think it should be.

9.   It's easier to work with shape hints with snapping turned on, so make sure **Snap to Objects** is checked in the **View** menu.

10. Click on the shape hint and drag it onto the top left corner of the head:

It's still a red color.

Shape hints work best if you start with the top left-most point that you want to control, and then work counter-clockwise around the shape. They can produce some beautiful, but unexpected results if you get them in the wrong order.

11. Now click on the keyframe in frame 30, and you'll find a corresponding '**a**' shape hint (also red) there: we've added a shape hint to the start image, so Flash assumes we want one for the end image too. Attach the shape hint in frame 30 to the top right-hand corner of the face.

Notice that when you click away from the shape, the shape hint has turned green. This indicates that it's properly attached to the shape and that its corresponding shape hint in the first frame is also attached properly. If you click back on the first frame, you'll see that it's turned yellow. This green-yellow signal means that shape hint '**a**' is locked on and ready to fire.

12. If you preview your movie now, you'll find that it's still not looking entirely natural. A few more shape hints will sort this out, so go back to your first keyframe and add another **three** shape hints.

If you ever find that **Add Shape Hint** isn't available in the menu, go back to your keyframe and make sure everything on it is selected. Shape hints can only be added when the object that you're tweening is selected. If you ever lose sight of your shape hints, make sure that the **View > Show Shape Hints** menu option is checked.

When you add the three shape hints in succession, they'll all be added one on top of the other on the stage. This may seem a bit confusing at first, but you'll soon get used to it. The top-most hint will be '**d**' as that's the fourth one that you created.

13. Drag the three new shape hints out to the other three corners of the rectangle, working counter-clockwise from the first point:

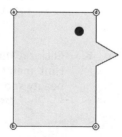

14. Now go to your end keyframe and drag the hints out from their little cluster in the center, but this time, reverse the relative left/right positions of the shape hints. The 'chin' shape hint in the first frame should still be on the 'chin' in the last frame, but it's on the other side of the stage because the face is turned around. Your finished shape should look like this in the last frame:

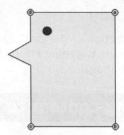

15. Preview your movie now, and the face should look as if it is turning from right to left. It's still not quite right though, as the eye seems to float through an out of body experience before returning to normality in the last frame. Ick. Guess what? Time for some more shape hints.

16. Go back to the first frame and add another couple of shape hints. Place the hints on either side of the eye:

17. Now go to the last frame and place the hints in the same relative (but horizontally flipped) positions on the final face:

18. If everything has worked correctly, your face should turn when you preview your movie. If you'd prefer the eye to blink as the tween flows, just add another couple of hints to the eye, one at the top and one at the bottom, the same in both keyframes. The face should now flip perfectly and wink at you cheekily.

    To remove shape hints you only need to grab and drag them off the stage, just as you would do to get rid of a guide. Dragging the hint off the stage in any frame will affect *both* frames that the hints are in. The alternative method to dragging is to delete all the hints at once, and start again: this can be achieved via the **Modify > Shape > Remove All Hints** menu option.

Shape hints can be kind of confusing at first, but it's important to be aware of what they are, what they can do, and how you can use them to add more control to a shape tween if you need to. If you're dealing with a complex shape tween, and no amount of shape hints seems to help, you may want to try adding a 'staging post' frame for your animation half way through, with a keyframe containing the desired 'half-way through' image showing what the animation should look like at this point. You can then add two tweens, one on either side, to link the three keyframes. This makes it a little easier for Flash to follow and should give better results. This is more time consuming, but it may wind up easier than letting Flash decide how the tween will work, as well as saving you the hassle of adding and positioning multiple shape hints.

Case study

In this section of the case study we'll build the content for the skills area of our web site. We'll be adding some shape tweening effects to make it a bit more interesting. Open your case study movie and let's start work on it again.

Adding content to the skills area

This page is where we're going to list our computing skills, so let's make a suitable background that relates to the content area. We've used a digital photo of a mouse and named the file `trackball.jpg`. We're going to import the picture and make it fade into the background, slowly changing color as it does so.

You can take a picture of something you'd find interesting for this section or find a photo on the Internet you can use (royalty-free, of course). Otherwise, feel free to use `trackball.jpg` (included in the download files for this case study).

1. Once you've decided which image to use, double-click on the **content** movie clip on the main stage to go into Edit Symbols mode.

2. Your movie clip should only have content on frame 1. On the **interface** and **scroll buttons** layers, select frame 10 and insert blank frames using F5:

3. Create a new layer folder called `work history`, and drag the **web site thumbnails** and **web site info boxes** layers into this new layer folder:

    Eventually we'll have layer folders for all the different areas of the web site that our buttons will take us to. This will help us to stay organized and give us more room to work on our timeline.

4. Create a new layer folder called `skills` and place it underneath the **work history** layer folder.

5. Create two new normal layers called `text` and `trackball` and drag these into the **skills** layer folder:

We've made a layer called **trackball** because we're going to place the trackball image on its own layer and then apply some shape tweening to it. You may want to name your own layer a different name depending on the image you are using.

6. Select frame 10 of the **trackball** layer and insert a keyframe (F6). Then go to **File > Import** and import trackball.jpg (or the image you have chosen):

7. Let's keep our Library organized now we're adding more and more content – drag the imported trackball image into the **skills** folder.

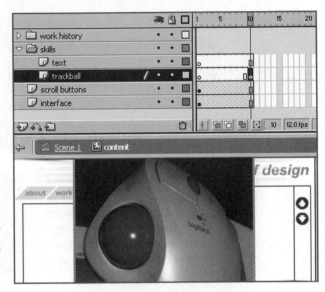

We now need to delete all the background from our image so that only the mouse itself remains. You looked at how to do this in Chapter 5, but here's a quick refresher just in case...

8. Select the trackball image and choose the **Modify > Break Apart** menu option.

9. Using a combination of the Lasso tool and the Magic Wand with the Eraser tool, trace the edge of the mouse out and delete the background. All you should be left with is the actual mouse shape.

10. Once you've done this, scale the mouse down (using the Free Transform tool or by entering values in the Property inspector) and position it in the right-hand corner of the interface:

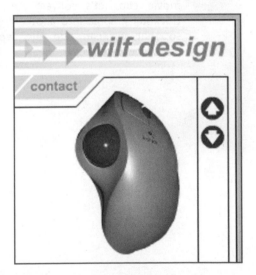

Before we move forward we need to think about how we want our trackball animation to work. We want its color to constantly transform – this means it's going to have to be in its own movie clip. We also want the mouse to be slightly transparent, which means the mouse will also have to be a graphic symbol too.

So here's our structure:

- trackball movie clip (for constant color transformation)

and within this movie clip:

- a layer for our color rotation shape tween.

- a layer for changing the alpha of the trackball graphic symbol (for transparency).

This trackball movie clip will loop over and over again producing the effect we want.

Color shape tweening the trackball

1. Open up your Library. Select the trackball image on the stage and drag it into the **skills** folder of the Library to convert it to a symbol. Give it a central registration point, set its behavior as a movie clip, and call it trackball mc:

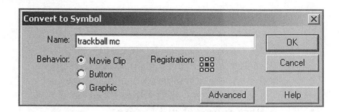

2. Double-click the trackball again on the stage, taking you into Edit Symbols mode.

Now that we are inside our trackball movie clip, let's convert the actual trackball graphic into another symbol so that we can add the separate transparency effect to it:

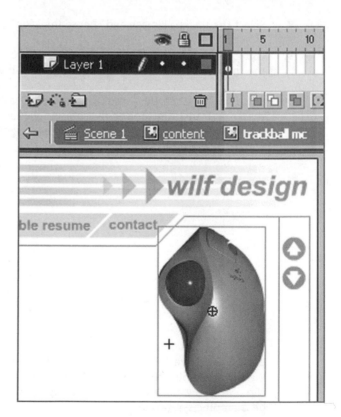

3. Select the trackball again and drag it into the **skills** folder of the Library. Make it a graphic symbol and call it `trackball graphic`:

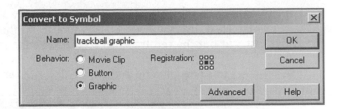

4. Make sure you're working in the **trackball mc** movie clip. Your **trackball graphic** symbol should be on **Layer 1** of the **trackball mc** movie clip. Rename this layer `trackball graphic`:

5. With the trackball graphic selected on the stage, go to the Property inspector and change its Alpha value to 50%:

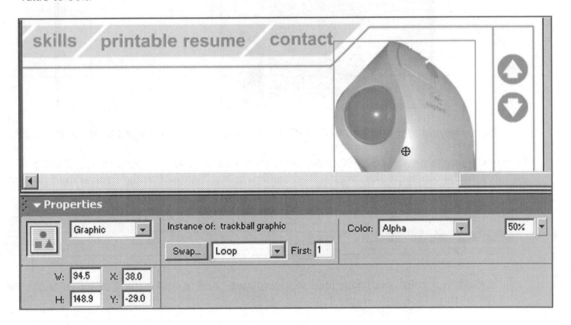

6. Insert a new layer called `color fades` above your **trackball graphic** layer. Select your trackball graphic and copy it.

7. Click on frame 1 of the **color fades** layer and use **Edit > Paste in Place** to paste the copy of the image. Hide the **trackball graphic** layer, so that only the trackball image on the **color fades** layer is visible:

8. Working on the **color fades** layer use **Modify > Break Apart** to break your trackball graphic into a fill. Next, use the Paint Bucket tool to fill the trackball shape with a slate blue color. (You can also cut out the red trackball so that only the mouse area itself will change color).

9. Select this new blue fill and, in the Color Mixer panel, set the Alpha value to 30%:

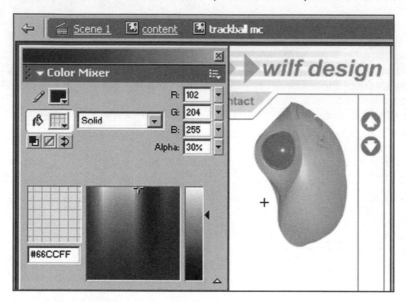

10. Insert a keyframe (F6) at frame 50 of the **color fades** layer and change the fill color to a green shade.

11. Add a keyframe at frame 100 and change the fill color to red. Be sure to set all these fill colors to 30% Alpha otherwise the original trackball image won't show through. You should now have three keyframes in the timeline where the fill color changes:

To make our color animation loop seamlessly we need to make the end fill color the same slate blue it started life as in frame 1.

12. Copy frame 1 (**Edit > Copy Frames**), then go to frame 150 and use the **Edit > Paste Frames** menu option.

13. Now to complete building the color fade animation – select all the frames in the **color fades** layer, from frame 1 through to frame 149, and insert a shape tween using the Property inspector:

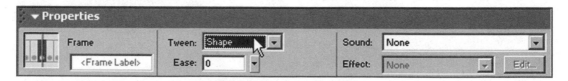

14. On the **trackball** layer select frame 150 (where the animation will end) and add a blank frame (**Insert > Frame**). This will allow your trackball graphic to shine through the color shape tween throughout the animation.

OK, that's the color shape tween animation finished for now. The last thing to do in this section, of course, is to actually add your skills to the page!

15. Go back into your **content** movie clip. On frame 10 of the **text** layer (within the **skills** layer folder), insert a keyframe (F6). Draw several static text fields on the stage, and enter any relevant information about your computing skills you wish:

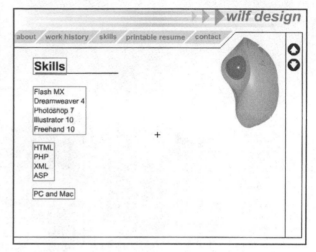

16. Save your case study movie and close it.

That's all for the case study in this chapter.

Summary

In this chapter, we took a gentle canter around the world of shape tweening, adding another tool to our increasingly powerful armory.

We saw that:

- **Shape tweening** complements motion tweening. It enables us to morph shapes into other shapes, shapes into text, and more.

- Shape tweens operate on **lines and fills** rather than the grouped shapes and symbols that motion tweens act upon.

- We can combine shape tweening with color changes and movement.

- **Shape hints** give us a fine degree of control over the way that a shape tween will work.

In the next chapter, we're going to look at a technique that can add really engaging visual effects to your Flash movies, especially when used in conjunction with shape and motion tweens – **masking**.

8

Masks and Masking

What we'll cover in this chapter:

- ***Masks*** *are a powerful feature in Flash that allow you to selectively show and hide content. You can create a mask and apply it to a layer so that only content 'underneath' the mask shows through. We'll explore their basic principles and see a range of different examples and applications.*

This chapter introduces the use of **masks** in Flash. Masks act as a way of selectively showing and hiding content in a Flash movie, based on the position of the mask, which lives on a separate layer from the content that it's masking. Using masks, you can create great effects in your movies: illusions of depth, movement, illumination and more – as you'll see in this chapter.

Masks are strange creatures, but we think you'll find them indispensable once you grasp the techniques for using them. Some Flash designers don't seem to embrace the usefulness of masks, possibly because the effects you can create with them are more at home in animation than standard web site design. But, once you've seen the results that masks help you achieve, we think you may well be a convert.

What is a mask?

Very early in this book, we discussed layers, and saw you how they can be used to simulate depth. If you're animating a character – let's call her Jane Doe – walking across the stage and behind a house, you'd put the house on a layer at the front of the movie, and Jane on a layer behind the house:

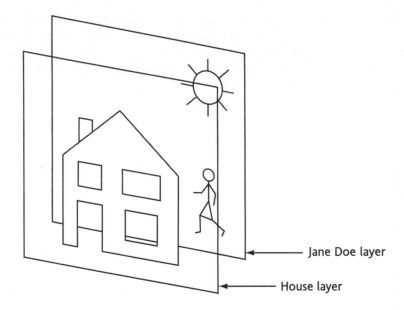

Jane Doe layer

House layer

As Jane walks across the area occupied by the house symbol, Flash knows that we wanted the house to stay in front because of the layer order that we've assigned. In effect, this will give the appearance that Jane has walked behind the house, and would create a sense of *depth* in the animation.

This effect can be achieved without masking, but suppose we wanted to show Jane walking around *inside* the house? That's more difficult, isn't it? You'd want Jane to be *visible* when she was behind a transparent part of the house front – the windows – and *invisible* when she was behind an opaque object such as a solid wall:

The requirement here is to make part of the front layer opaque, and part of it transparent. To do this in Flash, you need a mask.

When we create a mask, it's as if we lay a piece of card over our animation and block it all out. We then cut a window in the card and reveal a section of what's underneath. In Jane's case, we'd need to create a piece of card shaped like a solid-fronted house, and then cut holes in the card where the windows and door should be:

Once we've cut out the holes, we can hold the card in front of the background animation of Jane walking across the stage. We can then either move the card – our 'mask' – around so that different sections of our animation are revealed, or make the objects in the animation pass across the holes, appearing and disappearing as they do.

That's the basic principle of masking in Flash – we just use electronic layers to create our masks, rather than card and scissors.

When else would you need to use a mask in Flash? Here are a few examples:

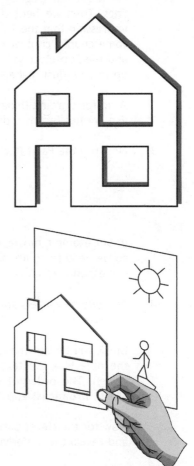

- When you need to show text scrolling from left to right across a TV screen. We'd only want the text to be visible when it was behind the area corresponding to the *screen*.

- When you want to zoom into an area on a picture and keep the viewable area inside a constant-sized window. As the picture is magnified and gets bigger, we only want to show the zoomed area of the picture, and hide all other areas.

- You want to simulate text being typed on the screen, making it appear, letter by letter, from left to right.

None of these effects can be created using layers alone. In each case, we want to hide *part* of our object, and that's exactly what a mask will do.

To illustrate the use of masking, let's create an animation based on the first example listed above: text scrolling across a TV screen.

Putting on your mask

First, we need our TV set.

1. In a new movie, rename the default layer as TV.

2. In the default keyframe at frame 1, create your TV by drawing a shape that looks something like the image on the right:

    Create the TV any way you like.

    We made our (slightly retro) TV by drawing the basic shape with straight lines. Then we bent the straight lines using the Arrow tool to give the impression that the TV is a freehand drawing, and added the antenna and some chunky control knobs. If you wanted to, you could use the Pen tool and the Subselect tool to create a Bezier-finessed masterpiece – it's really up to you. (Just make sure you end up with a TV that has a screen!)

    A tip for drawing things in the cartoon style we've used here is to draw with thick black outlines, like Warner Brothers did in the psychedelic 60s.

3. Now use the Paint Bucket tool to fill your drawing with color:

    In our example movie, we want our text to appear only on the TV's *screen*, so we need to create a mask that will only show the text when its position corresponds to an area inside the boundaries of the screen.

4. Add two new layers above the existing TV layer – Broadcast and Mask:

    Mask will be our mask layer, and **Broadcast** will contain all the objects – the text – that we wish to show on the TV screen. The order of the layers is crucial, and must read **Mask, Broadcast** and **TV** from top to bottom.

    Now for the clever part. Remember that the **Mask** layer is the piece of card that we'll use to hide and reveal the underlying **Broadcast** layer. We're going to cut a hole in our card that's the same shape as the screen of our TV, so that whatever we put on the **Broadcast** layer will only be visible when it is inside the TV screen.

5. Select the filled screen area of the TV – not the stroke. (You'll notice we've not made the TV into a symbol yet; this is so we can select the screen on its own):

6. Now copy the screen part into the clipboard with **Edit > Copy**.

    The next thing to do is use this screen shape to create the masked area on the **Mask** layer.

7. Select the **Mask** layer and paste the screen in place with **Edit > Paste in Place**.

8. Hide all the layers except for the **Mask** layer, and you should just see the pasted screen as shown here:

    It's a good idea to make your mask areas a striking color so that you can easily differentiate them from other movie content. Using a color that you'd rarely use in your movie designs is a good way to help you make that differentiation. Let's choose a bright pink.

9. Select the Paint Bucket tool and fill the screen shape on the **Mask** layer with a bright pink:

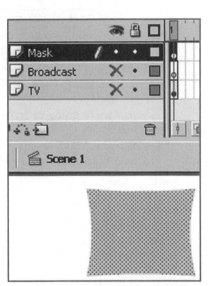

Although it might seem counter-intuitive for a mask to be a solid filled color, trust us. Flash isn't constrained by the same laws of physics that stop light passing freely through a piece of card. As long as Flash knows the *shape* of the mask, we can make it any color we like – Flash just ignores the color and sees only the shape.

When this TV screen-shaped mask is being used, you'll be able to see anything on the underlying layer that falls *behind* the pink area, and nothing that's in the areas outside the mask.

10. Lock the **Mask** layer so that you don't select anything on it by accident, and unhide the **TV** and **Broadcast** layers.

11. On the **TV** layer, select the whole of the TV and convert it into a new graphic symbol called TV Symbol.

> *Converting the TV set to a symbol is absolutely essential. Flash masks won't work unless your fills and lines have been converted to a symbol.*

12. Now lock the **TV** layer and unlock the **Mask** layer:

13. Select the screen-shaped mask on the **Mask** layer and convert it into a graphic symbol. Name it Screen Mask.

> *When you're working with masks on one layer, it's always a good idea to lock the layer containing the masked objects so that you can't inadvertently select both objects at once.*

Now we're going to tell Flash that we want our floating TV screen shape to act as a mask.

14. With the **Mask** layer selected, choose the **Modify > Layer** menu option and click on the **Mask** radio button in the **Layer Properties** window:

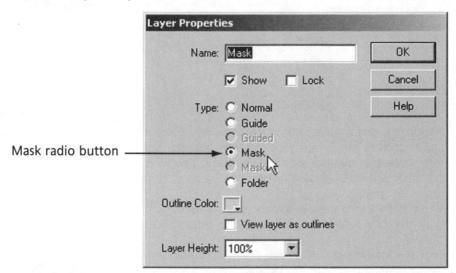

Mask radio button

15. Leave all of the other values as the defaults, and click **OK**.

We've now converted the **Mask** layer so that it will act as a mask. All that Flash sees on this layer now is the screen shape that we want to use as the mask.

Notice that the **Mask** layer's appearance has changed in the timeline:

The little checkered oval at the left identifies this layer as a 'mask' layer.

Now we have to tell Flash which layer we want the mask to be *applied to*.

16. Select the **Broadcast** layer and choose the **Modify > Layer** menu option. This time, select the **Masked** radio button to designate the **Broadcast** layer as the one that we want the TV screen shape to mask:

Masked radio button —————→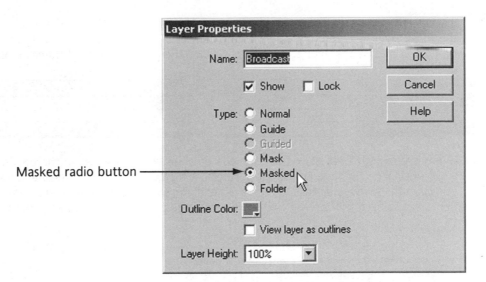

17. Click on **OK**.

Again, there's been a change with our layers in the timeline:

Note that the **Broadcast** layer now has an indented icon that looks like a folded sheet of paper, indicating that this layer has a mask applied to it.

Unlock the **TV** layer and your layers should now look like this:

The checkered oval icon on the **Mask** layer tells us we have created a mask, and the indented checkered icon in the **Broadcast** layer tells us that *this* is the layer we've placed our mask over the top of. The **Broadcast** layer is the one that the screen shape on the **Mask** layer will apply to – hiding part of it from view.

It's vital to note that the layer, or layers, that you want to be partially hidden must be placed below the mask you've created.

We won't see the effects of the **Mask** layer yet because the **Broadcast** layer currently has nothing in it. Let's put a message on the TV.

The first thing we need to do is increase the length of our movie to give us enough time to read the text that will shimmy across the TV screen.

18. Increase the movie length so that it lasts for a hundred frames. To do this, click on frame 100 in the **Mask** layer and, before you release the mouse, drag the cursor *down* to select all three layers. When you release the mouse, press F5 and you'll then have a hundred frames in each layer:

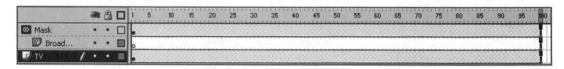

If you ever want to see more frames in the timeline (as you can see in the previous screenshot), you can click on the little **Frame View** button at the top right of the timeline. Clicking the button brings up the menu you see in the screenshot. If you click on **Small**, Flash will compress the frames that are displayed horizontally, and you'll see a greater number of frames in the timeline.

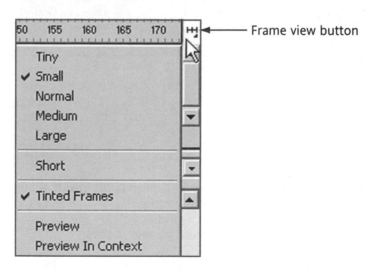

Frame view button

19. Now for the content. In frame 1 of the **Broadcast** layer, use the Text tool to add the text 'Stay tuned to this channel…' to the right of the TV, and level with the center of the TV screen. We've used a black, 26 point Comic Sans font:

20. Convert the text into a graphic symbol called Text.

    Now we'll make the text move across the screen.

21. In the **Broadcast** layer add a keyframe in frame 100. With the new keyframe selected, move the text to the *left* of the TV to establish its end position after it has scrolled across the screen:

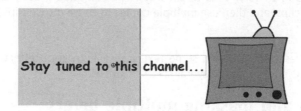

22. Click on any frame in the middle of your timeline. Now use the Property inspector to add a motion tween between frames 1 and 100 of the **Broadcast** layer:

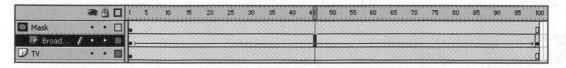

23. The last thing to do to make our mask work is to **lock** both the **Mask** layer *and* the **Broadcast** layer:

> *Flash will only show the effects of a mask when all the affected layers are locked. If you want your masks to work, always lock all affected layers.*

24. Press CTRL+F12 to preview your movie in a browser.

This is what you'll see when you test your movie: the TV with the scrolling text appearing only on the screen where the mask is. With a little extra work, this would make a good loading page for someone's web site...

You're now seeing how this can be a very powerful technique. The TV screen is a totally non-uniform shape, as is the rest of the TV. Simply by defining the area we wanted to display using a mask, we're able to achieve the complex effect we wanted with very little effort. The sequence of steps needs to be maintained, but after a little more practice and experimentation, you'll be turning out masked movies of your own.

Remember that when you create a mask, you have to specify the layer or layers that you want it to act upon. Only the sections of these layers that lie under the 'cut-out' shape(s) you draw on the mask layer will be visible in the finished movie.

Another thing to be aware of is that all the mask effects that we're creating here can be embedded inside movie clips and reused in all sorts of different ways. You can build great little animated masking effects, embed them in movie clips, and then use multiple copies of those movie clips to get all sorts of impressive action on the stage.

OK, we've created a mask and tweened some text across it, to good effect. How about we see how to animate the *mask*? And how to mask several layers at once?

Animated masks and masking multiple layers

In contrast to the example we've just seen, you can also use masks and keep the background stationary while the mask itself is animated, selectively hiding and revealing different parts of your animation. We're going to learn how to do this now. We'll also see how one mask can be used to cover and reveal several layers at once, by creating a spotlight effect on some text.

Moving the mask

1. Create a new movie.

2. Change the movie's background color to black using the Property inspector.

3. Using the Text tool, add some large bold white text in the center of the stage as shown here and rename the layer Text:

4. Add a new layer, and name it Spotlight. In this layer, draw a filled white circle that's a little bigger than the height of the text.

5. Convert the circle into a graphic symbol and name it Spot:

6. Make your animation 50 frames long in both layers by clicking, dragging, and pressing F5 in the same way that you did in the last exercise.

7. Add a keyframe in frame 50 of the **Spotlight** layer. Your timeline should now look like this:

8. With the new keyframe selected, move your **Spot** symbol to the far end of the text, after the '**u**', and create a motion tween between the two keyframes.

The circle will now move over the text when you play your movie. Here's a preview of its motion with **Onion Skin Outlines** turned on:

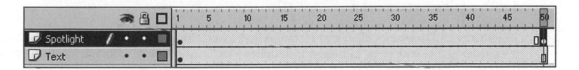

9. Finally, turn the **Spotlight** layer into a mask layer as you did earlier via the **Modify > Layer** menu option. Select the **Mask** radio button from the Layer Properties window for the **Spotlight** layer, and select the **Masked** radio button when you repeat the process for the **Text** layer.

10. Now lock both the layers and test the movie – the layers in your timeline should now look like this:

There's a problem with the movie at the moment: we see the text revealed by the round shape of the spotlight as it travels along, but the circular shape of the spotlight doesn't really come across fully. That's because the background is totally black – a real spotlight would illuminate the background as well as the text. Let's remedy that.

What we need to do is make the spotlight illuminate the background slightly. To do this, we'll draw a gray area behind the text on a new layer. This will be lit up in contrast to the text as the spot passes across it.

You must do this exactly as shown; otherwise the **Spotlight** layer won't act as a mask to the new layer.

11. Select the **Text** layer and add a new layer. Name your new layer Gray:

    We want our **Gray** layer to be *behind* the text, so we must move it to the bottom of the stack of layers.

12. With **Gray** still selected, drag the layer to the bottom, under **Text**. Your timeline should now look like this:

    Notice that both the layers **Gray** and **Text** have the indented icons next to them, signifying that *both* will be masked by **Spotlight**. Flash has automatically made our **Gray** layer a masked layer because of its adjacency to the mask layer when we created it.

13. Select **Gray** and draw a medium gray rectangle that covers the whole area that the circle will travel over. Unlock the **Text** layer to help you decipher exactly where your rectangle needs to go and how big it should be:

14. Lock all the layers again and test the movie.

    You'll now see what looks like an illuminated spotlight move from left to right, lighting up the darkness to reveal your text. This screenshot shows a graduated interpretation of the spotlight moving across the text in the movie we just created:

    What's actually happening is that our circular 'window' is moving across white text on a gray background – but the effect is quite striking. How about adding more keyframes to the mask layer and more motion tweens, creating a sweeping searchlight effect that moves up and down as well as from side to side. Or maybe a motion path that sweeps out in a spiral? Or a spotlight that starts small and grows bigger as the animation continues? Or...

We've only touched on the power of animated masks here. The number of effects that you can create with these features in Flash is limited only by your imagination. So practice, practice, practice....

Now let's look at some more text/mask combinations.

Using masks with text

Masks can be used particularly well with text. Text can act as the mask itself, as we'll see later, and an effect that can be easily simulated with masks is making words appear on the screen as if they were being typed. This is achieved by another method of animating the mask: instead of moving the mask around the stage, we *scale* it to make it grow – revealing more of the layer beneath it as it does so. Let's see how...

Simulating typed text

1. In a new movie, rename the default layer to Text, and add a new layer above it called Mask. We now need to turn our layers into mask and masked layers, and we're going to show you a quick alternative to the **Modify > Layer** menu option approach that we've used in our last two exercises

2. With the **Mask** layer selected, right-click on that layer and select **Mask** from the context-sensitive menu that pops up. **Mask** becomes a *mask* layer, and **Text** automatically becomes a *masked* layer. Note that both layers are locked:

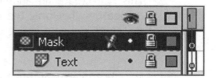

3. Unlock both layers by clicking on the topmost lock icon, so that we can add some content to them.

4. Change the movie's background color to a hue of your choice, and then add some text in the **Text** layer:

We've used a pale green on a dark green background – just in case there are any of you out there who are nostalgic for the days of corporate dumb terminals...

5. Now we want to make the text look as if it's being typed in letter by letter. In the **Mask** layer, create a long white rectangle that completely covers the text, and then convert it into a graphic symbol with a center left registration point. Call the new symbol Mask:

We've given this shape a left hand registration point as we're going to make the text gradually appear by scaling the white rectangle – a little like a preloader bar. If we scale the rectangle with the registration point in the center, then both ends are going to get shorter or longer, because scaling is done relative to the registration point.

At this point, ensure the rectangle is positioned correctly, covering our text. Make any adjustments to its position until you're happy that the text is fully obscured by it.

6.   Make the movie 50 frames long in both layers and then add a keyframe to the **Mask** layer at frame 50:

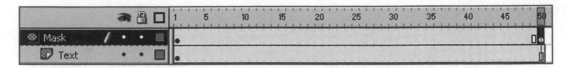

7.   In frame 1 of the **Mask** layer, shorten the mask using the Free Transform tool and dragging the right side of the rectangle to the left so that it's too short to cover any of the text:

8.   Click on any of the frames between 1 and 50 and add a motion tween with the Property inspector. This will create an animated mask that slowly reveals more and more text as it gets bigger. Remember that only the text that's *covered* by the mask will show up in the final movie – the rectangle growing is like a cut-out window on card gradually being torn open to reveal what's underneath.

9.   Lock both layers and test your movie. Your text will gradually appear as the mask rectangle scales up out to the right.

Don't worry that the mask will show *parts* of letters: the transition is usually too fast for the viewer to see that it isn't actually typing a word at a time, but revealing the words bit by bit. If it starts to look too obvious when you come to test the movie, simply shorten the motion tween by ten or so frames by choosing the **Insert > Remove Frames** menu option – making sure that the playhead is not on a keyframe. Alternatively, if you really want to emphasize words as they're created, rather than a constant wipe, add some extra keyframes along your timeline, stop the motion tween for the desired time and then pick up the tween again.

Now for another mean text-related masking technique.

A text shaped mask

One of the easiest ways to create instant masks is to use *text* as the mask. When using text in this way, it's a good idea to use a simple, heavy, bold and closely spaced font: using this kind of font will mean that a larger proportion of the image behind your mask is shown. For this reason, Impact is a good choice, as is the Haettenschweiler font shown here:

Haettenschweiler

Let's use this meaty-looking font as a mask in a practical example.

Masking with text

In this effect, we'll create a color gradient and mask it using a piece of text.

1. Open a new movie and rename the default layer to Text.

2. Now create a text field in the center of the stage using a bold thick font, similar in length to this:

    We've used a black 65 point Haettenschweiler.

3. Create a new layer below **Text** and call it Gradient. In this layer, create a filled gradient that's taller and considerably wider than the text like this:

We've used a blue and gold color spectrum gradient, selected from the bottom of the color palette for the **Fill color** box in the Property inspector.

4. Make sure that the **Gradient** layer is underneath the **Text** layer by dragging it in the timeline:

5. We want to motion tween the rectangle, so convert it into a graphic symbol with a central registration point and name it Rectangle.

6. Now make **Text** into a mask layer and **Gradient** into the layer that's being masked. Remember, the quick way to do this is by right-clicking on the mask layer and selecting **Mask** from the context-sensitive menu.

7. Make your animation 50 frames long by clicking, dragging, and pressing F5 in the now familiar way.

8. At frame 50 in the **Gradient** layer, add a keyframe. Move the **Rectangle** graphic symbol in this frame to the left:

9. Select any frame between 1 and 50 on the **Gradient** layer and add a motion tween from the Property inspector. Your timeline should now look like this:

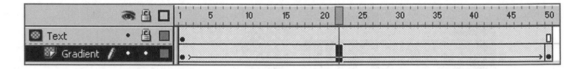

10. Lock both layers and test your movie. You'll see the text cycle through several colors as the gradient moves past it:

There's an additional cool modification you can make to this effect, and that's to add a *border* to the text. This will improve the effect because, as it stands, the lighter colors in the spectrum can make the outline of the text difficult to see on some screens.

11. Select the **Text** layer and create a new layer above it. Call the new layer Text Outline.

12. Unlock the **Text** layer and then copy the text to the **Text Outline** layer using the **Edit > Copy** and **Edit > Paste in Place** menu options.

13. With the text field on the **Text Outline** layer still selected, break the text apart **twice** with the **Modify > Break Apart** menu option. Hide the other layers.

14. Then, select the Ink Bottle tool and change the **Stroke Color** to black in the Tools panel.

15. Click on all the outlines in the text. To do this for the word '**spectrum**', you'll have to click on the *interior* outlines inside the '**p**' and the '**e**'. You might want to zoom in to get a better view while you're using the Ink Bottle tool.

16. Finally (with the inner text still selected), press your DELETE key or go to **Edit > Clear** to delete filled areas of each letter so you only leave the outline:

17. Test your movie. You'll see the color of your text change again, but this time with a more clearly defined outline:

Notice that the **Text Outline** layer doesn't need to be locked for the mask effect to be seen, as it's not masking anything or being masked.

A really cool variant of this is to use a bitmap instead of a gradient. In a similar way to the computer 'typing' we simulated earlier, you can even use a bitmap to gradually fill your mask and reveal your text. Here's how...

Filling your text with an image

We're now going to use a bitmap image called `skyline.bmp` to slowly fill a text mask. This image is included in the downloadable files from our web site – or you can use any image of your own choice, of course.

1. Set up a new movie. Rename the default layer to `Image` and add a second layer called `Text` just above it.

2. Make **Text** into the mask layer and **Image** into the masked layer:

3. Unlock the layers by clicking the topmost lock icon and in the **Text** layer, create a text field containing the word or words that you want to make appear, in the center of the stage:

4. Bring `skyline.bmp` (or your own image) onto the **Image** layer by selecting the layer and then using the **File > Import** menu option to navigate to the image in the dialog box:

5. Convert the imported image to a graphic symbol called `Skyline Object` and give it a center registration point.

6. Scale **Skyline Object** so that it's about the same height as your text, and place it on the stage so that its *right* edge is nearly at the *left* edge of your text:

7. Make your animation 50 frames long and insert a keyframe at frame 50 on the **Image** layer:

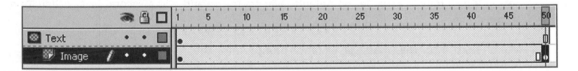

8. With the new keyframe still selected, move **Skyline Object** so that it's behind the text. Next, click anywhere on the **Image** layer between frames 1 and 50 and then assign a motion tween from the Property inspector.

9. Lock both layers and test your movie. Here's an interpretation of the effect you'll see:

Because your bitmap is moving, you can get away with quite a low resolution quality, so the download time can actually be surprisingly quick. Be aware that an effect like this, combined with a large bitmap, can become quite slow on older computers if your text fills the full screen. Try applying text outlines to this example like we did in the previous one.

You can now create a layer that's a mask, and apply this mask to a layer, or layers, that are labelled as 'masked'. This is yet another powerful feature that you and your imagination can implement in conjunction with other techniques such as tweening, animated fades and so on.

OK, that's it for the basic masking techniques. We think you'll agree that you can create some scintillating effects with them. The best way to learn more from here is to experiment and let your imagination run riot.

Later in the book we'll look at how to use movie clips as masks, using a little bit of ActionScript to create some interaction with them.

Case study

In this section of the case study, we're going to use our new masking skills to create a smooth rotation effect over some text. The text will form the content for the 'about' page of our portfolio, where we'd typically tell prospective employers all those impressive, interesting and endearing things about ourselves. Let's get to work.

1. Double-click on the **content** movie clip icon in your Library to go into Edit Symbols mode. In the movie clip timeline, insert a new layer folder called about.

The 'skills' section we were working on in the last chapter ends at frame 10, so we'll start the 'about' section at frame 20.

2. Create a new layer in your **about** folder and call it `text`. Next, select frame 20 and insert a keyframe (F6):

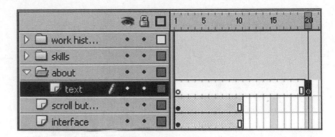

3. Insert frames (using F5) at frame 20 on both the **scroll buttons** and **interface** layers so that they're visible on the stage throughout the whole of the timeline:

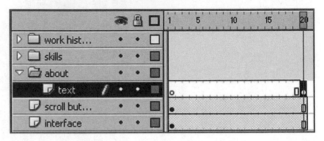

4. At frame 20 on the **text** layer, use the Text tool to place two static text fields in the content interface. In the first field type a suitable heading for your 'about' page and in the second text field, type in some details about yourself – we've used 20 pt Arial bold for the heading and 12 pt Arial for the main text. Make the main text a light gray color (but still readable):

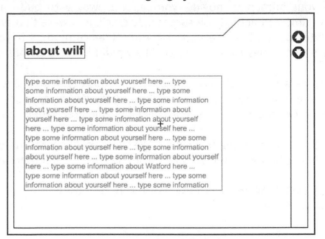

5. Insert a new layer in the **about** folder, directly above the **text** layer. Call it `masked star` and insert a keyframe at frame 20:

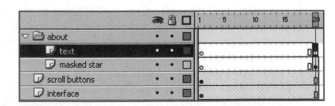

We're using a star-shaped graphic created in Adobe Illustrator that we've imported into our case study Library. We've converted it into a graphic symbol called `star shape`. You can substitute any shape you like for this mask, or use the star shape here as an example. If you want to use the star shape, download a copy from our web site and drag a copy into your Library.

6. In frame 20 of the **masked star** layer, drag an instance of the **star shape** graphic directly on top of your text on the stage (if it's too big, scale it with the Free Transform tool):

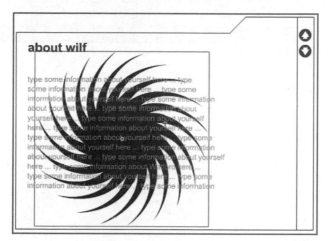

7. Double-click on the **text** layer icon to bring up the **Layer Properties** dialog box – check the **Mask** radio button:

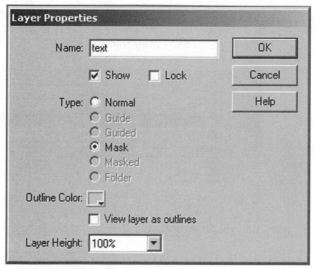

8. Repeat this step for the **masked star** layer, this time checking the **Masked** radio button.

9. To see the effect of the mask, make sure you lock both the **text** and **masked star** layers. Your text should now have a black area where the star is located:

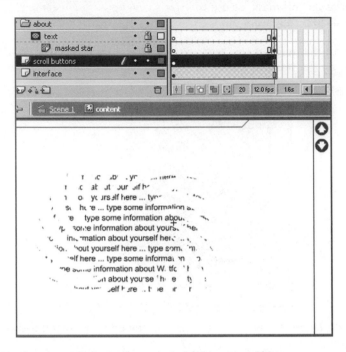

10. Insert a new layer and rename it text stay – drag it into the **about** layer folder underneath the **masked star** layer (remember that when you drag it, the folder icon will be highlighted brown to show that your selected layer is within the folder):

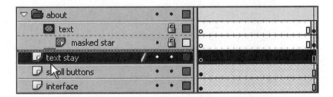

11. Remove any additional frames from the **text stay** layer so that you have just 20 frames. Select frame 20 of the **text** layer, and choose the **Edit > Copy Frames** menu option.

12. Next, select frame 20 of your new **text stay** layer and choose the **Edit > Paste Frames** menu option.

13. You'll notice that the **text stay** layer now has a mask layer icon:

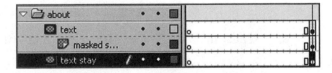

We want this layer to be normal, so double-click on the layer icon and select the **Normal** radio button in the **Layer Properties** dialog window and click **OK**.

14. Lock the **text stay** layer. Your timeline should now look like this:

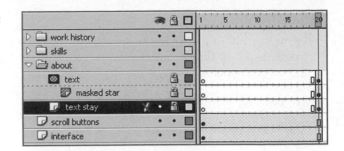

We're now going to animate the star shape to achieve a smooth rotating effect in our text.

15. Unlock the **masked star** layer and select the star shape on frame 20. Convert it to a movie clip symbol with a central registration point, and call it `star shape mc`:

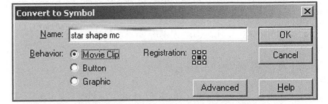

16. Now we can tween our star to make it slowly rotate. Double-click on the movie clip you just created and insert a keyframe (F6) at frame 100 (the only layer is the default **Layer 1**).

17. Click anywhere on **Layer 1** and use the Property inspector to add a motion tween. Set it to rotate clockwise (**CW**) just once:

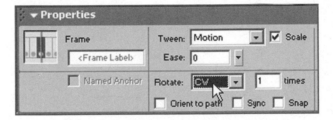

Although testing your movie at this point will cause it to loop too quickly to see our text masking effect, you can check the motion tween works via the Library preview pane (select your **star shape mc** in the Library and click on the play button icon in the top left of the preview pane).

18. Let's keep our Library tidy and move the **star shape** graphic symbol and **star shape mc** movie clip into the **about** folder.

19. Finally, save your case study movie and close it.

That's everything for now. In the next chapter's case study we're going to make our movie come alive with some ActionScript.

Summary

We've seen here that masks in Flash can help achieve a range of pretty darned snazzy effects. You can make masks as simple or complex as you wish, and you can encapsulate masking functionality inside movie clip symbols.

We saw that:

- **Masks** are created on a special mask layer.

- The **mask layer** is applied to a **masked layer** (or layers).

- The mask layer and all the layers it's being applied to must be locked for the mask effect to be seen.

- Masks can be static or animated.

- Masks are useful for:

  - Hiding and revealing selected parts of an animation.

  - Achieving a sense of depth.

  - Animating bitmap images as if they're vectors.

In the next chapter, we're going to start on the next very exciting leg of our journey: delving into the world of **ActionScript**.

Actions and Interactions

What we'll cover in this chapter:

- Introduction to **interactivity** – the fundamentals of **interaction**, **events** and **event handlers** in Flash.

- Introducing **ActionScript** – the programming language that makes Macromedia Flash so powerful.

- Creating interactive Flash sites with buttons and basic ActionScript:

  - **Animating** buttons

  - Adding **sound** to buttons

  - Invisible buttons

  - Attaching ActionScript to buttons and frames in the timeline to control the way the movie plays back, and to provide navigation features.

This chapter moves us a significant way along in our Flash journey. We're coming to the brow of a hill, and a whole new vista of Flash possibilities is going to open up before us, and there, bathed in sunlight, is the land of **ActionScript.**

ActionScript is what makes Macromedia Flash a living, breathing, responsive program rather than just a brilliant linear animation tool. ActionScript is what enables Flash to be **interactive.**

Interactivity

Interactivity, in this context, means that your Flash movie, when it's running in the user's browser, *responds* to something that the user does, or *reacts* to a pre-defined set of conditions. For example:

- Branching out of the movie's linear playback and playing a different movie clip when the user presses a button, or when the playhead hits a particular frame.

- Saving the user's name and e-mail address, which they've typed into a couple of text boxes.

- Confirming the user's order when they've added items to their shopping cart in a Flash e-commerce site.

- Playing different songs on a Flash jukebox.

- Dragging around pieces of a puzzle in a Flash jigsaw.

All of these examples rely on Flash's ability to respond to **events**. An *event* is simply something that *happens*. When you create an interactive movie, you plan the things that can happen, build an interface (buttons, text-entry boxes, etc.) that will allow the user to *make* those things – events – happen, and you create the ActionScript that will *handle* those events.

Events and event handlers

In order for interaction to take place you need to have an **event** and an **event handler**. When you call on a friend, you walk along the street until you reach their building. When this 'reaching their building' event takes place, the 'I've reached their building' event *handler* in your brain responds by turning your steps towards their door. Something of significance – an event – has occurred, and a piece of processing has been carried out to handle it.

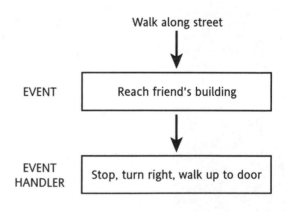

Now you push the doorbell or intercom button to let your friend know you've arrived. Your friend will then come to the door, look out of the window to see who's disturbed them, or grunt down the intercom.

Pressing that button was another event, and this time your friend responded to it – they 'handled' it, in that they were stimulated to *do something* by the buzzer sounding. From here you can discuss what you're going to do with your day – your extended interaction with your friend starts with the push of a button. If your friend had been out, or hadn't answered the door, your very own 'they're not there, I'll go to the mall' event handler would have kicked in. In the real world, events and event handling are complex activities – infinite, even. In Flash, you can control the environment more, and in your interactive movies you can plan for the anticipated range of events and handle them all.

And that, more or less, is everything that interaction is.

Let's examine one of the primary and most intuitive of tools that Flash gives us for interaction with the user – the **button**.

Buttons as interactive elements

In an interactive Flash movie, an *event* will be triggered by the mouse clicking on, or being dragged over, something on the screen – typically a button. The event *handler* here will be a set of instructions that we've attached to the button. These instructions will tell Flash exactly what we want it to do when the user clicks on that button and triggers the 'click' event. These instructions are written in Flash's internal programming language – **ActionScript**. ActionScript is really a set of instructions and structures that we can use to tie together all of the components in our movies so that they function as an integrated and coherent whole.

It's important to realise that a button on its own does not 'produce' interaction. A button placed in a movie has its default states – Up, Over, Down, and Hit – but they won't actually *do* anything interesting unless we explicitly tell them to. We've already seen that we can add keyframes to the button's internal timeline and change its display in each state, which makes the button more interesting to *look at*. But the button is still essentially 'dumb' – all it can do at the moment is *detect* events, such as when it's rolled over or pressed. To boost the button's intelligence we have to attach ActionScript to its different states: it's the ActionScript element that decides what to do when the button is pressed, and it's ActionScript that creates the interaction:

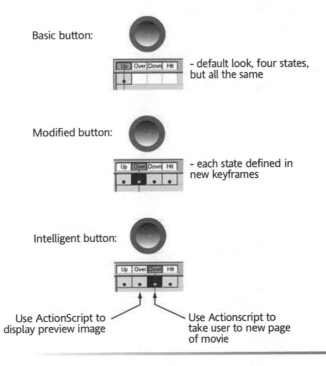

Basic button:
- default look, four states, but all the same

Modified button:
- each state defined in new keyframes

Intelligent button:

Use ActionScript to display preview image

Use Actionscript to take user to new page of movie

When you've attached the ActionScript to your button and added an instance of the button to your movie, the button will sit there, just itching for the user to interact with it.

In some programming languages – BASIC, for example – once your program starts, the program code is *always* running. In Flash, your 'program' – the ActionScript – is attached to a button, and will only run *when the button detects a particular action carried out by the user*. As your knowledge of Flash increases, you'll see why this is a much better way of creating user interfaces. One of the main features of advanced Flash sites is their use of buttons to start off lots of simple little sequences that, together, form a complex, fully animated, and interactive user experience.

As we progress in the next couple of chapters, you'll see that a button in Flash can be much more than just a switch; as well as detecting simple things like mouse clicks to provide navigation, the button can be used to start whole *avalanches* of actions in motion.

Let's start with a simple button.

Creating a simple button

To create an interactive element in our movie, we need a button on the stage waiting to be pressed – giving us an event – and some ActionScript attached to it to handle the event and tell Flash what to do.

Before we look at attaching ActionScript that responds to mouse clicks, let's make sure we're getting the most out of our buttons by creating a simple button and slowly developing its abilities.

1. Create a new movie and rename the default layer `buttons`.

2. Go to **View > Grid > Show Grid** and then **View > Grid > Snap to Grid**, and ensure that both are checked – this will help us position our symbols on the stage more accurately.

3. Insert a new graphic symbol and name it `circle`. Make it a red circle with a black outline. Don't put your new symbol on the stage just yet:

The reason we've created a graphic symbol before making it into a button is that we'll be using the circle many times within the button itself. By making the circle a symbol beforehand, we're allowing Flash to re-use the circle symbol, thus saving time and space.

4. Back on the main stage, click on the **New Symbol** button in the bottom left of the Library window and create a new button symbol called `button`:

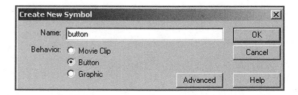

You'll now be inside the button symbol for editing, and you'll see a blank stage with the button icon at the top. The timeline contains the four button symbol states – **Up**, **Over**, **Down**, and **Hit**:

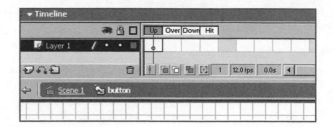

Remember the definitions of the four states of the button symbol:

- The **Up** state is how it looks in its original size and position.

- **Over** is how it will look when the user's mouse passes over it.

- **Down** is how it will look when it's clicked.

- **Hit** contains filled spaces that denote the areas the user must be over to press the button.

5. With the playhead at the Up state, click on the **circle** graphic symbol icon in the Library and drag an instance of it onto the stage inside the button:

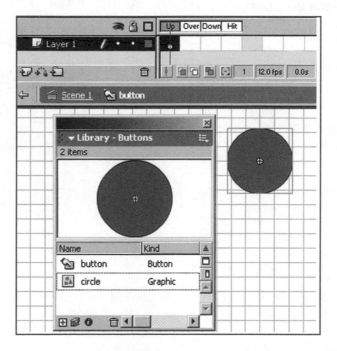

We're going to need to know the *exact* position of our symbol in the Up state – this is so that we can make the different visual renderings of the button's other states consistent. To do this, we'll use the Align panel to place it in the exact center of the stage.

6. Click on the **To Stage** button in the Align panel. With your circle symbol selected inside the button symbol, click on both the **Align horizontal center** button and the **Align vertical center** button:

 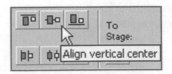

Only the Up frame of the button's timeline currently has a keyframe in it. To start bringing the other states to life, we need to add keyframes.

7. Add a keyframe (using F6) to each of the other three states. You've now put an instance of the graphic symbol **circle** into each state of your button symbol:

In the finished movie, we want to make this button get bigger when it's rolled over, and smaller when it's pressed. We can do this by scaling the instance in each of the button's 'state' keyframes, and we're going to scale each one by a specific amount.

8. Bring up the **Transform** panel using **Windows > Transform**, and select the **Over** state in the button timeline.

The Transform panel is useful for adding precise rotation, skewing, and scaling to symbols and shapes:

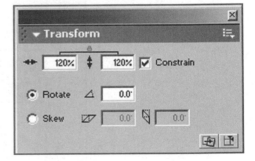

9. Make sure that the **Constrain** box in the Transform panel is checked – this ensures the proportions of the circle are maintained – then type 120 in either the horizontal or vertical scale fields and press the ENTER key to apply the scaling.

10. Make sure that the center position of the button stays in exactly the same place as in the Up state, otherwise the button will appear to move slightly when animated. You might need to drag the scaled version back to the central position – or you can use the Align panel again.

Also, don't make the **Over** state much bigger than the **Hit** state. You'll see why when you test the button: the parts of the **Over** state that are outside the **Hit** state won't respond to the mouse.

11. Now select the **Down** state and scale the circle instance down to **80%**.

Although it's not vital in this exercise, it's a good idea to make the Hit area a solid black object to avoid missing unfilled holes that, as explained earlier, could result in the button working erratically.

12. To do this, select the keyframe in the Hit state and then click on the circle on the stage. From the **Color** drop-down menu in the Property inspector, select **Brightness** and move the slider to -100%:

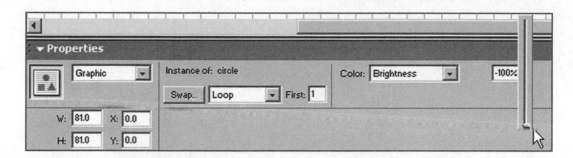

You can confirm that the Hit state circle has the same location and size as the Up state instance either by looking at all four states simultaneously using the Onion Skin tool, or by checking that the values in the Property inspector match for each state.

13. Click on the **Scene 1** icon under the timeline and put an instance of the button symbol at the center of the stage by dragging it out of the Library.

14. Test the movie. You'll notice that when the mouse goes over your button, it changes from a pointer to a hand icon and the button gets bigger. When you click and hold the button, it gets smaller:

Up state   Over state   Down state

That's the basic button defined. Time to accelerate its evolution into a more intelligent species of button.

Creating animated buttons

Flash allows us to define a *movie* as one of the button states. This feature allows us to create buttons that have complete animations within them. Let's create a simple animation and add it to the Over state of our button.

Putting a movie into a button

1. Double-click on the button symbol in the Library to edit it. Select the **Over** and **Down** states of the button from the previous exercise in turn, and press the **Reset** button in the Transform panel (or use **Modify > Transform > Remove Transform**). This will return both states' circle instances back to the same size as the Up state:

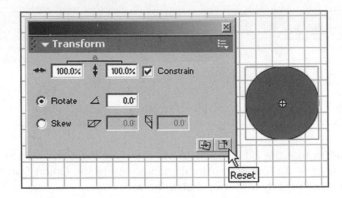

Now we'll create a simple movie that'll play when the user activates the button.

2. In the Library window click on the **New Symbol** button and create a new movie clip symbol called `circlemovie`.

3. In frame 1 of the new movie clip place an instance of the **circle** symbol at the center of the stage – use the Align panel to correctly center this horizontally and vertically (or enter X and Y coordinates of (0,0) in the Property Inspector):

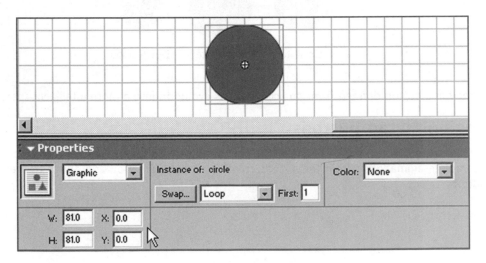

4. Add a keyframe at frame 10 and then use the Transform panel to reduce the size of the frame 10 **circle** instance to 40%:

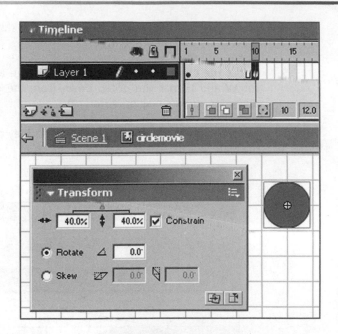

5. Add a motion tween between frames 1 and 10. If you turn on onion skinning between frames 1 and 10 you should see the button make the vaguely psychedelic pattern shown in the screenshot – simulating the way your button will shrink when its Over state is activated:

Once you've finished looking at the groovy pattern, click the Onion Skin mode button again to turn it off.

We're now going to put our animated **circlemovie** symbol into the Over state of our **button** symbol – replacing the instance of the graphic symbol **circle** that's currently there.

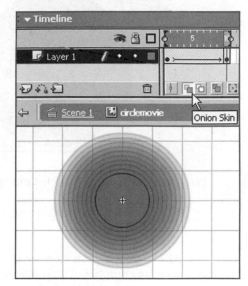

6. To edit the **button** symbol, double click its icon in the Library, and then select the Over state.

7. Select the **circle** symbol instance in the Over state and, using the Property inspector, make a note of its **W** and **H** (width and height) attributes. Then delete the symbol from the stage.

Now we want to put an instance of our **circlemovie** animated movie clip in place of the **circle** symbol we just deleted.

8. Make sure that the playhead is on the Over state, and then drag an instance of **circlemovie** from the Library and onto the stage.

9. Select the **circlemovie** instance on the stage and, in the Property inspector, enter the attributes for **W** and **H** that you noted down from the graphic symbol **circle** before (ours is 81 pixels in diameter – yours may be different).

10. Next, change the **X** and **Y** coordinates so they are (0,0): this way, we can ensure that it's in *exactly* the right place:

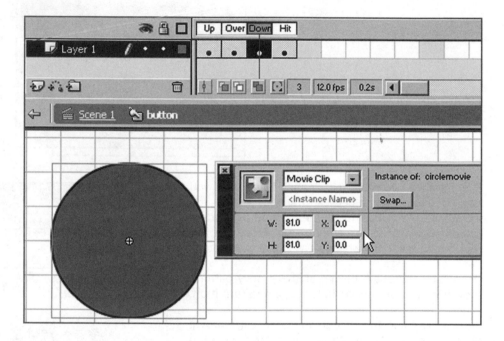

11. Now test the movie with **Control > Test Movie**.

Notice that when your mouse goes over the button, you see a looping animation of a smoothly receding button.

Although the animation we've chosen here isn't really *that* impressive, remember that you can have any number of animated effects embedded in a movie clip inside the button. All you have to make sure is that the first frame of the animation is the same size as the rest of the button states – from there, your Over state button image could morph into a mushroom, a dog... anything you like. Also, note that you should never animate the button's Hit state (unless you *really* want to mess with the user's mind!).

Although we now have a button with visual feedback, the button is still silent. Real buttons tend to click or squeak or ring. Let's add a sound.

Creating buttons that talk

The first thing we need is a sound file. You can use any kind of sound file you may have on your computer or you can download them from the Internet. It's beyond the scope of this chapter to specify the ins and outs of sound issues, so instead let's simply use an appropriate sound from the Sounds Library supplied with Flash.

> *Check out the Sound Sampling appendix at the back of this book for sites where you can download sounds. If you don't want to download from the Internet right now, you can use a sound from Flash's Sound Library. Alternatively, you can search your computer for an appropriate short sound clip – a WAV file on the PC, or an AIFF on the Mac.*

Making our button buzz

The first thing to do is to get the sound into our movie's Library.

1. Open the Sounds Library, using **Window > Common Libraries > Sounds**, and choose an appropriate file (click on the play icon in the top right corner of the Sounds Library window to preview the sound):

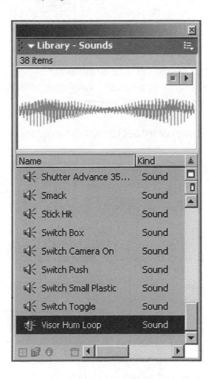

2. To import your chosen sound file, select it and drag it across into your own Library.

    Your Library window should now look something like this:

    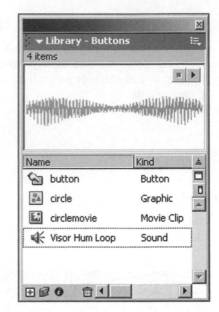

    Ideally, we would now edit the sound to optimize it, but we'll leave all that until our dedicated 'sound' chapter. Right now, what we need to do is attach the sound to the button.

3. Double-click on the **button** symbol in the Library to go into Edit Symbols mode.

4. Create a new layer called sound – this layer will be used to hold the sound our button will make.

5. Now add a blank keyframe to each of the button states using F7.

6. Select the **Down** state on the **sound** layer:

    This is the most usual button state to attach a sound to, and putting our sound here will make the button 'sound off' when it is pressed.

7. In the Property inspector, click on the **Sound** drop-down menu – this will show you all the currently available sounds. Unimpressively, only the one you just imported will be there. (Also ensure that the **Sync** drop-down is set to **Event**).

8. Select your sound. The Property inspector should now look something like the one shown here:

    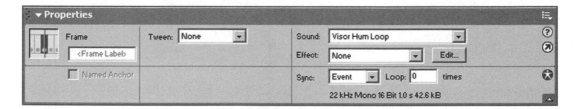

    Look closely at the **Down** keyframe after you've done this. There's a tiny blue waveform shown on the keyframe to signify that a sound has now been attached there:

9. Test the movie. Hear your sound when you press the button? Yes? Then we're done!

10. Save your movie.

When you add sound to a button's Down state in the way that we've done here, you're adding sound to *all* instances of the button. This is a major advantage for adding sound to a previously silent web site: if your web site uses many instances of a single button symbol, you only need to add sound once for *all* your buttons to start making sounds.

When you attach sound to a button using ActionScript, it's only added to that particular *instance* of the button on the stage, and only that instance is affected. We're going to look at ActionScript properly right now.

Introducing ActionScript

Earlier, we likened clicking on a Flash button to what happens when we ring on someone's doorbell. Having a Flash button all by itself is like ringing the doorbell at a house where nobody's home, or where the wiring's been disconnected. The button we've just created looks pretty enough, but beyond the default state-related behavior that we've just explored, it doesn't actually trigger anything when you press it. It doesn't really *handle* the 'click' event: when we click on a button as a user, the sound or embedded animation that plays isn't what we're really concerned with – what we're really interested in is where that button's going to take us, or what it's going to make happen. We need to *wire the button up*.

By adding ActionScript we can make our buttons actually take us somewhere. The ActionScript, remember, is the exact instructions that Flash follows when responding to an event. ActionScript *is* the wiring.

To start demonstrating ActionScript's features, we're going to create a simple movie where Flash asks the user to pick one of two options, and then responds differently for each of the two possible responses. This implies a logical 'branching' in our movie rather than a straightforward linear playback: we'll present the user with two colored buttons and the user will press one of them, causing Flash to go to one of two possible places. This ability to branch and make alternative choices is an important principle in creating interactive movies.

Before we can add an ActionScript and make an interactive movie, we need to create a basic 'front end' for the user to interact with: this will contain buttons that access the different places the user can be taken to. We're going to set these up now.

Creating a basic front end

1. Carry on working with the **button** movie from the previous exercise.

2. Drag another instance of your **button** symbol from the Library out onto the main stage – make sure you drag in the button symbol and *not* the graphic symbol.

3. Position the two button instances so they're next to each other in the center of the stage.

4. With one of your **button** instances highlighted, select **Tint** from the **Color** drop-down menu in the Property inspector, and make the button blue using the color palette to the right of the **Color** drop-down.

You've just altered the properties of this specific instance of the **button** symbol: the underlying symbol has remained the same. Remember that each individual instance has a range of properties that we can change via the Property inspector.

5.   Repeat this tint change for the other button, but make this one *pink*.

6.   Create a new layer called text and use a static text box to type pick your favorite color above the two buttons.

Your stage should look like this:

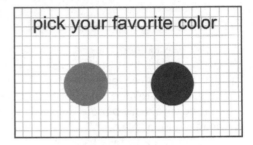

Here, you've used the same **button** symbol twice, but made them look different by changing the color of the two instances. This is a timesaving trick used by many Flash web designers to help workflow when creating sites that have many different buttons on them. They just create one 'master' button and then change the appearance of each *instance*.

Now we need to set up two areas of our site that Flash will take us to when each button is pressed – one area for the pink button, and one for the blue button. We're going to put these areas in a separate scene from the default Scene 1 where we've just created the front end.

7.   Bring up the Scene panel if it's not already open by going to **Window > Scene**. This will show you that you only have one scene at the moment, **Scene 1**.

8.   Double-click on the clapperboard icon of this scene – this will allow you to rename it. Call it Scene 1 Buttons.

9.   Create a *new* scene by clicking on the **+** button at the bottom right of the panel. Call this Scene 2 Choice.

10.   Click once on **Scene 2 Choice** to select it:

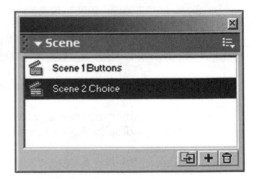

Inside the new scene, there'll only be one empty layer called **Layer 1**. Don't worry – you haven't deleted everything! We're looking at our new scene, which is currently empty. You can check that you're actually in the new scene by looking on the left, below the timeline – this will say **Scene 2 Choice**:

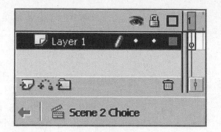

11. Rename the default layer in Scene 2 as text, and then add a new layer called labels.

12. Click in frame 30, and press F5 to add frames to both layers to make the scene 30 frames long in total:

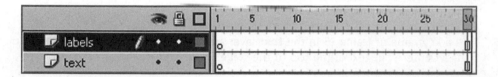

When the user presses any of the buttons in Scene 1, we want Flash to jump to particular points in Scene 2 – points which are related to whichever button the user chooses:

We'll now label these points in Scene 2 so that they're properly signposted – which means that we can then use ActionScript to jump straight to them.

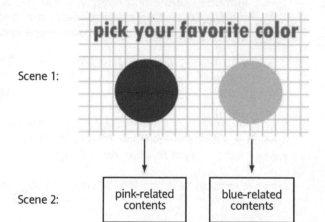

Scene 1:

Scene 2:

13. Select frame 1 in the **labels** layer. Go to the Property inspector and type pink in the **Frame** field:

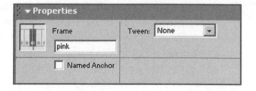

What you've done here is specifically attach a label to frame 1 of the **labels** layer. With this label in place, you can use ActionScript to jump directly to this frame, in this scene, from anywhere else in the movie. That's a pretty powerful thing to be able to do – bypass the linear tyranny of the timeline and jump around inside the movie.

Notice that Flash has added a little flag in the timeline and is displaying the label name next to it:

We can use this label as a reference point for the pink button-related content that we want the user to be able to jump to.

Now we need to partition off this 'pink-labeled' section of the Scene 2 timeline from the part that we want to set aside for the stuff related to the *blue* button.

14. Click to select frame 15 in the same layer and add a new keyframe. In the Property inspector use the **Frame** field again to label the new keyframe blue:

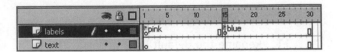

Now, on the text layer, we're going to type the content the user will see when they press either of our two colored buttons. This is the content that's associated with the respective blue and pink parts of the timeline as marked by the labels.

15. Add a keyframe at frame 15 in the **text** layer and use a static text box to type in You selected blue! Center your text at the top of the stage.

16. In frame 1 of the **text** layer, type You selected pink! in the same place on the stage. You can use the Onion Skin mode to view both sentences at the same time if you want to place them precisely, or match the width and height values in the Property inspector.

Your Scene 2 timeline should now look like this:

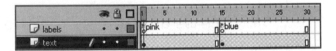

So, what we've done here is create two separate messages, each of which lives on its own separately labeled section of the timeline in Scene 2. We know that we can use those labels as reference points that we can jump straight to using ActionScript.

Now we're ready to go back to Scene 1 and start getting our hands dirty by adding some ActionScript to do the jumping!

Attaching ActionScript to timelines and buttons

We now have a simple front end for the user to interact with and two alternative locations to move on to from the two buttons. However, when we play the movie at the moment, the playhead will zip through the movie in a resolutely linear fashion: Scene 1 will go straight into Scene 2 and not give the user chance to choose a color. We need to shout 'STOP!' at the end of Scene 1 so that the front end hangs around and gives the user time to ponder the alternatives and make their choice.

To do this we add some ActionScript to a frame in the timeline, telling the movie to halt at a particular point: this will give the user all the time in the world to choose a button, and when they do we need to make sure Flash knows which part of Scene 2 to take them to. To do *this* we attach an ActionScript **to each button**. Once we've added our ActionScript we'll have a fully working interactive movie.

To summarize:

- We can add ActionScript **to a frame** so that the ActionScript is triggered when the playhead reaches that frame.

- We can attach ActionScript **to a button** so that the ActionScript is only triggered when the user clicks on the button. Here, the user triggers the event and the ActionScript handles it.

Let's add the ActionScript that'll hook up the front end with the specific chunks of content in Scene 2.

Adding ActionScript to a frame

1. Go back into Scene 1 using the **Edit Scene** button (the clapperboard icon at the bottom right corner of your timeline):

2. Add a new layer to Scene 1 called halt. Select frame 1 in this layer and open the Actions panel if it's not already visible with **Window > Actions**.

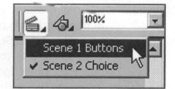

Up pops up an interesting looking panel:

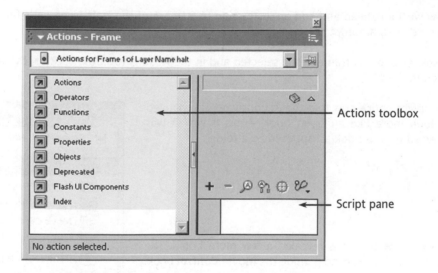

Actions toolbox

Script pane

Don't worry. The reason this window looks a little daunting is that it's showing a whole *range* of ActionScript possibilities at the same time. Let's take a look at some of the basic elements of the Actions panel:

- The Actions toolbox shows the available ActionScript elements stored in folders.

- The Script pane (currently empty) will display the specific elements that we've chosen to apply to this particular frame or object.

- The uppermost pane (the drop down menu) displays the keyframe or object that we have selected. This is particularly helpful for keeping tabs on which elements of the movie have code attached when our movies get more complex later on.

When the arrow to the right of this pane is clicked, a drop-down menu is displayed showing all of the keyframes and objects for which we can add or amend ActionScript . However, the selections in the drop-down are only relevant to the *current* position of the playhead – the drop-down doesn't display all the available objects and keyframes in the movie.

We'll take a look at some of the panel's other elements in a moment.

The Actions toolbox, the left-hand pane, consists of a list of folders, also known as books – you'll see why they're called this later – containing categorized elements to add interactivity. Don't worry too much about exploring these at the moment. For now, just remember that implementing ActionScript rests on your having an idea of what you want your movie to do, and then finding the particular ActionScript element (or combination of elements) that'll let you achieve your aim – don't worry that you have to learn each and every element that's hidden away in this collection of books. ActionScript is a rich and powerful language in its Flash MX incarnation, and you can go as far as you like with it. We'll go into more detail about the extended functions in the next chapter, and also later in the book, but for now we're going to use the Actions panel to give our movie a single, simple, instruction.

Now we'll go ahead and add an instruction to frame 1 of the **halt** layer. Let's find the instruction that we need amongst the books.

3. Firstly, ensure this frame is still selected and in the Actions toolbox, click on the **Actions** book to open it.

You might notice now that the Actions icon has changed to look more like an open book – this is why it was referred to as a book as opposed to a folder:

The **Actions** book has revealed a few more books. The instruction that we need is inside the **Movie Control** book.

4.   Open the **Movie Control** book by clicking on it:

The little blue circles you can now see are ActionScript **commands** or **actions**. These are the instructions we can give to our movie to tell it to specifically do something or go somewhere.

The **Movie Control** folder has a number of ActionScript commands that control navigation around Flash movies, along with a few other basic, but essential, actions.

5.   Double-click on the fourth command down, called **stop**:

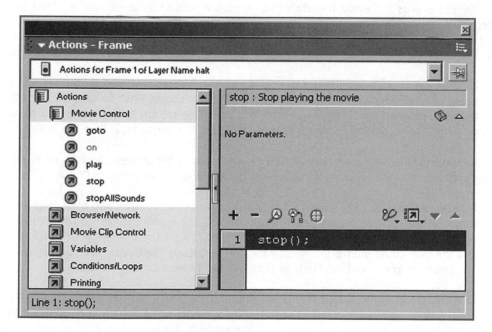

Two things happen.

Firstly, there's now a little '**a**' in the first frame of the **halt** layer. This signifies that this keyframe has a piece of ActionScript attached to it.

Secondly, a little bit of text has appeared in the Script pane of the Actions panel. This is the piece of ActionScript itself – an ActionScript command telling frame 1 to do something when the playhead hits it.

What we've done so far is add a one line ActionScript command to the first frame of Scene 1, telling Flash to 'stop when you get to this frame'. Let's be clear about exactly how Flash will respond to this instruction: Flash will **not** turn off the animation – it'll merely *pause* it and wait to see what happens next. Our buttons will still be active, and all the visual content will remain on display in the user's browser. This stop action is simply our way of saying 'keep those buttons on display where the user can see them'.

6. If you preview the movie now, your two buttons will be on permanent display, and if you move the mouse over them, they'll go through the animated scaling behavior we built into the Over state.

We've used ActionScript to achieve our first objective of keeping the buttons up so that the viewer can choose their favorite color on the buttons.

What Flash needs to know *next* is where we want to take the user when they click on one of those buttons. To do this we're going to attach an ActionScript to each button. These pieces of ActionScript will hook up each button to its dedicated piece of content – we can use the labels to tell Flash and ActionScript *where* to go. But Flash also needs to know *when* to move to Scene 2.

Remember the **events** and **event handlers** that set off our 'visit a friend' interaction at the beginning of the chapter? Well, we want our interaction in this movie to start with the user doing something with their mouse on or near our button. What we're trying to detect here is called a **mouse event**. You can ask Flash (which acts as the event handler) to detect one or more types of mouse event. The most common ones are:

- A **Press** event occurs when the user *clicks* on the button. You may think that this would be the event of choice to ask Flash to detect, but it actually causes Flash to race off and start doing new things as soon as the button is pressed. This doesn't leave any time for the user to see the button working – for instance, running the nice animation that we've built into the button.

- **Release** is when the user *releases* the mouse button after a press, and it's what we use in many situations, because it allows us to see the button in its Down state.

- A **Release Outside** event occurs when the user presses our button and then drags the mouse away from the button while keeping the mouse pressed. The event is triggered when the mouse is finally released. Why would you use this event? Well, you might use it when your buttons are very small and the user could inadvertently drag the mouse outside the button area before they release it. In this situation you could ask Flash to detect either Release *or* Release Outside.

- The **Roll Over** and **Roll Out** events are used to detect whether or not the mouse is *over* a certain area. Buttons set up to detect only these two events don't usually look like buttons at all. For example, if you had a bitmap picture of the world and you wanted a bit of text at the bottom of the map to change to reflect which country the mouse was over, you would add a lot of country-shaped buttons. Think of buttons asked to detect Roll Over and Roll Out events as 'mouse position sensors' rather than true buttons, and this class of mouse event will start to make more sense.

Notice in the Actions toolbox that the on command is grayed out. This is because we currently have a *frame* selected on the timeline. In a finished and published flash movie, the mouse will only be able to generate mouse events on or around a **button**. Next we'll take a look at how ActionScript can control frames and the timeline, and how buttons can supply a little interactivity. So, let's move straight on and see how to attach actions to our buttons.

Adding ActionScript to a button

1. Still in Scene 1, select the **pink** button with the Arrow Tool.

Notice that the title bar in the Actions panel has changed from **Actions – Frame** to **Actions – Button** (telling us that we're attaching this ActionScript to a button and not a frame). This is because the Actions panel is context-sensitive depending on where you are attaching your ActionScript. Also notice that the on ActionScript element is now available in the Actions toolbox.

2. Double-click on in the Actions toolbox:

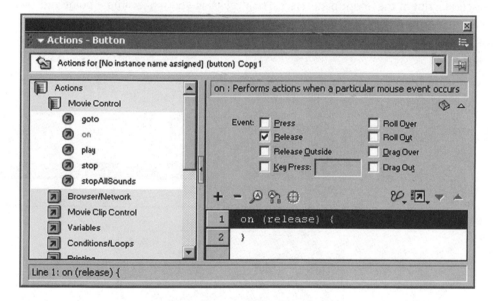

In the right-hand pane, this ActionScript command appears:

```
on (release) {
}
```

This may look a bit too nerdy for some, but remember that you didn't actually have to write it – Flash is generating the 'code' for you: you're just choosing the actions from the Actions toolbox. When the code appears in the Script pane (on the right of the panel), Flash has recognized that you've attached it to the button in question.

The curly brackets at the end of the on (release) are a necessity of ActionScript's syntax, but the core part of the code is in the on (release) statement: this is now attached to our pink button, and it tells Flash 'when the user clicks on me and releases the mouse button, I'm going to ask you to do something'.

> *It's possible to type the code directly into the Script pane if you know the correct syntax to use. At the moment, we're using the Actions panel in 'Normal' mode, but 'Expert' mode is available to you if you want to dispense with the tremendous amount of help that Flash gives you in Normal mode. You can switch between modes by clicking on the Actions options drop-down – located at the very top right of the Actions panel with an icon resembling a list with a downward-facing arrow.*

Above the Script pane, where it says **Event**, you can choose *which* of the available mouse events you want Flash to detect. Try checking and unchecking the different fields to see how it affects the ActionScript in the Script pane. Here, Flash is letting you make simple point and click choices that automatically alter the ActionScript attached to the button:

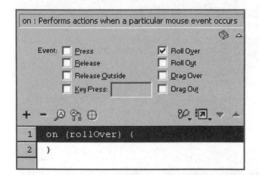 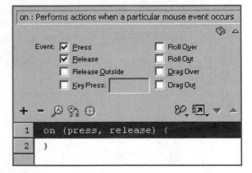

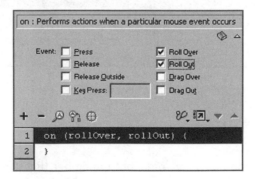

3.   When you're done experimenting with the mouse event check boxes, make sure that you leave only the `release` event checked.

We now need to tell the event handler (Flash) exactly what to do when it detects the mouse being clicked and released over our pink button. This instruction will be appended to the `on (release)` code.

4. Double-click on the `goto` action in the toolbox. This will add a new piece of code into the Script pane:

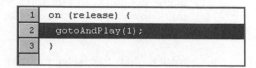

This is the default option for the `Play` ActionScript element. Essentially, the ActionScript we've assembled in the Script pane is saying to Flash: 'When the user releases the mouse on this button, go and play some content that's stored elsewhere.'

We now have to point Flash at that specific content.

5. Now look at the options that have appeared above the Script pane:

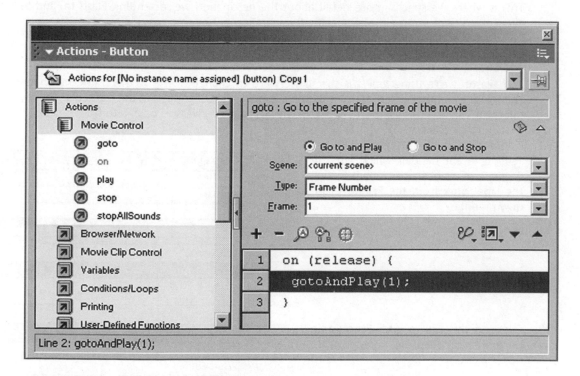

These options help us make the choice about *exactly* where we're going to send Flash to find the content that we want it to play when the user clicks on the button. As we already know, we've created that content in Scene 2, and given each chunk of content labels.

BACK BUTTON

301

6. Click on the **Scene** drop-down menu above the Script pane and select **Scene 2 Choice**. (If you can't see the pull down menu tabs, make the Actions panel a bit wider).

Notice that this selection has now been incorporated into the `gotoAndPlay` statement:

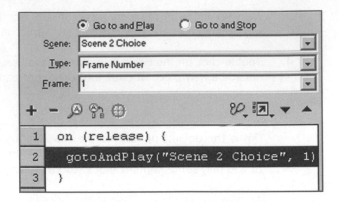

7. Next, click on the **Type** drop-down menu.

This is where we specify more detail about the destination we're sending Flash to, and tells the event handler to go to either a specific *frame* in Scene 2 or to a specific *label*.

8. Select **frame label**.

The reason we're using *labels* is that if we were to change Scene 2, the frame numbers would change as we add or delete frames. By using a label, we're signposting the particular frame we are interested in, and this signpost will move with its frame as we add or delete frames on either side of it.

9. Tell the event handler which label in Scene 2 we want to go to by selecting the label **pink** from the **Frame** drop-down menu:

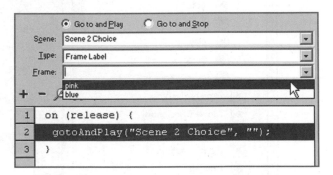

10. Click on the **Go to and Stop** radio button just above the **Scene** drop-down menu:

Notice that the second instruction in the Script pane is now `gotoAndStop`, not `gotoAndPlay`, and that the **pink** label is now inserted into the code.

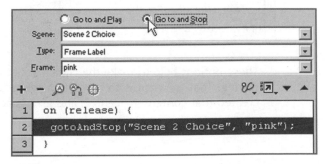

This means that Flash will stop when it gets to the **pink** label, keeping the display of Scene 2's content on the screen. It's worth remembering that the stop command doesn't quit the Flash movie – it simply pauses the playhead. In this example, the playhead would pause on the frame labelled pink.

> *It's important to note that the ActionScript is added to an instance of a button symbol on the stage, not the symbol itself in the Library.*

11. Without closing the Actions panel, select the blue button on the stage.

    The Script pane of the Actions panel will now be empty, as we haven't yet attached any actions to the blue button.

12. Repeat the steps you took to add the ActionScript to the pink button, this time telling the event handler to take the user to the **blue** label in **Scene 2 Choice**:

    - Add the on ActionScript element.

    - Add the goto element.

    - Check the **Go to and Stop** radio button.

    - Select the appropriate **Scene**, **Type**, and **Frame** from each of these drop-down boxes.

13. When you're done, the Actions panel for the blue button should look like this:

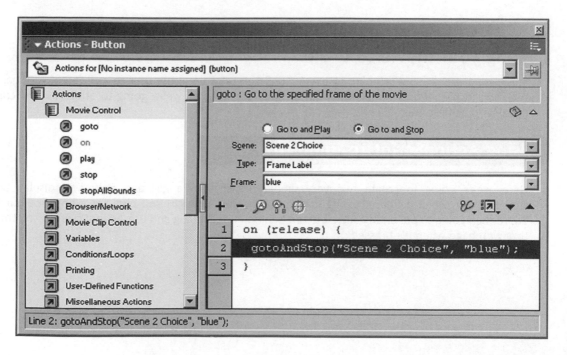

14. Test the movie (CTRL-ENTER) and see if it's interactive!

When you click and release the mouse over one of the buttons your movie should take you to the appropriate part of Scene 2. You'll notice that once you've made a selection you can't go back and try the other option. You can re-run the movie from the preview movie by pressing CTRL-ENTER (or APPLE-ENTER on the Mac), or use the Controller panel (**Window > Toolbars > Controller**):

pick your favorite color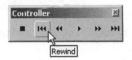

Although this interactive movie is very simple, the way we took the user to one of a choice of places depending on which button they pressed is the key to building web site navigation. Instead of just two colored buttons, we could have used a whole menu of buttons, each taking us to a different part of the web site.

What if our movie was actually part of a children's wear web site, and we were asking the question because we wanted to know if the user's child was a boy or a girl? We could enable the user to jump from our movie to another Flash page that presented either boys' or girls' clothes.

Lets do it!

Linking your movie to a URL

In this next exercise, we're going to use ActionScript to redirect the user to a different web page, with a specific URL, depending upon which button they press. Again, we're going to attach ActionScript to the buttons to achieve this.

Using ActionScript to jump to a URL

Here, we're going to create two very simple drawings of a girl and a boy to display below the stereotypically color-gendered content in Scene 2 (pink for a girl and blue for a boy, like our buttons). We're then going to put an **invisible button** behind each drawing and use ActionScript to link the drawing to a web page when it's pressed:

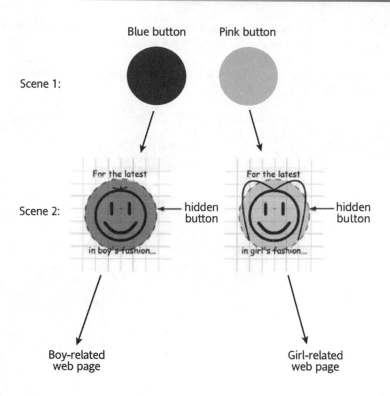

Scene 1:

Blue button   Pink button

Scene 2:

hidden button   hidden button

Boy-related web page   Girl-related web page

1. Continue using the same button-based movie.

2. Create two new graphic symbols called girl and boy, and in each one, draw an image of a girl and a boy respectively.

We'll leave it to your own ingenuity and good taste to create your own boy and girl drawings, but make sure you include a line of text that'll entice the user to push the invisible buttons that we'll add soon:

3. In Scene 2, select frame 1 of the **text** layer and drag an instance of **girl** out of the Library and position it under the 'you selected pink!' text.

4. Now select frame 15 and position an instance of **boy** under '**you selected blue!'**

5. Still in Scene 2 create a new layer called buttons and drag it down so that it's underneath the other two layers. Create a keyframe in this layer at frame 15.

6. Select frame 1 in the buttons layer, click on your button symbol in the Library, and drag it onto the stage behind the **girl** symbol.

7. Scale the button so that it completely surrounds **girl**. You should have something like this:

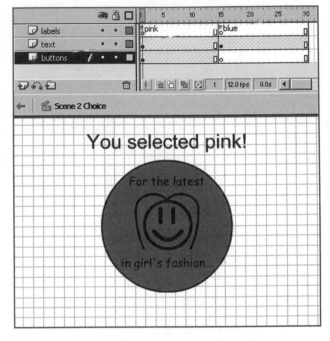

Now we want to take the user to a new web page when they click on the button behind **girl**. The ActionScript we attach to this button will tell Flash 'when the user clicks and releases the mouse over this button, go to the web page we specify'. We do this using the getURL action.

8. With the new button selected, open the Actions panel if it isn't already open. Open the **Browser/Network** book in the Actions toolbox:

This will reveal a number of ActionScript commands associated with browser and file control from within Flash. Don't worry too much about the other commands at the moment.

9.   Double-click on the second action in the **Browser/Network** book – **getURL**:

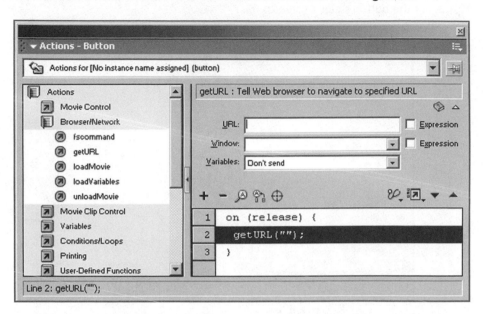

Notice that the event handler automatically assumes we want it to detect an on (release) mouse event. This is the default setting, and if you know you're going to use it you don't need to double-click on, but can go straight to your second piece of ActionScript. The event handler will detect the mouse being released over the button just as it did in previous exercise.

10.   In the **URL** field above the Script pane type 'http://www.friendsofed.com' – or a URL of your choice – it can even point to a file on your own machine if you wish.

You'll notice that we've added the whole URL here, including the http:// bit, making the address an *absolute* one. It's always a good idea to do this in Flash, otherwise the command may have strange effects on certain servers.

Our button will now take the user to a web page (not exactly full of suitable clothes, but you see the principle...). However, the button is spoiling our lovely drawing. An *invisible* button would make our movie look much more pleasing.

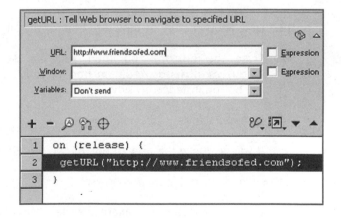

11. With the button still selected, open the **Color** drop-down in the Property inspector and choose **Alpha**. Set the button's alpha value to 0%:

This is a very powerful but simple technique. By making our button transparent, we can put it on top of or below any other bitmap or symbol, making the user think that the symbol or bitmap is the button. And to do all this, we've still only used the same old master button symbol we created.

We'll now create the invisible button and URL specification for the blue option.

12. Drag another copy of the button out of the Library and onto frame 15 of the **buttons** layer.

13. Scale the button, and then add the ActionScript to it – this time make the URL **http://www.friendsofed.com/fmc** (or your own choice), and then use the alpha effect to make the button instance invisible. *WWW.MACROMEDIA.COM FRIENDSOFED.COM*

14. Test your movie.

It will now take the user to one of two new destinations.

We've learnt a lot in this chapter so far...

We've learnt that buttons in Flash are a prime means of adding interactivity and sound to a web site. We've seen that buttons do not have to actually look like real life buttons, and can be anything from invisible ghosts to entire movies in their own right. They can be any shape or size we choose, and we can use the same button over and over again and make each one look different.

We've learnt how to give Flash instructions to jump to new parts of our movie when it detects the user pushing a button. Not only have we learnt how to attach ActionScript to buttons that tell Flash what to do, we've learnt how to add ActionScript to the timeline as well, so that we can make Flash go through its timeline in a non-linear way if we choose to do so.

Let's finish off with the case study.

Case study

In this section of the case study we're going to add some basic actions to our main timeline and also to the **content** movie clip so that it doesn't continue to loop. We'll make the movie stop looping continuously so the user can read the different pages until they decide where they want to go on our site. In the next chapter we'll be able to attach more advanced targeting actions to our buttons to complete the navigation functions. For now, we'll be using stop and getURL.

1. Open up your case study movie from where you saved it last.

2. At the very top of your main timeline create a new layer called **Actions**. (It's good practice to keep all your frame actions in one location, as it makes them much easier to organize and, more importantly, easy to find.)

3. Insert a keyframe at frame 56 on this **Actions** layer. Then open up the Actions panel and add a **stop** action to that frame:

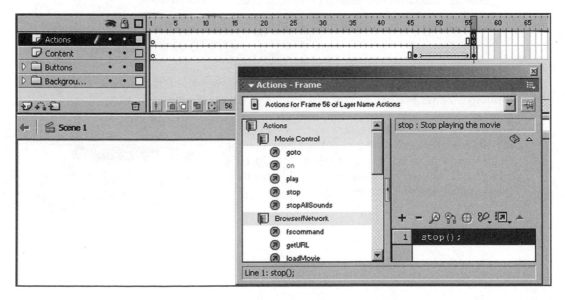

4. Double click your on your **content** movie clip to edit it. At the top of the timeline add a new layer called actions.

    In this timeline, the *work history*, *skills*, and *about* sections of our web site start at frames 1, 10, and 20 respectively. So, in order to make the movie pause at each of these sections until the user wants to leave (by pressing a button), we need to attach a **stop** action to each of these frames in the timeline.

5. On the **actions** layer, insert a keyframe at frames 10 and 20. Then attach **stop** actions to frames 1, 10, and 20 using the Actions panel. Now our movie will no longer loop if we were to test it. It would simply stop at the work history section (when it meets the first **stop** action):

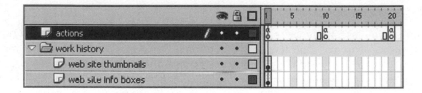

6. In the **work history** layer folder, select the **web site thumbnails** layer. Insert a new layer above it called **invisible buttons**. It'll cover frames 1 to 20. Select all the frames *except* frame1, right-click and choose **Remove Frames**. We're doing this so that our *work history* section doesn't display over the other sections of our web site:

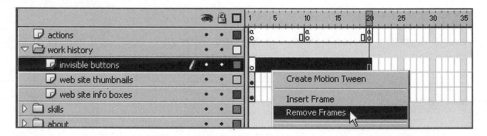

7. On frame 1 of this new layer, draw a solid rectangle over your left-hand web site thumbnail image. It doesn't matter what color it is, just as long as it's exactly the same size.

8. Convert the rectangle to a button symbol (F8) called **invisible button** and double-click this symbol on the stage to edit it. Select the keyframe in the **Up** state and drag it into the **Hit** state. You should only have the rectangle shape in the **Hit** state:

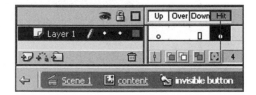

9. Go back into the **content** movie clip's timeline and you should now see a transparent aqua box over the left-hand thumbnail. This is your **invisible button**. You can apply actions to this button and re-use it over and over again to keep the file size down:

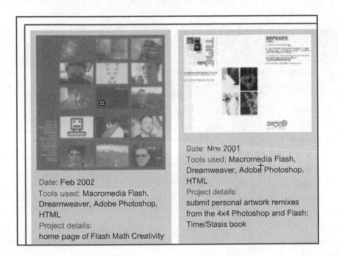

We now to want add some ActionScript to this invisible button so that when the user clicks on it, they'll be taken to this example web site where they can view our work. However, we also want the user to come back and explore the rest of our portfolio, so we'll make this example web site open in a new browser window.

10. Select the **invisible button** and open up the Actions panel. Add an **on (release)** action:

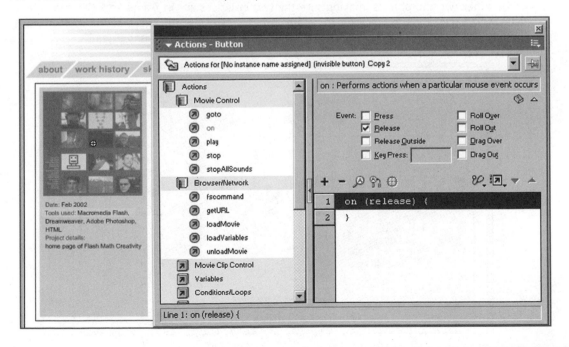

11. Next double-click on the **getURL** command (it's located in the **Actions > Browser/Network** book in the Actions toolbox). In the **URL** field, type in the appropriate URL of the web site (including the **http://** part) and select **_blank** from the **Window** drop-down menu (this will make the web site we have specified in the **URL** field open in a new browser window):

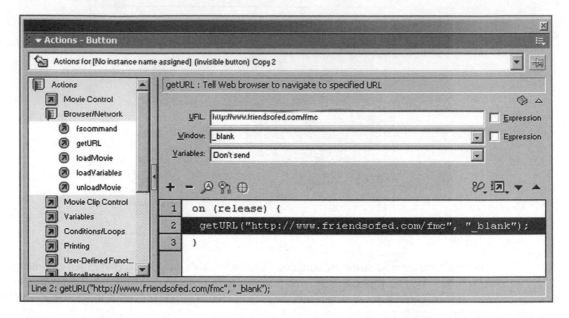

12. Go into your Library and drag the **invisible button** symbol into the **Buttons** folder to keep things organized. Next, drag two instances of the **invisible button** out of the Library and place them over the other two thumbnails, making sure the two instances are in frame 1 of the **invisible buttons** layer. If necessary, use the Free Transform tool to resize the instances of the **invisible button** so that each one perfectly matches the dimensions of the thumbnail underneath:

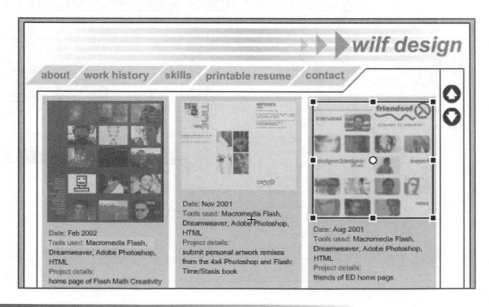

13. Select the new instance of each **invisible button** and repeat steps 10 and 11 to activate them. Remember, first add an **on (release)** command and then attach the **getURL** command to each of the invisible buttons. Here's the example for the center invisible button:

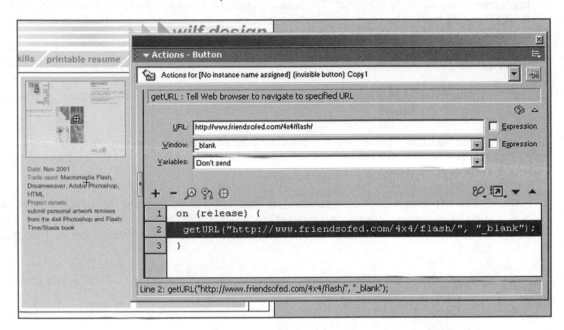

Go ahead and attach the same ActionScript to the last invisible button, but change the *URL* to match your example site accordingly (in our example, the URL is **http://www.friendsofed.com**). Remember to add the **http://** part at the beginning of the URL, and choose **_blank** from the **Window** drop-down.

14. You can now test your movie and check if these buttons work. You should be able to click over the thumbnails and the example web sites will open in your default browser.

Notice that our case study web site loads up with the work history section and then rests there. This is because we added a **stop** action to frame 1 of the content movie clip – the movie is waiting for an instruction from the user before it goes on to play the rest of the movie. This is what we're going to enable in the next section of the case study – we'll be using some more ActionScript to make the main navigation buttons function effectively.

15. Save your case study movie and close it.

Summary

In this chapter, we introduced the important concept of interactivity, and we started to see how Flash implements this using ActionScript. This was an important chapter because the simple applications of ActionScripting that we've seen here will be a foundation that you can build on, both in the next chapter specifically and in the rest of the book more generally.

We saw that:

- **Interactivity** is about bringing the Flash movie to life, and giving the user an interesting and satisfying experience.

- At the heart of interactivity are the principles of **events** and **event handlers**. Things happen – events – like a user clicking on a button, and we create **actions** or behavior that will respond and cope with these events.

- A powerful way of adding interaction in Flash is by using **buttons**. Buttons can have behavior – such as animation, sound, and movie clips – embedded in their default states, and they can be made even more intelligent by attaching **ActionScript** to the mouse events that buttons can detect.

- **ActionScript** is the string that ties together all the components of a Flash movie or web site.

- ActionScript is the internal programming language that Flash uses to create actions in the Actions panel, either in Normal or Expert mode.

- ActionScript can be attached to **frames** in the timeline, or to **objects** – typically buttons – on the stage.

- We can use ActionScript to jump to specific areas inside our movies, and we can even jump to specified web pages and sites.

In the next chapter, we'll explore ActionScript in more depth and see more ways that it can work for us.

Intelligent Actions

What we'll cover in this chapter:

- *Further ActionScripting:*

    - *Increasing interaction.*

    - *Using ActionScript to direct instructions to specific objects on the stage and tell them what to do.*

- *Variables and conditional statements:*

    - *Storing values for later use within scripts.*

    - *Letting Flash make choices about what to do.*

In the previous chapter you used ActionScripts to make a multi-scene, multi-section interactive Flash movie that allowed the user to navigate their way through the alternative routes.

That was just the beginning. ActionScripting can be used to do much, much more: frames and buttons that have ActionScripts attached to them suddenly become supercharged and much more talented than their ordinary cousins. This is at the heart of why Flash is a much richer and more flexible environment for web page production than HTML, and the reason why Flash can be used to produce sites that are more interactive and dynamic in the way they allow the user to move around. Some Flash sites even appear to think for themselves.

This chapter will show you how to start giving your Flash sites these qualities.

You may find this chapter a little daunting at first, particularly because ActionScripting may appear frightening to those of you who are coming into Flash from a Photoshop/graphic design background. You don't need to worry though: Flash actually helps you so much that it practically writes the ActionScript for you! As a beginner, you only have to do two things:

1.   Have a clear idea of what you want your ActionScript to do.

2.   Press some buttons and check boxes to make Flash build up the ActionScript code.

Trust us, there's no need to use math or obscure logic unless that's what you want to do.

The power of ActionScript

We discovered in the previous chapter that ActionScripts are *event driven*. This means that the actions we've told Flash to perform are only carried out when an event we've specified takes place – when the mouse cursor does something specific, or when a frame containing an ActionScript is encountered on the timeline. This makes ActionScripts easy to write. For example, once you've created a working button, all you have to do is attach an ActionScript to it telling Flash what the button should do. There's no long obscure program to write – you just decide what you want Flash to do, generate the appropriate bit of ActionScript, and then move on.

A designer wrote recently: 'whenever I think of Flash scripts, I have this irrational mental image of a little superhero with a letter 'A' on their chest. Made up of normal Flash Frames, they have come to us from the planet Interactivity to free us from the clutches of their archenemy, a secret organization known only by the initials HTML. Ridding the world of boring, static web pages wherever they may exist, with powers that give one command the abilities of 100 lines of JavaScript...Is it a bird? Is it a plane? No. It's *ActionScript!*'

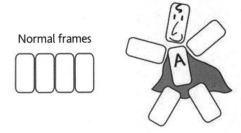

Normal frames

ActionScript is fundamentally much more dynamic than, say a button rollover or an animated movie. With ActionScript, you can control just about every attribute of just about everything on the stage. Surreal as it sounds, ActionScript enables individual elements of your movie to talk to each other. A button symbol can say to a movie symbol, 'When instance X of me is pressed, you start playing from frame Y'. Buttons no longer just control navigation as in plain old HTML; *they also control other objects,* such as movies and graphics. This is done using a type of ActionScripting known as **dot notation**.

Defining instances for dot notation

With dot notation we can make one object in our animation – a button for example – tell another object what to do. Before we can demonstrate this concept we need to create a couple of symbols so that one can boss the other around.

Let's create a little face to talk to. Something we can tell to be happy or sad, depending on our mood!

> *Make sure you save the 'smiler' movie we work on throughout this chapter: we'll be enhancing its capabilities with ActionScript as we progress through the book.*

1. In a fresh Flash movie, create a new movie clip symbol called `smiler`.

2. Inside **smiler**, create two new layers. From the bottom up, rename your three layers `face`, `eyes` and `smile`. These layers are to hold the separate parts that will make up our face:

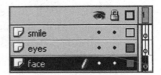

3. Place a yellow circle with a black stroke 8pt thick in the center of the stage on the **face** layer. Center the circle by entering 0 in the **X** and **Y** boxes of the Property inspector, or by using the **Align** panel. If you have **Show Grid** (CTRL+#) and **Snap to Grid** (CTRL+SHIFT+#) on, you'll have no problem doing it by sight:

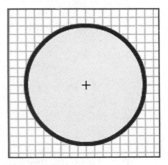

4. In the **eyes** layer, add, well, two eyes. Use two lines with the same stroke width as your circle:

5. Select the **smile** layer and add a horizontal line approximately where the mouth should be:

We know what you're thinking: our face should be smiling.

6. Make all the layers 15 frames long and add a keyframe in the **smiler** layer at frame 15:

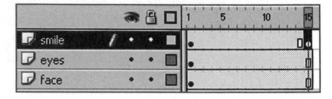

What we'll do next is animate the mouth so that it goes from a smile to a frown, passing through all the intermediate mood expressions in between. To do this we'll set up a shape tween from frame 1 (smiling) to frame 15 (frowning). For the next part to work, you must *not* have the mouth selected (if you find you have, simply click on a blank part of the stage).

7. Select the Arrow tool and go to frame 1. Put the pointer on the mid-point of the mouth until the cursor develops the curve attachment and drag the center of the mouth down to make your face smile:

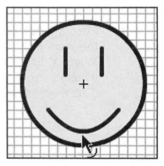

8. Using the Property inspector, add a label happy to this frame and select **shape** from the **Tween** drop-down menu:

A light green shape tween will now extend from frame 1 to frame 15.

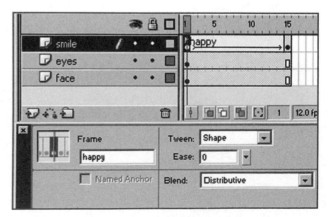

You'll notice that we have nothing else on the **smile** layer. This is a requirement in *all* tween animation, as you'll remember from earlier in this book: you'll confuse Flash if you have more than one item in the layer, and your tween won't work. Also, note that the smile object is just a drawn shape and *not* a symbol – if it was, this would also prevent the shape tween from working.

9. Now select frame 15 of **smile**. Your face here is in its expressionless, or neutral position. By using the pointer in the same way as before, make the face *frown*.

10. Use the Property inspector to add a label called sad to the keyframe at frame 15. (You won't see this label on the timeline because there's not enough space to show it, but you *will* see a little flag in the frame to show that it's been labeled):

11. You can see the motion **smiler** will perform by selecting it in the Library window and clicking on the **Play** button, or by using the Onion Skin tool to see all the frames at once, or by dragging your playhead through the timeline:

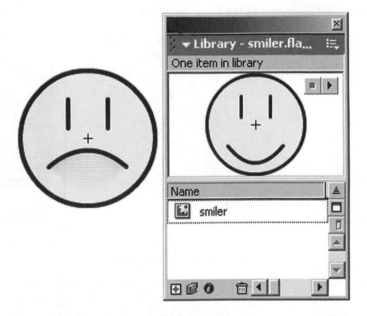

We also want to label the 'neutral' face expression. The exact position of this will depend on how you drew your mouth, but it should be somewhere near the middle of the movie.

12. Click and drag the playhead up and down the timeline until it is on the frame where the 'smile' is closest to the straight horizontal line you drew originally.

13. Insert a keyframe at this frame. Use the Property inspector to label it neutral:

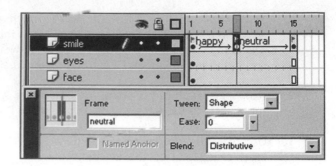

Each of these labels corresponds to a different expression: we want to be able to target the expression we want to see. To do this, we need a button to press...

14. Create a new graphic symbol and call it rectangle. This symbol will form the basis of our button.

15. Inside the graphic symbol, draw a yellow rectangle:

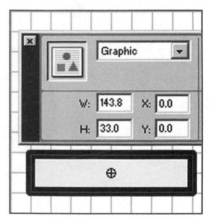

We're going to be putting text over the top of our button eventually, so make sure the body of your rectangle is an appropriate size for typing onto.

16. Now create a button symbol called rectangle button.

17. Inside the button symbol, drag an instance of the **rectangle** symbol onto the screen and center it by entering 0 in the **X** and **Y** boxes in the bottom half of the Property inspector:

> As we've mentioned before, it's important that the graphics in a button's states all line up. For that reason, it's a good idea to always center buttons. Then, if a button ever starts to look wobbly when it's used in your final movie, you'll know all you have to do to correct the problem is set its position in all states to X:0.0; Y:0.0 with the Property inspector.

18. Add keyframes to the Over state and the Hit state.

We suggested earlier in the book that it was a good idea to make the 'hittable' shape in the Hit state a distinctive color. Here, however, because we know that the square is solid, we don't need to change the shape in the Hit state from yellow to a distinctive black by adjusting the brightness, but you may wish to do so for practice.

We'll let the user know they're over the button's 'press' area by making the button become a lighter shade in the Over state.

19. Select the button in the Over state. Now choose the **Brightness** option from the Property inspector's **Color** drop-down menu and set it to **40%** using the slider:

 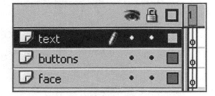

20. Go back to the main stage in Scene 1 and add two new layers. Rename your three layers, from the bottom up, `face`, `buttons` and `text`:

21. Select the **face** layer and drag an instance of **smiler** onto the stage from the Library. Then, in the **buttons** layer, add two instances of the **rectangle** button symbol. Your stage should look like this one:

Now to give the user some hints about which buttons they might want to press.

22. In the **text** layer, use the Text tool and the Property inspector to add the words 'better' and 'worse' on top of the buttons as shown, and along the top of the stage type 'How do you feel?':

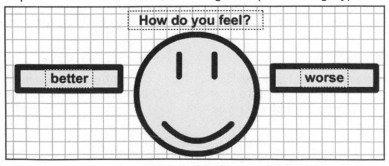

You can test the movie now if you wish. When you go over the buttons, they should become lighter, and the face will continuously animate from happy to sad, but nothing will happen when you press either button.

The next step is to use the buttons to control what mood smiler is in, but before we begin adding the ActionScript that'll tell smiler how it feels, let's look at how dot notation works in theory.

Dot notation

It may not sound very exciting, but dot notation will give you and your movies incredible possibilities.

Dot notation in Flash and ActionScript is a way of expressing a **path** through a movie: it gives us a way of targeting a particular object and telling it what to do, irrespective of its position in the movie's structure. So, if we want to direct a particular piece of ActionScript at a specific movie clip, or if we want to tell an instance of a 'square' symbol to change its alpha value to 10, we can do that by specifying that object's location using dot notation.

A typical line of dot notation ActionScript would look like this:

```
square._x = 100
```

This line would move the **square** instance to an **x** (horizontal) position of **100** on the stage. Notice the dot before the **_x**? Perhaps this is what gives dot notation its name!

Dot notation enables us to reference any instance or object within the Flash movie, but for this chapter, we'll stick to one location for all of our instances – we'll take a look at how to reference different locations in the movie later in the book. Dot notation only works on individual, *named instances* of a symbol. Let's make sure we're clear on what an instance is and why we use them.

The original 'master' symbol that sits in the Library is the *template*, and any instances of it that we put on the stage will be replicas of this master symbol. While the version in the Library is the original, think of the instance on the stage as a clone, permanently linked to its master. An instance will *always* look and behave like its original: when the original changes, *all* its instances will change also. This characteristic is what differentiates an *instance* from a *copy*: if you simply draw a square on the stage, copy and paste it next to the original and then go back to the original and change it, the copy would not be affected in any way as a *copy* has no link to its original.

You can see this link between originals and instances for yourself by altering the rectangle symbol you created in the last exercise.

Let's learn how to enter dot notation code with the ActionScript Panel's **Expert mode**.

Expert mode

To enter dot notation into our Flash movies we have to change the Actions panel so that it functions in Expert mode. Expert mode is different to Normal mode because it allows us to type ActionScript freely – like you would in a word processor or text editor.

We used the Actions panel in Normal mode in the last chapter when we were able to double-click on a command to select it, and enter the properties in a number of input boxes. Expert mode assumes the user has certain knowledge, but provides a number of aids to help less advanced users, so we don't need to feel daunted by using this particular mode.

Many of you might be thinking right now – what's wrong with using Normal mode? In a nutshell, Expert mode allows you to enter dot notation code manually, whereas Normal mode doesn't. You will eventually find that Expert mode is faster to work in, and it will enable you to learn ActionScript a little quicker (but you might not be aware of it!).

We'll see how Expert mode works and how it can help us to learn ActionScript as we work through the next exercise.

Originals and instances

1. In the Library window, double-click on the **rectangle** symbol to go into Edit Symbols mode.

2. Select the whole of the yellow rectangle with the Arrow tool and use the Free Transform tool to stretch it at the top and the bottom. Once you've changed the size of your rectangle, re-center it by entering 0 in the **X** and **Y** boxes of the Property inspector:

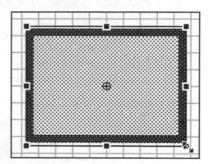

3. Click on **Scene 1** at the top of the timeline to go back to the main stage and notice that *both* the instances of **rectangle** have mimicked the change made to their parent:

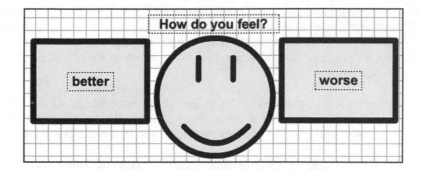

The instances of **rectangle** we put in each state of **rectangle button** have changed and consequently, the instances of **rectangle button** on the stage have changed as well. The changes we made to the original symbol have rippled through to all of the instances associated with it. This is a big advantage for editing and changing your web site – Flash can just follow the link to each instance of the original and make the necessary changes.

When we change a symbol, we alter its **attributes**. Attributes are the features of our symbol and include things such as size, position, and color. For a *movie clip*, attributes also include values like its 'current frame'. We'll be looking in more depth at this aspect of Flash in the two *intermediate ActionScript* chapters later in the book.

So, Flash is able to change the attributes of smiler because it knows what a 'smiler' type of object is – thanks to the template in the Library. However, in a truly interactive and flexible movie, we want Flash to be able to change the attributes of single, *individual* instances on the stage, while leaving the original untouched. For Flash to do this, each instance must be *unique* and identifiable. In propeller-head computing languages, making a specific incarnation of a symbol identifiable is called **instantiation** – which basically means giving each instance a *name*.

Changing attributes with dot notation

Let's instantiate – *name* – the instance of **smiler** we have on our stage.

1.   Select **smiler** on the stage and open the Property inspector.

2.   The Property inspector tells you that this is an instance of a symbol called **smiler** and that it's a **movie clip**. In the **Name** field, give this instance the name face and press ENTER.

Because we've now given this specific instance of **smiler** a name, Flash now knows enough about it to let us control it directly. It knows that this particular instance is called **face**, and can now differentiate it from any other instance of **smiler** we might place on the stage in the future. Additionally, we can now direct commands to this instance in a way that parallels our use of labels in the previous chapter.

The **face** instance is now going to be the 'target' of our ActionScript. At the moment, **smiler** plays continuously during our movie, but we want it to stay on the neutral expression until one of the buttons is pressed – one button will make it happy, and one will make it sad.

To do this we're going to control the **smiler** instance's **current frame** attribute.

3. At the top of the movie's main timeline, create a new layer called `control`. Select the first frame on this new layer and use the Property inspector to add a label to it called `initialize`. Then, with the frame selected, go to **Window > Actions**, or click on the arrow icon on the far right-hand side of the Property inspector:

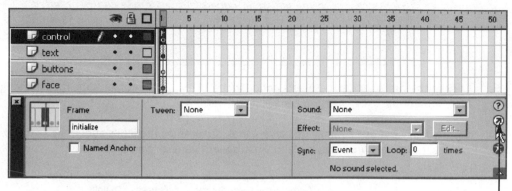

Object Actions

This will open the **Actions – Frame** panel in Normal mode. Let's change it to Expert mode so that we can start entering our ActionScript code.

4. Open the Actions options by clicking on the drop-down icon at the top right of the Actions window:

5. Select **Expert Mode** (the second option on the menu) to switch the **Actions – Frame** panel to Expert mode.

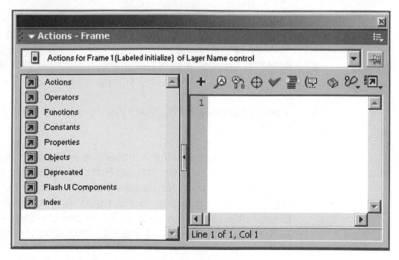

The bottom right-hand pane has expanded to cover all of the right-hand side. This is because Expert mode will not give us input boxes to enter parameters for our code. Additionally, there are significantly more commands available to us in the left-hand pane.

Expert mode has given us a little more responsibility already!

> *The commands in the left-hand pane of Expert mode can be inserted into the code by double-clicking on them in the same way as in Normal mode.*

6. Click in the right-hand pane. You'll notice that a blinking text cursor appears, signifying that we can type something. Well, we're not quite ready, yet!

Before we begin our coding, let's take a look at some of the icons above the text box in the right-hand pane to see what they do and what benefit we can gain from them:

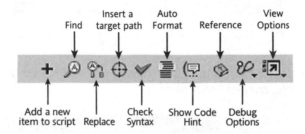

- **Add a new item to script**: Opens a list of all the ActionScript commands available for adding to your script. You can select a command from this menu and it will appear in the script, similar to Normal mode.

- **Find**: Allows you to locate a piece of text within the active script pane.

- **Replace**: Locates a text string and replaces it with another string, (similar to the 'Find & Replace' found in most text editing programs).

- **Insert a target path**: Locates instances in our Flash movie. We'll look at this in more detail in a moment.

- **Check Syntax**: Receiving ActionScript errors after waiting for a Flash movie to publish can sometimes be really frustrating. Fortunately, Flash has this button for checking the validity of our code. If Flash locates a script error, an output box appears on screen, detailing the location and reason for your error(s). As you learn ActionScript, you'll begin to see the Output window more and more – don't worry – this is normal for anyone learning ActionScript (and even the masters from time to time!).

- **Auto Format**: Formats your ActionScript to look neat, tidy and correctly indented.

- **Show Code Hint**: This makes Expert mode a lot easier! Code hints appear to suggest the correct parameters required for ActionScript commands:

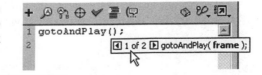

You can hide the code hints by clicking on this button, but for now we'd recommend that you leave this on until you're fully familiar with ActionScript.

■ **Reference**: Flash MX comes with its own ActionScript guide, which is really useful when writing your scripts. You can open the Reference panel by selecting a command from the left-hand pane or highlighting a command in the code pane:

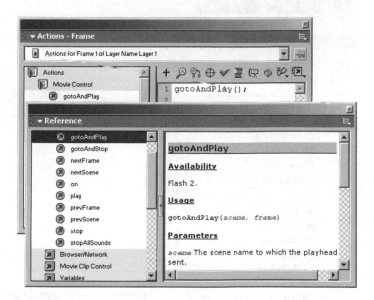

■ **Debug Options**: Debugging is the process of checking your ActionScript and removing any glitches contained in it.

■ **View Options**: Switches between Normal and Expert modes. From here, you can also activate line numbers for code in the right-hand pane. This makes it easier for you to locate errors in your script that appear in the Output window when you test your movie:

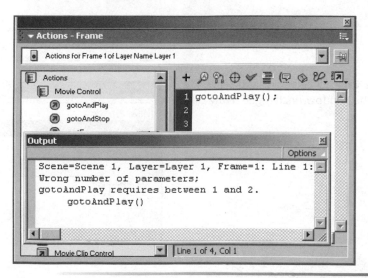

Now that we've looked at all the buttons in the Actions panel, let's give one of them a try.

7. Make sure that you have frame 1 of the **control** layer selected and click on the **Insert a target path** button:

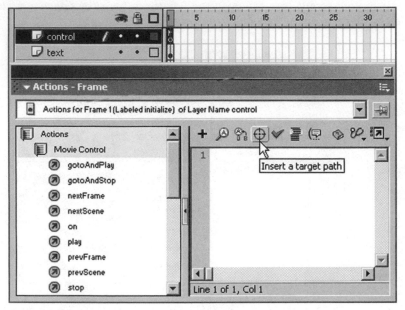

This reveals all potential targets in the movie that you can control – all of the symbols that have **instance** names:

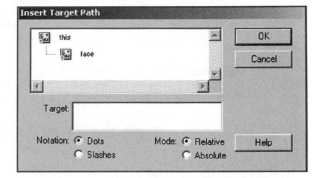

8. Click on **face** to select it, and leave the rest of the window unchanged. Now click **OK**:

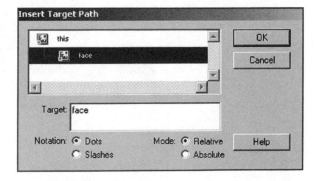

The right-hand pane in the Actions panel now contains the word **face**:

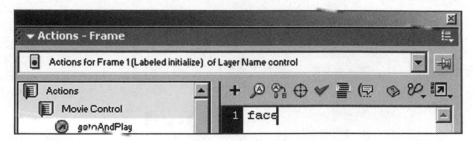

We've now pointed Flash at the correct target – next, we need to tell Flash what we want it to *do* with that target.

What we want Flash to do is make the smiler movie start on its neutral, expressionless face. Remember, we're attaching this ActionScript to the first frame of our main timeline, so what we really want to say to Flash is: 'when you encounter the frame labeled **initialize** in the timeline (the first frame), tell the instance **face** to jump to the **neutral** label on its internal timeline and stay there':

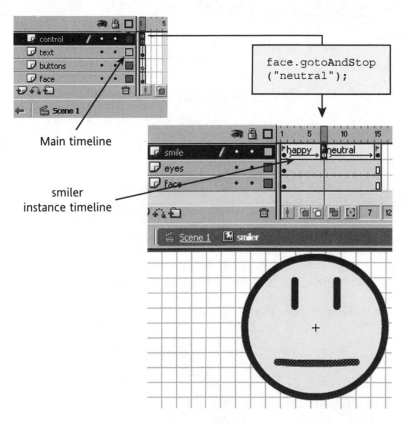

Main timeline

```
face.gotoAndStop
("neutral");
```

smiler
instance timeline

Let's tell Flash exactly where to go...

9. Type a dot after **face** in the right-hand pane of the Actions panel:

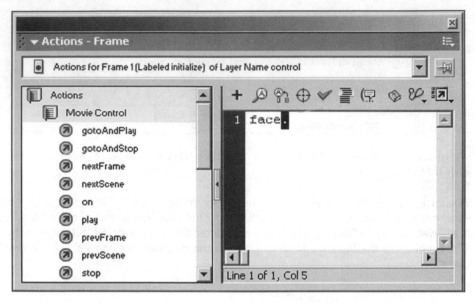

10. Next, type:

```
gotoAndStop(
```

...into the right-hand pane after the dot you just entered, you will now see the following:

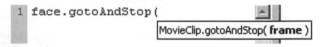

The box that has appeared is a code hint. (If you're not seeing it, click on the **Show Code Hint** button in the Actions panel:

Flash is showing us the correct syntax for the **gotoAndStop** command. We already have the first two elements in place: the field that is required is shown to us in bold text – **frame**.

11. Complete this line of ActionScript by typing:

```
"neutral");
```

A semi-colon signifies the end of a line of ActionScript.

The last piece of ActionScript we need to attach to this frame is a **stop** action. This is telling Flash to stop the main timeline animation at *this* frame.

12. Press ENTER so that the blinking cursor is on a new line below the previous line of code.

13. Type `stop ();` on this new line or double-click on the **stop** command in the left-hand pane:

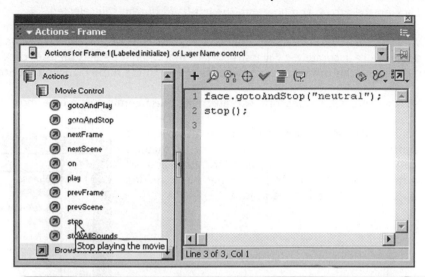

> *Even though you are working in Expert mode, you can still select the commands in the left-hand pane by double-clicking on them. While you are learning ActionScript, there is no right or wrong way to work in Expert mode – do whatever suits you until you feel familiar and confident enough to decide which mode you prefer.*

This particular movie would run in exactly the same way with or without this command. However, if you were to add a second scene the movie would run straight into it before the user had a chance to interact with **smiler**.

Now we need to add ActionScript to the buttons.

14. Click on the button on the left and make sure that the Property inspector is open.

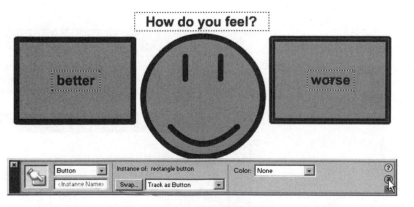

Remember, the arrow icon at the far right of the Property inspector can be used to open the Actions panel for this button.

15. Click on the arrow icon now with the left-hand button still selected.

We want to create ActionScript that basically says to Flash, 'When this button is pressed, make **face** smile'. More accurately, it will instruct Flash that when it detects the user clicking and releasing their mouse over this button, it must make **face** jump to the **happy** label on the **smiler** movie's timeline.

Now we've used ActionScript, we can create these commands a little more confidently.

16. Double-click on the **on** command from the **Movie Control** folder in the left-hand pane of the Actions panel. Notice that as you do this, a **ScrollPane** appears in the right-hand pane. This is another of the helpful attributes available in Expert mode:

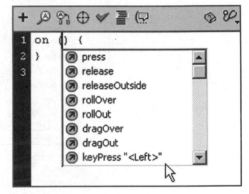

With the blinking cursor in between the brackets following the **on** handler, Flash is prompting us for the parameter from the list, that we want to appear between the brackets.

17. Double-click on **release** from the ScrollPane to select it. The **on** handler will change to look like this:

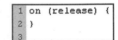

18. Place the cursor after the first curly bracket and press ENTER. The cursor should now appear on the next line and will be indented a little:

This is because anything within the curly brackets is part of the **on** handler and will be performed when the mouse is released.

19. Click on the target icon and then click on **face** in the **Insert Target Path** window that appears and click **OK**:

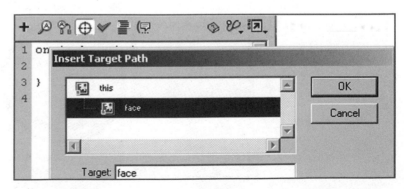

20. As before, type a dot after **face** and then type:

        gotoAndStop("happy");

```
1  on (release) {
2      face.gotoAndStop("happy");
3  }
4
```

21. Select the right-hand button and repeat steps 15 through 20, but this time type sad in the gotoAndStop brackets. This button will then make **face** frown.

22. Test your movie.

Smiler will now start off on its neutral face position because of the ActionScript we attached to the timeline. When we press the **better** button, **face** smiles, and when we press the **worse** button, **face** frowns.

The ActionScript attached to each button is controlling the attributes of another object (the instance of our **smiler** movie symbol). This very simple way of linking elements together is extremely powerful and can be extended much further to link more and more objects to each other.

We now know how to use dot notation to control instances and enable bits of our animation to boss each other around. But we can also give Flash the power to make decisions for itself by using two more of ActionScript's special powers: **variables** and **conditional statements**.

Teaching your movie to think for itself

The ability to use ActionScript to help Flash make structured decisions means that very advanced Flash interfaces can be built. This feature allows Flash to move beyond being merely a graphical interface for web pages and to enter the domain of fully-fledged web applications and games. By adding ActionScript to a Flash web page you can do more than just make it interactive. You can give it a brain.

At the moment we only ever see the frames of the **smiler** movie that we labeled: **happy**, **neutral**, and **sad**. It would be nice if we could see all the intermediate frames and expressions as well.

When you press the **better** button at the moment, it takes you to the 'best' expression, and the **worse** button takes you to the 'worst' expression. What we want to be able to do when we press the **better** button is to make the movie go *one frame* nearer the **happy** label, or frame 1, and show us a *slightly* happier expression. Similarly, when we press the **worse** button, we want the movie to go one frame nearer the **sad** label at frame 15, and show us a *slightly* sadder expression. We want to give smiler a more nuanced range of expressions rather than the two extremes it presents us with at the moment.

Essentially, what we want to do is go to the *previous* frame if the *better* button is pressed, and to the *next* frame when the *worse* button is pressed.

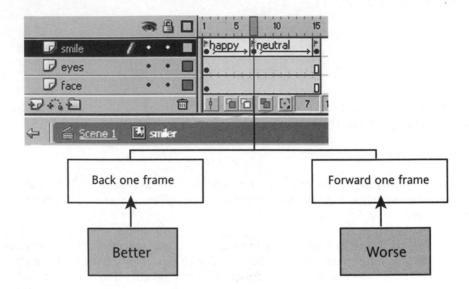

So, we want the ActionScript we create to say to Flash, in simple terms, 'When the **better** button is pressed, make **face** move *back* one frame in the **smiler** movie timeline' and 'When the **worse** button is pressed, make **face** move *forward* one frame in the **smiler** movie timeline':

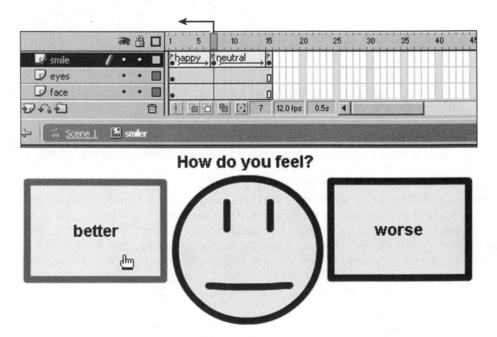

But – and it's a big 'but' – what happens when we reach the first or last frame of the movie?

If the **better** button is pressed when face is at frame one, or if the **worse** button is pressed when face is at frame 15, the actions we told Flash to carry out will be impossible and our instructions won't make any sense.

We need Flash to be able to decide what action it should take in these circumstances – whether it should move to another frame, or stay where it is. To be able to do this Flash must know what frame it's currently at. We can tell Flash where it's at by making use of **variables.**

Variables

A variable is a named container where you store values or data that you want to use again and again while a program – or Flash movie – is running. A variable is essentially a bit of computer memory that you give a name to. You store information in this memory location, and when you give Flash the name of the variable, it knows where to go and look for the information you stored.

There are two types of variable in Flash we need to look at here – **literal variables**, and **expressions.**

A **literal** variable is a value that you want to treat as a 'literal' value: that is, whenever you send Flash to find that variable, the value that it finds in the memory location will be something like a name, an address, or the color of your eyes. It's a value that you want to read directly from memory once you've set it.

The color of your eyes, for example, could be stored as a literal variable. If you wanted to tell Flash your eyes were blue, you would define this variable like so:

```
Eyes = "blue"
```

The "" around the value denotes that it's a literal variable. It won't change until you change your eye color. Although your eyes could have been any color at all, Flash will deduce that now they're blue, they'll always be blue – until you tell Flash otherwise. Whenever Flash uses this variable, it will read it as a single, integrated value.

An **expression** is different from a literal variable. An expression doesn't necessarily have a fixed value that's waiting to be read out of a particular memory location. Instead, an expression has to be *evaluated* – Flash has to do a little figuring out before it can decide what the value of the expression is.

For example, the statement 'Number of dollars in my pocket + number of dollars in my pay check' is an expression: it has two component parts, each of which needs to be evaluated and added together before a final figure can be calculated. Essentially, an expression is any statement that will ultimately return a value.

You could call the money in your pocket 'Dollars', and tell Flash you had 10 of them by writing:

```
Dollars = 10
```

Notice that when we write an expression variable we don't enclose it in `''`. By writing our variable like this Flash knows it's an expression. (Not all literal variables need to be enclosed in `''`, but for now we'll assume they do).

Having given Flash this information, you can now forget how much money you have and get Flash to keep track of your accounts. If you were to now find a dollar on the floor and put that one in your pocket, you could just say to Flash, 'I now have one more dollar than I had before.' You would write this:

```
Dollars = Dollars + 1
```

Flash will now make the value of dollars equal to eleven, so if we find another dollar under the couch we would again say, 'Flash, I have one more dollar than I had before.'

We can apply this knowledge to our movie and get Flash to keep track of what frame of **smiler** we're on. We'll create a variable, and we'll call it smilerframe. We can store the current frame number inside this variable. Once Flash looks at this variable and knows which frame we're starting from, it can add or subtract one frame from this variable each time a button is pressed. The value of **smilerframe** will change using an expression that essentially says:

```
smilerframe = smilerframe + 1
```

or

```
smilerframe = smilerframe - 1
```

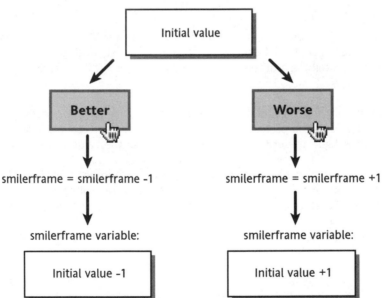

These expressions will create the new value of **smilerframe** and store it in the variable.

Let's put this into practice.

Using variables

Our first step is to find the frame number that corresponds to the neutral expression of **face**. We can then store this value in the **smilerframe** variable and use it as the starting point for the frame-by-frame movement from 'happy' to 'sad'.

Earlier, we attached ActionScript to the **initialize** frame, which told Flash that at the start of the movie, **face** should be on the frame labeled **neutral**. This is the frame number that we'll use as the initial value for our **smilerframe** variable.

1. Double-click on the movie symbol icon of **smiler** in the Library to go into Edit Symbols mode.

2. Move the playhead to the frame containing the **neutral** label. You'll be able to see exactly what frame this is by looking in the little frame-counter pane at the bottom of the timeline:

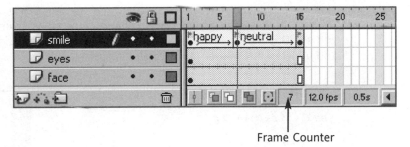

Frame Counter

In this example, **neutral** is on frame 7, but in your movie it could be different depending on how you drew the mouth. We can now make our **smilerframe** variable equal to 7 (or whatever the value is in your movie).

3. On the main stage, click the **initialize** frame on the **control** layer and click on the arrow icon on the far right of the Property inspector to bring up the Actions panel for this frame.

    The Actions panel that opens is titled **Actions – Frame**, and the drop-down menu below displays the information for this particular frame. The ActionScript that we have already entered is also present:

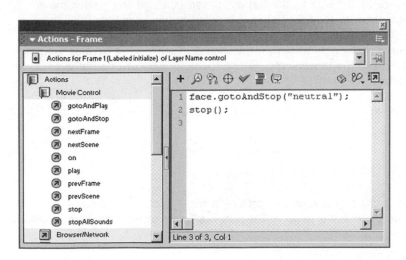

As you begin to create more ActionScript, you'll find yourself using this drop-down menu more and more.

Setting the variable here is designed to 'initialize' it at the beginning of the script so that Flash can use it later: this is a discrete piece of information that we're giving to Flash for future reference so that it knows what the initial value of **smilerframe** is. For this reason, we need it to be the *first* line of ActionScript.

4. Click to position the cursor before any of the other code in the right-hand pane, then press ENTER to push the first line of code onto the next line:

```
1
2  face.gotoAndStop("neutral");
3  stop();
4
```

Now we can set **smilerframe** to equal 7. During our movie, as the user clicks on the **better** and **worse** buttons, we're going to want the value of **smilerframe** to change to anything between 1 and 15. This means that **smilerframe** has to be an expression variable that can be operated on and updated as the user makes their choices.

5. Type the following into the additional line you've just created in the script pane:

```
smilerframe = 7;
```

```
1  smilerframe = 7;
2  face.gotoAndStop("neutral");
3  stop();
4
```

So far, our ActionScript for frame 1 looks like this:

This script now sets the **smilername** variable to its initial value at the center of the happy/sad continuum as soon as the movie starts. It also directs the movie to the middle of the **face** instance's timeline, pausing the movie there with a neutral facial expression and waiting for the user's input.

Now we need to change the ActionScript instructions that are attached to each of the buttons. Instead of telling **face** to go all the way to the **happy** or **sad** labels of the **smiler** movie clip as soon as they're clicked, we want them to tell **face** to move forward or back *one frame*.

When we found a dollar, the new value the money in our pocket became Dollars + 1. Similarly, when a button is pressed and the timeline moves one frame forward or one frame back, we want to *update* the value of **smilerframe** as either:

```
smilerframe = smilerframe + 1
```

or:

```
smilerframe = smilerframe - 1
```

We'll still be using the **gotoAndStop** action to make **face** move up and down the **smiler** movie clip timeline, but we'll now tell it to go to the *previous* frame or the *next* frame. Fortunately, Flash has built-in facilities to help us do this.

However, we still have the problem of what Flash will do when we get to either end of the timeline and it can't physically *go* to the previous or next frame. How do we stop Flash going off the end of the movie? Well, to solve this, we use a **conditional statement**.

Conditional statements

A conditional statement allows our Flash movie to make choices, based on the situation it finds itself in. This means we can tell Flash to only follow the instructions we've given it *if* certain conditions apply. Helpfully, '**if**' is the name of the action we'll use to insert a conditional statement in our button.

If, in our 'dollars' example, our pockets were only big enough to hold a hundred dollars, we'd add a conditional statement in our instructions to Flash. We'd say, 'Every time we find a dollar, only put it in our pocket **if** Dollars (the variable) is less than one hundred.' If Dollars was already equal to one hundred, Flash would know to ignore the rest of the instruction.

Let's define the conditions that must apply in our **smiler** movie for Flash to follow our instructions. When the **better** button is pressed we want it to tell **face** to go to the previous frame of **smiler** if – and only if – ñ **smiler** is not *currently* on frame 1. If **smiler** *is* currently on frame 1, then the **smilerframe** variable will equal 1. If **smiler** is *not* on frame 1, then **smilerframe** will be greater than 1.

Flash will now understand that we're happy to go to the previous frame if we're at a frame greater than 1 (**smilerframe > 1**). If **smilerframe** actually equals 1, then the movie will know not to move when the **better** button is pressed:

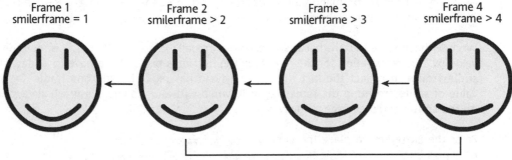

| Frame 1 | Frame 2 | Frame 3 | Frame 4 |
| smilerframe = 1 | smilerframe > 2 | smilerframe > 3 | smilerframe > 4 |

(go to the previous frame if smilerframe >1)

Let's add this instruction and conditional statement to the **better** button.

Updating the buttons with sexier ActionScript

1. Select the **better** button and open the Actions panel with the arrow icon on the far right of the Property inspector.

    We're going to change the ActionScript for this button, so we'll need to remove the current actions within the **on** handler.

2.   Highlight the second line of code.

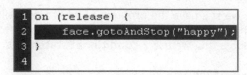

3.   Press the DELETE key. This will leave us with the following:

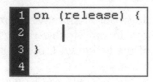

Before we tell **face** to go to the previous frame of **smiler** when it's clicked, we need to add our conditional statement. Remember, we only want our instructions carried out if **smilerframe > 1**.

4.   Type the following in the right hand pane of the Actions window:

```
if (smilerframe > 1) {
```

```
1  on (release) {
2      if (smilerframe > 1) {
3  }
4
```

Be careful to get the spelling of **smilerframe** exactly right, otherwise Flash will think you're talking about something else.

As you typed the **if** command you probably noticed the code hint tool tip. Remember that this is the Expert mode's way of helping you.

We now have to tell Flash that if **smilerframe** actually *is* greater than 1, it should decrease that value by 1 in preparation for the next time the button is pressed: we have to update the value of **smilerframe** to reflect the fact that the playhead has moved along one frame. By tracking the value of **smilerframe** in the same way as it would with our dollars, Flash will always know where on the **smiler** timeline **face** actually is.

5.   Press the ENTER key to place the cursor on a new line.

Notice that the cursor has been indented again:

```
1  on (release) {
2      if (smilerframe > 1) {
3
4  }
5
```

6.   Now type the following:

```
smilerframe = smilerframe -1;
```

...and press ENTER to place the cursor on a new line.

We now need to tell Flash what to do next – actually move the playhead along the timeline in **face**.

7.   Click on the **Insert a target path** button, and then select **face** as your target, as we did earlier in the chapter. Then click **OK**.

8. As always, place a dot immediately after **face** and type:

    ```
    prevFrame ();
    ```

    ```
    1  on (release) {
    2      if (smilerframe > 1) {
    3          smilerframe = smilerframe -1;
    4          face.|
    5  }
    6
    ```

9. Finally, press ENTER for a new line.

    Our code for the **better** button is almost complete. As with an **on** handler, an **if** statement requires that it is closed with a curly bracket. Let's place one.

    ```
    1  on (release) {
    2      if (smilerframe > 1) {
    3          smilerframe = smilerframe -1;
    4          face.prevFrame ();
    5      }|
    6  }
    7
    ```

10. Type a closing curly bracket on the new line. It will immediately realign itself, in line with the **if** statement above.

    Press the **Auto Format** button above the right-hand pane to clean up your code so that it looks all neat and tidy.

    The **better** button is now ready to use.

11. Test the movie. You'll see that **face** will get happier each time the **better** button is pressed, whereas it will go straight to its sad expression when you press the **worse** button.

    OK, now to make the **worse** button fully functional. We need to repeat the same sequence of steps as we did for the **better** button, but with some significant changes to our conditional statement and to the instructions we shoot at **face**. Follow through the next set of instructions carefully.

12. Select the **worse** button and open its Actions panel.

13. Remove the line of script within the curly brackets.

14. Type the following code as you see it, taking care to spell everything correctly and case everything as seen:

    ```
    if (smilerframe < 15) {
    smilerframe = smilerframe +1;
    face.nextFrame ();
    }
    ```

15. Press the **Auto Format** button and all of your code for the **worse** button will now look like this:

    If it matches up, the **worse** button is ready to roll!

    ```
    1  on (release) {
    2      if (smilerframe<15) {
    3          smilerframe = smilerframe+1;
    4          face.nextFrame();
    5      }
    6  }
    ```

16. Test the movie again. Now *both* of the buttons will make the mouth move incrementally. You'll see **face** change its expression smoothly from happy, to neutral, to sad, and back again as the buttons are pressed.

17. Save the movie. We'll work on it some more later.

There has been a lot to take in through this chapter, but we've learnt fundamental concepts for creating top quality Flash sites.

Understanding what instances are and how dot notation can be used to control them will enable you to give your sites a far greater degree of interaction for the user to enjoy and marvel at. They will be able to do things like start or stop movies, affect the appearance and behavior of movie elements, all in addition to merely navigating the site. You can actually do a whole lot more with dot notation, and the basic skills you've gained here will provide a solid footing for learning the more fancy stuff later in your Flash career. Indeed, we have two more advanced chapters on ActionScript later in the book, so we hope that this has whetted your appetite.

You've also been introduced to the use of variables and conditional statements. These are the features that give Flash the ability to think for itself. When used together, they give Flash some fairly powerful decision making abilities.

Case study

We still have two sections of our portfolio site left to build into our Flash movie. We'll add them in now for future use, but the main part of this chapter's case study is using some ActionScript to finally make our navigation work. This ActionScript will mean that when the user clicks on a button at the top of our web site, Flash will go to the relevant frame in our **content** movie clip and display the content we've been building.

1. Open up your case study movie file.

2. Double-click on your **content** movie clip and create two new layer folders called `resume` and `contact`. In each of these layer folders, insert a new layer called `text`:

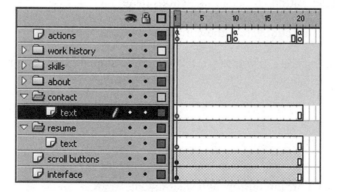

Now we need to extend both these **text** layers and also add two new **stop** actions at the appropriate frames in the **actions** layer.

3. In the **contact** layer folder, select the **text** layer and insert a keyframe at frame 30. Also add a keyframe at frame 30 of the **actions** layer and attach a **stop** action to that frame.

4. Repeat these steps for the **resume** section, only this time place the keyframes at frame 40:

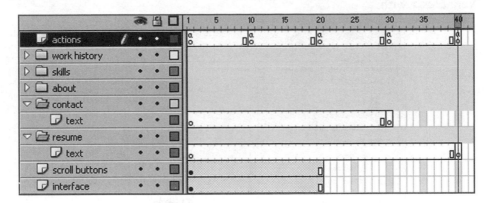

Now let's give each section of this movie clip a label that refers to the five different sections of our web site. By doing this we'll be able to reference these sections much easier in our ActionScript when we activate the navigation buttons.

5. Select frame 1 in the **actions** layer. Go to the Property inspector and type `work history` into the **Frame Label** field. When you hit ENTER you'll see your label appear in the timeline next to the little red flag.

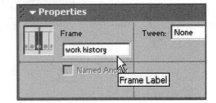

6. Repeat this last step, adding appropriate labels to frames 10, 20, 30, and 40 (we've included a blank keyframe at frame 50 in the screenshot below so that you can the last frame label):

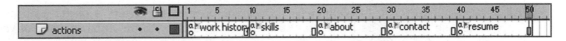

Now that we have all the sections created and labeled, we can start to add the ActionScript to our main buttons so that they target these labeled sections – navigating the user to them when they're pressed. This is where all the true interaction takes place in our Flash movie.

7. Go back into your main timeline, click on frame 46 and select your **content** movie clip on the stage. In the **Instance Name** field of the Property inspector, give the movie clip an instance name of `content`. Repeat this step at frame 56:

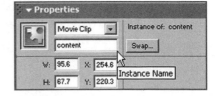

8. Select the **about** button on the main stage and open up the Actions panel (F9).

9.   Next, click on the **Add a new item to the script** button (the plus sign) and select **Actions > Variables > with**:

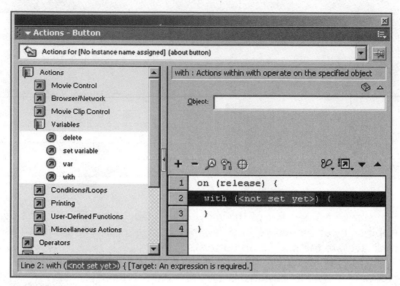

In the Script pane you can see:

```
on (release) {
    with (<not set yet>) {
    }
}
```

We need to enter a target path so that Flash knows how to get to the **about** section of the content movie clip.

10. Place your cursor in the **Object** field. Once you do that, the **Insert a target path** button (the target-like icon) will be highlighted so that you can browse to the instance name of your movie clip to control it. Click on this button to open the Insert Target Path window.

11. In this window set the **Mode** to **Absolute**. You can see your **_root** level (your main timeline) in the window with all the instance names you have given to movie clips below it. Select the **content** instance and press **OK**:

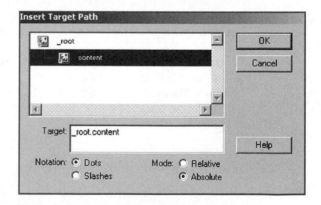

This target to your movie clip has now been entered into the Script pane:

At the moment Flash knows *what* movie clip it's talking to – it now needs to know *where* to go in this movie clip. The last thing we need to do to make the **about** button target our **about** section correctly is just give it a simple **goto** action. So let's do just that:

12. Go to the **Actions > Movie Control** book, and insert a **goto** command underneath your target path line.

13. Check the **Go to and Stop** radio button, select **Frame Label** from the **Type** drop-down menu, and type about in the **Frame** field (remember the **about** section is at frame 20 in the **content** movie clip with the label **about** at its start):

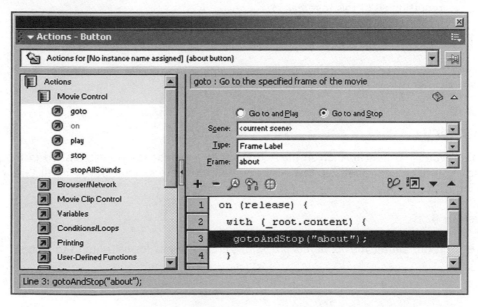

14. Go ahead and test your movie. It'll load up with the **work history** section first, but the **about** button is now fully functional – clicking on it will take you to the **about** section of your web site.

15. Go back into your main movie and we'll now add the same ActionScript to the remaining four buttons in the navigation bar. The target path will always be the same – it's the **goto** actions that will change. Here are the steps again:

    1. Select the button on the stage.

    2. Double-click **with** in the **Actions > Variables** book.

    3. Specify the target path like we did previously by first clicking in the **Object** field above the Script pane, opening the Insert Target Path window, and then selecting the **content** instance name.

    4. Add the **gotoAndStop** command.

    5. For each individual button, be sure to specify the Frame Label you want Flash to go to for that particular button: **work history**, **skills**, **resume**, or **contact**.
    (Remember, you can double-click your movie clip at any time to check the names of the frame labels that you've assigned.)

16. Test your movie.

    Phew! That's everything done on the buttons. You should now be able to directly access all sections of your web site using the buttons on the navigation bar. Although the **contact** and **resume** sections don't presently have any content in them, you can see that the buttons work and navigate to the specific area of the movie clip. You can now see the other three sections with content previously built in fully working – remember the color animation on the mouse in the **skills** section and the text mask effect on the **about** page? Sit back and appreciate the hard work you've done in putting all of this together.

17. Save your case study movie and close it.

In the next chapter we're going to add some sound to our case study movie, but as you can see, this portfolio web site is now substantially finished.

Summary

This chapter has built further on the ActionScripting foundation we established in the previous chapter. We've taken an important step towards being able to create well integrated, intelligent, responsive movies using ActionScript.

We saw that:

- In our **smiler** movie, **labels** provide reference points for us to jump to using ActionScript.

- We can name specific instances of movie clip symbols on the stage using the Property inspector. Naming an instance – instantiating it – means that we can use that name in scripts and manipulate that instance using ActionScript commands.

- We can use actions to 'point' at particular instances on the stage and pass them instructions about how they should behave.

- The **goto** action is used to jump to an individual frame number or label within a movie clip's timeline.

- We can add intelligence and decision-making to our movies using variables and conditional statements:

  - **Variables** are memory locations where we can store values and information for later (re)use.

  - We use the **Set Variable** action to initialize a variable by entering its **name** and **value** in the Actions panel.

  - **Conditional statements** let Flash decide what action to take, depending upon the conditions it finds.

  - We used the **if** conditional statement to move the playhead backwards or forwards based on the value of the **smilerframe** variable.

If you want to do serious, industrial strength work with Flash, you need to learn ActionScript. We'll be returning to explore ActionScript in much more detail later in the book.

In the next chapter – **sound and video**.

Multimedia: Sound and Video

What we'll cover in this chapter:

- **Creating sound** – creating or acquiring sounds and music to use in your movies.

- **Importing and exporting sound and video** – looks at the types of sound and video that Flash can handle, and the best ways to get sound into and out of Flash.

- **Using sound and video in Flash** – manipulating sound and video inside of Flash once you've got it there.

- **Flash sound issues** – tips on sound implementation in Flash, such as potential pitfalls and strange effects.

- **Flash video issues** – tips on when it's best to compress imported videos, depending on their content.

This chapter is about using sound and video to enhance your Flash movies. We've already attached sound to a button in a previous chapter, but here we'll be opening up the world of Flash multimedia and climbing right inside.

Multimedia web sites have previously separated the sound and video content from the rest of the site. For example, embedding a video into a separate, standalone application was the norm with standard HTML web sites.

The key to getting multimedia onto the web without compromising loading times is *optimization*, so we'll go through all the things you'll need to consider when you finally come to exporting your movie. We'll look at sound and video elements separately, considering the implications of each when we add them to our movies. The introduction of sound into previous versions of Flash helped enhance the user experience, but Macromedia Flash MX now has the ability to embed video, so the experience can only get better!

In this chapter, we'll be constructing a soundtrack that will play alongside your web site's visual content. In this example, we'll separate the soundtrack and the visual content to minimize download time. By doing this, the web site will load first, allowing people to begin navigating, while the soundtrack loads in the background and starts playing when it's ready. There's another advantage to keeping the sound and visual components apart: if you want to change or replace your soundtrack at a later date, it's much easier to implement this on a separate soundtrack rather than extracting sound files from within your movie and then inserting new ones.

Before we go ahead and take a look at sound in the first section, we recommend that you download the set of sounds from our web site to get the most out of the examples in this chapter.

Plug in those speakers and let's rumble.

Sound on the web

Sound on the web was always problematic, and then a little thing called MP3 came along and blew everything else out of the water. Before the advent of MP3 there were really only two options for the web designer: **MIDI** and **sampled sound files**. MIDI (Music Instrument Digital Interface) is a format that's understood by all digital music instruments, all music cards, and most soundcards.

For most sound formats, the sound file contains a *digital representation* of the actual sounds, with the corollary that a higher quality representation of the sound implies a larger file. The advantage of MIDI is that it doesn't hold representations of the sounds themselves, just the instructions for how to *play them* on a specific instrument. This means that MIDI files are very small and compact compared to other formats. It's a bit like raster and vector graphics: a MIDI file is similar to a vector in that it's an *instruction* to do something, and not a direct representation of the thing (the sound) itself. MIDI can also be embedded in simple HTML.

A MIDI soundcard contains a bank of instruments which the MIDI file instructs to play at certain times, at different volumes, pitches and so on. This can be a problem in that only the instruments embedded in the card can be played. New instruments can sometimes be added to the card, but this means a loss of standardization, as you can't guarantee that everyone will have the correct instrument, resulting in another instrument being substituted for it.

The problems with MIDI are that it's not a universal standard, and that the final sound output depends on the quality of your MIDI-compatible synthesizer or music card. More importantly, MIDI is a music language only: it can't be used to create vocal sounds or non-musical effects – such as a door slamming.

The other pre-MP3 option was to have sampled data via the various sound formats of the time – things like WAVs, SNDs and AIFFs. These were big and bulky, and tended to be a major headache during download. Waiting an extra thirty seconds for a voice to say 'Hi there!' at a web site homepage didn't really cut the mustard! Additionally, not all sound formats were understood by both PC and Mac platforms, causing further bugs and uncertainties.

Then along came MP3. This was a sound format that compressed sounds intelligently via several different filters to give a much smaller file size for a given quality than any other sound compression system (with the exception of MIDI, which as explained above, is really an electronic music language for instruments). MP3 is now *the* standard for music files on the web, in the same way that Macromedia Flash is the standard for high-impact, highly interactive web sites. It therefore comes as no surprise that Flash supports MP3.

Flash and MP3

When using Flash and MP3, once the music is embedded into Flash, it can be listened to on the web but can't be copied in the same way that normal MP3 data can be downloaded across the web.

Although MP3 simplifies the sound export options available from Flash considerably, there's still the problem of getting the sound *into* Flash in the first place. In this section we'll briefly experiment with different ways of doing this.

So, without further ado, let's start honing our Flash multimedia skills by using sound. Creating and manipulating sound is probably something novel to many new Flash users, so we have some separate tutorials in this chapter. The Sound Sampling appendix at the end of this book describes the fundamentals of digital sound. You might like to look at that too if you're totally new to digital sound.

Let's begin – logically enough – with how to create or source the sounds we want to use.

Creating sound

The first problem with getting sound into Flash is acquiring your sound files. There are generally only two options:

- Get them from a sound library CD or from a web site offering public domain sounds.

- Create the sound samples yourself.

There are a lot of sites out there that rip off their sounds from obscure dance or hip-hop records. The implications of this may not be too serious when you're starting out, but when you create sites commercially, being found out can be both costly and embarrassing. The easy and safe option is to get your sounds and loops from a royalty-free web site. For those who go for this option, there's a list of useful sources that you can also find in the Sound Sampling appendix, so just nip to the web, download a couple of sounds, and fast-forward to the next section.

Now we'll briefly illustrate a typical route for *creating* sounds for Flash.

There are two main types of sound you'll want to capture: incidental sounds and music. Incidental sounds are things like doors slamming or cows mooing, which can easily be recorded with just a microphone, a handy cow, and the free sound recording software that comes with your computer (Sound Recorder on the PC or the Sound control panel on a Mac). You could record music in the same way, but the results would be huge files with poor quality. The best way to get high quality music onto a computer is to create it yourself.

One of the techniques that you'll learn later in this chapter is how to create a full sound score, optimized for the web. One of the best ways to utilize sound on the Internet is by creating a **sound loop**. This means that you start and stop with exactly the same noise, meaning that you can repeat the sound endlessly and smoothly without any obvious breaks in it. The advantage of this is that you only need to download one small file that can carry on playing for a long time. Because music loops are one of the hardest sounds to create well, we'll work through the thought process that goes into them, then finally onto the actual creation itself.

To create music professionally, you'd use a sequencing program along with a battery of expensive synthesizers and instruments, but you can obtain simple (and relatively cheap) entry-level sequencers from the web (see the Sound Sampling appendix for a few to try). Instead of using expensive 'physical' instruments, you can actually use the sequencer to control your soundcard's *built-in* instruments via MIDI. The real advantage of this method is that all current soundcards support playback of sampled sound (as well as sound capture via a microphone). If you have a half-decent soundcard, you probably have a full synthesizer and sampler sitting in a slot in your computer even as we speak. The sound quality of internal soundcards won't be a problem because you'll be compressing the sounds extensively for web transport, and in the end there won't be much difference between them. Once you've created your musical masterpiece, it's necessary to *export* it from your sequencer as audio.

We created this chapter's accompanying sound files by importing the sequencer/synthesizer output into Sound Forge – a popular sound editing program made by Sonic Foundry, with a cheaper cut-down version available – at 44 KHz and 16 bit, which is the equivalent of CD quality. Using Sound Forge, you can also *normalize* the sounds. Normalization takes the loudest sound in the sample and increases/decreases the overall volume based on this level, setting it as the highest point in the possible *range* of sounds in your movie. This ensures that there's a much greater range available for the quieter sounds in your file, thus avoiding excessively loud quantization noise (hissing) during the sampling process (see the Sound Sampling appendix for an explanation of quantization). If you don't have any really quiet sounds in your file, then this isn't really necessary.

After this Sound Forge based processing, the sounds were passed through a package called ACID (from the same makers as Sound Forge) to create a seamless loop, then saved on to the computer. If you're using a Mac, use Macromedia's SoundEdit to edit your sounds and the built-in Loop Tuner to perfect your loops. The most common formats for saving in are WAV files (PC) or AIFF files (Mac). We'll be using WAVs as the default file format for our sounds throughout this chapter, but if you're using a Mac just substitute this for AIFFs – all of the processes will remain the same.

The files are now ready for importing into Flash.

To allow you to use the individual sounds, we've included them amongst the files at the download section of our web site. We've kept the sound files at CD quality throughout the sound capture process, for two reasons:

- The maximum (best) sound quality that Flash can export is limited by the sound quality at which you choose to *import*. The better your input, the more flexibility you have with the output. There's always the chance that you may want to use better quality sounds as Internet transmission speeds creep up and more people have faster connections. By keeping the files at CD quality, you're never in danger of having to re-record samples.

- You may want to create screensavers or other non-web applications, and these will be able to use CD quality sound because bandwidth won't be an issue. In this case, you wouldn't have to re-record the sounds, as they would already be at the highest quality.

Of course, you may not have CD quality *output* available, particularly if you're using non-optical connections and/or a soundcard as your synthesizer. In that and any other case, keep your sounds at the highest quality your setup can manage – you may just save yourself from major hassle later on.

Importing and exporting sound with Flash

In the last section we gave a brief overview of how to get audio onto your computer so that it's ready for importing into Flash. We'll now look at how to actually get it into Flash, and how to optimize it for *export* onto the Internet.

To import a sound, all you have to do is use the **File > Import** menu.

Flash can import a number of sound formats: WAV, AIFF, and MP3 probably being the three most popular. If you've created your own sounds, it's strongly recommended that you keep them as full quality WAV files, because MP3 is what's called a **lossy** format. This means that to get the highest amount of compression, the computer intelligently discards sounds that it thinks you won't hear. The problem with this is that there's a drop in quality, and once the sound information is discarded, it's lost forever. Although you may not be able to hear the differences, you'll see them in programs like Sound Forge and ACID, and you may start to have trouble synchronizing the lower quality sounds as precisely: this is because the waveforms have started to 'blur', making accurately locating the sound's start and stop positions much more difficult.

Let's get our fingers busy and work with some real sounds.

> *If you haven't already visited our site and downloaded the sound files that accompany this section, do so now. Go to* **www.friendsofed.com**, *follow the links to the* **Code** *page, find the correct code download page for this book and download the relevant sounds file. We've included both CD quality and Flash-optimized (and therefore smaller) versions of the files.*

Bringing sound into the mix

1. Open up a new movie and save it away as Soundtrack.fla.

2. Use the **File > Import** command to open up the **Import** dialog box, and select **All Sound Formats** from the drop-down menu:

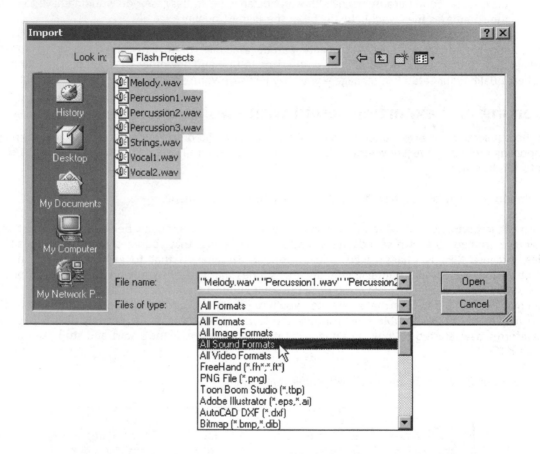

3. From here, navigate to where you've saved your downloaded sound files and **Open** them all, adding them to your Library (you can do multiple selections in the PC dialog box using SHIFT-click or CTRL-click).

4. Once the sounds are imported, they'll appear in your Library:

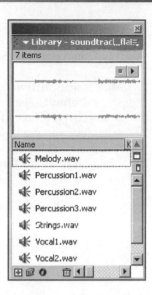

The preview window will show a waveform representation of the selected sound. If you see *two* separate waveforms it means that the sound was imported in stereo. If you click on the **Play** button in the preview window, Flash will play one loop of your *original* sound. It's important to remember this, as Flash will play the sound as it was when you imported it, ignoring any compression you may have added inside of Flash since the original import.

5. Bring up the **Sound Properties** window for the **Percussion1** sound either by double-clicking on it in the Library, or by selecting it and pressing the **Properties** button at the bottom of the Library window:

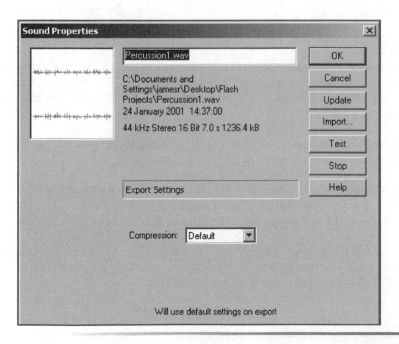

This window displays the basic information for the selected sound file, and also shows how the sound will be exported in the final movie. The form Flash will export the sound in is dependent on the selection that we set in the **Compression** drop-down menu.

6. Click on the **Test** button, and your sound will play in its original state. If you leave this set to **Default**, Flash will take the settings from your **Publish Settings** window (this window will be covered fully in Chapter 13). At the moment, the default compression settings are **MP3** at 16 bit, but you won't *hear* this difference until your movie is published.

7. Next, in the **Compression** drop-down menu of the **Sound Properties** window, change the setting to **MP3**:

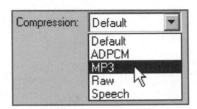

This will open up another list of options:

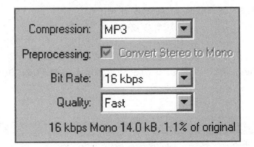

The important part to look at here is the text at the bottom of the window. This text tells you how big your file is, and how much it has been compressed. For example, the original file was 1236.4 KB. Using MP3 compression, we've got the size down to 14.0 KB, an amazing 1.1% of the original file size.

8. By clicking on **Test** now, you'll hear the compressed sound. Notice that it doesn't sound quite the same as your original sound.

    You can juggle the file size against the quality by playing with the MP3 settings until you reach a happy medium. The **Bit Rate** is another way of expressing the sampling rate of the sound: it's found by multiplying the *sampling* rate (in Hz) by the *number of bits* per sample.

9. When you've tweaked your sound to what you consider to be the best balance, click **OK** to choose the settings. If you decide later that your sounds are taking up too much room, you can always go back and change the settings to give a smaller size.

10. Now tweak the rest of the sounds to give the best results that work for you. We'll use these optimized sounds later.

11. Save the movie.

> *Sounds can form a major part of the download for the final movie. If you're using sounds, then it's recommended that you do not simply accept the default sound settings or set the export options globally. Play around with the settings for each sound individually, and choose the most appropriate setting for each one by considering the sound quality you hear and offsetting this against the relative importance of the sound. Be fairly brutal in this, because sound files may make your final web site unviewable if they are allowed to stay large and uncompressed.*

In particular, you might consider:

- Making button 'click' sounds as small as the compression allows – the sounds will be a lot deeper and a bit muffled, but hey, what's the difference between one momentary click sound and another?

- Making less prominent sounds lower quality – if you have a big thumping bass line and percussion up front, do you really need all those background effects to be high quality?

- The human ear is very poor at sensing the direction of deep sounds, so stereo isn't really necessary for them. MP3 takes this into account during its compression, but other methods may not.

We'll end this section with a discussion of the different sound compression methods (called **codecs,** which stands for **CO**mpression – **DEC**ompression). In practice, the only way to be really sure you've used the best settings is to keep on tweaking and testing until you're happy with the audible result.

ADPCM is mainly there for compatibility with Flash 3. It can sometimes give good results for short sounds such as button clicks, but for longer sounds or musical samples it's best to stick with MP3. As always, the only way to be certain is to try them all and pick the one that's best for you.

MP3 is the compression codec of choice for the Internet in general. You'll find that it tends to give the best sound for the smallest file size. It works by splitting the sound up into frequency bands and then applying numerous filters and tricks, based on which sounds the human ear would actually hear. This weeds out redundant information before recompiling the sound.

If you've a definite maximum file size that you can use, then just work your way down the **Bit Rate** menu until the desired file size is reached. You can also select a *quality* to encode the file at. It's recommended that you leave this set to **Fast**, as on slower machines a higher quality may result in your sounds playing out of sync with the rest of your movie. MP3 also allows you to select stereo when going above 16 KB per second, but because of the way MP3 compression works, this won't always make a huge difference. Often on a stereo track, most of the sounds in one channel are mirrored in the other: part of the MP3 compression cycle is to compare the two channels and delete all of the mirrored information from one of them and then just mark the differences in the other channel. When the track is played back, one channel plays in stereo until it comes across a marked difference and it plays that difference in the other channel. By this method, the size of the track is almost halved while still remaining true to the original. MP3 then performs a number of other more complicated routines to get the track size down even further.

Raw has no compression routine and, as its name suggests, it exports raw digitized sound. You can actually reduce the file size by specifying a lower quality, but your final file size will generally be much higher than using any of the other methods. You would only use this method if you were running the final movie from a hard drive in applications such as Flash screensavers.

Speech is a form of compression that is best, predictably, for use on recorded voice tracks. Because voices record at a lower frequency than most sounds, including music for example, this allows you to use a lower sample rate – 5KHz or 11KHz are acceptable. Use this when you have a voice track for your Flash movies.

> *In all the options listed above, it's important to note that putting the sound quality higher than the original imported sound won't produce better quality sound. The quality setting adjusts how good a job Flash makes of compressing the sounds into the SWF and doesn't affect the performance of playback. So, putting the sound quality higher than the original will increase the final file size and add lots of redundant bits that do nothing useful.*

Using sound in Flash

We've already looked at how to attach sound to buttons in our Actions and Interactions chapter. Attaching sound to the timeline is almost identical in nature, but there are additional sound features Flash offers that we've not yet touched on. We'll repair that state of affairs right now.

Attaching sounds to the timeline

This is as easy as it sounds: you create a keyframe, and attach a sound to it. There are, however, several options that can be selected to make full use of the sound, and extra optimization facilities offered by Flash. Although the number of drop-down menus may seem a little daunting, it all fits together in a fluid movement when you're actually adding sound. The best way to illustrate this is to try it.

Attaching sounds to the timeline

1. Continuing on from the last exercise, change the name of the **Soundtrack** movie's default layer to `Percussion1`. Next, insert a keyframe in frame 5. You should now have this basic set-up:

2. Now open up the Property inspector if it's not already open. From here we can attach our sound, and add effects and different timings to it in the process. If the keyframe in frame 5 is not already highlighted, click on it now. Open up the **Sound** drop-down menu from the Property inspector – all of the sounds in your Library will appear in a list:

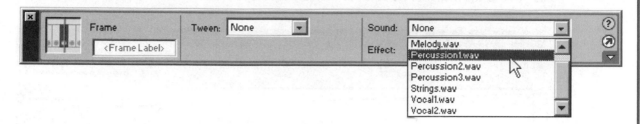

3. To attach a sound to your keyframe you just select it from this list – scroll down the list and click on **Percussion1**. Once you've selected your sound, a little waveform appears in the keyframe:

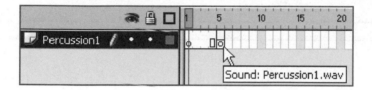

At the moment it will just look like a straight horizontal line because you can only see a small fragment of it.

4. To rectify this, add additional frames by pressing F5 at frame 90 so that you can see the end of the waveform just poking into frame 89:

5. Now test your movie. You should hear a short pause, and then the sound will begin playing at frame 5.

6. Next, click on your sound in the timeline and return to the Property inspector. The next thing to look at is the **Effect** drop-down menu:

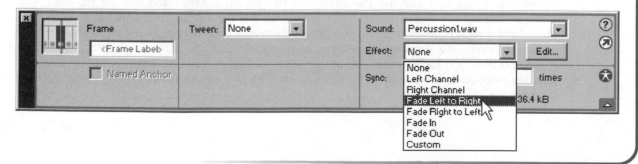

This option allows you to add audio effects via a **volume envelope**. The envelope allows you to see and control the volume in different parts of the sound.

7.   For an example of this, select **Fade Left to Right** from the **Effect** drop-down menu, then click on **Edit** (next to the menu) to be taken to the **Edit Envelope** window:

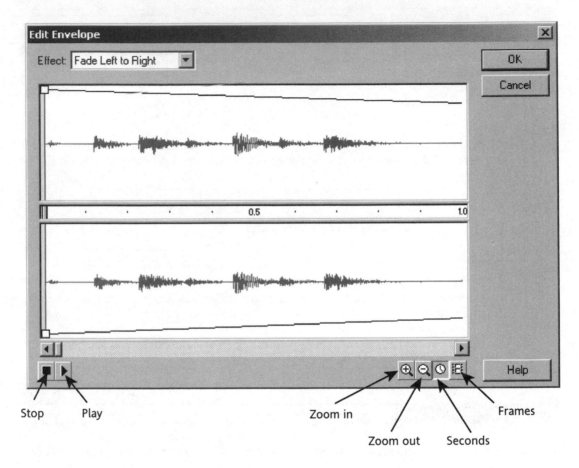

Once the Edit Envelope window appears, use the **Zoom** buttons on the bottom right until you can see the full waveform.

Stereo sounds are split into two **channels**, one for the left speaker, and one for the right. This window contains two panes, showing the waveforms for the left audio channel at the top, and those for the right channel at the bottom. You'll always see two channels, even if the sound you're editing is mono – the one channel will just be repeated twice. The scale between the two panes represents time, and can be measured in seconds or in frames. You can toggle between the scales with the two buttons on the bottom right. You can test your sound at any time by using the **Play** button.

Superimposed on top of the waveforms are a couple of lines with little white squares on either end. These lines depict the volume envelope, and they can be used to control the volume of your sound. The top of the pane represents 100% volume, and the bottom is silence. Because we've selected **Fade Left to Right**, the top pane (the left channel) will have a diagonal line running from the top at the beginning of the sound to the bottom at the end, while the bottom pane will show the opposite. This will mean the sound in the left speaker will start at full volume and drop to nothing, and the sound in the right speaker will start at nothing and rise to full volume, giving the effect of the sound panning from one side to the other.

8.   Press the **Play** button now to hear the effect.

9.   The squares on the lines are control points, much like on Bezier curves, and they can be dragged to change the shape of the envelope – try it now.

10. Drag the control points higher and lower, and use the **Play** button to preview your changes. You can add more control points, up to a maximum of 8, by clicking anywhere on either the top or bottom pane. When you add a point in one pane, Flash adds an identical point in the other. You can easily make some pretty strange sound effects by playing with these settings:

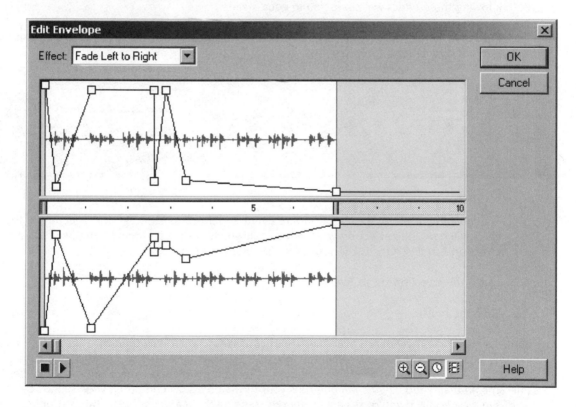

11. To get an idea of some basic effects, run through the **Effect** drop-down list at the top of the window, and notice how the envelope changes to reflect your selection.

Always play your sounds after you make an alteration to ensure you're achieving the effect you want. As with most things, the best way to appreciate how it works is to play about with it and learn by listening to the effects you make. Notice that you can still zoom in and out using the magnifying glass icons while you're editing the envelope – this allows you to be more precise with the timing of the control points.

12. We're going to set the **Effect** to **None**, as we want the sound to start straight away, but feel free to leave your experimental effects on if you wish.

13. Click **OK** to close the window with your chosen effects applied to your sound.

    As you may already have begun to realise, the volume envelope can be very powerful when creating sound effects. For example, the sound of an approaching car can easily be simulated by importing a basic engine noise, and using the envelope controls to make it slowly increase in volume. The same engine noise could also be used to simulate the car moving from left to right across the screen by using the **Fade Left to Right** effect. By clever use of the envelope controls, you could even incorporate both of these effects into the same sound. Many more complicated effects are possible with these controls, but they're beyond the scope of this book. For now, just knowing these basics will stand you in good stead.

14. Open the **Sync** drop-down menu in the Property inspector. This will give you a list of four options – **Event**, **Start**, **Stop**, and **Stream**:

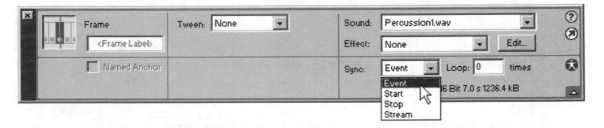

The most important of these options are **Event** and **Stream**. Although the selection of these **Sync** types will have little effect on your movie while you're testing it within Flash, they have a profound effect on how Flash loads the sounds during Internet playback.

15. Leave this selection set to **Event**.

16. Save the movie.

Sounds in Flash take precedence over animations and videos, and follow their own separate 'lifetime'. For example, imagine you have an animation that's 10 seconds long, and a sound that also lasts for 10 seconds. You could tell Flash to *start* them both at the same time and expect them both to *finish* at the same time. In reality though, if someone runs your movie on a slow computer, your sounds can easily get out of sync, especially if you're streaming sounds (sending the file down bit by bit as it plays). If you ran the 10 second animation/sound example on a slow computer, it might get half way through the sound and animation without a problem, but then have to pause the animation as it waited to load the next part of the sound as it arrived down the wire. If it was the other way and the animation was the problem, Flash would try to skip frames to allow the sound to play smoothly.

- The **Event** option tells Flash to treat the sound in the same way as it treats movie symbols. It will only load one version of the sound into its Library when the movie is first played, and will re-use the sound if it has to play it more than once. Event sounds are not played until the whole sound has been loaded, and they're not locked to the timeline. If you have an event sound lasting 10 seconds, but the user's computer is too slow to maintain the frame rate, the frame you would have expected the sound to end on may not be the one that the sound actually *does* end on. The problem with this is that your movie may take longer to begin playing, because Flash is loading all of the sounds before it starts.

- **Stream** tells Flash to start loading the sound directly from the Internet as a constant sound stream. Flash starts playing the sound as soon as it has approximately 5 seconds of the sound loaded. If you repeat the same sound several times, Flash will reload the sound each time, as it's not kept in the computer's memory. Where you have several sounds all streaming at the same time and stopping at the same time, Flash will mix them all together when it creates the SWF file for Internet playback, and will stream back only one channel. Additionally, Flash will lock the sound to the timeline. This means that if the sound gets ahead or behind of the main timeline, Flash will stop or skip frames to make sure the sound stops at the right instant. This can cause choppy animations as Flash tries to keep the frame rate up with the sound, but does ensure your animation keeps in sync with your soundtrack.

Having said all that, the choice of whether to use **Event** or **Stream** is usually easily made. If the sound is relatively short and will be played more than once or looped, select **Event**, and if your sound is a long, non-repeating, introductory tune that has to start playing immediately, then select **Stream**. It's usually more economical to purpose-build tailored sounds from scratch for your movies, which can be easily looped if they need to be. In this case, you'll rarely have to use the **Stream** option, and will therefore save your sounds from having to be reloaded when you want to re-use them.

- The **Start** option is almost identical to **Event**, except that it won't allow more than one version of the same sound to play at the same time. For example, if you have a long sound attached to a button it will normally replay every time the button is pressed and, rather than stopping the first sound if the button is pressed again, Flash will just start playing the new sound over the top of the original one. As you can imagine, this can make a mess of your carefully constructed sounds!

- The **Stop** option does just what it says it does. There's an action to stop all sounds at once, but if you just want to stop one sound, or a limited group of sounds, you would make the soundtrack jump to a frame with this command attached to it. This comes in useful when you have a soundtrack playing in the background and button click noises over the top. If you had an option to turn the soundtrack off, but you still wanted to have your other noises, you would use a button linked to this option to stop the soundtrack playing.

These options will become a lot clearer when we discuss streaming and publishing your movies in the next two chapters.

- The final sound option in the Property inspector is **Loop**. Flash will play the sound from end to end as many times as you specify here. If you leave this set to 0, the sound won't loop – it will play once and then stop. There are numerous tricks you can perform with this option: for instance, if you set **Loop** to a huge number like 9999, and then put a **Stop** action in the keyframe containing the start of the sound, you could create a sound that will effectively play forever – certainly longer than anyone is likely to listen to it. When you have a looping sound, the volume envelope will extend across all of the loops, allowing you to apply fades and effects across the whole sound, not just each individual loop. This is useful for repetitive sounds like car engines and helicopter whirrs.

Now let's examine some of quirks of sound in Flash.

Flash sound issues

There are a fair number of unexpected things that can happen when you're using sound in Flash. These 'features' have put off many otherwise competent Flash web designers from dabbling much further than adding sound to the odd button click in Flash. It's important that you're aware of these from the beginning so that you won't have too much trouble with them later.

- Flash sometimes doesn't seem to like it if you play sound in the first frame of your movie. The Flash Player sometimes seems to get its synchronization wrong if all the sounds start on the first frame of your movie or the first frame of any scene. For this reason, it's a good idea to start all sounds at about frame 5. It's also worth noting that if you have a sound on a `gotoAndPlay` action in a movie with a long timeline and high frame rate, it's a good idea to put the sound a few frames after the destination frame.

- From time to time, Event synchronized sounds may not last as long as they should, or may not sound as if they start on the same frame, even though they are set to do so on the timeline. There's a little trick that you can use to correct this: as well as starting your sounds at frame 5, try adding a new layer with a one-frame sound in frame 4 and setting it to **Stream**. We'll call this a 'kicker' layer, because it seems to kick the Flash Player into action, and make it behave like it should. It doesn't matter which sound you use, but remember to set its volume envelope to nothing, so you won't hear anything when it plays. You'll need to do this for every new scene you have that contains any Event sounds that are supposed to start at the same instant. Alternatively, you can create a very short sound sample specifically for use as the kicker in all your projects. A potential danger with this technique is that if you have a movie with very intense animation, the streamed kicker will force frames to be skipped, including the possibility of skipping other code and sound keyframes.

- **Event** sounds are only synchronized to the timeline when they're started. If, for some reason, the computer fails to keep up with the frame rate, your carefully triggered sounds can start to play too late, leaving gaps and – worse – becoming unsynchronized. There are three ways around this:

  - Change scene often, and have a kicker at the beginning of each to bring Flash back in line. Although this fixes the problem after it has occurred, it doesn't stop the problem occurring in the first place.

  - When you come to publish your movie (more on this in the **Publishing** chapter), set your movie playback to **Auto High**. If you've set your movie to **High** quality, Flash will try to maintain the picture quality of your animations at a maximum, and won't be too bothered about maintaining a constant frame rate. This may result in your sounds being triggered too late, because the timeline itself is 'getting behind'. You can lower the quality to **Auto High** from the **HTML** tab of the **File > Publish Settings** menu. This tells Flash to maintain a high quality until it's in danger of becoming too slow, at which point Flash will drop the picture quality to keep up. Flash can therefore compensate intelligently.

- Drop the frame rate.

- Whether you're producing a professional or home web site, it's still best to test it out on a minimum spec computer. Although this used to be a major issue, it's becoming increasingly less so as the average computer becomes faster. The other option is to forget the issue completely unless someone reports a problem, which is less likely as time goes on, but which still might stop that person from ever returning to your site.

Now that you know about how to acquire or create sound loops, and how to avoid some of the pitfalls associated with sound, it's time to do something a bit more useful than attaching the odd click to a button or a few low-quality sound effects to the timeline.

Integrating sound

In this part of the chapter we'll create a full soundtrack. There are few web sites that actually have such a thing, possibly because of all the problems that've been encountered with Flash's **Event** sound type, so you're now beginning to walk a trail less trodden, one that many before you have been afraid to follow. You may be a beginner, but that's no excuse for being afraid. Enjoy.

Creating a movie soundtrack

A feature of Flash that we've not talked about yet is the **loadMovie** action. This action allows Flash to run *more than one movie at the same time*. One of these movies could be your web site's visual content, and the other one could be the soundtrack.

In this chapter we'll create a soundtrack movie, and we'll show you how to add it to a web site movie when we talk about publishing later in Chapter 13. Our soundtrack will not be like a traditional Flash movie, because it'll have a blank stage – the timeline in the soundtrack movie will control sound only. Don't be put off by this, as it will all begin to blend together when we get to the Publishing chapter. For now, let's paste together the loops we imported earlier and make a polished soundtrack.

1. In your `Soundtrack.fla` movie, you should already have a full, optimized Library, and one layer containing a percussion sound:

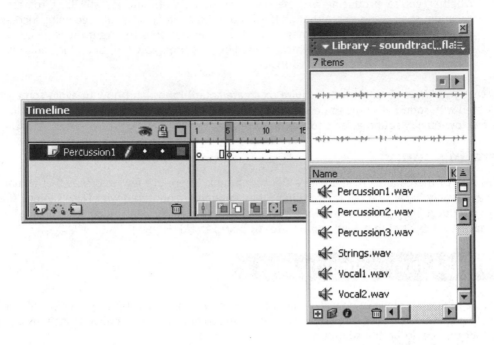

These sounds have been specially selected to allow the creation of a number of different compositions, or in the more modern parlance, they allow different remixes of the same tune. So you can bring certain elements to the fore or delete others to give completely different styles. For example, using strings and melodies for an ambient sound, or focusing on percussion for a more insistent dub sound.

As you saw earlier, the sounds were created for looping and re-use, so we'll be using **Event** syncing throughout. Taking into account the problems that can occur with **Event** sounds, the first thing we must do is add a 'kicker'.

2. Create a new layer and name it `Kicker`.

3. Insert a keyframe in frame 4 of the **Kicker** layer, then attach the **BassLine** sound (although you can use any sound) to the keyframe:

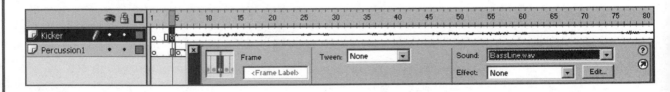

4. In the Property inspector, set the **Sync** drop-down menu to **Stream**.

5. Insert a blank keyframe in frame 5 of the **Kicker** layer. As we've set the sound to **Stream**, we want to make sure that the sound only plays for one frame before stopping. This will do that for us.

6. Click back onto frame 4, and then click on the **Edit** button in the Property inspector to open the **Edit Envelope** window for the **BassLine** sound. Drag the control points to the bottom to set the volume to zero, then close the window:

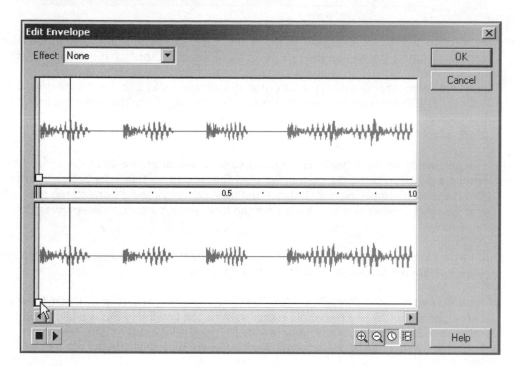

There's no need to change the **Loop** option in the Property inspector because we only want our sound to play once.

7. Because this composition will be long, and it's imperative to know where in the timeline you are at all times (you'll have to be constantly counting beats and frames to sync everything up just right), we'll also add a long 'comments' layer to hold labels. Add a new layer above your **Kicker** layer, and name it Comments.

   The layer will automatically be made to the length of your longest layer – in this case, the **Percussion1** layer. If it needs to be any longer at any stage, you can always lengthen it later. You could also make this layer a guide layer if you wanted, so that it doesn't get exported into the final movie, but since it actually contains nothing but labels, it won't make much real difference.

8. Insert a keyframe in frame 4 of the **Comments** layer, above your 'kicker' sound. Use the **Frame** field on the left of the Property inspector to put a label in this keyframe that reads Kicker & Percussion1 – don't worry if the label is too long for the text field. The labels on this comment layer (overleaf) will let you quickly see what's happening, and when, in your soundtrack (overleaf):

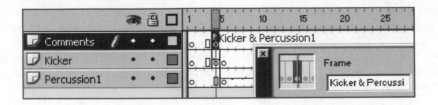

9. Make sure that your percussion sound is set to be an **Event** sound that doesn't loop. Unless otherwise stated, this will be the setting for all of the other sounds, too. Don't forget!

    Just as a safety check, let's make sure that this sample looks like we're expecting it to. In Sonic Foundry's ACID program, the samples were 7 seconds long each. The movie is playing at 12 frames per second, which for seven seconds equates to 84 frames. The sample starts at frame 5 and ends at 89, which seems about right.

    The percussion sound is two bars long, and so for that matter, are all of the other samples. We're writing a dance track, so the pattern we must follow is to do four bars before inserting a change. This is the standard pattern for all dance and most pop music, so it's one to remember. This means that we need another two bars before we can have a new pattern, so we must repeat this pattern once more.

10. Insert a keyframe in frame 89 of the **Percussion1** layer, and attach another **Percussion1** sound using the **Sound** drop-down in the Property inspector.

11. Now play your sound through to make sure there are no glitches in it. Insert frames as you did before, until you can see the whole sound wave on the timeline – this will allow you to easily sync other sounds to the end of it. If your sounds do sound a little out of sync, try moving their starting keyframe forwards or backwards until you find where they sound best.

    You may be wondering why we didn't just repeat the first sample for two loops using the Property inspector. You *could* have done that, but remember that **Event** sounds are only synchronized to the timeline *when they're started*. The longer the event sound lasts before you attach a new version to the timeline, the more chance there is of your sound getting slightly out of sync with the timeline.

    Next, you'll be adding a new loop, **Percussion2**, which is a slightly fuller rhythm with more bass.

12. Firstly, add a new layer called `Percussion2` to put the sound in, and move this layer to the bottom of the list. This means that your layer order follows the order of the samples in the soundtrack. If you need to see all of your layers at once, click on the bottom of the timeline and drag it down until they're all in view.

13. Now add a keyframe in this layer at the frame immediately after the first percussion loop finishes, and attach the **Percussion2** sound to it:

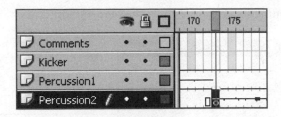

14. Add a keyframe to your **Comments** layer above where you started the new sound and label it `Percussion2`:

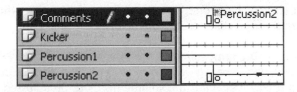

This label is there to remind you that you're now in the second set of four bars, and that you're using the second percussion sample. Documentation of music files is pretty much a necessity. You may recognize all the individual waveforms now, but in six months time when you want to spruce up your web site, and decide on a celebratory remix, it may take you some time to find where each new sound comes in on the composition.

15. In accordance with the four bar rule, repeat the **Percussion2** sound in the same way as you did for **Percussion1**.

16. Next we'll be adding two sounds that will start at the same time in the third set of four bars. Prepare the timeline by adding two new layers to the bottom, calling them `Percussion3` and `BigBang`:

Insert your new sounds in their respective layers immediately after the end of the second **Percussion2** sound:

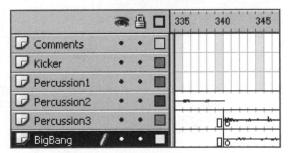

17. Update your **Comments** layer to include the new sounds:

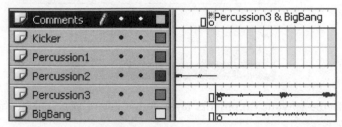

18. Preview your movie to hear your soundtrack. Now that you've more than one sound playing at the same time, you start to have one being overshadowed by the other. This can be corrected by messing about with the relative volume of each track to make for a more pleasing composition.

19. We want to bring the **BigBang** sound to the fore, so open up the **Edit Envelope** window for the **Percussion3** sound, and lower its volume by dragging the control points down a bit. Now return to your movie and play it again. If the volume needs to be adjusted again, go back and drag the points a little lower. Repeat this until you're happy with the results:

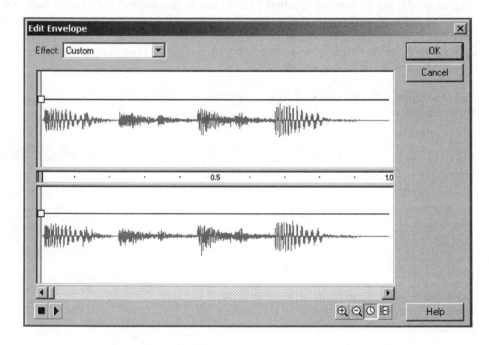

You can also easily bring the volume back up to 100% after the **BigBang** effect has played. By doing this, you can then insert another **Percussion3** track afterwards at full volume without having a noticeable jump in the sound.

20. Look on your timeline, and note which frame the **BigBang** sound finishes in:

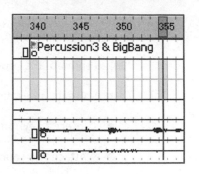

21. Now go back into the **Edit Envelope** window for **Percussion3** and change the timer to frames (click on the button next to **Help** and you'll see the frame numbers of your movie appear in the **Edit Envelope** window).

22. You can now move along the sound until you come to the frame where you noted the **BigBang** sound as finishing, and put another control point in:

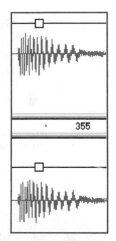

23. Then move about 10 frames forward, to give a gradual volume increase, and put in another control point at 100% in both panes and press **OK**:

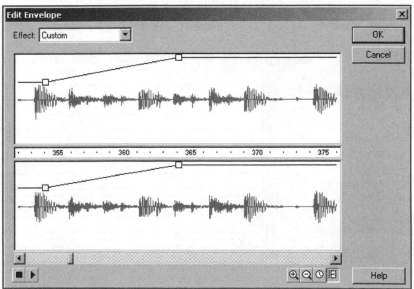

24. Now play back your soundtrack. It should play smoothly all the way through, and you probably won't even notice the change in volume at the end.

So, to sum up, the process for adding new sounds is:

- Create a new layer and name it after the sound.

- Insert a keyframe in the new layer where you want the sound to start.

- Attach the sound to the keyframe using the Property inspector.

- Add a label to your **Comments** layer so you can track what's happening.

- Add enough frames to the layer until you can see the end of the waveform.

- Play the soundtrack and decide if you want to make any volume or syncing changes.

- Make any changes you need to, and play the sound again to make sure you're happy with it.

- Either add another copy of the sound afterwards, or start a new sound on its own layer.

25. Now use the other sounds we've provided you with – or ones you've created yourself – and put them together to create your own complete soundtrack. Don't worry if it ends up quite long; that's what the soundtrack is for – to provide a backdrop while the visitor is at your site.

At the end of the soundtrack, we're going to put in a loop so that a section of it will carry on playing forever.

26. Add a label in your **Comments** layer at the end of your last sound and call it End Loop.

27. Now insert one set of the sounds that you want to carry on looping. Here's our final selection:

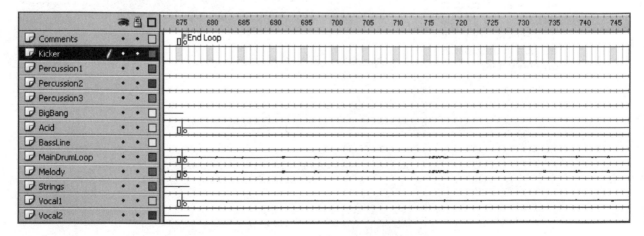

28. Using the sound section of the Property inspector, set all of the sounds in your final loop to play 999 times, which should be longer than even the most avid fan of your music will remain:

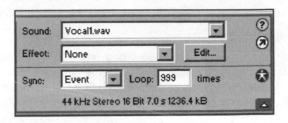

Because the sounds start at the same time, they're synchronized to each other and won't fall out of time with one another. They may fall out of time with the *timeline*, but that doesn't really matter anymore, as no new sounds will be started that need to be synchronized to any particular event.

29. The final thing to do is to put a **Stop** action in the **End Loop** keyframe in the **Comments** layer. If you wanted to have a number of separate soundtracks, say for different sections of your movie, then you could keep them all as different scenes in your one main soundtrack movie, and call them when required. By putting a **Stop** action in here, you're making sure that Flash won't start playing these when it gets to the end of your first soundtrack. Just select **Stop** from the **Sync** drop-down menu in the Property inspector.

That's it, your musical masterpiece is finished. Now just crank up the volume, press play, kick back your heels and enjoy – until you get sick of it and turn it off.

30. Save your movie.

And that's more or less all there is to the basics of putting music in Flash. Simply add or subtract sounds every 4 bars and you're away. The only thing we haven't talked about sound-wise is how to allow the user to turn the sound *off*. Because the control for this will have to be in your web site movie and not the soundtrack, we'll leave that for later.

Well designed sounds that can be seamlessly looped are gold dust to the Flash designer, because they make the production of optimized soundtracks to go with your web site just a matter of dragging and dropping sounds onto the timeline. Also, an understanding of how and how not to lay down sound in Flash will prevent you falling into the traps that befall many Flash beginners. The use of sound in Flash for soundtracks and incidental effects will hopefully help lift your web site design above its mute contemporaries.

Next, let's have a look at how we can enhance our Flash movies using **video**.

Video on the web

The utopian idea of television via the Internet has always been obstructed by user technology in one way or another. The lack of broadband availability is the prime restriction, with streaming being the best solution for large amounts of content.

Video on the web is primarily served through three players – QuickTime, RealPlayer, and Windows Media Player. The most common problem with using these formats within a web site is their lack of integration with the site interface. However, we now have the ability to embed video into Flash itself, eradicating the need to worry about issues such as integration. Now that Flash has this capability, the only real concern is whether the user has Flash Player 6.

Flash uses the Sorenson Spark codec to embed video into Flash movies. Other Sorenson codecs are commonly used to create streaming content for QuickTime, amongst others. The Sorenson Spark codec works by encoding the video data on import, and embedding the encoded video within the Flash movie. When you import a video file from an external source, Flash embeds it directly within its Library.

Let's talk about how to make some video content before we get 'stuck in' with Flash.

Creating video

If you have a Mac with FireWire or have upgraded to Windows XP, then you already have your own resources for generating video content. For several years now, Macs have come with a free version of iMovie, and more recently, Movie Maker was bundled with all copies of Windows XP, meaning that there's an increasing pool of computer owners with the resources to carry out non-linear video editing on their machines.

Non-linear video editing means that your video is on a storyboard that you can edit any part of. Traditional 'linear' video editing dictated that you had to start at the beginning and work your way through the video. If you got to the end and wanted to go back to edit a few frames near the beginning, the likelihood was that you'd destroy anything after those frames.

Digital video (DV) cameras now regularly come with desktop editing software. This was made a lot easier by Apple and Sony's recommendation and development of the FireWire interface (also known as iLink on Sony products), along with powerful yet affordable software like Apple's Final Cut Pro and Adobe Premiere. This has meant that creating movies of excellent picture quality at home has been made possible – somewhat of a revolution. The revolution, which has taken Hollywood by storm, allows anyone to shoot and edit their own features without the expense of reels of film and edit time.

The uses of these technologies aren't exclusive to the bedroom filmmaker. Many Hollywood productions have embraced the DV format, including director Mike Figgis on the film *Time Code*. If all of this talk of DV and FireWire doesn't apply to you though, don't worry – there are still many options available to you.

- **Windows users** – If you don't have a system with FireWire ports, there are many cheap capture cards available that work with analog and DV cameras. Most of these come with some basic editing software to get you going and will enable you to export in a format suitable for importing into Flash. Alternatively, you can buy a cheap FireWire expansion card and join the DV revolution!

- **Mac users** – There's a good chance that if you're reading this, then you have built-in FireWire capability and a copy of iMovie. If you don't have FireWire, then you'll need a capture card or FireWire expansion card to bring in video content. You can then get the latest versions of QuickTime Pro or iMovie for a reasonable price.

With all import options considered, you'll benefit greatly if your footage is shot on a DV camera using miniDV format tapes. The ability to shoot high quality videos is increasing as the price of DV cameras drops and higher quality cameras are released onto the market.

As a cheap investment, FireWire is also worth considering. It is fast enough to comfortably import video, and also allows the application to take control of DV cameras for reviewing rushes – removing the need to fiddle with the tiny play, rewind and stop buttons on the camera!

Flash-friendly formats

Making video suitable for use in Flash is easy. Most (if not all) video editing applications will enable you to export your footage to a suitable format, such as MOV or AVI files. In all cases, try to export the content without any compression and at a reasonable size, because Flash will take care of any scaling or compression on import. Just for the record, here's a list of all the footage that Flash can import on both platforms:

- If QuickTime 4 (or higher) is installed on Macintosh or Windows:

    AVI, DV, MPG, and MOV

- If DirectX 7 (or higher) is installed on Windows:

    AVI, MPG, WMV, and ASF

There are occasions when Flash has issues with importing sound with video clips. To save yourself any problems, it's best to keep your footage saved in its original format wherever possible. That way, you can export the footage in a suitable format for the Flash codec to import the sound with the clip.

Before we begin, make sure you have some video clips handy, or have downloaded the video files that are available on our web site.

Using video with Flash

Now that we know which formats we need, let's import a video clip into Flash.

Importing video

1.   Open up a new movie.

2.   Use **File > Import** to open the **Import** dialog box, and select **All Video Formats** from the drop-down menu.

3.   Navigate to where you have saved the download files and select `redcar.mov`, or locate another clip from your hard disk. Select the clip you wish to import and press **Open** (overleaf).

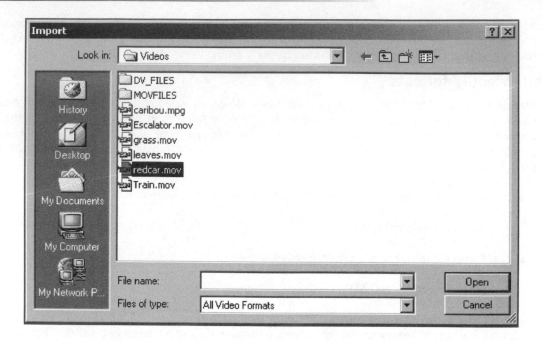

4. In the dialog box that appears, leave the default selection checked – **Embed video in Macromedia Flash document** – and press **OK**:

The other option is used when exporting a Flash movie as a QuickTime document.

5. You'll now be faced with the **Import Video Settings** window and a multitude of sliders and buttons:

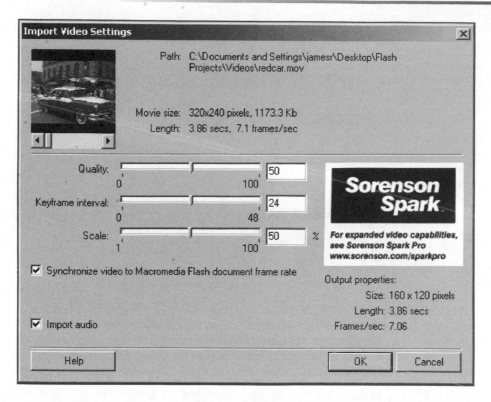

For now, we'll concentrate on importing the video, and will look at the import options available to us in a moment.

6. Drag the **Quality** bar to **100** or type it into the box on the right.

7. Set the **Keyframe interval** to **0** and the **Scale** to **100%**:

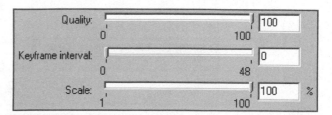

8. Make sure that the two boxes on the left are checked, and that the drop-down menu in the center is set to **1:1**. Your import settings should look like this:

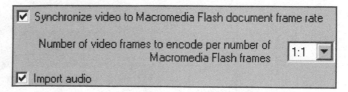

9. Click **OK** to confirm and import the video. You should now be greeted with a progress bar which might take a while – depending on the file size of the clip you imported:

Once this is done, another dialog appears:

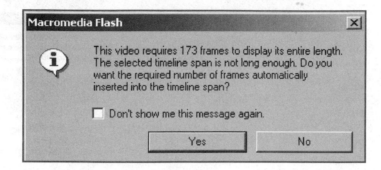

Flash is offering to save us a little time by expanding the timeline to cover the whole contents of the movie – how considerate!

10. Click **Yes** to allow Flash to extend the timeline. You'll now see that the frames in **Layer 1** are extended (up to frame 46 if you've imported the redcar.mov) and the movie is placed on our stage:

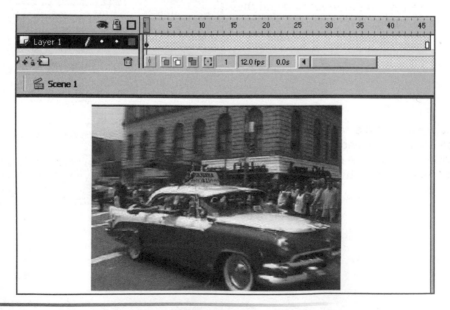

11. Drag the playhead along the top of the timeline and you'll see that the content of the movie changes according to where we are in the timeline:

 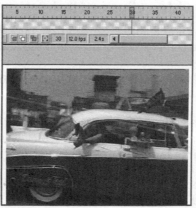 

You might have noticed that although we've imported sound with the clip, there's no visual identifier for the sound. The sound of the clip is embedded within the video timeline and is only heard when the movie is published or tested.

12. Test the movie with **Control > Test Movie**. It's worth comparing our movie's file size – with no obvious compression applied – with the original MOV file. We can preview file sizes with the **Bandwidth Profiler**, which we'll have a more detailed look at in the next chapter.

13. With the test movie still open, select **View > Bandwidth Profiler**:

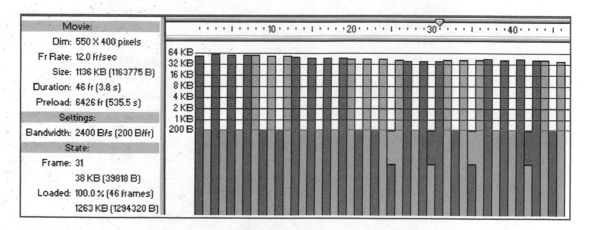

If you look at the left-hand pane of the top part of the screen you'll see that the file size, listed under the **Movie** category, is listed as 1136 KB. The size of the original MOV file is 1174 KB, which isn't a huge saving, but all video clips will compress differently. Clips with a lot of flat color and little motion will compress the most and you'll really be able to make drastic savings in the relative size of your video files.

Let's now move on to have a look at **optimizing** your movies so that your audience get the best experience they can.

Importing and managing video clips in Flash

So far we've imported a video clip file into Flash and have published the movie to see how it runs. We'll now take a detailed look at the compression options, and see how to manage video clips on the timeline.

1. Open a new movie. Choose the **File > Import to Library** menu option, and select the files `Train.mov` and `Escalator.mov`.

   These clips were shot inside the London Underground in miniDV format, imported through FireWire and trimmed in iMovie 2. From iMovie, they were exported as generic QuickTime MOV files in **Full Quality, Large** format in order to maintain a reasonable degree of quality.

2. Click **OK** to begin importing the video files. Flash will now import them one at a time, and present you with the relevant dialog boxes for each clip.

3. In the dialog box that appears select **Embed video in Macromedia Flash document** and click **OK**.

   You should now be presented with the Import Video Settings window for `Escalator.mov`. Let's take a look at the available options in this dialog:

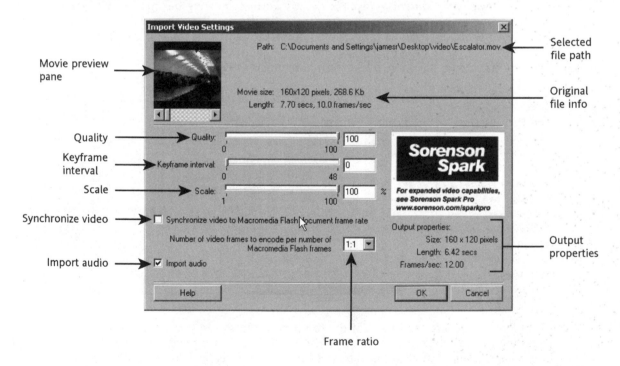

The top half of the **Import Video Settings** window gives information about the clip being imported and the bottom half gives you all the compression options. Let's have a closer look at some of the window's features:

- **Movie preview pane**: A simple preview of the clip being imported. Use the scrollbar to scroll along the timeline of the clip.

- **Selected file path**: The stored location of the clip being imported.

- **Original file info**: This displays the imported video clip's original properties. It shows the physical size (in pixels), the file size (in kilobytes), the length of the clip, and the frame rate. This is a useful field to check against the output properties below.

- **Quality**: The required quality of the clip after importing and applying compression. If you set this to 0, the compression will be high, but the image quality will be very poor. The more compression you apply to the clip, the smaller it will become – at a sacrifice to the image quality. It's best to try changing the settings here for different clips, as you might find that some clips will look better than others following the same amount of compression. The project you're working on might also be restricted by file size, so you need to take this into account too.

- **Keyframe interval**: This is used to control the frequency of complete frames, or keyframes, in the clip. The number you choose here determines the number of frames before the *next* keyframe. In between keyframes, only parts of the image that change are stored, meaning that the file size is smaller. If this is set to a low number, such as 1, a complete frame is stored for each frame of the clip, resulting in a larger file size, but enables the movie to run much better on slower machines.

- **Scale**: This allows you to change the scale of the imported clip. Reducing the size of a clip can save you many kilobytes. Larger movies mean larger file sizes. Videos with lots of movement and fast pans will require more bandwidth and therefore smaller pixel dimensions. For an idea of file size guidelines for different bandwidths, use the following common pixel sizes:

    - Modem users: 240 x 180

    - ISDN: 320 x 240

    - Broadband: 480 x 360

- **Synchronize video**: This option allows you to synchronize the video clip's frame rate to that of the Flash movie. In the event of synchronizing, if the frame rate of your Flash movie is slower than the video clip, some frames are lost on import. This will also reduce the file size as frames are spaced out to replace those that have been removed. If you have synchronized your clip, and choose later to change the frame rate of your Flash movie, you will need to re-import the clip – we'll look at how to do that in a moment. You can get some wacky effects by experimenting with this option!

- **Import audio**: This gives you the option of whether or not to import the audio along with the visual content. In a few cases, such as importing an MPEG through QuickTime, you may not be able to import the audio and will see the following instead of a check box (overleaf):

⚠ The audio in this file can not be imported.

To overcome this, export the movie again from your initial source in an uncompressed format and you should then be able to import it.

- **Frame ratio**: This is the ratio of video frames to encode for each Flash frame. With this option Flash will space out your frames, making the clip run less smoothly, but saving you a few kilobytes.

- **Output properties**: This reflects all the changes that you have made in the options above, showing physical size (in pixels), clip length, and the number of frames per second.

> *Flash caps the maximum frame rate at the frame rate of the movie, so if your clip has a high frame rate that you intend to keep on import, be sure to increase the frame rate of your Flash movie beforehand.*

Now back to the exercise...

4.   Set the Import Video Settings for both clips to those shown here:

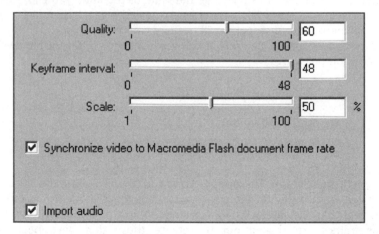

For now we'll be quite conservative with the compression on the clips and then we'll change settings depending on their quality and how much file size we think we should save.

5.   Insert two new layers into the Flash movie and rename your three layers Comments, Train, and Escalator:

As we did earlier in the sound section of this chapter, the **Comments** layer will hold labels signifying cue points, and the other two layers will hold the content. Even though we only have two video clips, it's a good idea to do this in case you expand your movie later on.

6. On the **Escalator** layer, drag a copy of the imported **Escalator** clip from the Library onto the stage. You'll now get a dialog box asking if you want to extend the timeline to the end of the clip:

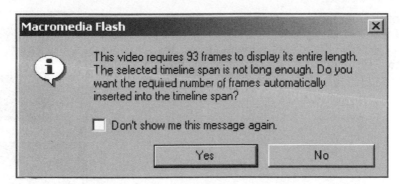

7. Click **Yes** and then center it to the stage with the Align panel.

8. Select the clip on the stage and convert it to a symbol by pressing F8. Make it a movie clip with a central registration point and name it `Escalator mc`. You'll see the same dialog box as before – this time it relates to the movie clip's timeline being extended. Click **Yes** to extend the movie clip's timeline.

Agreeing twice to the same action might seem a little counter-intuitive, but we've extended the length of the main timeline so that our movie clip will play all the way through before reaching the second clip. If we had placed the clip straight into a new symbol on importing to our movie, we would have needed to add frames ourselves. This way, Flash has done it for us.

9. With the Property inspector, label frame 1 of the **Comments** layer `escalator start`. Insert some blank frames to extend the timeline on this layer so that you can see the label clearly:

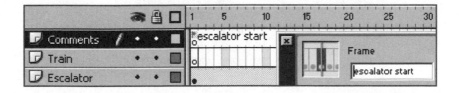

We now need to insert the second clip so that it runs smoothly after our first one – giving our London Underground movie a sense of that Monday morning commuter urgency.

10. Locate the final frame of the escalator movie in the timeline and insert a keyframe on the next frame of the **Train** layer (frame 94):

385

11. Drag a copy of the imported **Train** clip from the Library onto this new keyframe. You'll be greeted with the same dialog about extending our keyframes – click **Yes** to extend the frames in the main timeline. Remember to also insert a keyframe on the **Comments** layer at frame 94 and add the frame label `Train start`.

12. Convert this to a movie clip (F8) called `train mc`, again with a central registration point.

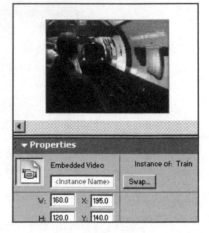

We want the transition between the two clips to be smooth – like a real 'cut' in a movie. So, make sure that your **Train** clip has exactly the same dimensions as the previous **Escalator** clip and is center-aligned to the stage. My dimensions here are 160 (width) x 120 (height) pixels:

13. Once you're happy with how you've arranged your movie, select the **Control > Test Movie** menu option.

14. Before closing the movie, open the Bandwidth Profiler with **View > Bandwidth Profiler**.

You'll notice in the left-hand pane that the size is 378 KB – this figure represents both parts of our movie:

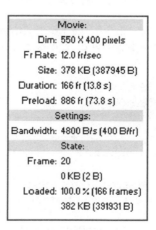

Let's see if we can compress the movie a little more.

15. Double-click on **Train** in the Library to bring up its properties:

Changing your video's visual apppearance

1. Open the `trains.fla` file from the previous exercise.

2. Select the **Escalator** movie clip on the stage.

3. From the **Color** drop-down in the Property inspector, select **Tint**.

4. Tint the video a pink color. As you can see, a color tint can really help to change the ambience of your video clip.

5. Now select the **Train** movie clip, choose **Advanced** from the **Color** drop-down in the Property inspector.

6. Click on the **Settings** button and set the colors as in the screenshot below to invert the color of the movie clip:

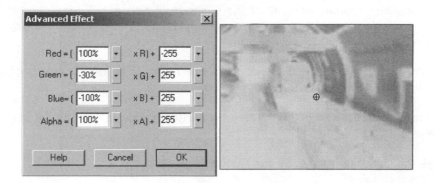

7. Now test the movie and pretend it's a Monday morning after a long Sunday night – the look and feel of our movie has certainly changed from the previous exercise.

What we've done here is just scratch the surface when it comes to using video in Flash. As with other aspects of Flash, video comes alive when you start using ActionScript to manipulate it. Combined with the effects you can achieve by simply adjusting color settings or using the Free Transform tool, you can easily achieve some good-looking results.

The best thing you can do now is go ahead and experiment, but don't forget about the rest of the book – there's lots more for you to learn that can help enhance what you've already discovered so far!

Case study

As a quick amendment to our navigation bar, we're going to add a sound to the buttons' Down state to make them a little more intuitive – when the user clicks on the button they'll hear a short 'click' sound. In this case study we'll import a simple sound from the Flash sound Library.

1. Open up your case study movie.

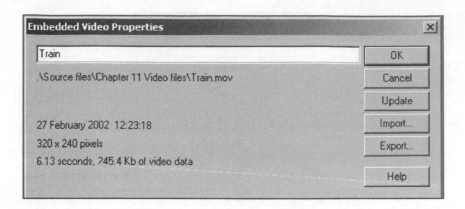

This movie is 245.4 KB, which represents over half of our final movie size. Video with lots of motion does not compress well with most codecs because there is little to reproduce and carry forward from the previous frame. Videos that have a similar background to reproduce on each frame will compress well, such as a newsreader for example – the only changing parts of the image will be the newsreader's motion, while all of the things around them will remain static (unless they're doing an outside broadcast at a speedway competition). This is where the **Keyframe Interval** setting is particularly useful.

We can't really compress this clip much more with regard to reproducing parts of the image. Let's turn the quality down a little to see how it looks.

16. Click on **Import** in the **Embedded Video Properties** window. Select the file again and you'll see the familiar Import Video Settings window.

17. Change the **Quality** setting to **30** and then re-import the clip.

    The Embedded Video Properties window will be updated and this time the size is 163 KB. We've managed to shave a third off its size, but does the image quality make it worthwhile? Test the movie to find out. While certain parts of our movie look a little blocky, the video is still recognizable.

    As we mentioned previously, different videos will all compress differently in Flash and it's best to experiment with each one individually to establish compression settings that best suit the clip you are working with.

18. Save the movie as `trains.fla`.

    OK – that's enough about compression and codecs – let's see what we can do with the video clips to have a bit of fun.

Treating video clips like any other Flash symbol

If you thought being able to import video into Flash was enough – you don't know the half of it. The real power of using video in Flash is that it can be used like any other symbol in the Library. Let's quickly see what we can do with it to make our videos more fun than the Monday morning depicted in the last movie.

If you fancy writing a soundtrack for your web site, don't forget to take a look at the **Sound Appendix** at the back of this book. You could add a background soundtrack for the whole site. Simply create a new layer in your file on the main timeline and import your loop onto the first frame. Set it to loop 10,000 times, which should be long enough for any user's visit at the site.

These are just a few ideas on how you can creatively utilize sound in your Flash movies, but the scope is endless, so go on and experiment.

Summary

If used well, sound and video can add an extra dimension to your Flash movies and web sites. We already knew that we could attach sounds to buttons, and in this chapter we've also looked at how to incorporate multiple sound elements onto the Flash timeline.

We saw that:

- You can import generic or purpose-built sounds and videos into your Flash movie.

- You can process and optimize the **properties** for a sound or video once you've imported them into the Flash Library.

In the **sound** section of this chapter, we saw that:

- You attach sounds to keyframes in the main timeline (or inside a movie clip's timeline) using the Property inspector, which gives you access to an extensive range of panning, volume, syncing and looping effects.

- You can create a complete, independent, soundtrack movie that will play alongside your visual movie – we'll see how to integrate these two components in the **Publishing** chapter.

Finally, in the **video** section, we saw how to:

- Import video clips into our Flash Library and how to manage them on the timeline.

- Re-import videos to optimize their compression settings in the **Import Video Settings** window.

- Affect the visual appearance of our video clips through our old friend, the Property inspector.

We have briefly discussed optimizing our movie settings in this chapter – in the next chapter we'll examine this aspect of creating Flash movies in a little more detail.

2. Double-click on your **about button** symbol in the Library. Create a new layer called sound and insert a keyframe on this layer in the button's Down state. It's a good idea to always add a new layer for the sound element, keeping it separate from the other elements of the button:

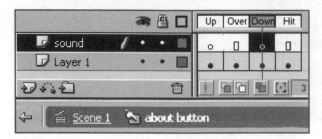

3. Next, let's get our sound. It's up to you what to use here – you could import any sound you've got on your computer, but for this example we're going to use a 'click' sound that's supplied with Flash.

4. Choose the **Window > Common Libraries > Sounds** menu option and choose an appropriate 'click' sound that a button might realistically make when it's pressed, such as the **Plastic Button**. Drag it out onto the stage and it will appear in your **sound** layer:

5. Make sure that the **Sync** is set to **Event** in the Property inspector.

6. Repeat these three steps for the other four buttons in the navigation bar. This time though, you don't need to open up the Common Library as you can retrieve the sound from your own movie's Library.

7. When you've finished adding the sounds, test your movie. All the buttons should now play the sound when you click on them.

8. Let's keep up our good housekeeping habits by dragging the **Plastic Button** sound into the **Buttons** folder of our Library.

9. Finally, save your case study movie and close it.

You now have the beginnings of a burgeoning multimedia web site – animation, sound, interactivity – they're all here.

As this site is our web-based portfolio that we want potential employers to view, it's appropriate to just use a simple 'click' effect here, but the principles of adding sounds to buttons and keyframes in general are the same. It would be exactly the same process as we've done here to add a full-on drum roll or a blood-curdling scream to play when the user's mouse moves over an invisible button – although potential bosses may be a little bemused when they hear a scream as they click to view your work history!

The data that's passed between different IP numbers is directed across the Internet by special communications computers called **routers**. Routers are like switching stations that direct data to its target destination. Each router passes the data that it receives on to the next closest *working* router to the target address. The routers are arranged to be intelligent enough to pick the fastest available route for the data to take. As the network is in a constant state of flux, your data might be directed via an infinite number of possible routes – but the router will do its best to pick the best route for you.

TCP (Transmission Control Protocol) is the technology that *verifies* the data actually got to its destination. IP doesn't care if the packets of data are sent out of order, or even not sent at all. It's up to its big brother TCP to make sure that all the data eventually gets to where its sender intended.

In terms of *hardware*, the Internet looks like a lot of nodes (or computers) all connected together. Although it may seem rather anarchic and organic, there is actually a broad structure.

Nodes tend to be grouped together in clusters, and these have a large, high bandwidth transmission point called a **hub** at their center. Such hubs are sometimes connected together by very large bandwidth links called **backbones**, which connect large population areas or continents.

The Internet then, is a network of physical networks across which you can send, receive, and view text files, using the transport methods of TCP/IP. The **World Wide Web** is a more recent development that came about because there was a need to access multimedia files containing music, pictures, and video across the network of machines.

The World Wide Web

The web consists of two parts: **Browsers** – software that allows the computers that are part of the Internet to read and view multimedia files; and **Servers** – computers that can host and disseminate these documents.

It's the universally agreed components of the web, coupled with the expandability and versatility of the underlying TCP/IP and communications hardware that have made the Internet such a success. One of the key web components is **Uniform Resource Locators**, or URLs. We use these in the same way we use file names, but a URL designates a file that can exist on any computer within a network, such as the Internet. Another component is **HyperText Markup Language** (HTML), which is a system-independent way of telling a browser how to render information.

So, when a client asks you what the Internet is, you can tell them. But one of the key things we need to know about before we put our work out on the net is **bandwidth**.

Bandwidth

Whenever people talk about the future of the Internet, one of the things that's invariably discussed is bandwidth. Bandwidth essentially denotes how much data will travel along a given path in a given time, or how much information a modem can download and how quickly.

Bandwidth is measured in bits or bytes per second – a bit being the smallest individual morsel of computerized data. The higher the bandwidth, the faster things get to and from your computer. Different types of content demand different amounts of bandwidth to let them be used effectively – for example, it takes more bandwidth to download an animation in one second than it does to download a static text page in the same time. Because the size of the 'pipe' you send the data down to a user's computer is fixed by the capacity of their modem, you need to think about the size of your movie, and how long it's going to take to get down the pipe and onto their screen. Photographs, sound files, and video clips all add to the bandwidth required to quickly download a file.

Data sent over the Internet will usually get to its destination, but neither the sender nor the receiver knows *when* this will occur, or the *route* that will be taken. Over time, the average transmission rate becomes fairly constant, but because of the nature of TCP/IP and the way that it parcels data into little packets as they're transmitted, it's unwise to assume a given transmission rate over a short period. Again, there are implications here for the way you design your movies – as you'll see when we discuss *streaming* later.

A full Internet connection is only as fast as the *slowest* node, meaning that slow sections will tend to drag down the average transmission time across the whole network – the difference between a 33.6K modem and a 56K modem in download times was not that great until the transmission lines across the Internet began to be upgraded. Although this 'lowest common denominator' factor is not so much of a problem now, it can still rear its ugly head during peak times, when it's the Internet itself that's the slowest component in the whole system. Here's an example:

A large number of people are trying to access the same server or web page. The closer a router is to the target server, the number of available alternative routes drops, whereas the amount of data being shuttled goes *up*, creating a bottleneck of queuing information. So what do the poor routers do? They give up and throw your data away! You, and everyone else, try again, and the re-tries generate even more traffic, grinding the whole thing to a standstill.

These problems show up sometimes as numerous re-tries and connection losses when trying to connect to popular pages, or a sudden drop in bandwidth for no apparent reason (but most likely due to the loss of a route, causing traffic to be suddenly shoveled onto your local routers!)

So, the important thing to remember is this: the time it will take your potential viewer to download your Flash site file depends on what's in your file and (within the constraints of the Internet we've just discussed) how quickly their computer can read it. This means that when you make a Flash site you not only have to consider *what* you put in your Flash movie file, but *who* you want to be able to see it. Who is your audience, and what assumptions do you make about their computer equipment?

The end user – your audience

If you're coding your site on a super fast dual-G4 Mac, what happens if the user has a slow PC? There have been all sorts of little discussions about this on the Flash newsgroups for some years, spilling over into accusations of elitism and/or Flash snobbery on the one hand, and the 'take no chances' corporate Flash designers on the other.

Here are some general rules to keep in mind before putting your site on the web:

- No user will wait more than fifteen seconds for your site to download if nothing *interesting* is happening at the same time (now read that again) unless you're a cool enough Flash designer to warrant the wait.

- A cutting-edge, designer Flash web site should be viewable using a standard two-year-old computer's hardware configuration.

- A commercial Flash site should be viewable on a standard three-year-old computer.

- The speed of connection you can assume is largely dependent on two things:

  - Whether your target is a business or design audience (assume whatever was 'cutting-edge' 18 months ago), or a domestic user (assume the worst!)

  - The relative affluence of your target audience.

Now you've absorbed all this techno-jargon, you'll be aware just how easy it is to lose your movie file in the digital jungle that is the Internet. To ensure your file survives that jungle environment, it's essential to understand the concept of **streaming**, and to consider how to use it when designing Flash movies for the Internet.

Streaming

As we've said, the bits of your Flash file that will make your site stand out from the crowd – your movies, sound effects, and so on – are the bits that will take a long time to download. If you have them all at frame 1 of the timeline, your user's modem will be unable to download your movie straight away and the user will have to sit and look at nothing until the download is complete. They'll most likely get bored and take their business elsewhere.

However, when streaming is used, your Flash presentation starts playing before all of it has loaded into the user's browser. By starting the Flash page as soon as there is enough information to show *something* rather than waiting until the whole thing has loaded up first, the user has much less time to wait before they can see part of the web site. This means that you can hold the user's attention while the cast of your all-singing, all-dancing, interactive masterpiece of a site is downloaded by the their computer.

> *Well thought-out Flash sites often have a specific scene at the beginning that loads up immediately, allowing the viewer to watch it as the rest of the movie is downloaded. This type of scene is called a* **preloader***, and we'll look at preloaders more thoroughly later in the chapter.*

Streaming, as we saw when using sound in our movies earlier on, is therefore a very good thing. Although it doesn't actually make things load faster down the user's pipe, it intelligently organizes what's needed in the movie and when, so that everything is loaded up in the best order. Used efficiently, streaming can ensure that everything in your movie is downloaded *before* it's needed on the stage, meaning that the movie will play smoothly without any pauses to wait for an image or a movie clip to appear.

When a user requests a Flash web page across the Internet, Flash has to send the user two things:

- The Flash movie's timeline, including attached ActionScripts and 'non-instanced' components (things that aren't stored as symbols) such as text and drawn shapes that haven't been converted into symbols.

- The Flash Library, including the sounds, symbols, and bitmaps used in the movie.

When Flash sends this data across the net, it will send the movie timeline *in frame order*. If the movie is split into separate scenes, it will send the scenes in the order they appear in the Scene panel. Flash will also arrange the transmission of Library symbols so that they're sent in the sequence in which they appear in the timeline.

You can think of our web-bound movie as having two markers traveling along its timeline. The first one is the **streamer**, which tracks how much of the movie has been downloaded and is ready to play. The second is the **player** – which points to the current frame being played:

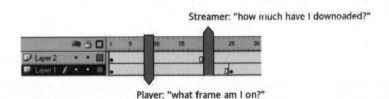

For streaming to work, the streamer always has to be in front of the player. If the player catches the streamer the movie will pause, as it means that the next frame of animation has not yet been loaded. To avoid the player constantly playing tag with the streamer, causing a pause every time it catches up, it's a good idea to give the streamer a head start. We call this head start a **streaming buffer**. A streaming buffer operates by starting off the streaming process before the playback is started, giving Flash the chance to download some of the movie onto the user's computer in advance of the playback starting.

To illustrate this, imagine a movie that has a movie clip symbol called **A** in frames 10 and 30, a graphic symbol **B** at frame 20, and a drawing on frame 40 that isn't a symbol, like this:

Flash would follow this sequence during streaming:

- Start off the streamer, sending the timeline data, beginning with frame 1. As it sends each frame, Flash will also send all timeline ActionScripts. If the streamer reaches frame 10 before the player, movie clip A will start to load. If, during this process, the player catches up to the streamer, the movie will pause as it waits for the movie clip to load.

- Once the movie clip A has loaded, the streamer will race on towards frame 20, leaving the player plodding along the timeline, playing back the content that's been downloaded so far. Hopefully, the graphic symbol **B** will have loaded by the time the player reaches frame 20.

- At frame 30, the streamer sees a new instance of the movie clip symbol **A**, which it's already used once before. It doesn't have to load it up again because the information is already in the Library.

It just adds the instance name (and any other instance-specific information on the timeline) to the symbol template in the Library and recreates the instance without having to download it again.

- At frame 40, the streaming marker sees a drawing on the stage that has not been converted to a symbol. The information for this drawing is not in the Library – instead, it's attached to the frame in which it was drawn. The *streamer* will load the information as part of the frame data, but because the data isn't in the Library, the drawing cannot be re-used in the same way as happened in frame 30, and it will have to be loaded again if it's encountered in another keyframe.

The idea of streamers and players may be a little hard to visualize, but Flash has something that actually lets you see these two markers in action, allowing you to work out how Internet download times will affect your Flash presentation's delivery to the user's browser – and that's what we're going to look at next – the **Bandwidth Profiler**.

The Bandwidth Profiler

The Bandwidth Profiler lets you preview how your movie will behave as it downloads in the real world.

The first thing to be aware of is that Flash's Bandwidth Profiler assumes *constant* transfer rates. Having read the introduction to what the Internet actually is, you'll realize that this is a close approximation at the best of times, and a downright fiction at peak traffic times. However, you can use the profiler to get a good idea of which stages of your movie are going to be problematic for a user to download, even if you can't get *exact* precision for all times.

Using the Bandwidth Profiler

1. Create a new movie and make it 20 frames long by clicking on the timeline at frame 20, and pressing F5:

2. In frame 1, type this – 'This is a test to see how I can optimize this movie using the Bandwidth Profiler' – into a static text box in the center of the stage in 24 point Times New Roman:

> This is a test to see how I can optimize this movie using the Bandwidth Profiler

3. Convert the text into a graphic symbol with F8 or by choosing the **Insert > Convert to Symbol** menu option. Call the symbol **text1**.

4. At frame 1, and under the text you've already placed on the stage, add a new static text box containing this text: 'Flash will be made to load two pieces of text in different fonts, and we'll use the Bandwidth Profiler to optimise the movie'. Use 16 point Arial for this text.

5. Make the text a graphic symbol as before, and call it '**text2**'. Your stage will look something like this:

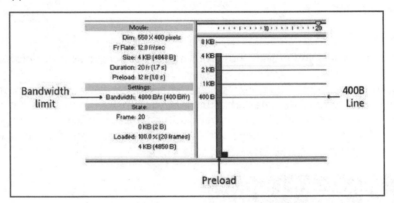

This is a test to see how I can optimize this movie using the Bandwidth Profiler

Flash will be made to load two pieces of text in different fonts and we'll use the Bandwidth Profiler to optimize the movie

6. Test your movie by pressing CTRL-ENTER.

7. While the movie's playing, go to the **View > Bandwidth Profiler** menu option or press CTRL-B. A graph will appear:

At the far left of the graph there's lots of useful looking information under the headings **Movie**, **Settings**, and **State**. To the right is a little bar graph that tells you how much data is downloaded during each frame. Under **Settings**, you'll see something like **Bandwidth: 4800B/s (400 B/fr)**. This tells you the amount of information, in bytes, that can be read per second and per frame. The red line at the 400B point on the graph also shows this. This is the **Bandwidth Limit** and it represents the maximum throughput a particular modem can handle.

Your Bandwidth and Bandwidth Limit figures may read differently from those shown in the screenshot: there are three different values it can have, as you'll see now.

8. Look in the **Debug** menu:

You'll see the numbers **14.4**, **28.8**, and **56K** listed on this menu, with one of them ticked. Do those numbers sound familiar? They're modem speeds, and these options represent the download rates that the Bandwidth Profiler can simulate.

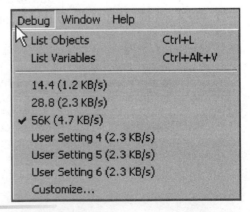

9. Our Bandwidth Profiler is currently simulating download using a 56K modem – set yours to the same.

   If you look under the **Movie** heading in the left of the profiler window, you can see **Size 4KB** and **Preload: 13fr (1.1s)**. This is telling us that the movie is a 4KB download in total. Because everything appears in frame 1 of our movie, Flash has to preload everything *before* frame 1 can be played. This preload time, the time the user will wait to see the movie, is 1.1 seconds.

   Try changing to simulate a 28.8 modem, and if you really want to see how we used to live, try out the 14.4 modem as well. As you can see from the **Size** and **Preload** figures at these different settings, some people are going to have to wait longer than others to see this movie. Now you have a feel for how different modems have different download times, let's see what we can do about it.

   If you look towards the top of the profiler, you can see a little marker that whizzes back and forth while the movie is running. This is the player we described earlier. What a help it would be to see the streamer as well. We can...

10. Select **View > Show Streaming**. Did you catch that? Let's see it again in slo-mo.

11. Choose the 14.4 modem setting from the **Debug** menu and select the **View > Show Streaming** menu option again.

   Nothing happens for a second or so, except some frantic activity going on under the **State** heading at the bottom left of the profiler. Then you'll suddenly see a green band along the top of the profiler. The data in the frames covered by the green band is what has already been loaded.

   The leading edge of this band is the streamer, and the distance the green band is ahead of the player is our streaming buffer.

   In this movie we have no streaming buffer at all. The player catches the streamer at frame 1 as it waits for our symbols to load. We need to go back and redesign our movie to allow streaming to take place so we can spare our user that 1 second of waiting. As I'm sure you'll appreciate, this wait can be a lot longer for more complex movies – but the method needed to avoid it is the same as we're about to use.

12. Close down the test movie screen and go back to the main stage.

13. Delete all the text from frame 1 and add two new blank keyframes at frames 5 and 15:

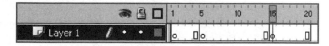

14. With the keyframe at frame 5 selected, drag an instance of the **text1** graphic symbol onto the center of the stage. At frame 15, do the same with **text2**.

15. Test the movie – making sure the Bandwidth Profiler is still running (CTRL-B) – and use the **Debug** menu to set the modem to 14.4.

16. To see the streamer again, go to **View > Show Streaming**.

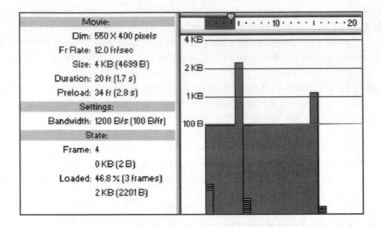

You will see something like the graph above to start with. The green bar, or streamer, will race ahead to frame 4 almost straight away – even on the 14.4 modem – because these are blank frames. These blank frames are our streaming buffer – the time we have to start streaming before the player starts trying to play back the movie in the user's browser. The player will move along at its usual 'frame every twelfth of a second' pace until it catches the streamer at frame 4, where the streamer has been delayed by the first peak in the data graph.

Frame 4 is the *end* of the streaming buffer. The player will now have to wait while the extra data that's needed for frame 5 *(the* **text1** *symbol)* is loaded before it can play that frame.

When you test the movie with **Show Streaming** turned *off*, the extended pause at frame 4 is not shown. By using **Show Streaming**, we're simulating what the movie would actually look like during transfer and playback across the Internet.

However, we can see that there will be a pause before frame 5 just by using the graph. The first download spike on the graph is telling you that the modem can't preload all the data needed before the frame is due to be played:

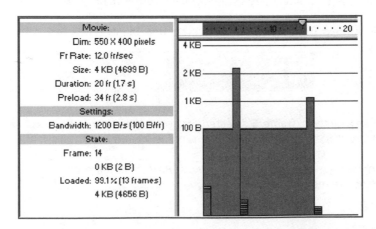

This is perhaps not surprising for a 14.4 modem, as the bandwidth limit allows only 100 bytes per frame to be downloaded.

The spike on the graph also tells us how much we've exceeded the bandwidth limit by, enabling us to judge how long the pause in playback will be.

> *Notice that the profile scale is not linear. This scale, from the 1KB line upwards, is an exponential function of 2. Don't worry if you never paid attention in math when you did exponential functions, all it means here is that every value on the scale is double the value below it. Flash will create an appropriate scale for whatever amounts of data it needs to display.*

We can see that the data contained in frame 5 is over 2KB more than can be downloaded in one frame. The modem we're currently simulating takes a second to download 1200 bytes, so the movie will pause for almost two seconds. To give the modem enough time to download the data for frame 5 we'd need to add over 20 blank frames to the start of our movie – keeping the viewer waiting for playback to start and giving them a very dull first impression of our site.

Even then, our movie will pause once more at the second spike on the graph where **text2** is being loaded, and fixing this will require yet further lengthening of our already protracted movie.

So, on a 14.4 modem it's still very difficult to avoid pauses due to the very low bandwidth limit. In this case you may have to accept that even streaming can't solve the problem. You can easily switch to something more current by selecting the 56K modem from the **Debug** menu:

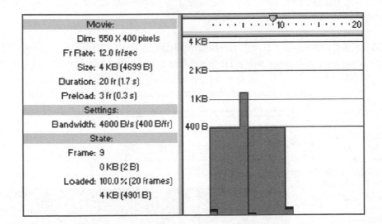

As you can see above, the use of a 56K modem makes the second spike disappear, but you're still stuck with the first one at frame 5 when the data required for **text1** again takes us over our bandwidth limit.

17. Go back to the movie and add three blank frames (F5) before the first keyframe:

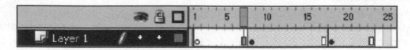

18. If you test the movie now, you'll get a bandwidth profile like this:

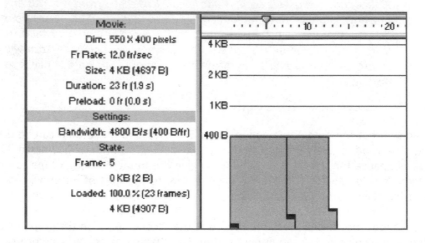

Notice that the bars *never* go above the bandwidth limit. This means that when downloaded by a 56K modem, the movie will run smoothly with no pauses. The streamer will always be ahead of the player because all the data needed for each frame is loaded before it needs to be played – we have given our movie a sufficient streaming buffer.

In short, the movie will look and behave the same whether it is viewed from your hard drive or over the Internet with a 56K modem.

The movie we just created was fairly simplistic, but the theory we applied is the same when you start creating much bigger sites. Here's a bandwidth profile for a real commercial site:

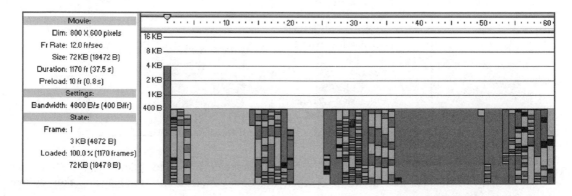

There's an initial preload at frame 1, but after that, the site is always inside the bandwidth requirements of a 56K modem. Why did its designer choose a 56K modem? Well, this particular site was for a nightclub. Its designer considered two of the guidelines we spoke of earlier: who the target audience for the site was, in this case 18 to 26 year olds; and the relative affluence of this audience. Thinking about these factors allowed the designer to reason that the people coming to view the site would have at *least* a 56K modem at the time the site was going out. He or she reasoned rightly, because the hit rate for the nightclub trebled when this Flash site was used!

> *If you see a peak on the Bandwidth Profiler for one of your movies and want to know which frame is causing it, click on the peak and the movie will go directly to the offending movie frame. Remember though, the bar graph is arranged in the order that streaming will take place, and the bar you click on will rarely represent the frame that the numbering along the top of the graph (which is the current frame being played) suggests it should. You can see which frame you have clicked on by looking under* **State** *to the bottom left of the screen.*

As you can see, the Bandwidth Profiler is a vital tool. With it, you can tailor your movie to meet the bandwidth constraints of your target user. With the **Show Streaming** option activated, you can actually see how bandwidth will affect your movie in real time, and alter things accordingly.

There are some sites that don't use streaming at all. Instead, they load the whole movie in one go. For example, Flash animations that lip-sync to sound don't use streaming, as even a slight slowing down of playback would greatly affect the movie. However, the designers judge that their viewers will be prepared to wait for this spectacle.

A lot of 'unstreamed' sites are Flash showcase sites where Flash designers show off to other Flash designers or potential clients. As fledgling Flash users you're unlikely to be aiming your sites at these people and consequently your audience is unlikely to have the same level of technical equipment to view sites as these people do.

For most web audiences, long waits for web sites are a real turnoff. Although the Internet is getting faster all the time, low bandwidths will be with us at least for the shelf life of Flash MX, so we must learn to overcome them. The Bandwidth Profiler is a powerful weapon to have in your armory in this respect.

However, you're lucky that Flash MX is the first version of Flash to harness the advantage of SWF compression. You may not be aware of it, but content created for the Flash Player 6 is compressed when published. Vector objects, text, and ActionScript are all compressed. But be aware – if you are authoring for the Flash Player 5, you'll need to switch this compression off. You can do this by going to **File > Publish Settings** and unchecking the **Compress Movie** option on the **Flash** tab.

Optimizing and fine-tuning Flash movies

There are a number of things you can do to make your movies more lean and compact for Internet download. In this section, we'll summarize all the Flash methods that allow you to achieve responsive sites, before looking at how to optimize space for content on the stage. Firstly, we'll look at what to consider when planning your site.

Structure

Perhaps the most important aspect to get right for a responsive site is a well-defined structure and download flow. You need to sit down and think about which scenes the user will see, and in what order, before you jump into Flash and start creating the movie. For example, an MP3 site would probably consist of the following scenes:

- Preloader

- Intro

- Main

- About

- Downloads

- Links

When visiting the site, the viewer would most likely:

- See the *preloader*, and be taken to the *intro*.

- From there, end up in the *main* scene.

- Because he or she has come here looking for MP3 files, go straight to *downloads*.

- Once they've set off a music file download, the viewer will probably browse the *about* scene to find out more about the music.

- Finally, the viewer will most likely exit from *about* or via your *links* section.

This analysis of the way that your site will be used dictates that you want *preloader*, *intro*, and *main* to be your first three streamed scenes, because these are the scenes that the viewer is likely to look at first. Remember, Flash will stream the scenes in the order that they appear in the *Scene* panel. You can choose which scene to follow these with, but by second-guessing what your audience will do, and streaming the scenes in the appropriate order, you'll make your site more responsive for most visitors. In this case, our preference would be to make *downloads* the next scene, followed by *about*, and finally *links*. If you put your scenes in a random order you have no way of ensuring that the scenes will be loaded and ready to use when they are accessed by the user.

In a slightly more subtle vein, the average user in this example will spend little time in the *main* section, seeing this as just a route to the *downloads* section. You can design that into the site by making the *main* scene easy for the user's modem to download, thus buying time for the *downloads* section to be loaded more quickly as well. Structuring your Flash site in this strategic way is the hallmark of a good web designer. It will come with practice, and all designers will always be somewhere on that particular learning curve, struggling with the same problem you'll face as a beginner!

Use the right components in your movie

Choosing the correct basic pieces to build up your site with is another area where forethought is required.

It's wise to use symbols wherever possible – the reason being that symbols possess two very desirable properties that make them bandwidth friendly. These are:

- The attributes of a symbol (size, color, etc.) can be changed for an individual instance via the Property Inspector.

- Flash downloads each symbol only *once*, and bases all instances of the symbol on the single downloaded version in the Library.

This means that instead of building a blue button and a red button separately, you can have a single gray button that Flash will only have to download once but will use to produce two tinted instances. If you don't make an object a symbol, Flash will not store it in the Library once it has downloaded it, and will have to download it again the next time a separate copy of it appears in the movie.

There's one part that's an exception to this rule: a 'starting credits' movie that you want the user to see first. If this is the case, and you make your starting credits a movie clip symbol, Flash will not begin playing it until it has completely loaded. If, however, you created it as the first scene of your movie, Flash would begin to play the movie as soon as the first frame had streamed in.

The way you use *fonts* in your final movie will also affect the download time. If your movie contains text written in a sans serif font such as Helvetica, a serif font such as Times, and a Typewriter style font such as Courier, all three font files will need to be downloaded before the movie can be viewed. If, however, you use the generic *_sans, _serif* or *_typewriter* styles to write your text in your original file, the text in the downloaded version will be written using fonts on the user's hard drive that match these styles. No font files will have to be downloaded as part of the Flash file, and the download time will be reduced.

In general, every time you use a new font face, Flash will have to download the font shapes you've used. If you're designing a site that contains a lot of text, make sure that you use the same font throughout. Because some fonts look very similar on the screen, you may not notice you're using two different fonts and are inadvertently adding to the download time of your movie. Be wary, also, of using complex font faces:

Before you use such fonts, look to see how big the font files are. They may really look cool, but some really complex font faces can take up to 32K just for ten or so characters, and lead to unnecessary download delays...try before you buy!

Optimizing various elements

It's important to do everything possible to keep the file size of your Flash movie as low as you can. We're going to have a quick look at the tools Flash provides for lowering the amount of data taken up by the *individual elements* of a movie.

Reducing the memory used by vector shapes

1. Create a new movie and add three blank keyframes to the timeline so that there are four in total:

2. Use the Pencil tool, in the **Ink** mode, to draw an abstract shape at frame 1. Make your shape excessively curvy, like ours:

3. Select your shape and copy it. Next, select frame 2 and use the **Edit > Paste in Place** menu option to copy your shape onto the stage in this frame. Do the same at frames 3 and 4.

4. Select the shape in frame 2 and go to **Modify > Smooth**.

5. Select the shape in frame 3 and go to **Modify > Straighten**.

6. Finally, select the shape in frame 4 and go to **Modify > Optimize** and drag the slider to maximum.

The **Smooth** option will make our shape more rounded, in the way that shapes drawn with the 'smoothed' Pencil tool appear, and **Straighten**, as you've no doubt surmised, will make our shape more angular in the way shapes drawn with the 'straightened' Pencil tool appear. These commands can be repeated over and over again to make the shape more and more rounded, or more and more angular.

The **Optimize** option will reduce the number of curves that make up the shape. Like the previous two commands, it can be applied multiple times – but only until Flash reaches a point where no more curves can be removed.

7. Test your movie, and make sure the Bandwidth Profiler is turned on (**View > Bandwidth Profiler**):

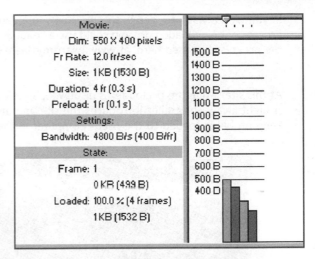

The graph will be the same shape whichever modem setting you use. It shows us that the modified versions of our shape will download more quickly than the original drawing. As designers, we must decide how much we're prepared to alter the appearance of our movie components in our quest for a lower download time.

One designing eye also needs to be kept on the size of any sound clips or bitmap images we use, as the bigger they are, the longer they'll take to download. We discovered how to optimize bitmaps and sound files earlier in the book. We need to balance how much they add to the movie's appeal against how long the user has to wait to see them.

Optimizing tricks and tips

Here are a few ideas that'll get you started on the route to efficient and responsive sites.

As we've said earlier in the chapter, the key to good design is structuring your site so the elements load in the order they're needed. Make sure you load up all the functional and informative components first, such as the buttons that enable the site to be navigated, and let the eye candy that you have put in to show off appear later, as not everyone will be prepared to wait for it.

One question that sometimes pops up is: how do you make Flash load up symbols *before* they're needed? You would need to do this if, for example, you wanted a responsive site and were prepared for Flash to pause at the beginning while essential symbols were loaded up. It's done using a **preloader**. A preloader is a scene created purely to occupy the user's attention while the symbols your site requires for later use are downloaded. Remember, once they're in the Library, Flash doesn't need to reload them every time they appear.

In order to load the symbols without the user seeing them, you tell Flash they're appearing in the frame that's playing, but you place them in the work area *outside* the visible stage. However, you'd want the viewer to be looking at something so that they didn't get bored and lose patience with your downloading site.

So, what a good preloader needs is a simple animation to play as the download takes place, and some informative text to let the user know they won't have to wait too long. You can see a good example of utilizing such a technique while content loads at **www.2advanced.com/perspectives**:

If you don't want to detail specific items that are in the process of being loaded up, you could use a 'loading bar' (like the progress bar used here, at **www.iwantmyflashtv.com**):

At this site, while the preloader is displayed, an initial Flash animation trailer is being loaded that will play straight away. The trailer introduces the site and also simultaneously allows large amounts of content to keep on being loaded to the user's computer in the background.

To give the viewer a 'percentage loaded' figure you would arrange all the objects you needed to download amongst ten frames of the preloader so that each contained 10% of the total download (the Bandwidth Profiler could be used to fine-tune this).

These two methods, however, can be seen as overkill! If you have to give 'percentage loaded' figures as your site is downloading, your download may be too long! Be warned – while Flash designers expecting a fantastic Flash interactive experiment may be prepared to wait for this content, the average web surfer will leave the site before it has even completely loaded. As always, the decisions taken on whether to use a preloader or how you organize the loading of your site's content should always be determined by the user's hardware and motivation for visiting the site.

Loading multimedia on demand

A great tactic for optimizing your web site is to load the content required on demand. Using the `loadMovie` and `loadSound` commands from your base Flash file, you can call in another SWF, MP3, or JPG file. The bonus of doing this is that you only have to call content when the user requires it, meaning that the initial download overhead is much lower. In previous versions of Flash, a Macromedia product called Generator was used to create content featuring MP3s and JPGs, but Flash MX has the ability to call in these files on-the-fly all by itself.

The `loadMovie` command works by loading content into a level above the main movie or into a movie clip target. Here's an example of how the ActionScript command would look when loading a SWF file into a movie clip:

```
mymovieclip.loadMovie ("myfile.swf");
```

It's worth mentioning that content loaded with the `loadMovie` command does not replace any of the content stored in the base SWF. Let's try this out to get a better idea of what options it gives us.

Using LoadMovie to create a functioning record player

1. Open a new Flash movie and save it as `record_base.fla`.

2. Rename the default layer `record player`. Create another two layers called `actions` and `blank`.

3. Draw a simple record player on the **record player** layer. Our attempt is a lovely orange and yellow, with a red arm:

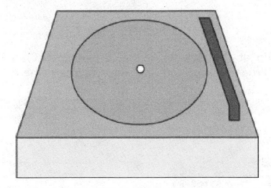

We're going to give the record player a record to play by loading an external SWF file. Until then it's a sad and lonely record player.

4. On the **blank** layer, create a new movie clip symbol called `blankClip`. This movie clip will be used in its current form – totally empty. The reason for this is that we will load the external SWF file into this movie clip.

5. Without editing or adding anything to the movie clip's timeline, click on the back button to return to the main timeline. Drag a copy of the **blankClip** symbol from the Library and place it on the stage:

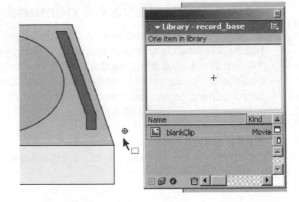

You'll notice that because the symbol is empty and it's selected, it is represented on the stage by a circle and a cross. If you deselect the movie clip by clicking elsewhere (such as on the record player graphic), it's represented by just an unfilled circle:

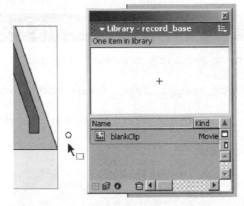

6. Place the **blankClip** at the very top left of the stage (0,0) by selecting it and entering the coordinates in the Property inspector. Give it an instance name of `target`:

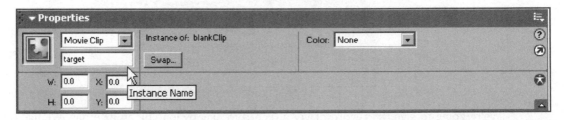

This will be used to load in the external SWF file. Let's add the code to load into our (as yet, uncreated) SWF file.

7. Insert a keyframe (F6) on frame **25** of the **actions** layer. Select frame 25 of your **record player** layer and extend your frames up to frame 25 by pressing F5.

8. Now select the keyframe back on frame and open up the Actions panel (F2).

9. Make sure that the Actions panel is in Expert Mode and type the following into the Script pane:

    ```
    target.loadMovie("record_on.swf");
    stop();
    ```

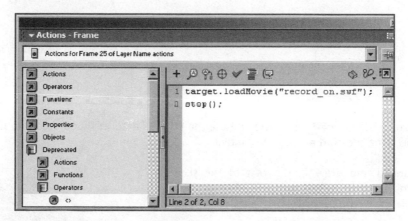

The code here might look a little familiar from the dot notation we looked at in Chapter 10. The **target** instance of **blankClip** will load a movie clip into itself. The movie is then stopped.

If you test the movie now, nothing will happen – if you go to **Window > Output** you'll simply get an error message in the Output panel where Flash tells you that it can't find the file you specified:

So let's give our record player something to play – a nice tune.

10. Save the current `record_base.fla` but leave it open.

11. Open a new movie and save it as `record_on.fla`. If the name sounds familiar, that's because it's the same as we entered in the code earlier.

    The first thing we need to do is match up the record player from the `record_base` file with the new file.

12. Return to the `record_base` file using the **Window** menu and select the record player graphic.

13. Select all the shapes, fills, and lines that form your record player, and copy them (if you're using the graphic from the download FLA, you'll need to ungroup the graphic using CTRL-SHIFT-G):

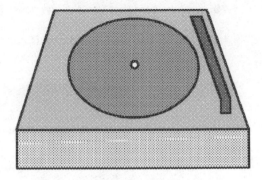

14. Return to the `record_on` movie and use the **Edit > Paste in Place** menu option to position them in the same location as the other movie.

15. Go ahead and draw in the rest of the scene, placing a record on the turntable and moving the needle on to the record:

You may find it easiest to construct the 'playing' record player by drawing each shape or fill on separate layers.

16. Once you are done, save the movie in the same location as `record_base.fla` – this is very important as otherwise the `loadMovie` command will not work. Use **Control > Test Movie** to publish the **record_on** file.

You might not be aware that **Test Movie** actually produces a SWF file. This is all we need.

17. Return to the `record_base` movie and use **Control > Test Movie** again. If all has been done correctly, the record player will be lonely for a short while, and will then be given a lovely record to play. If this hasn't worked, make sure that you gave the **blankClip** an instance name and that both your files are saved in the same folder – these are the most common places to go wrong.

And that's our turntable movie finished. It could do with a little sound and a button to start the record, but now you know how to load in external SWFs, we'll leave this for you to play and experiment with.

Loading video files, MP3s, and JPGs

Now that you've seen how to use the **loadMovie** command using an external SWF file as an example, it's worth knowing how to work with other file formats so that you're able to call these on demand too.

Video

A typical system for working with video files on popular sites (such as **www.quicktime.com**) is to provide the user with a number of different files for their relevant bandwidth. QuickTime in particular has movie trailers for users with 56k, 100k, and 300k bandwidths. The files for the different users have been specifically sized and compressed so that the user gets the best possible experience without the long download time.

What you can learn from this is that this technique can also work for you. By creating a number of different sized SWF files from the same video clip, you can use the `loadMovie` command to simply load in the required file size content on demand. This means that lower end users will not have to wait, and higher end users can view the content in full-blown luscious quality. Neat, huh?

JPG

Flash MX now has support for importing JPGs on the fly, meaning that – as with the video tip above – you can load in content that specifically caters for the user's bandwidth (and patience level!) JPG files can be imported directly using the `loadMovie` command, for example:

```
movieclip.loadMovie ("mypicture.jpg");
```

If you're new to Flash – this will make your work a lot easier!

MP3

As with the JPG import, the ability to import MP3 files is also new in Flash MX. This is a little more difficult to work with and is really beyond the scope of this book. If you are bold enough to try it use:

```
target = new Sound ();
target.loadSound ("mysounds.mp3", true);
target.start ();
```

Now that you've seen how to load content only when it's required, you have a valuable insight into how many web sites are created with multiple SWF movies and dynamically loaded content.

Making the most of space in your Flash movies

Sometimes even the biggest canvas is not big enough to let us splash on a little more paint. If you get the feeling that you're running out of stage space in your Flash movies, then **components** are for you.

Components are objects built into Flash MX for things like forms (such as radio buttons and check boxes) and instant navigation – drop-down go menus, for example:

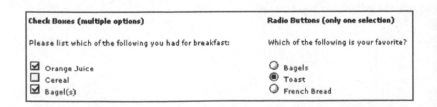

Let's take a look at what components Flash MX has to offer. Open the Components panel using **Window > Components**:

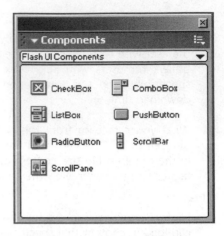

If you're familiar with HTML forms then you will instantly recognize the majority of Flash MX's built-in components. For now we'll be leaving the majority of these alone and concentrating on two component types which can be used to save some valuable space on the Flash stage.

The two components that we'll use in the next exercise are the **ScrollBar** and **ScrollPane**. The **ScrollBar** component is used to provide scrolling functionality for a text box, meaning that any text too big to fit into the text box can be stored easily and the user can scroll through it:

To create a scrolling text box in previous versions of Flash, you would have needed to use quite a bit of ActionScript and also drawn a number of graphics to make the physical shape and color of a scroll bar.

The **ScrollPane** component is similar to the ScrollBar component, but is not limited to textual content and can scroll both horizontally and vertically. The ScrollPane can contain movie clips, graphics, and even video clips. It also has the added bonus of being scrollable by dragging – making navigation even easier.

Both components are excellent for storing extra content that doesn't all fit on the stage, and this extra content can be easily accessed by the user as required.

Let's see how they work.

The ScrollPane component

In this exercise, we'll create a **ScrollPane** to show off a few images within a frame:

1. Open a new Flash movie and save it as `photo_scrollpane.fla`. The first thing to do is create the content for the ScrollPane. All of the images will be placed within one movie clip, like so:

2. Create a new movie clip called `photoClip`.

3.   Use **File > Import to Library** and locate the three image files from the download file for this chapter (ch12_image1.jpg, ch12_image2.jpg and ch12_image3.jpg), or use some pictures of your own:

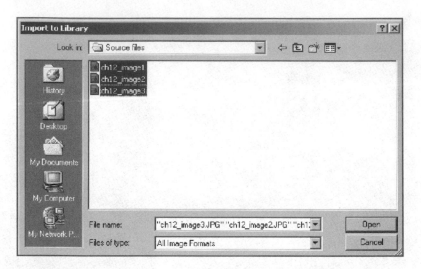

4.   Click **Open** to import the files into your Library.

5.   Within the **photoClip** timeline, drag an instance of the ch12_image1.jpg image from the Library and center it on the stage (check that it's dead center in the Property inspector):

8. Drag a copy of the second image out of the Library and place it to the left of the center image. Use the Align panel to ensure that it's vertically centered:

9. Now drag out a copy of the third image and place it to the right of the center image. Make sure that the images are all vertically centered, and try to position them as close to each other as possible:

10. Select all the images on the stage, group them using the **Modify > Group** menu option and then use the Property inspector to align the whole group on the center of the stage.

The content for the ScrollPane is now complete. Let's use our first component.

11. Return to the main timeline using the back button. Open the Components panel with **Window > Components**.

12. Drag a copy of the **ScrollPane** component out of the Components panel and onto the stage. The parameters for this component will then appear in the Property inspector:

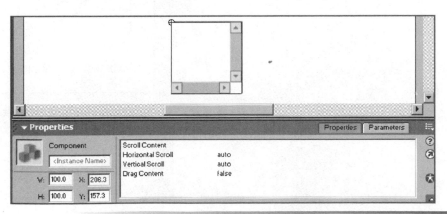

Notice that a new folder has appeared in your Library called **Flash UI Components**. This is where Flash stores all the elements required for this component. You won't need to edit any of the contents of this folder — these are the pre-built component elements that come with Flash MX, saving us some work.

You might also have noticed that the ScrollPane is a bit too small for our images at the moment. It will scroll, but we won't be able to see more than a portion of each image at the same time. Let's resize the ScrollPane so that it's large enough to cover the height of our images.

The height of all our images is 296 pixels. (We can check this by going back into the **photoClip** timeline, selecting the images, and looking in the Property inspector):

13. Back in the main timeline, select the ScrollPane component and set the height (**H**) to 296 and the width (**W**) to 448:

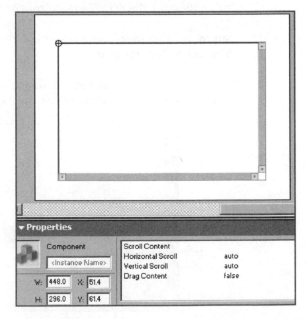

14. We've made the width 448 pixels because this is the combined width of our `ch12_image2.jpg` and `ch12_image3.jpg` imported images. This means that we'll be able to view the left and right-most images in the ScrollPane in their entirety.

15. Center the ScrollPane to the stage using the Align panel with the **To Stage** button switched on.

Now that we've resized the ScrollPane and our image content has been prepared, there are a couple of things left to do: identify the content, and tell the ScrollPane which content to scroll.

16. Right-click on the **photoClip** movie clip in the Library, and select **Linkage** from the drop-down menu. The following Linkage Properties dialog box appears:

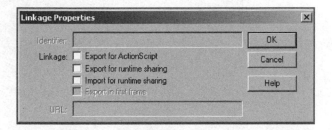

Linkage names are very similar to instance names, but are Library-based instead of being placed on the stage. We won't go into too much detail here because it's getting a little outside the scope of this book, but we'll use it here just this once.

17. Check the **Export for ActionScript** box. The **Identifier** input box at the top of the dialog will now become available. Type the word `photos` into this text box, and click **OK**:

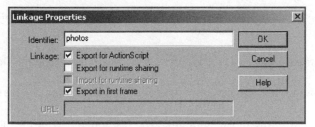

18. Now select the ScrollPane component on the stage and make sure that the Property inspector is open.

We're now going to tell the component what content to use – the **photoClip** movie clip that we just gave a linkage name to.

19. Click next to the **Scroll Content** text in the Property inspector and a blinking text cursor will appear:

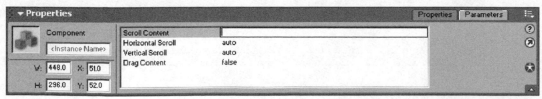

20. Type photos into the box and press ENTER.

21. Now we are ready to sit back and enjoy our hard work. Select **Control > Test Movie** to preview the movie:

The vertical ScrollBar has disappeared from the preview because it was set to **auto** in the **Component Parameters** (listed in the Property inspector). **Auto** means that it will only scroll when necessary, and because our ScrollPane is large enough to house the full height of our **photoClip** movie clip, is doesn't need to include the vertical ScrollBar.

So that's the ScrollPane component. You could go ahead and experiment with the Component Parameters in the Property Inspector.

22. For a good example of how useful the component can be, try setting the **Drag Content** option to **true**:

23. Test your movie again – you can now drag your images around the ScrollPane with the mouse.

24. If you are happy with the movie, and intend to use some of your own images in it, save the movie and close it.

Next, let's take a brief look at the ScrollBar component.

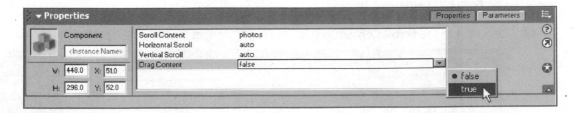

The ScrollBar component

1. Open a new Flash movie and use the Text tool to place a text box on the stage and type the following into it (we're using 40 point _sans):

2. Use the Arrow tool to select the text box and open up the Property inspector.

3. Change the text box type to **Input Text** in the **Text type** drop-down menu:

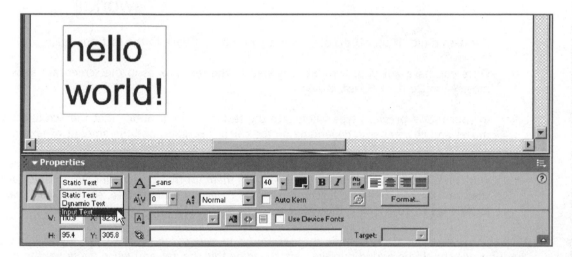

An input text box is a field that will appear in the movie, and which the user can select to type their own text inside.

4. In the lower half of the Property inspector, change the settings for the selected text box so that it is a **Multiline** text box, is selectable, and has a border:

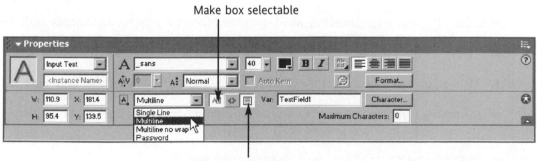

5. Open the Components panel with **Window > Components**.

6. Drag the **ScrollBar** component onto the stage and place it so that it's just inside the left edge of the text box:

7. When you release the component, it should turn into a familiar scrollbar graphic, resized and snapped to our text box:

If it hasn't, pick it up off the stage and try dropping it back in the text box again.

8. Once you have got your ScrollBar snapped to the text box as in the screenshot above, test the movie with **Control > Test Movie**.

9. In your movie preview, type wildly into the text box. You'll notice that the ScrollBar on the left moves and changes size, depending on the cursor's position and the amount of text in the box.

That's our quick example finished. Although ScrollBars don't work with static text boxes, they do work on dynamic text boxes, so you could use them for making scrolling news panes for your web site, for example. Dynamic text boxes will be covered in Chapter 14, so then you'll have the full knowledge to go ahead and create one.

Now that we've finished our section on useful ways to save space on the stage, let's summarize a few questions we should be asking ourselves after reading this chapter and when we are authoring our web sites in Flash.

Last minute checks

Armed with the information from this chapter, we're now able to ensure our Flash sites will be suitable for exposure on the web. When you complete authoring a Flash movie, view it with **Show Streaming** on and ask yourself the following questions:

-   Does the movie run smoothly when using the modem my target audience is most likely to have?

-   Does it ever pause at inappropriate times because of streaming?

-   Is the user made aware that they'll have to wait (and for how long) whenever a preload is required?

-   If my site is running slow because of high bandwidth, what can I get rid of – is the tune that plays every time a button is pressed *really* necessary?

-   Would it be better to load my content on demand?

-   Am I making the most of the space available on the stage and how can I utilize the space better?

Case study

In this section of the case study we'll build the **contact** section of our web site. We'll design the whole **contact** section in a separate Flash movie, and then use the loadMovie command to load in this file when the user requires it so as to save on the initial download time. We'll also import images into Flash from an outside source.

loadMovie is a good way of splitting a large initial download into lots of smaller downloads that can occur on demand. For example, it's more important for the user to see the navigation and structural elements of a web site appear first on the screen prior to any of your content. So, following this scenario, you'd have your movie's main components – such as navigation buttons and the overall shape – download first with the Flash file, and then call the actual content in from outside the movie.

That's precisely what we're going to do now with our case study.

Loading an external SWF on demand

1. Open up your case study movie.

2. Create a brand new Flash file that has exactly the same stage dimensions as the portfolio movie you've been working on (500 x 400 pixels) and name it contact_info.fla.

3. On this new blank stage design your **contact** section information. Bear in mind that you need to keep all this **contact** content within the boundaries of your main movie's content interface, so it might be a good idea to copy the interface shape and use it as a guide in this new movie (but don't forget to delete it when you've finished). Here's a shot of our contact_info file as an example, but feel free to put anything you want in here:

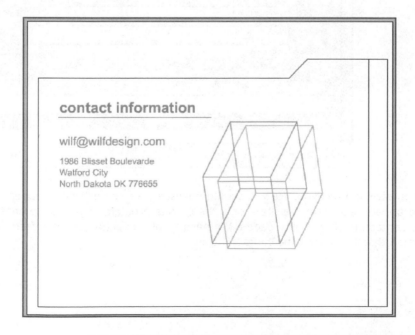

4. Once you've finished designing your contact Flash file, (making sure the interface guide shape is gone) test your movie, automatically creating the contact_info.swf file that we're going to import into our main movie.

5. Open your main case study movie again and double-click on the **content** movie clip. We want the folder interface to be visible throughout the movie, so extend the **scroll buttons** and **interface** layers up to frame 50.

6. Select the **contact** frame on the **actions** layer (it should already be labeled):

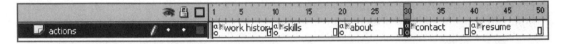

7. Open up the Actions panel (F9) and add a loadMovie command (located under **Actions > Browser/Network > loadMovie**).

8. With loadMovieNum selected in the script pane, type contact_info.swf in the URL field – the name of the SWF file you've just created. Also, change the **Location Level** from **0** to **1**. This will make our loaded SWF sit on top of our main case study movie rather than replace it:

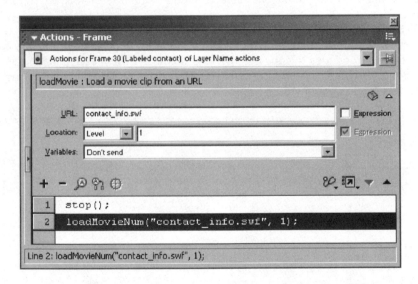

If you save and test your file you should now see your contact movie appear when you go to the appropriate section of the site – only there's one problem: if you go to another part of the site, the contact movie remains loaded. We need to put an action on each frame at the start of each section that will *unload* the contact movie.

9. Select the **work history** frame in the **actions** timeline and go to the Actions panel. Add an **unloadMovie** action using **Actions > Browser/Network > unloadMovie** and set the **Location Level** to **1**:

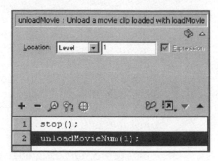

10. Test your movie again, click on the **contact** section, and then go back to the **work history** section you'll now be able to see that the `contact_info.swf` has been unloaded.

11. Add an `unloadMovie` action for the remaining 3 sections of our web site (remembering to always change the **Location Level** to 1). Test your movie and make sure all areas are working properly.

    OK – that's the Contact area of our web site completed. Remember you can keep on customizing these sections we're building as we go along.

Loading external JPGs into movie clips

Let's take a little bit of time to think about how we can optimize our movie further by removing the thumbnail images currently embedded in our file, and making Flash import them when required.

Before starting this exercise, make sure that the three thumbnail images you imported into your main movie's Library are stored in the same folder directory as your case study FLA on your computer. Resave them as JPGs through your computer's default image-editing application as `thumbnail01.jpg`, `thumbnail02.jpg` and `thumbnail03.jpg`.

1. In your **content** movie clip, go to the **work history** section and open up its layer folder.

2. Lock all the layers inside the folder except the **web site thumbnails** layer. Select the first thumbnail on the stage and convert it to a movie clip symbol called `thumb01`.

3. Double-click on it to edit it and delete the picture from the **thumb01** movie clip. Go back into the **content movie clip** – you should now see nothing but the cross hairs in the position where the image used to be. Move the cross hairs to the top left corner of the aqua **invisible button** (it's easiest to do this with **Snap to Objects** switched on):

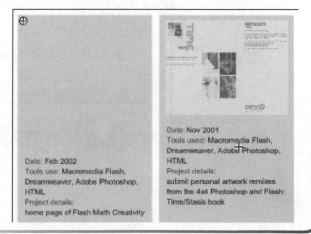

4. Repeat this same step for the other two thumbnail images, converting them into movie clips called thumb02 and thumb03. Delete the images from the clips and, back in the **content** movie clip, line the cross hairs up with the top left corner of their corresponding invisible buttons:

5. Before we start assigning actions we need to give each of these movie clips an instance name. Go to the Property inspector, select each movie clip on the stage in turn (you'll need to click on the cross hairs), and individually give them instance names of **thumb01**, **thumb02**, and **thumb03**, corresponding to their respective number in the movie clip names.

   Now we just need to add the actions to our **work history** section to call the images into these empty movie clips.

6. Select frame 1 of the **actions** layer (the start of the **work history** section) and open up the Actions panel. Add a **loadMovie** action using **Actions > Browser/Network > loadMovie**:

7. Type the file name we want to load (thumbnail01.jpg), into the URL field.

8. Select **Target** from the **Location** drop-down menu and use your **Insert a target path** button to select the movie clip we want to import the image into (deleting the 0 that's in this field already). If you'd rather type the location manually, the path would be:

   _root.content.thumb01

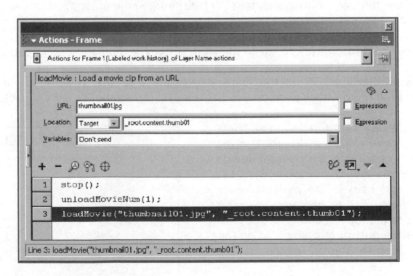

9. Repeat this process so that `thumbnail02.jpg` and `thumbnail03.jpg` will be called into their own unique target movie clips. When you've finished this, the Script pane for frame 1 of the **actions** layer should look like this:

```
1  stop();
2  unloadMovieNum(1);
3  loadMovie("thumbnail01.jpg", "_root.content.thumb01");
4  loadMovie("thumbnail02.jpg", "_root.content.thumb02");
5  loadMovie("thumbnail03.jpg", "_root.content.thumb03");
```

10. Test your movie. Instead of downloading in the Flash file Library, the thumbnail images are now called by the `loadMovie` actions.

11. We'll now go back and organize our Library. Remove the three thumbnail bitmap images you imported earlier in this case study. Importing the images direct to the movie will help to reduce the Flash file size as well as spread the initial download bottleneck on the user's computer, because the images are no longer downloaded with the Library. Also, move your `thumb01`, `thumb02` and `thumb03` movie clips into your work history folder.

12. Finally, save your case study file and close it.

Summary

We've now seen the technicalities of how we make sure our Flash movie gets where we want it to go in the form we intended, and in a way that's satisfactory for the user.

We saw that:

- The **Bandwidth Profiler** lets us see:

    - how our movie will play on the Internet.

    - where the pauses in playback will occur.

- **Streaming** is used to smoothly download the components of our movie before they are needed on the stage.

- A **preloader** can buy us time to download our entire movie in one go.

In the next chapter, we're going to look at the issues involved in preparing our movie for publishing on the web.

Publishing

What we'll cover in this chapter:

- *The different formats available to you for publishing, and when to use them.*

- *How to create the necessary files to get your movie ready for the Internet.*

- *The principles of putting your files on the Internet.*

- *Adding **anchors** to your movie to enhance the user's navigation options.*

OK, so you've spent days – weeks, maybe – creating the perfect movie, and you're bursting to show it to the world, but so far only your dog and a few bewildered family members have been able to see it. Relax – the waiting is over – this chapter is here to help you and your movie make the transition from the cozy world of the local hard drive to the hustle and bustle of the Internet. It's time to go public.

The essential process is this: when you're happy with your movie, you use Flash's **File > Publish** menu option to create a viewable file that you can share with the world. This file can then be put on your web site.

When you're preparing your movie for display on the web, there are a number of different output formats you can choose from when you finally publish the movie.

Web formats

One of the things that's made Flash so successful on the web is its small file size, and this is where publishing comes in. Up until now you've only been working with FLAs – the authoring files where you work on your movie as its creation is in progress. When you publish your movie, Flash compresses the FLA and removes all of the redundant information leaving just the instructions for a sleek, streamlined, multimedia presentation. The default output file from the Flash publishing process is a SWF ('swiff'), but there are several other formats available to you. The more common ones you'll come across, and their usual file extensions, are:

- Flash – `.swf`

- HTML – `.html`

- Animated GIFs – `.gif`

- QuickTime – `.mov`

There's a rich choice to choose from, and you can make things as simple or as complicated as you want. Flash's publishing process means that you point and click to select the output options you want, and Flash does the rest for you, producing files that can be migrated straight onto your web site and put into the public domain.

Let's look at each of the common output formats in turn.

Flash

The full name for the standard Flash file format is **Shockwave for Flash**, hence SWF. The Flash Player is the piece of software that plays these SWF files on the user's browser. The Flash player is now a standard across the Internet, and you can more or less assume that anyone who wants to watch Flash movies already has the Flash Player installed on their machines. In the transition from Macromedia Flash 5 to Flash MX, there's a slight hitch: new movies built in Flash MX are not compatible with the old Flash Player 5, so people will have to download the new Flash Player 6 to be able to see your movies. There *is* an option to export your movie in older Flash formats when you publish it, but by doing this you won't be able to use any of the new features in Flash MX. For most of the things we've covered so far in the book, this won't be a problem, but if you intend to embed video or use some of the more advanced ActionScript techniques you'll have to export your movie in the Flash Player 6 format. It's a trade-off: if you want to reach the widest audience, you'll be advised to always put a Flash 5 compatible movie onto the Internet at the moment, at least until Flash MX has been around for a few more months. However, if you want to show off some of the new functionality you've learned or simply want to publish your Flash movie in a compressed format, you'll have to use Flash MX.

The Shockwave for Flash format is part of a larger standard called Shockwave. This standard is used in Macromedia's Director software, and it means you can incorporate your Flash movie seamlessly into Director. Director is a general multimedia-authoring tool, and is designed to produce multimedia presentations for applications such as CD-ROMs and screensavers, as well as web applications and interactive 3D environments. The main difference between Flash and Director is that Director has been designed for general multimedia, and not just small, size-optimized, web graphics. Director can do many things that Flash is not designed to do, such as use real 3D (using 3D models and cameras) and provide greater synchronization between multimedia streams.

If you ever reach the point where you want to create more heavy-duty multimedia presentations, Director is a good place to start.

HTML

HTML stands for HyperText Markup Language. HTML is not a language in the same way that ActionScript is – it's a **formatting** language whereas ActionScript is a **scripting** language. This basically means that HTML consists of special instructions telling the browser how to format the text and graphics on a web page. It's these instructions or *tags* that are the heart of HTML, and they are also its major weakness. HTML was only designed to present simple text data and static images. At its inception this was enough, but as the Internet has taken off, HTML has looked more and more old-fashioned and heavy. On the plus side, HTML is an integral, universal feature of the World Wide Web. Its ease of use and total compatibility make it a good choice if you want simple information to be readable by absolutely everyone. One of its main features – the ability to have links from one page to any other – was a defining feature that led to the current popularity of the web as a tool for quickly acquiring information. Additionally of course, you don't need a plug-in or player for HTML to work.

The real problems with HTML start when you want to do multimedia. Because HTML wasn't designed for this, you have to use JavaScript (the scripting language that ActionScript is based on), over the top of it, and by doing this you start to lose compatibility. There are new versions of HTML, and other supporting languages for multimedia and wireless devices in the works, but for the time being at least, there will be much less support for them on the web than there is for the Flash Player.

As a Flash designer, you have to know a bit about HTML because it's what carries your movie on the web: to make your movie accessible over the web, your movie file will be hosted inside an HTML file. Luckily, it's easy to publish your movie embedded right in an HTML file, which you can then simply integrate into your web site. As we'll see later in this chapter, all you have to do is tell Flash a few simple things about how you want the final movie to behave in the browser window, and it will generate the appropriate HTML file. You still may need to do other things with this Flash-generated HTML, however, because parts of your HTML document can perform tasks that Flash does not do, like making descriptions and keywords for the web page available to search engines.

Furthermore, most Flash web pages don't just consist of a Flash movie on its own: they're usually made up of many separate elements – things like hit counters and advertising banners – and your Flash movie must integrate seamlessly with these. In this chapter, we'll be discussing Flash's HTML publishing controls, but not the HTML site design and creation side of things: that's a whole subject of its own. We've included a couple of good HTML resource sites in Appendix B, and there are many books dedicated to HTML if you want a more thorough understanding.

Animated GIFs

Animated GIFs were an early attempt at animated content on the web. We've already touched on them briefly when we imported them into Flash in an earlier chapter, but you can also *export* your Flash movie as a GIF. Why would you want to do this? For the simple reason that you don't need a special plug-in to view them. You can guarantee that everyone who can view images on the web (and that really is just about everyone) will be able to view your movie. This is the reason why all banner ads are created as animated GIFs – they're universally viewable, and thus assault the maximum number of eyeballs. You can harness this accessibility in your own sites by having both a Flash, and an animated GIF/HTML version of your site on the Internet, allowing people to visit either depending on their preferences. It's possible to export some or all of your Flash movie as animated GIFs, via the export options, which we'll touch on later.

QuickTime

QuickTime is Apple's Internet multimedia technology. The advantage of using QuickTime rather than Flash is that it can be integrated with other compatible technologies, can be set up to run with QuickTime server-streaming content, and has a large user base. You can embed a Flash SWF file in QuickTime as a multimedia channel, but at the time of writing, Flash MX is not supported – QuickTime 6 (the latest version), only supports up to Flash 5 content. You can also export your Flash presentation as a QuickTime MOV file via the publish options.

So, how do you actually publish the movie?

Putting on the show

Once you've produced your movie, you have to create the necessary files for people to view it outside of the Flash authoring environment. The way this happens is controlled by the settings in the **File > Publish Settings** window:

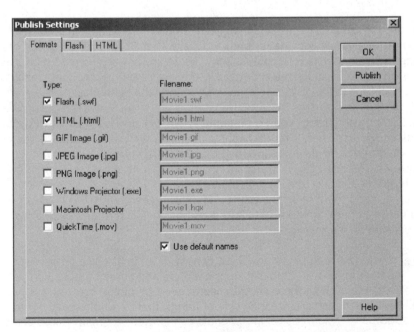

Each of these different formats is for playing your movie in a different environment, such as the Internet, a QuickTime movie, a standalone file that can be run on a computer without the Flash Player installed, or even as a static picture. It's important to realise that the file you've been creating so far won't be the file that's finally used in any of the above applications. The 'work in progress' FLA file will be converted to one or more new files that can be read by the target software.

The general method is as follows:

- Select how you want to publish your movie via the **Publish Settings** window.

- Preview the movie.

- Once you're happy with your Publish Settings, publish the movie.

- Transfer the published movie onto your web site.

Let's walk through the publishing process.

Creating and publishing a basic movie

To start off with, we'll concentrate on the simplest and easily the most popular option: publishing a Flash movie in a form that'll be viewed by anyone who's got a browser with the Flash Player attached. Firstly, we'll create a simple movie to publish.

1. Start a new movie and on the stage write This is a test movie in a static text box using a big, bold font:

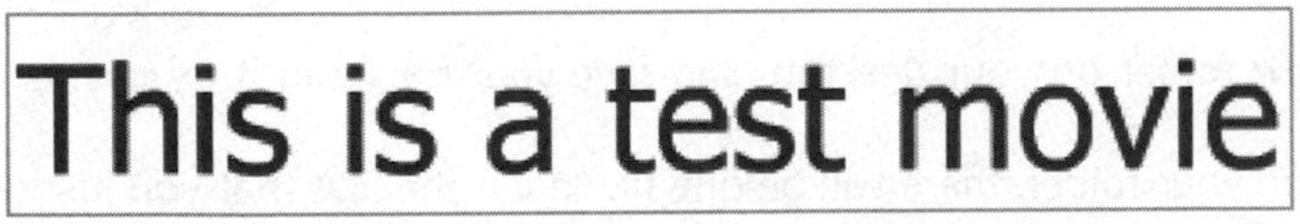

This is a test movie

2. Use the Align panel to make sure your text is in the exact center of the stage.

3. Convert the text into a graphic symbol called **text graphic** with a central registration point.

4. Insert a keyframe in frame 20 of your movie.

5. Using the Property inspector, add a motion tween between the two keyframes and set it to rotate clockwise one time:

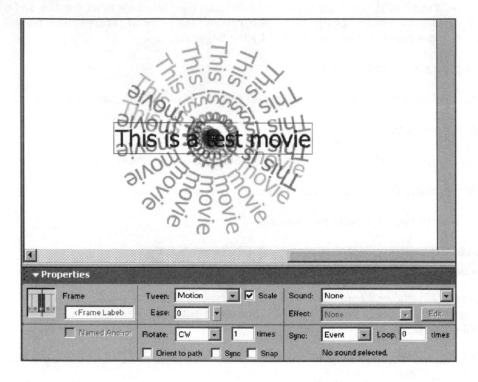

6. Test your movie (CTRL+ENTER). It's a simple movie, but it'll be effective for our purposes here.

7. Create a new folder on your desktop, and save your movie in it as `movie.fla`.

If you look in your folder, there will be one file in it – the FLA that you just saved. When you publish your movie, Flash will automatically put all of its output files in the same folder as the one your FLA is saved in, so if you're building a big project it's a good idea to keep everything in a dedicated folder.

8. Go back into Flash, and select **File > Publish Preview**. A sub-menu will appear with the publishing options on it:

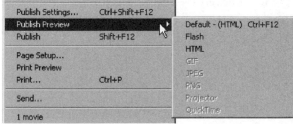

If your copy of Flash is in the same condition it was when you installed it, you'll see three options available: **Default**, **Flash**, and **HTML**. When you publish your movie, Flash will create output files in all of the formats that are in bold letters on the **Publish Preview** menu – in this case, SWF and HTML. By previewing a file, Flash will still publish all of the highlighted file types, but it will open the one you've selected in its associated viewer.

9. Select the **Flash** option: this will take you to the familiar 'test movie' screen.

    When you're on this screen, Flash is showing you what the movie will look like on its own. It has compiled your source FLA file and produced a SWF file, which is what you're seeing being played.

10. Go back to the **Publish Preview** menu and select the **HTML** option. You'll see the same movie, except this time it's being played in your default browser. When you select this option, Flash will create an HTML file and embed the SWF into it.

11. Go take a look at the folder you stored movie.fla in. You'll see that there are now three files in it:

Name ▲	Size	Type	Modified
movie.fla	16 KB	Flash Document	09/03/2002 16:06
movie.html	1 KB	Microsoft HTML Document 5.0	09/03/2002 16:07
movie.swf	2 KB	Flash Movie	09/03/2002 16:07

The SWF is the Flash Movie file that's playable in the Flash Player, and the HTML file is just a text HTML document containing the formatting tags needed to display the page in a browser, plus a link to the SWF (on the eleventh line down in this text):

```
<HTML>
<HEAD>
<TITLE>movie</TITLE>
</HEAD>
<BODY bgcolor="#FFFFFF">
<!-- URL's used in the movie-->
<!-- text used in the movie-->
<!--This is a test movie--><OBJECT classid="clsid:D27CDB6E-AE6D-11cf-96B8-444553540000"
  codebase="http://download.macromedia.com/pub/shockwave/cabs/flash/swflash.cab#version=6,0,0,0"
  WIDTH="550" HEIGHT="400" id="movie" ALIGN="">
  <PARAM NAME=movie VALUE="movie.swf"> <PARAM NAME=quality VALUE=high> <PARAM NAME=bgcolor VALUE=#FFFFFF>
  <EMBED src="movie.swf" quality=high bgcolor=#FFFFFF  WIDTH="550" HEIGHT="400" NAME="movie" ALIGN=""
  TYPE="application/x-shockwave-flash" PLUGINSPAGE="http://www.macromedia.com/go/getflashplayer"></EMBED>
</OBJECT>
</BODY>
</HTML>
```

SWF file
link →

When this HTML file is loaded into the browser, it will give you this result:

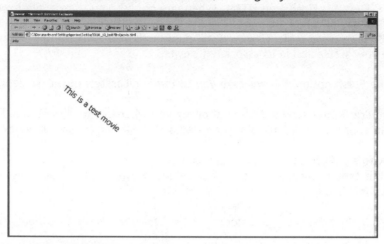

There's a slight problem with the way our movie is being shown in the browser. The size is right – its dimensions are the same as we set in the **Document Properties** dialog box – but it appears in the top left corner of the screen. We can change all that by giving Flash some different publishing settings to work with.

12. Select the **File > Publish Settings** menu option and bring up the **Publish Settings** window:

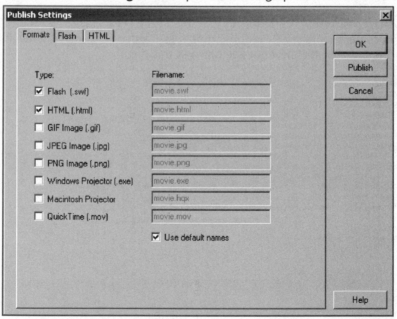

The **Formats** tab of the **Publish Settings** window is where you can select the file formats your movie will be published in. You'll see that at the moment there are check marks in the boxes for **Flash** and **HTML** – these correspond to the options that were available to us on the **Publish Preview** menu. At the top of the window there are tabs corresponding to these two selected options.

13. Click in the **GIF Image** check box, and you'll see a new **GIF** tab appear at the top of the window:

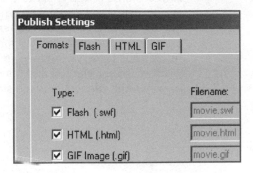

14. Uncheck the box, and the tab will disappear. The tabs contain the individual settings for each of the file types that you've got checked in the **Type** list.

15. Click on the **HTML** tab to go to the **HTML Publish Settings** window:

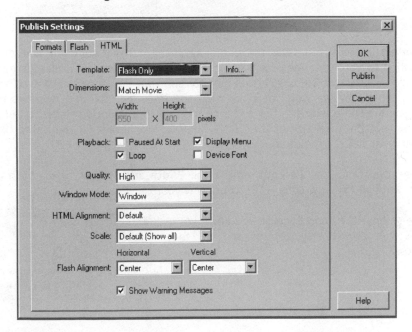

We'll be covering all of the options in detail later in the chapter, but for now, let's sort out getting your movie to play how you want it to.

16. We want the movie to take up the *whole* of the screen when it plays, and this is done through the **Dimensions** drop-down menu:

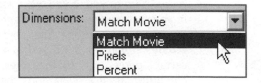

At the moment, this is set to **Match Movie**, so your browser will always keep the movie at the size set in the **Document Properties** window – in this case, the default 550 x 400 pixels. If you resize your browser window, your Flash movie will stay at the same size and will begin to be cut off when the window gets too small:

The other problem with using a pixel measurement is that if someone is using a different screen resolution to you, your movie will come out a different size. If you design your movie to be the perfect size on your 1280 x 960 pixel monitor and your audience are viewing it on their 800 x 600 screen, what they see won't be quite what you intended. You can stop this from happening by changing the **Dimensions** setting to **Percent**. The **Percent** option refers to the size in the browser window, not the pixel size of the movie, so 100% will always fill the entire browser window, no matter what size or resolution it is. Neat.

17. Change the settings to **Percent**, ensure the **Width** and **Height** boxes both read 100, and use **File > Publish Preview** (CTRL+F12) to preview your movie again.

These settings are *good* because you know your movie will always stay central and fill the window:

The choice of which of the **Dimensions** options to use is up to you: if you want your movie to be in an exact area on your web page and remain in the same proportions, then leave the **Match Movie** settings on, but if you want it to play at a certain percentage of the screen size on any computer at any resolution, then choose the **Percent** setting.

18. Go back to the **Publish Settings** window and click on the **Formats** tab.

Notice that each of the file formats has a grayed-out box next to it with the name of your movie in. These boxes show what your movie will be called when you publish it. It's vital to be able to see which of your files corresponds to which format, and if the extensions are not visible on your computer then it can be a problem telling them apart at a glance. For example, GIF, JPG, and PNG will often all have the same icon, as they can be associated with the same program. To make this difference more obvious, it's useful to be able to change the names of the files to suit the format you're saving it in.

19. Uncheck the **Use default names** box:

The grayed-out boxes will now become editable. Change the names of your two selected file types to `movie_flash.swf` and `movie_html.html` respectively:

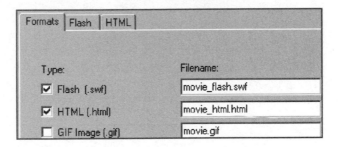

20. Now click on the **Publish** button. If you look in the folder where you originally saved your movie, you'll see a whole host of files there now:

Name △	Size	Type	Modified
movie.fla	32 KB	Flash Document	09/03/2002 16:41
movie.html	1 KB	Microsoft HTML Document 5.0	09/03/2002 16:58
movie.swf	2 KB	Flash Movie	09/03/2002 16:58
movie_flash.swf	2 KB	Flash Movie	09/03/2002 16:59
movie_html.html	1 KB	Microsoft HTML Document 5.0	09/03/2002 16:59

You can see how much quicker and easier it is to locate specific files, and this can be a lifesaver in a large project. Looking in the **Type** column of the screenshot shown above, the **Flash Document** file is your original FLA, and the **Flash Movie** files are the SWFs that'll open in the standalone Flash Player. When you were using the Bandwidth Profiler in the last chapter, the SWF was the file you were testing. You can see here how much smaller the compressed SWFs are compared to the original FLA.

21. Double-click on the `movie_flash.swf` file shown in your folder, and your movie will start to play in the standalone player (provided you installed the Flash Player when you loaded Flash onto your machine, of course!):

22. Close the player and double-click on the `movie_html.html` file, and your movie will now start playing in your web browser.

> *These two files – the SWF and the HTML file – are all that you need to put your movie on the Internet.*

If you wanted, you could delete your FLA file now, and still be able to display your work on the web. This isn't recommended though, as if you ever wanted to go back and edit your movie, you'd need to have the FLA. You should try to keep all of your project files in one folder so you can easily find them again if you need to. It's also always a good idea to archive your FLAs onto CD or some other backup medium.

Now that you've gone through the process once, we'll take a more detailed look at the different publishing options, examining how and why you'd use them.

The many faces of Flash

Flash is a powerful creature, but it's a modest creature as well. It recognizes that while it can do a lot of things, it can't do *everything*. For this reason, there are many different publishing options, allowing you to do much more with your Flash movie than just create a SWF.

1. Open the **Publish Settings** window, and check *all* the **Type** boxes. A tab will appear for each type.

2. For ease of reference later, go through and change the name of each file to include its format as you did before. The **Projector** files are standalone executable files that don't have any options, so we won't be looking at them here. These files are used if you're creating movies for viewing off-line, such as screen-savers, or if you want to e-mail your movie to a friend, and they don't have the Flash Player. The projector files contain a miniaturized Flash Player inside them so people can view your movie even if they don't have a Flash Player installed.

3. When you've finished, you'll have a screen like this:

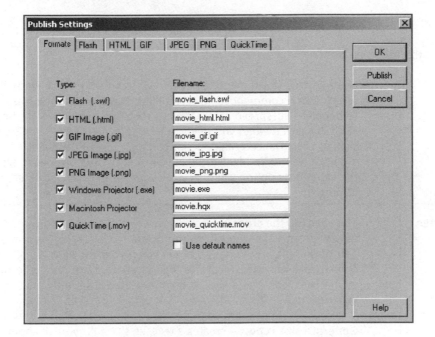

The two most important and influential tabs are **Flash** and **HTML**, so we'll focus on these two.

Flash file publishing options

The **Flash** tab is where you specify exactly how the SWF file will be created:

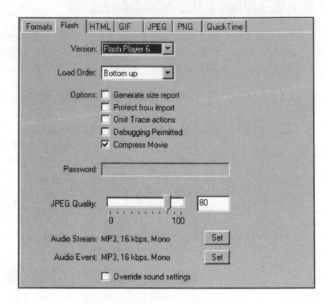

It contains the following options:

Version	Use this drop-down menu to specify which version of the Flash Player you want to use. You're recommended to select Flash Player 5 until the Flash Player 6 has time to become widespread across the Internet. The only time you should definitely use Flash Player 6 is when you need to include some of Flash MX's extra functionality, such as the advanced ActionScript commands. You can tell which commands these are because they're highlighted in yellow in the Actions panel. Also remember that the QuickTime option will only work with Flash 5 files (or earlier versions of Flash) at present.
Load Order	This specifies the order in which Flash will load the *layers* for the first frame of your movie. It can either load from the bottom layer up, or from the top layer down. This option only really has an effect when your movie is being viewed over a slow connection, when the failure to load layers that are critical to display first – such as the layer containing the navigation buttons – could result in a degraded user experience.
Options	**Generate size report** – creates a text file that tells you all about the final SWF file. The file can be useful when you're optimizing your movie, as it gives you a frame by frame breakdown of the movie's size, and useful information about any symbols, sounds, pictures, and text that you have in there. The exact content of this file is a bit beyond the scope of this book, but it's fairly straightforward when you view the file. **Protect from import** – this stops anyone from taking your SWF file and importing it back into Flash, and then copying all of your hard work.

Omit Trace actions – makes Flash ignore any **Trace** actions you might have included in your movie. **Trace** actions are commands that allow you to track the value of a variable in your movie and display it in the Output window while the movie is running. This is very helpful for you when you're debugging your movie, but you don't want it popping up when someone else plays your file.

Debugging Permitted – allows you to use the Debugger panel on the final presentation, which can be selected from the Flash Player pop-up menu. This is useful for you when you're trying to track any bugs in your final movie, but again, it's not something that you normally want other people to be able to use. It's also possible to password protect this option by putting a word into the **Password** box. This permits only those who know the password to use the debugging options.

Compress Movie – allows Flash to compress the Flash movie on publishing. As mentioned earlier, ActionScript code, video, and text benefit most from this, but vector shapes are also compressed. This option cannot be used for movies intended for use with player versions earlier than Flash Player 6.

Quality

There are **Quality** settings for imported artwork and sounds. These are global settings, and they will only affect the movie components that you did not optimize separately. As you discovered in earlier chapters, it's always best to optimize all aspects of your movie separately, as this allows for the best compression to quality ratio. There's an option to **Override sound settings**, but you should never need to do this.

HTML file publishing options

The **HTML** tab specifies how you want to configure the HTML file that will be published. For those of you who want to fine-tune the default Flash-generated HTML by hand, the appendix on HTML and Flash at the back of this book explains the key issues, and expands on the use of Macromedia Dreamweaver with Flash.

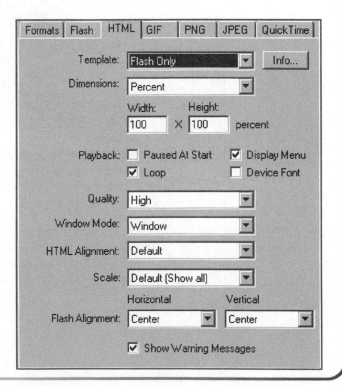

Template

This specifies the type of HTML file you want the SWF to be embedded into: each different template will include specific types of HTML tags that allow you to extend the HTML file's functionality:

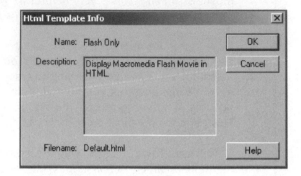

The **Info** button will give you a brief description of the selected template, and which file it is. The HTML template files are actually kept in the **Flash MX/First Run/HTML** folder, so if you're an HTML whiz and want to change them, back up the originals and have a play.

The **Flash with Named Anchors** option is a major new addition in Flash MX:

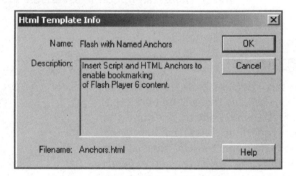

This option allows you to take control of the browser's back and forward navigation buttons, allowing a more familiar form of interaction for the less experienced web user. We'll look at this in more detail shortly.

In most cases, the **Flash Only** option will be fine.

Dimensions

As you've already seen, this allows you to change how your movie is displayed on the screen. You can use your movie dimensions, specify another movie size, or scale your movie to a percentage of the user's browser dimensions.

Playback	**Paused At Start** – means the user has to tell the movie to play before it will do anything.

Checking the **Display Menu** option will allow the user to see a menu if they right-click on your movie:

This menu allows the user to control the playback of the movie, change the movie quality, and zoom in and see all that lovely vector detail. Switch this off if you want to stop the menu appearing.

Loop – will play your movie continuously if selected, or only once if it's not. This option is overridden by any stop actions that you have, and can also be overridden by the user.

Device Font – replaces any static text in your movie with a system font, which can cut down on file size.

Quality	This option allows you to set the rendering quality that your movie will play at – the lower the quality setting, the faster it will run on a slower computer. You're recommended to set this to **Auto High** to allow Flash to drop the quality to maintain frame rate and synchronization if it needs to. It's not worth worrying about setting this to a low quality – if the user's having problems with the quality, they can change it themselves at their end.
Window Mode	These options affect how some advanced Dynamic HTML commands can interact with your movie in certain browsers. Most of the time, you'll want to leave this set to **Window**.
HTML Alignment	This allows you to specify the position of your movie window inside the browser window. **Default** will center the movie, and the other options will align it along the desired edge.

Scale	If you've changed the size of your movie with the **Dimensions** option earlier, you can use this option to define how your movie is scaled to fit into the browser window.
Flash Alignment	These two options allow you to set the vertical and horizontal alignment of your masterpiece inside the movie window, and how it will be cropped if it needs to be.
Show Warning Message	When this box is checked, any errors that are discovered when the HTML file is played – things like images that aren't where they say they are – are displayed as messages on your screen.

Until you become more familiar with the intricacies of HTML coding, you won't need to alter many – if any – of these options. The **Dimensions** are the most important things to be aware of at this stage, and you can experiment with the rest when you become more experienced.

Using anchors in Flash

In previous versions of Macromedia Flash there were a few flawed usability issues, one of which was the Flash movie ignorance of the browser's back and forward buttons.

Because of the way that HTML web sites have conditioned the user into pressing the back button frequently during a session, coupled with their unawareness of the medium, some web sites constructed entirely in Flash quickly became annoying. Many of these web sites simply had unclear navigation, and the button issue didn't make it any easier.

With the release of Flash MX, this issue has now been overcome by using **anchors**. Anchors are major stop off points along the main timeline that enable the user to navigate around a web site using the browser's back and forward buttons.

Let's go and try out this new feature to get a clearer idea of how these anchors work.

Placing anchors in your Flash file

Anchors are placed by adding a frame label and ticking the named anchor box below it in the Property inspector:

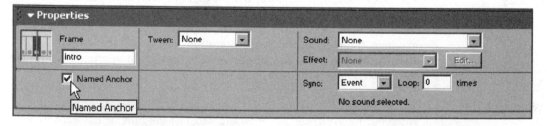

Anchors can only be placed on the main timeline of your Flash movie.

Let's make a quick example to see how they work and how the Flash file is published:

1.   Open a new Flash movie and save it as `anchors.fla`.

2.   Add four layers to the existing **Layer 1**. From the top downwards name your layers: `Actions`, `Anchors/Labels`, `Buttons`, `Fruit`, and `Text`.

3.   On the **Buttons** layer, create four buttons named Main, Apple, Orange, and Pear:

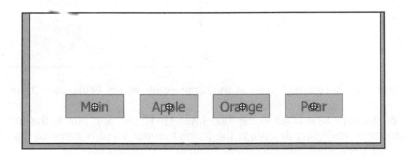

4.   On the **Fruit** layer, insert keyframes at frames 10, 20, and 30.

5.   At frame 10 draw an apple...

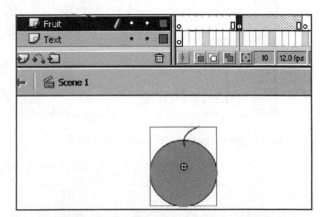

...on frame 20 draw an orange...

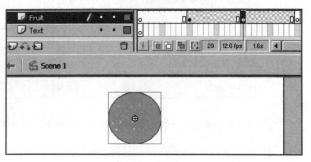

...and on frame 30 draw a pear:

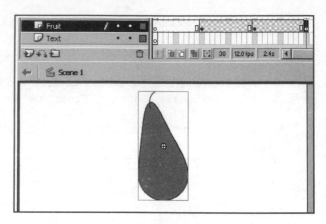

These will signify different parts of our movie's timeline as we move between them. To be extra sure that we know where we are when the SWF is running, we'll add some text to the fruit keyframes.

6. On the **Text** layer, insert keyframes at the same points as the **Fruit** layer (frames 10, 20, and 30).

7. At each of the four keyframes in the **Text** layer (1, 10, 20, and 30), in the top left corner of the stage, add some static text describing the frame number and the name of the page, for example:

 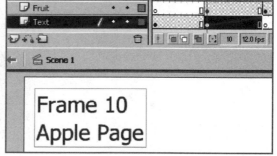

So far, your timeline should look like this:

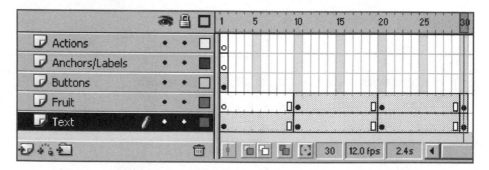

Now we need to add some anchors to our movie.

8. On the **Anchors/Labels** layer, insert keyframes at frames 10, 20, and 30.

9.　Label frame 1 `main` and tick the **Named Anchor** box below the **Frame** box in the Property inspector:

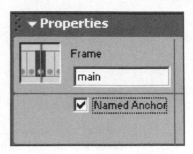

You've just created your first Flash anchor. Congratulations. It wasn't so difficult was it? No time to bask in the glory; let's add the other anchors.

You might notice that the little red flag in the timeline (which denoted a frame label) has gone all sea-worthy and changed to an anchor shape now that you've checked the **Named Anchor** box.

10.　Insert the following anchors at the appropriate frames:

- **apple** at frame 10

- **orange** at frame 20

- **pear** at frame 30

11.　Click in frame 40 of the **Actions** layer and drag your cursor down to the **Text** layer. Press F5 to extend your timeline so that you can fully see the **pear** anchor label.

Your timeline should now look like this:

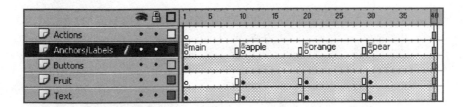

Now let's add some actions to our movie.

12.　Firstly, add keyframes at frames 10, 20, and 30 of the **Actions** layer.

13.　Select all the keyframes on this layer individually (not forgetting the keyframe at frame 1) and add a **stop** action to each one.

This will stop the timeline from running on to the next fruit before we have finished with the current one.

Let's now add some simple ActionScript to the buttons we made earlier.

14. Select the **Main** button and open the Actions panel. Attach this code to the button:

```
on (release) {
gotoAndPlay ("main");
}
```

15. Go ahead and add the same code to the other buttons, substituting the '**main**' anchor name for the individual fruits' anchor names. Make sure you get these right.

The quickest way to do this is to cut and paste the code from the **Main button** and make the minor anchor name change for each of the other buttons.

Once you've done this your movie is finished – the only thing left to do is publish the page correctly. Earlier on in the chapter we looked at the **Publish Settings** window, where the HTML template for publishing **Flash with Named Anchors** is located.

> *Testing that the anchors in your movie work must be done in a browser environment such as Netscape Communicator or Internet Explorer. If you were to test this movie within Flash, the anchors wouldn't function because there are no back and forward buttons.*

16. Open the Publish Settings window using **File > Publish Settings**.

17. On the **Formats** tab, make sure that both the **Flash** and **HTML** boxes are checked.

18. Go to the **HTML** tab and select **Flash with Named Anchors** from the **Template** drop-down menu:

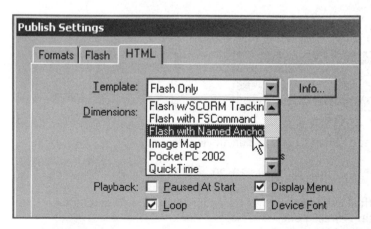

This will mean that when you publish our movie, a HTML document will be created with a little code included to make the anchors functional.

19. Now click **OK**. Select **File > Publish Preview > HTML** to open the Flash movie in a browser:

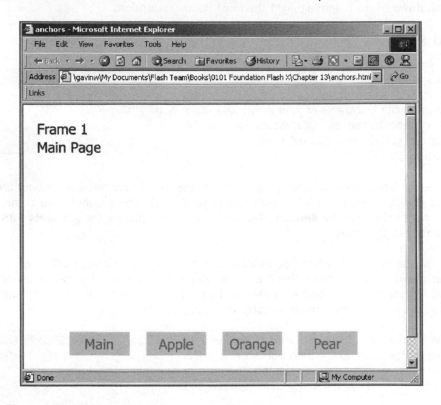

Go ahead and test the anchors. From the main page, click on the **Pear** button to open the Pear page and then press the browser's back button. It will return you back to the main page. Pretty neat, huh? This will save your visitors and yourself a lot of headaches and makes the whole navigation experience a lot more intuitive.

20. Save your file and close it.

Most web users don't care what application the page is created in as long as they can use the features familiar to them. This new anchors feature also enables the user to add the Flash page to their Favorites or bookmark it too.

> *At the time of writing, anchors inside Flash files do not work correctly in IE 6 browsers. Hitting the back button in IE 6 simply takes you to the previous anchor you set in your Flash timeline. So, evaluate whether or not you really want to include anchors in your Flash site, and then assess the proportion of your potential visitors who will be accessing your site using IE 6. The choice to include anchors is up to you, but be aware that they won't work properly yet in IE 6.*

The remaining publishing formats in the **Publish Settings** window are fairly self-explanatory. We'll give you a brief run down of them and highlight the most important options.

GIF, JPG, and PNG

These bitmap export options are of particular interest to the Flash designer, as they allow the easy creation of both a Flash *and* an HTML version of your web site. All of these formats will publish the first frame of your movie as a static image. The exception to this are GIFs, which can also be animated. You can specify an individual frame for Flash to publish by putting #Static as a label on that frame:

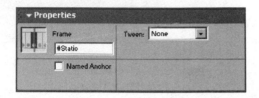

GIF seems to be the best option for publishing a static image, as GIF compression routines are well suited to Flash's solid colors. If you use a lot of gradients in your movie though, these can come out horribly dithered – it's worth checking the **Remove Gradients** box and replacing the gradients with solid colors to achieve a better quality image.

GIF files can also be *animated*. When you publish your movie as an animated GIF, Flash will save each frame of your movie as a GIF frame that'll then be played through in a flipbook manner to give the appearance of animation. This is best for HTML versions of sites, or for doing small animations such as advertising banners that you want to be viewable on all computers.

If the image you're exporting contains a lot of gradients or imported artwork, the best option is to publish it as a JPG file. As you move the **Quality** slider to the left, the file size gets smaller but the quality of the image deteriorates – and vice versa:

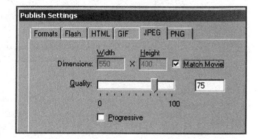

It's worth playing with this option in conjunction with the **Publish Preview** option to find the best balance for your image. There's also an option to set the image as a **Progressive** JPG. This is a method for loading images on slower computers: the computer will load an interlaced version of the file (say every 5TH line), then progressively fill in the image one set of lines at a time.

PNG is the only image format supported by Flash that includes an alpha channel for transparency. Remember that a transparent GIF can only be fully transparent, or fully opaque, but a PNG image can contain *degrees* of transparency. To use this option, you must have the **Bit Depth** set to **24-bit with Alpha**:

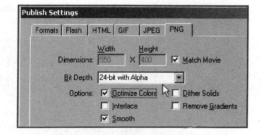

QuickTime movies

Publishing your movies in QuickTime format allows you to use it with other QuickTime files. The Flash movie will be published on its own 'track' inside the QuickTime file, and this can then be edited from inside QuickTime Pro – a program from Apple for the creation and editing of QuickTime files. The options here control how the Flash track will interact with other tracks inside the movie, and which type of QuickTime controller to use to play the movie. It's a good idea to check the **Flatten** box, as this tells Flash to build all of the external files (such as graphics or movies) into the final QuickTime file, allowing it to be played as a standalone file on any computer. If this box is *not* checked, the final file will be smaller, but it will depend on links to the external files. If these files are moved or renamed, the movie won't display correctly.

Now you've got your files together, the final hurdle is getting them up to the server and onto the Internet.

Uploading your files to the host web site

To finally make your movies available to the viewer, you need to upload them onto your hosting server so that people can access them over the Internet. This task is always fraught with danger the first time you ever do it, but like riding a bike, after you get it right once it'll just seem to come naturally. The options available to you when you upload your files will depend on the Internet Service Provider (ISP) you're using, and it would be impractical to provide you with instructions on how to do it all in detail. We'll cover some of the basic principles here, but always check with your ISP to make sure you know all of its distinctive ins and outs.

The key stages in the process are:

■ Choose your ISP and establish how much space they'll give you for your web site, and what features they'll support.

■ Find out the specific upload locations and procedures for your ISP.

■ Transfer your movie files up to the host site based on these procedures.

The first problem you come across when you're getting your web page up and running is knowing exactly which files you need to upload. The only files that you need are your SWF and HTML files: remember that the FLA file is just the authoring file, and it isn't required once you've published your movie. Also, you don't need to upload any of the fonts, images or other external files, as Flash will embed these into your final SWF movie.

The second problem you'll come across is knowing what to *call* your HTML file. If the file is going to be a page inside your web site then you can call it whatever you like as long as you include a link to that filename from another web page. If, however, your movie is going to be the *first* page of your web site, you'll need to rename it according to the protocols of your ISP. Typically, the first HTML page of a site is called index.html, but you'll need to check this with your ISP. When you type a web address into your browser, you'll normally just type the URL, for example **www.friendsofed.com**, and the browser automatically searches for the web page called **www.friendsofed.com/index.html**. It's just a convention designed to save people from having to type **/index.html** at the end of every web address. If you did not rename your file, the user would have to know to type **www.friendsofed.com/movie_html.html** into their browser to get to your movie.

The final hurdle is actually getting the files up onto the server. To perform file transfers to the server you use a special protocol called **ftp**, which stands for **file transfer protocol**. You can either use a shareware program to do this (see Appendix B for some web resources), or one of the many site creation programs, such as Microsoft FrontPage or Macromedia Dreamweaver, which contain built-in features to help you upload your files.

From here, you pass beyond the bounds of Flash, and out into the brave new world of the Internet.

Case study

We're almost there with our case study web site. With the addition of the **resume** section our content will be finished, but we're going to save that part for the next chapter when we'll have learnt some more ActionScript techniques.

For now, we're going to set up the necessary files on our hard drive that you'll need to upload your web site onto the Internet.

First, we want our movie to play back fast so that users don't have to wait as long when they navigate through the different sections of the web site. To do this we'll need to change the **fps** rate (frames per second) to a higher speed.

1. Open up your case study movie.

2. Go to **Modify > Document** and set the **Frame Rate** to 40 in the Document Properties dialog box. This will make our movie play back very quickly. There is no need to do this to the contact_info.swf file that is called in when the user clicks on the **about** button, since loaded movies will automatically match the fps of the base movie:

    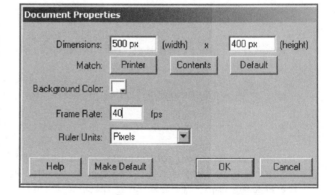

    (Remember, you can also adjust the fps through the Property inspector.)

3. Go to **File > Publish Settings** to bring up the **Publish Settings** window. On the **Formats** tab check the **Flash** and **HTML** boxes (the **Filename** may be different to the screenshot below — it'll be whatever you have chosen to save your case study movie as):

    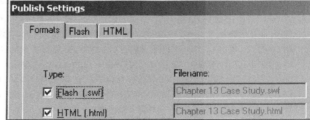

4. On the **Flash** tab set the **JPEG Quality** to **80%**. This will shear off a bit from the file size, but not so much that it will degrade the quality of the images we have imported:

5. On the **HTML** tab uncheck the **Display Menu** box so that the menu does not appear when users right-click on the movie.

6. We also want to make our web site scalable in the user's browser without distorting the proportions of the movie. To do this, select **Percent** from the **Dimensions** drop-down menu and leave the **Scale** selection as **Default (Show all)**:

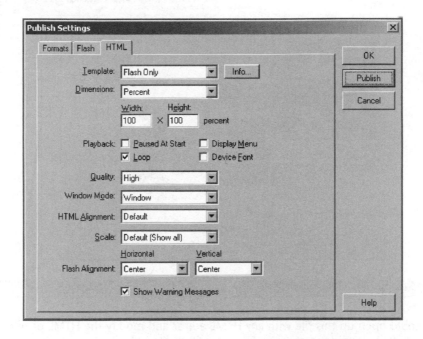

7. That's it! Press the **Publish** button and then look in the folder on your computer where you've stored all the files for this case study:

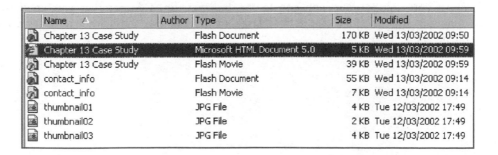

The HTML file has been added here and you can run it to test how your SWF file looks, embedded into the HTML page:

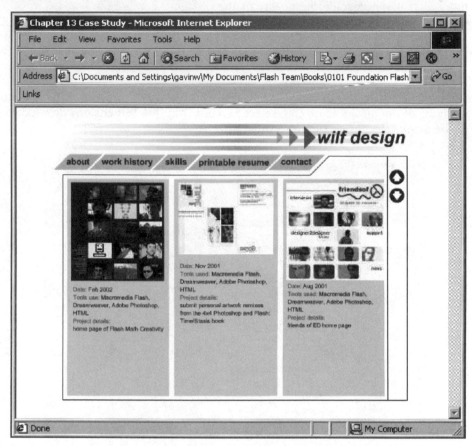

You could open up this file with any HTML editor and modify the HTML page or, indeed, create a new HTML page from scratch to place your Flash file inside.

8.   Save your case study file and close it.

When you upload your web site to the Internet, don't forget that you need to include the `contact_info.swf` and all the thumbnail images, because these are external files that your main movie will call on.

*To further optimize your movie, try checking the **Compress Movie box** on the **Flash** tab in the **Publish Settings** window. This is a new feature in Flash MX that significantly reduces the size of the final SWF you produce. However, player versions earlier than Flash Player 6 cannot decode this new compression feature, so you need to be sure about your target audience and what player version you expect them to have. To be on the safe side though, and to ensure that visitors to your site can definitely see your portfolio, publish without the new compression feature. This will make your movie suitable for Flash Player 5, and we know that most users will then be able to view our portfolio. Maybe later on – when more people have Flash Player 6 – you might want to reconsider whether or not you use this new compression feature.*

Summary

In this chapter, we've given a brief survey of the issues related to getting your finished movies ready for viewing up on the web.

We saw that:

- Flash has **publishing options** that will build all the output files you need to get your movie online.

- The most common publishing option for Flash is to embed a **SWF** file inside an **HTML** page.

- Flash will create the HTML file that hosts your movie, and you can tweak the HTML if you wish.

- You can adjust the way your movie displays in the user's browser – and other attributes too – by manipulating the values in the **Publish Settings** window.

- Flash MX includes the option to add **anchors** to your movie, enabling users to navigate your site using the back and forward buttons in their browser.

- Once you've created the viewable files, you need to consult with your ISP about getting your files up on your web site.

In the next two chapters, we're going to delve deep into the heart of ActionScript and give you a taste of the future.

Intermediate ActionScript, Part 1

What we'll cover in this chapter:

- *The first steps of intermediate ActionScripting:*

    - *Planning larger scale ActionScripts.*

    - *Basic input and output.*

- *Taking ActionScript further:*

    - *Flash MX dot notation: the logic of a Flash movie's internal structure, and why dot notation is a major advance.*

    - *Getting movies to talk to each other using dot notation in ActionScript.*

    - *Animating objects dynamically with ActionScript and user input.*

So far in this book you've gained enough Flash know-how to earn the grade 'beginner' – you're not a novice anymore, that's for sure. However, the rest of the book is going to take you beyond this and enable you to earn your wings as an 'intermediate' Flash user. The impressive effects on cutting-edge Flash sites will no longer baffle you – after the next two chapters you'll have an insight into the methods that top Flash designers use to create those cool-looking sites.

This is the starting point of your road towards mastering Flash and this chapter, along with the next, is going to teach you the three main programming techniques you need to get going on your journey. They are:

- Intelligently breaking down a problem and forming a structured plan to resolve it.

- Treating a movie clip symbol as an **object** and understanding its relationship to the main timeline *and* to other movie clips.

- Object-oriented programming.

We'll cover the first two points here, and introduce the basics of the third so you can hit the ground running when we get to Chapter 15.

From now on, the book has a much steeper learning curve than in the previous chapters, and assumes you know how to attach basic actions (which we covered in Chapters 9 and 10) without being shown all the steps explicitly. However, we want as many readers as possible to get their wings and so if, after reading the relevant section, you feel you haven't mastered one of these skills, go back and practice a little until you get the hang of it. The things we'll discuss in this chapter are the things that will make the difference between a plain vanilla Flash site and one that's packed with interesting and engaging features.

Planning a complex ActionScript: practical overview

This chapter's author has worked in several 'software heavy' environments before going into multimedia and web design. These were at the sharper end of the equation: from industrial display systems up to safety-critical computer-control systems at nuclear plants. Working with this intense level of coding teaches two things about effective programming which are equally applicable to complex ActionScripting – which is really programming by another name:

- You must start by looking at the *problem* and *not* the solution, and then refine the problem until you have a collection of simpler problems to solve.

- You must treat these individual problems as small, self-contained tasks, and be able to code and test each small solution as you go along to make sure it's working properly. Once the discrete components are tested and working, you can integrate them and test again.

We're going to put these ideas into practice by modifying the Smiler movie we created in Chapter 10.

Some people are very sensitive about their age, so when you're asked, 'How old do you think I am?' by anyone, you need to reply with care. If you guess close, you'll please them. But if you're a long way out, in either direction, you're likely to offend, and may need to retreat quickly.

We're going to make our Smiler equally sensitive about its age. Fishing for a compliment, it'll invite you to guess its age. If your guess is way wrong, it'll put on a big frown, but as your guesses get closer to its actual age, the happier Smiler will get. When you guess dead right, you'll see Smiler's broadest possible smile.

This is going to involve quite a big change to the existing Smiler code. Following the advice above, the first question we need to ask is, 'what exactly is the problem we're trying to address with our complex ActionScript?'

Defining a problem

Is 'guessing Smiler's age' the ActionScripting problem? No – that's the *user's* problem. We're creating the code for Flash to *deal* with the user's guess. Let's think about exactly what we want Flash to do by walking through the user's typical interaction with Smiler – this will help us identify the contours of the problem and the sub-problems that it's composed of:

1. We want to define a number that the user doesn't know – Smiler's age – and we want to constantly check this number against the user's guess.

2. We want to detect when the user is wrong and, if so, by how much, and then convert the size of the user's error into an expression on Smiler's face.

3. The more wrong the guess is, the more Smiler will move towards its biggest frown, at the 'sad' frame.

4. As the user's guesses get nearer to Smiler's age, the happier it'll get – moving towards the 'happy' frame. When the user guesses the exact value of Smiler's age, Smiler will put on its biggest smile and the game is finished.

How do we now check that we've defined the problem correctly? Well, we think it through in our heads and ensure there's nothing else we want our program to do. If necessary, we talk to our client to ensure that we've analyzed the problem correctly.

> At this stage, it's important to think only in terms of what you're going to want Flash to do – now isn't the time to think about exactly how you're going to make Flash do it. We need to keep our minds untainted by solutions until we've got a clear idea of the problem and its component sub-problems.

You'll find that most problems can be stated in a similar form to that we've just used, even if they're very complex. A programmer would call the list of things that the ActionScript needs to do a list of **requirements**. This list doesn't state the solution; it just states *what needs to be done*. Because these are the only requirements we have for the interaction of Smiler and the user, we can be reasonably confident that our list is a general statement of the *whole* problem. A programmer would call these the **high level requirements**, and would then break each requirement down into a list of smaller, more detailed, requirements for the program. This list is called a **requirements specification**.

The multi-billion dollar 'super-computer' programs that refuse to work don't usually fail because they've been coded incorrectly. They fail – almost without exception – because the *wrong problem* is defined at the planning stage, meaning that the programming solution that's built, based on that definition, doesn't fulfil the requirements of the *actual* problem that you set out to address! This can mean that the programmers are not all working towards the same clearly defined goal: although all the sections of the program work in isolation, when they're put together, the different chunks can't be integrated properly and nothing works. This emphasizes the importance of planning, and it's why we're not going to jump straight into creating the ActionScript for the new, improved Smiler. Instead, we're going to take things stage by stage, and guarantee that we come up with an effective solution.

Breaking down the Smiler problem

We now need to break down, or *decompose*, our high level requirements into more detailed basic requirements. We keep breaking things down in repeated iterations until we have the simplest list possible – things that can't be broken down any further.

A first iteration has sub-points of each original point (1.1, 1.2; 2.1, 2.2...) and a second iteration has sub-points of each of these (1.1.1, 1.1.2, 1.1.3...).

Let's work out Smiler's detailed requirements specification, based on the high level requirement we've already agreed above:

1. Define a number representing Smiler's 'age'.

2. Acquire a number – let's call it 'guess' from the user, and check it against 'age'.

3. Compare the difference between 'age' and 'guess' and apply this value to the Smiler movie in order to make it go to a particular frame to indicate how close the guess is.

4. If the difference is *zero*, make Smiler to go to the 'happy' label on the timeline – Smiler's biggest smile – and stop. If the difference is *not* zero, repeat from point 2.

We can now break this down further in our first iteration by asking ourselves more questions about the nature of the problem. For example:

- How big a number can *age* be? Can it be 450? Can it be 6.124569081?

- Can *guess* be the *word* 'five' or does it have to be *number* '5'?

- How many frames should Smiler have?

This is what our first iteration might look like:

- 1.1 – Get Flash to define a variable – *age* – which is between 1 and 99.

- 2.1 – Elicit a text entry from the user that's numeric.

- 2.2 – Assign this text entry to a variable, *guess*.

- 2.3 – If *guess* is not between 1 and 99, then repeat from 2.1.

- 3.1 – Create a new variable, *difference*, which is equal to *age* minus *guess*.

- 3.2 – If *difference* is a negative number, convert it to a positive number of equal magnitude.

- 3.3 – In the Smiler movie clip, go to a frame number that's equal to *difference* to represent how far out the user's guess is.

- 4.1 – If *difference* is zero, then stop. Otherwise repeat from 2.1.

Through refining our problem we've almost written ourselves a set of instructions to solve it with.

If we put 1.1 to 4.1 in order, we actually end up with a list of what we need to do to reach a solution to the overall Smiler ActionScripting problem. This powerful technique goes by the name of **top down design**: We've defined the high level problem – the 'top' – and then worked 'down' into the problem by splitting up the requirements into their simplest forms. By the end of the process we have a problem that's so well defined it has become the answer itself – and the path to the final specification is traceable all the way back to the top level problem we're trying to solve.

The Smiler example is a fairly simple problem, and we probably could have worked out the answer in our heads without listing our requirements. However, when you're working on a bigger coding project you won't have that luxury. The top-down method of planning and problem definition will save a lot of time and brainpower when solving more complex problems, and will help to ensure you're solving the right problem in the right way.

By giving your problem a defined structure, you are forcing your ActionScript to follow a similar, structured, form. You will write ActionScript that doesn't look like it was hacked together, but something that's well thought out, considered, and which addresses each requirement in turn.

For the beginner, thinking of the task in terms of the *problem* rather than the actual ActionScript has yet another, rather more subtle, advantage: if you think only in terms of the code solution, you'll only ever use the Flash skills you've already got to grips with. However, if you define the problem properly before thinking about the code, you may well hit upon the requirement for tasks you can't yet do, like creating a 'loop' where a set of instructions are repeated until a certain condition is met. You'll be forced to try new methods to achieve this – instead of repeating the knowledge you already have and allowing your Flash programs to become stale. By looking at what you need to solve a problem, rather than what problems you can solve with the skills you already have, you'll constantly improve your skills and upgrade your Flash technique.

We now know what we need to change in the old Smiler to create a new, age-sensitive, version. However, before we can solve the problem defined by our requirement specification, there're one or two pieces of Flash know-how we need to acquire. For instance, point 2 asks us to get the user to guess Smiler's age: so we need to know how to allow the user to *input* text and how to get Flash to *use* that input.

Basic input and output

So far in this book, we've seen that ActionScript allows us to create *variables* that we can store values in, and that Flash uses these variables in the background without the user being aware of them.

Sometimes, as in the Smiler movie, we want to have these variables visible on the screen so that we, and the user, can see what they are. In Flash, getting and displaying variables – whose values can change, remember – is done with **input text** fields and **dynamic text** fields. Although we have touched on using input text fields, most of the text fields we've used up to now have contained **static text**, which, as its name suggests, doesn't do anything but sit in its box (even if the box itself is animated). Before we explain the two new types of text, there's something about the text fields themselves that you may or may not already have noticed and needs to be explained.

If you just click once on the stage with the Text tool while you have Static Text selected from the drop-down menu on the far left of the Property inspector, you'll create a text field that will extend indefinitely as you type into it. The text field will only move to a new line when you press the ENTER key. This text field, with *undefined* width, will have a *circle* in the top right corner:

Undefined...

If, however, you *click and drag* on the stage with the Text tool and make your text field a wide rectangle, this field will have a width defined by the size of the field you just dragged out. The text you type into it will wrap onto the line below as the text reaches the edge of the field. This text field, with a *defined* width, will have a *square* in the top right corner:

This is a defined width...

An undefined text field will become a defined text field if you alter its width at any time. Additionally, you can revert a defined text field to undefined by placing your cursor over the little square and double-clicking.

OK – now to use text fields for input and update them dynamically.

Input text and dynamic text

Let's try an experiment.

1.   Create a new movie and use the Text tool to drag out a text field on the stage. Make it about two inches wide.

2.   In the Property inspector, use the Text type drop-down menu to change the text from **Static Text** to **Input Text**.

3.   Notice that the square at the top right of the text box has moved to the bottom right, and that there are also new fields visible in the bottom half of the Property inspector:

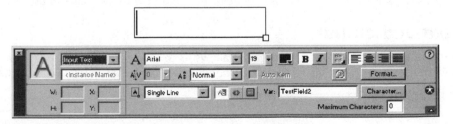

This text field is now enabled as an input field in the finished movie. The additional fields in the bottom section of the Property inspector allow us to control the behavior of that input field.

Let's use these fields to tell Flash that we want to store the user's input in a variable.

4. In the **Var** (variable) field, enter usertext, change the **Maximum Characters** field to **10**, set the line type to **Single Line** and press the **Show Border Around Text** button. Also press the **Left/Top Justify** button and your panel will now look like this:

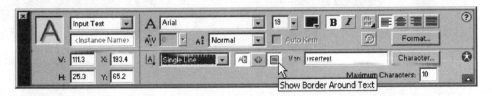

By entering **usertext** in the **Var** field, we're telling Flash that when the user enters text into this field in the finished movie, we want Flash to store that text inside a variable called **usertext**:

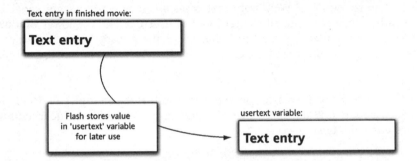

Selecting the **Show Border Around Text** option means that the outline of the text field will appear in the movie – this can be very important for the user, as they don't want to have to search too hard for the text input area.

5. Now test the movie.

6. Click on the box and try entering some text. You'll find you can enter up to 10 characters, the maximum we specified.

OK, we've created a text input area for the user on the screen, and the text typed into here will be *assigned* to the **usertext** variable. When we assign a value to a variable, we're just 'populating' that variable with a value we want to refer to later using the variable name.

We can now also create an *output* text area that'll keep us informed about the current value of the variable.

7. Paste a copy of the text field you just created underneath the original.

8. Working with the new text field, change the text type to **Dynamic Text** using the drop-down menu in the Property inspector.

9. Now *deselect* the **Show Border Around Text** button, and also deselect the **Selectable** button.

10. In the **Var** field, enter `usertext`, the variable name. This is the same variable we're inputting in the top window – we're telling Flash to display this variable in the new dynamic text box on the screen:

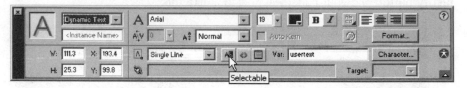

11. Now test the movie.

    You can enter text in the upper window, but you *can't* select the lower window. Whatever you enter in the upper window also appears in the lower window.

    What's happening here? Well, both text areas are showing the same variable, **usertext**. The top window has been set up to allow user input of **usertext**, and the lower window has been set up to display it. Rather than tell the user what he or she already knows, as we're doing here, we can instead make Flash do something useful to the data we input before it displays it, or outputs it, for viewing.

12. Select the lower text field again and change it so that it's an **Input Text** type field. Press the **Show Border Around Text** button so that it's selected, and enter `10` in the **Maximum Characters** field. In the **Var** field, type `usertext2`:

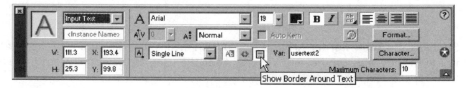

    We're going to get Flash to add the input to **usertext** and **usertext2** together and display the result in a third text area. We need to define this third text area next.

13. Draw a third text box and make it a **Dynamic Text** field.

14. Make sure the **Selectable** button is unselected, and that the **Show Border Around Text** button remains selected.

15. In the **Var** field, type `textadd`. Because **textadd** is the addition of the previous two variables, it may be up to **20** characters long. Make sure you create a large enough text field to fit all those characters in.

16. Place the two input fields on the left of the stage, one above the other, and the new, dynamic, text field on the right of the stage:

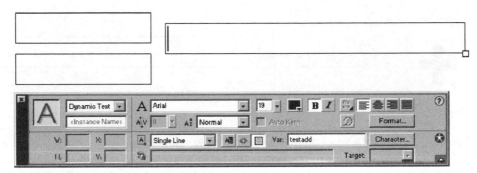

Now we need to let the user add the two text entries together.

17. Create a new button symbol and call it add.

18. Using a standard (static text) text field, type a large + sign in the button symbol's **Up** state, and add keyframes to the other states:

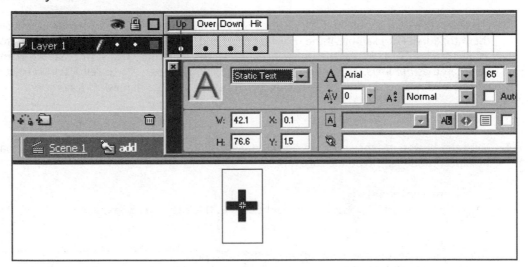

19. In the **Down** state, change the + in the text box to an = sign, and in the **Hit** state add a filled square that completely covers the +: this will give the user a larger button to press than just the + sign.

20. Back on the main stage, place an instance of the button symbol in the center of the stage next to the two input boxes:

That's the front-end part of the movie set up. Now we need to create a little ActionScript that will add together the contents of the two input fields and display the result in the dynamic text field on the right. This ActionScript will work with the two input variables and assign the result of the calculation to the **textadd** variable.

To achieve this, we'll create an ActionScript to calculate **usertext + usertext2**, assign the result to the **textadd** variable, and then display the result. We want the user to enter **usertext** and **usertext2** before we do the addition, so we'll attach the addition ActionScript to the + button that we just added to the movie. This way, Flash will perform the calculation when two numbers have been entered and the button is pressed.

However, there's a problem. If we just ask Flash to add **usertext2** to **usertext**, it will simply join them together. For example, if the user typed '35' and '45', Flash would assign the result to **textadd** as '3545'. Flash would treat the inputs as *string values* – ordinary text – whereas we want them to be treated as *numbers*. To do this, we use the function Number () to tell Flash to treat the value of whatever we put in the brackets (which will be our variable names) as a number.

Let's build that ActionScript.

21. With the button instance selected on the stage, go into the Actions panel, make sure that you are in Expert mode, and type the following:

```
on (release) {
    textadd = Number (usertext) + Number (usertext2);
}
```

The Script pane on the right of the Actions panel will look like this:

22. Now test the movie. Type two numbers into the input fields and press the big '+' button:

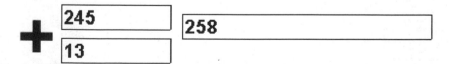

It works! And you can even add decimals.

23. Try typing letters into one, or both of the fields and pressing the + button. The **textadd** dynamic text field shows **NaN**, or 'Not a Number':

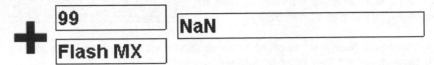

There's an informal rule in programming that states 'If you're taking input from the user, assume that the user is a monkey'. We're not talking about the monkey with a keyboard whose random typing produced, by chance, *Hamlet*. We're talking about the monkey next to it that *didn't*. Your input fields have to cater for all the *wrong* inputs as well as the *right* one. So your code has to be able to cope if the user types **'89g6!trc'** instead of **'896'**. Let's see how to add an 'intelligence filter' to an input field.

24. Select one of the input text fields and click on the **Character** button in the Property inspector to display the **Character Options** window:

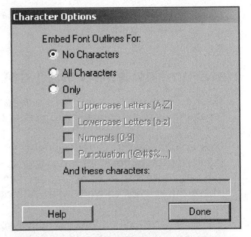

This window lets you specify what can be typed into or displayed in this input or dynamic text field. Flash assumes you want to allow input of *everything* unless you select any of the options.

25. We only want *numbers* to be entered in the input fields, so select **Only** from the window, and check the **Numerals (0-9) box**:

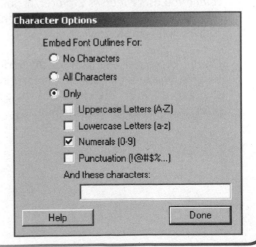

26. We also want to include the decimal point and the minus sign in case someone wants to enter a negative decimal like **-234.567453**. Enter a . (period) and a - (minus sign) in the bottom text field for each of the input fields, to specify that we want to be able to input these characters as well as numbers:

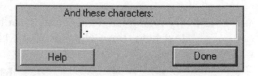

27. Test your movie again. Now you can monkey about all you want: Flash will only allow you to type in up to 10 characters, and they must be integers from 0 to 9 or '.' or '-'.

Flash possesses a math library, containing functions such as sin, cos, tan, etc., that would allow us to develop this simple movie into a working calculator program.

Remember the Smiler specification we were planning before? We've just discovered an important building block that allows us to code it up in Flash: now we've got the hang of input and output, getting the user to guess Smiler's age later in the chapter will be no problem at all.

First though, we need to learn a little more about **dot notation** and how to use it with paths in ActionScript.

Referencing paths with dot notation

As we discovered earlier, dot notation in ActionScript is a way of expressing a **path** through a movie, enabling us to reference any object in the movie.

Remember the structured planning we went through at the beginning of this chapter? We broke the Smiler problem down into manageable chunks or sub-problems. If we now structure our movie correctly, we can address each of our requirements *in a separate movie clip*. We can then use dot notation to make these movie clips converse with each other and control the movie as a whole.

Here's an analogy: on your computer you have a hard drive with various folders and sub-folders – often nested many deep. To get to a particular folder you use Windows Explorer, or you click on the drive's icon on the Mac to open up the folders you want to look at.

On our computer, the path for the folder of this text file (the one that's been edited, printed, and shipped to your bookstore), is based on its position in the folder hierarchy:

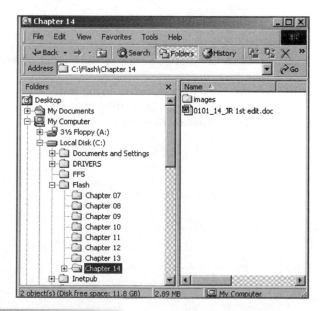

So, the actual path for this file is:

> **C:\Flash\Chapter 14\0101_14_JR_1st edit.doc**

This path tells us how to get to this text file starting from the hard drive, **C:**, which is the lowest level, or **root level**. (You'll note the tree-like nature of the way these networks are linked). What we're saying here is that to get to the file I have to go into a folder called *Flash*, where I'll find another folder called *Chapter 14*, and if I open *that* folder, the file I want will be there. This path through the folder hierarchy gives me the entire journey, starting from the lowest level – the hard drive. If I specify the path in this way, starting from the hard drive level, it's referred to as the total or *absolute* path.

If I was *already* at **C:\Flash**, then I could express the route to the document *relative* to where I'm starting from   I don't have to go back via the hard drive level. The path from **C:\Flash** would be expressed as:

> **Chapter 14**

This is saying, 'starting from where you are, open the folder *Chapter 14*, and you'll find the file you want'.

Flash uses a similar structure, except that instead of seeing levels of hard drives and folders, it refers to SWF files and movie clips or, to be more accurate, it refers to their *timelines* and *sub-timelines*. Consider a Flash movie that has:

- A main timeline (or *root* timeline, called _root in Flash) that has one scene – Scene 1.

- A movie clip called **FoED** on frame 27 of Scene 1.

- A movie clip called **FoundationFlash** on **FoED**'s timeline at frame 20.
  .swf file:

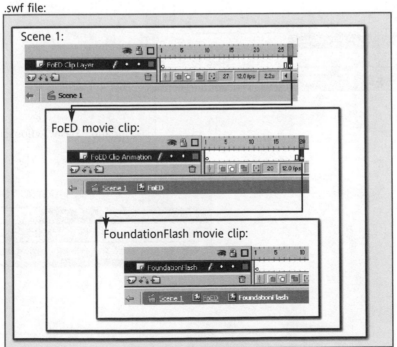

To access an object or frame on **FoundationFlash**'s timeline, I could use the following *absolute* path in my ActionScript:

```
_root.FoED.FoundationFlash
```

> *Because the path shown above is an absolute path, starting at the **_root** and working its way through the nested timelines, I can safely issue it from anywhere and know that Flash will be able to find its way, down the path, to the **FoundationFlash** movie clip's timeline.*

Note that each of the levels in this hierarchy is separated by a dot – hence the term **dot notation**. We can use this notation to specify the path that we want Flash to follow – and we can use it to point to any object, anywhere in the movie.

What if I wanted to access something in **FoundationFlash**'s timeline from within the **FoED** movie clip? I *could* use the full, absolute path defined above, but I could also use a simpler method, because I'm *almost* where I want to be; I can just give a shorter *relative* path in ActionScript as follows:

```
FoundationFlash
```

This path will start from where I am, and look for the next level of the path inside of the **FoED** movie clip:

FoED movie clip:

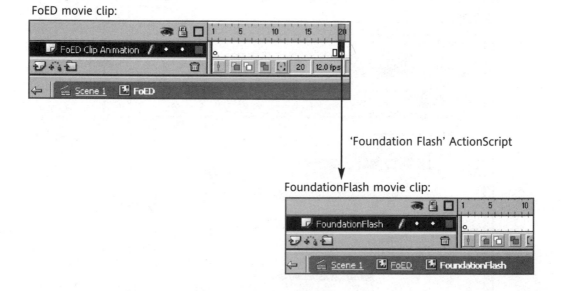

'Foundation Flash' ActionScript

FoundationFlash movie clip:

And there's a special ActionScript command if I want to go back a level: for example, from **FoundationFlash** back up to the **FoED** clip):

        _parent

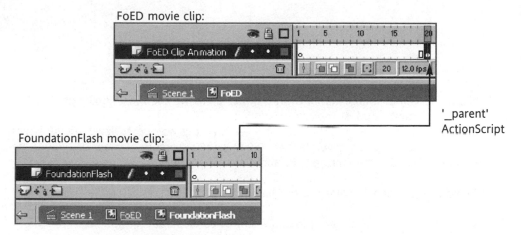

You can also string these commands together to go back *more* than one level:

        _parent._parent

Going back to our hard drive, you'll notice that we actually have more than just a **C:** drive. We also have A and D drives:

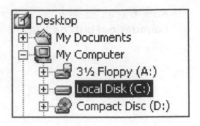

We can navigate to those drives by specifying their paths – such as **A:**.

Similarly, we can include *external* movies in the paths we use in ActionScript. To access a separate SWF using dot notation, you just replace `_root` with a reference to the external SWF's *level*, `_level0` for the SWF at level 0, `_level1` for the SWF at level 1, all the way up to level 16000 (which is the maximum number of levels you can have). In fact, 16000 is the maximum number of symbols you can have in the Library, and 16000 is the limit for just about everything in Flash.

In terms of the original analogy of our hard drive:

- SWF files – movies – are the equivalent of our separate hard drives.

- A movie's main timeline is the equivalent of the root path of each hard drive.

- Individual movie clips are the equivalent of folders and sub-folders.

On our hard drives, we use paths to access *files*. What will Flash allow us to access? Well, for a start, it allows us to access *variables*.

To specify a variable at the end of a path, as with other dot notation, you just precede it by a '.' (period). So, the full path for a variable called **userinput** in the **FoundationFlash** movie clip would be:

```
_root.FoED.FoundationFlash.userinput
```

or

```
_level0.FoED.FoundationFlash.userinput
```

In your Flash movies, you'll find the root level displayed as level 0.

Before we put this into practice, let's think about the dynamic animation we promised you at the start of the chapter.

Dynamic animation

For dynamic animation to work, we have to be able to target a movie clip and alter some aspects of its appearance or behavior. To do that, we work with a movie's *properties*. We can view these properties by looking at the movie in **Debug** mode.

Viewing a movie clip's properties

1. Open one of your movies – preferably one with a movie clip attached to the main timeline.

2. Now choose the **Control > Debug Movie** menu option to bring up the **Debugger** window with the movie in test mode.

3. Click on the **Properties** tab (about half way down on the left side of the Debugger window) and extend the size of the Properties pane if necessary.

> *Note that Flash sometimes doesn't work properly in Debug mode unless you have run the movie in test mode at least once. If the **Debugger** window appears completely blank, simply go back and do a **Control > Test Movie**, and then try the **Debug** menu option again. Alternatively, choose the **Control > Debug Movie** option.*

When you get the Debugger window up, you'll see something like this, though you may have to extend the size of the window and the Properties pane to help see what's inside:

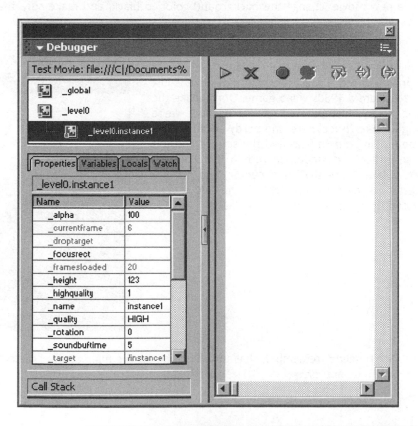

The top left pane here shows us the hierarchy of movie clips in the movie. It also gives us the path for each nested movie clip, starting at the root with the main timeline, down to the movie clip inside Scene 1. Note the dot separating the nested clip from the timeline:

Movie clips have other aspects apart from just the variables that we define and set. The names and values shown in the bottom pane of the Debugger window when you click on the different movie clips are the **properties** of the movie clip. All movie clips will have this same set of properties, but the *values* for the properties in an individual movie clip will differ.

Essentially, properties are just like variables except that they relate to a particular aspect of the movie clip such as its size, rotation, position on the stage, or whether all of its frames have streamed in yet. There's one difference between variables and properties that you may already have guessed: if we change a property of our movie clip at any stage, we'll alter its appearance on the screen – it'll be animated. We're going to do this now with dot notation.

Dynamic animation with dot notation

You can now use this knowledge of levels, variables, and properties to execute a simple example of a new kind of animation and control. We'll create a dynamic animation that responds to user keyboard inputs.

1. Open a new movie, change the background color to black, and make sure that the stage is 550 pixels x 400 pixels.

2. Create a new movie clip symbol called `spaceship`, rename the movie clip symbol's default layer `space` and draw yourself a spaceship that looks like it just emerged from a 1980s video game. Don't make the spacecraft too complicated: partly because we're aiming for a retro feel here, and partly because Flash will be moving our ship around the screen, and this will be easier and smoother with a less complex shape. Make sure that the center line of the spaceship is also the center of the movie clip (denoted by a little cross):

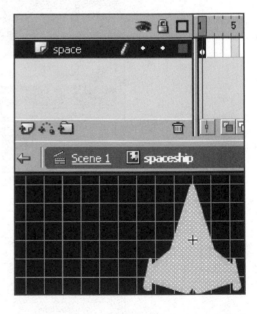

3. In the root timeline (remember, that's the timeline on the main stage) create three layers, called `actions`, `input` and `ship`.

4. In the new **ship** layer, drag an instance of your **spaceship** movie clip onto the stage. Position it at the bottom of the stage and scale it so that it looks like player 1's spacecraft from a Space Invaders arcade game. Using the Property inspector, give the **spaceship** movie clip an instance name – `ship`:

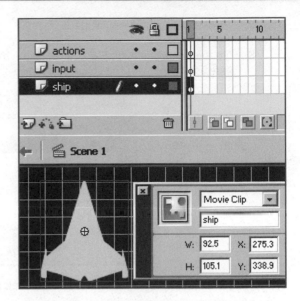

We want to be able to move this spacecraft left and right as it dodges the alien hordes in its epic battle to save the planet – whatever. To do this we need to know two things about this spaceship:

- Its position

- How fast it will move

To get this information all we need to know is the **spaceship** movie clip's **_x property**, which is its position on the x-axis of the screen – how far from the right of the screen the space ship is. The ship is at the extreme *left* when **_x=0**, and the extreme *right* when **_x=550**. Once we have this value, we can then assign it to a variable called **ship_pos,** which we'll use to keep track of where the ship is.

5. In the root timeline's **actions** layer, at frame 1, open up the Actions panel and type:

```
ship_pos =
```

6. Click on the **Insert Target Path** button and then select the **Absolute** radio button from the Insert Target Path window:

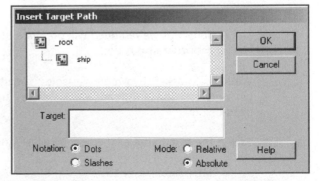

You'll now see that the paths are shown from **_root**, giving us an idea of where the ship instance is located from the main timeline of the movie.

7. Select **ship** as the target path.

8. In the **Target** field, type a ' . ' after **ship** – this is to tell Flash that we want to explore the properties that are associated with the **spaceship** movie clip:

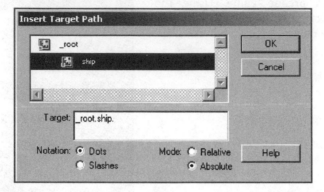

9. Click **OK** to return to the Actions panel. In the Script pane you'll see the following:

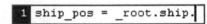

```
1  ship_pos = _root.ship.
```

10. Now add the following in the Script pane: `_x;`

Your ActionScript should now read:

```
ship_pos = _root.ship._x;
```

If you'd like to see the properties available to manipulate movie clips and other objects, open the **Properties** book in the Actions toolbox:

We'll be using some of these in the next exercise.

The ActionScript we've added will populate the **ship_pos** variable with the value of the ship movie clip's x (horizontal) position.

We need to assign two more variables: **speed**, to set how fast our spacecraft will move (in pixels per keypress) and **shipdead**, which will be either 'true' or 'false' depending on whether our ship is dead or not.

11. Still in the first frame of the **actions** layer, add the following ActionScript:

```
shipdead = false;
speed = 5;
```

This sets the value of **shipdead** to **false**, and the value of **speed** to **5**, leaving this frame's finished ActionScript looking like this:

```
1 ship_pos = _root.ship._x;
2 shipdead = false;
3 speed = 5;
```

12. Use the Property inspector to label this frame as **initialized**, to signify that this is the initialization of the variables.

    Now we'll add the *input* part. We've looked at keyboard input into text fields, but that's not really what we want to do here. Instead, we want our animation to react to a particular key being pressed – the LEFT arrow key. When this is pressed, we want to move the **spaceship** movie clip instance 5 pixels to the left. This works in a similar way to a button press, and we need to create a button to enable us to do it. This button will never actually appear on the user's screen, but it will act as a 'funnel' that captures their keyboard input and feeds it into Flash.

13. Create a new button symbol called **input** and on its **Up** state, in a **Static Text** field, type `input`.

14. We don't want this button to ever be selected, so insert a blank keyframe in its **Hit** state. To ensure that it's never seen (as well as never selected), go back to the root timeline and place an instance of the button *in the work area*, outside the stage in frame 1 of the **input** layer:

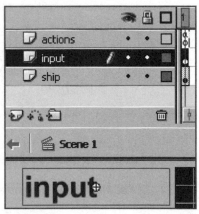

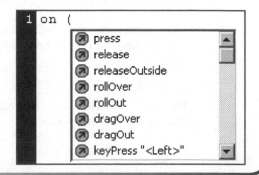

15. Select the button with the Arrow tool and bring up the Actions panel.

    Earlier in the book we discussed the alternatives to having an `on (release)` event. One we didn't mention was the `on (KeyPress)` event. We use this event to tell Flash to carry out an instruction when a *particular* key is pressed.

16. In the Script pane of the Actions panel, type:

    `on (`

    and the already familiar menu will appear to give us some assistance with our selection:

481

17. Select `keyPress "<Left>"` from the menu and your code for the **input** button will now look like this:

```
1 on (keyPress "<Left>"
```

The hidden button will now respond to the press of the LEFT arrow key.

Next, we have to tell Flash what to do when the LEFTarrow key is pressed. We want it to move five pixels to the left of its current position, or to **_x - speed**. Flash already knows that **speed = 5** from the initialization frame.

18. Close the **on** handler with a closing bracket and insert an opening curly bracket. Press ENTER to move the cursor to a new line:

```
1 on (keyPress "<Left>") {
2 |
```

Next, type…

```
_root.ship._x =
```

…into the Script pane of the Actions panel. We want to change the value of the movie clip instance's **_x** position, remember.

> *Notice this time that we haven't used the Insert Target Path button. If you are ever unsure of the location of one of your instances, be sure to use it.*

To subtract speed from the current **x** position of the movie clip, we need to reference its current position and subtract the speed variable's value away from it.

19. Add this to the previous ActionScript:

```
_root.ship._x-speed;
```

making our new line of code:

```
_root.ship._x = _root.ship._x-speed;
```

20. Finally, remember to include a closing curly bracket below the line you've just typed.

After pressing the **Auto Format** button, your code will now look like this:

```
1 on (keyPress "<Left>") {
2     _root.ship._x = _root.ship._x-speed;
3 }
```

This piece of ActionScript will now decrement the x position of **spaceship** every time the user presses the LEFT arrow key.

Now we're going to make the ship move five pixels to the *right* when the RIGHT arrow is pressed. This means we want the **spaceship** movie clip's **_x** property to *increase* by five, so we'll write **_x + speed**.

21. Repeat and adapt steps 16 onwards to create this next piece of ActionScript for the rightward movement of the ship:

```
on (keyPress "<Right>") {
_root.ship._x = _root.ship._x+speed;
}
```

Your script will now look like this:

```
1 on (keyPress "<Left>") {
2     _root.ship._x = _root.ship._x-speed;
3 }
4 on (keyPress "<Right>") {
5     _root.ship._x = _root.ship._x+speed;
6 }
```

22. Test your movie. You can use the LEFT and RIGHT arrow keys to move the spaceship left and right. How cool is *that*?

This is currently a pretty basic movement, but we're using the main principles of dot notation to alter the properties of the **spaceship** movie clip and are therefore able to move it at will – its movement is not fixed, as it would be in a simple motion tween. This kind of dynamic animation is often called **sprite movement.**

We haven't finished yet. Next, we're going to simulate the effect of our spaceship being killed by the marauding hordes of alien invaders. We're not going to create the aliens themselves, but your knowledge will soon be sufficient for you to do that yourself. When our ship is destroyed, we want to change the value of the **shipdead** variable we initialized in the movie's first frame: we want to change its value from 'false' to 'true'.

23. In the **root** timeline, select the button and open the Actions panel.

24. Add the following code to the previous lines:

```
on (keyPress "<Space>") {
_root.shipdead = true;
}
```

The **on (KeyPress)** event responds to the SPACE BAR being pressed, and when this happens, changes the **shipdead** variable to **true**. After pressing the **Auto Format** button, your ActionScript for the **input** button symbol will now look like this:

```
1 on (keyPress "<Left>") {
2     _root.ship._x = _root.ship._x-speed;
3 }
4 on (keyPress "<Right>") {
5     _root.ship._x = _root.ship._x+speed;
6 }
7 on (keyPress "<Space>") {
8     _root.shipdead = true;
9 }
```

OK, we've set the movie up for the entire user input. Now we need to make the **spaceship** display change in response to the SPACE BAR being pressed. We've just attached the code to the SPACE BAR for the sake of this exercise. It's actually intended to simulate the outcome of alien fire hitting our spacecraft.

25. Open the **spaceship** movie clip and create a new layer called `Actions`. Select the **Actions** layer and add keyframes at frames 2 and 10.

26. Using the Property inspector, label frame 2 of the layer `dead`.

27. On the **space** layer, place a keyframe at frame 2.

28. Now place blank keyframes at frames 3 and 10. Your timeline should now look like this:

29. On frame 10 of the **Actions** layer, add the code:

```
gotoAndPlay("dead");
```

This sets up a loop from frames 2 to 10, so when the spaceship dies, it will flash on and off, appearing at frame 2, and then disappearing until it loops around again.

30. Select frame 1 of the **Actions** layer and attach a **stop** command to halt the timeline. Frame 1 will be visible until the ship dies and then we'll send the playhead to the frame labeled **dead**.

Now we need to add some code to regularly check the status of **shipdead**. We'll attach this code to a new blank movie clip within the **spaceship** movie clip, **using** an ActionScript command we haven't yet come across – `onClipEvent`.

Attaching code to instances and objects

Now that we've become accustomed to paths and dot notation, the ability to attach code directly to objects might just seem like something else to confuse you on your way up the ActionScript ladder. If you've survived so far, then don't give up yet. The `onClipEvent` handler will give your objects their independence. It has a number of different event types, from mouse events to frame events, meaning that it can be set to trigger on different occasions by different things.

Flash 5 provided the ability to attach actions to clips directly, thus providing an object-based approach and moving away from previous timeline-based checks set in looping timelines. With Flash 4, to perform a check of this kind required the Flasher to create a 2-frame loop – the first frame to perform the required check and the second to loop back to the first.

Now we have the ability to encapsulate our checking code in one place.

Let's take a look at how a typical `onClipEvent` handler would look:

```
onClipEvent (load) {
    this._x = 200;
}
```

The code on the previous page is saying 'when I have loaded, set my x position on the stage to 200'. We use the first person because the code is self-referential – a bizarre concept – it is checking if it has loaded itself and, if it has, is then telling itself to move to the x coordinate of 200 on the stage.

this references the actual object that the onClipEvent is attached to.

The concept is relatively straightforward – let's try another:

```
onClipEvent (enterFrame) {
    this._x = this._x +1;
}
```

In this example our code is saying: 'every frame, add one to my x position'. If you noticed that it is not *literally* using 'every frame' in the code, you are correct; enterFrame is the event equivalent, and is run on every frame of the movie. We will use enterFrame to check the status of the **shipdead** variable. Because it is frequently updated, it will give us a pretty true and swift reading when **shipdead** changes.

Now that we have a little familiarity with the onClipEvent, let's get back to our spaceship.

Placing an onClipEvent handler in our movie

1. Create a new layer called blank in the spaceship movie clip.

2. Select the **blank** layer and insert a keyframe at frame 2:

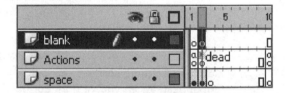

3. On frame 1 of the **blank** layer, draw a small square in the work area to the left of the stage:

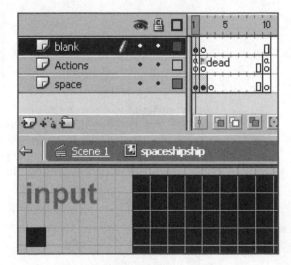

Traditionally, blank movie clips – with no visible content – are used to perform ActionScript checks so that they are not visible on the screen. For now, we'll use a shape to identify the movie clip before deleting the graphic later.

4. Convert the square to a movie clip symbol called `blankClip`.

5. Click on the **blankClip** movie clip and open the Actions panel. You'll notice that the window that has opened is titled **Actions – Movie Clip**. This is because we are attaching script directly to a movie clip.

6. Enter the following code:

```
onClipEvent (
```

You'll see a drop-down menu appear in the Script pane of the Actions panel. Select **enterFrame** from the drop-down. Your code should now look like this:

```
1 onClipEvent (enterFrame
```

7. Close the `onClipEvent` handler with a closing bracket and insert an opening curly bracket. Press ENTER to move the cursor to a new line and type the following code:

```
if (_root.shipdead ==   true) {
   _parent.gotoAndPlay ("dead");
}
}
```

After you've typed `_parent.` you'll see another drop-down menu appear. You can either select `gotoAndPlay` from the menu, or you can continue typing and the menu will automatically disappear. When you've finished, the Script pane in your Actions panel will look like this:

```
1 onClipEvent (enterFrame) {
2     if (_root.shipdead == true) {
3         _parent.gotoAndPlay("dead");
4     }
5 }
```

This ActionScript will check to see if the spaceship has been destroyed by the user pressing the SPACE BAR. If it has been destroyed, it will send the `_parent` (in this case the **spaceship** movie clip) to the frame labeled **dead**. Action will only be taken if `shipdead == true` (if the SPACE BAR has been pressed). If it is false, we simply go to the next frame, where the **onClipEvent** will check its status again. This will continue until the ship is dead or the user is bored and the movie is closed.

> The == symbol is an operator which means 'equals to' and is only used to compare, not to set.

8. Now that our code is attached to our supposedly blank movie clip, go ahead and delete the square from *within* the **blankClip** movie clip's timeline.

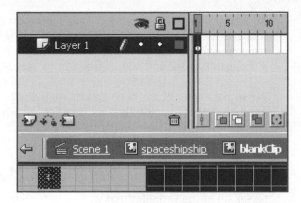

9. Return to the **spaceship** movie clip and you'll see that our **blankClip** is now truly blank. It is identified within our Flash authoring environment like this:

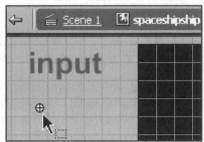

Even though we have been true to the blank movie clip concept by deleting the square symbol, as long as the movie clip is located off the stage (as with our input button) it will not be seen in the final published movie.

10. Now test the movie again. You'll see that when you press the SPACE BAR, the spaceship will flash. (You can add the obligatory 'blooop blooop...blooop blooop...ping!' noise later if you feel the need).

Note that if you try and publish the movie as it stands, the keys won't work until the user has clicked on the screen with the mouse.

When we press the SPACE BAR, the root timeline sets the **shipdead** variable to **true**. The **spaceship** movie clip is constantly looking at this variable's status via the onclipEvent check that's attached to the **blankClip** movie clip inside **spaceship**. As soon as it sees that it's true, it skips from the 'I am alive' frame to the 'I am dead' loop.

This is a significantly different setup from what we've done before. In particular:

- All animations in this FLA are created using ActionScript alone. No part of the animation process is tied to the timeline via tween keyframes, and as a result the animation is entirely controlled by the user, and will be different every time.

- Rather than being a way of separating out animations into different parts, movie clips are being used in a much more complex way. They are no longer just sitting on the root timeline and being told what to do. They are now actively controlling themselves based on variables derived from user input, and beginning to act in a much more proactive way.

As well as controlling the spaceship's position on the x-axis, you could just as easily control any other *property* of the movie clip. For example, using the *rotation* property you could get the ship to rotate clockwise and anticlockwise in response to the arrow keys. Another thing you could do would be to create a draggable slider and use its position to vary the *alpha* property of a movie clip instance.

We spoke earlier of the alien hordes we'd need to create in order to complete our game. Each alien would need to have variables such as **invader_pos**, **invaderdead** and **fire_photon_torpedo**. Controlling the properties of all of our invaders individually is much simpler than you may imagine, as the next brief example will illustrate.

Many movie clips, many variables

So far, all of the variables that we've used inside of our simple movies have been associated with the whole movie. That is, they were defined in ActionScript in the main timeline, and when their values changed, every movie clip that used those variables saw the changed value. These variables have what's known as **global scope** – they look the same to everything in the movie, and any changes in value are applied *globally* across the whole movie.

This is fine if we have a simple movie and a few variables – it's not too difficult to track and maintain these variable values in ActionScript. Imagine, though, if you had twenty aliens on your screen, each inside its own movie clip instance, each one of them needing to have its x and y positions tracked and amended as the movie played. In this situation, it's considerably more difficult to track and update these aliens' associated variables if these variables are all kept on the main timeline.

Fortunately, we can create variables that are *specific to particular movie clips*, and whose changes in value only affect the movie clip that the variable is associated with. This means that each alien movie clip can have its own **alien_pos** variable, independent of the other nineteen (or thirty-nine, or six hundred) aliens.

Let's look at how this works in a brief exercise.

Movie clip-specific variables

1. Open a new movie.

2. In the root timeline (that's on the main stage, remember – we're going to be speaking in this new jargon from now on) add three layers: actions, text and clips:

3. In frame 1 of the **actions** layer, open your **Actions – Frame** window and type:

        a=3;

4. In the **text** layer, add a **Dynamic Text** field using the Text tool and Property inspector. Make it non-selectable by switching the **Selectable** button to off, and give it a border by depressing the **Show Border Around Text** button.

We want the variable displayed in this box to be called **'a'**, so type a in the **Var** field (make sure the text font color you've selected is *not* the background color):

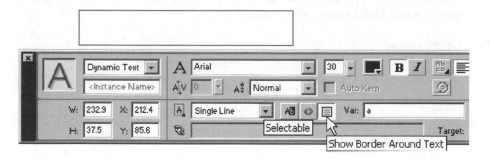

When you run this single frame movie, you'll just see a text box with the number **3** in it. Not the most exciting movie we've made in this book. Bear with us, though, as the point this example illustrates will open your eyes to a wealth of exciting possible movies.

5.   Back in the main movie, create a new movie clip called Mclip. Add new actions and text layers to it as you did for the root timeline.

6.   Create a similar non-selectable dynamic text field on the **text** layer and also press the **Show Border Around Text** button, but this time set it to display the variable **'b'**:

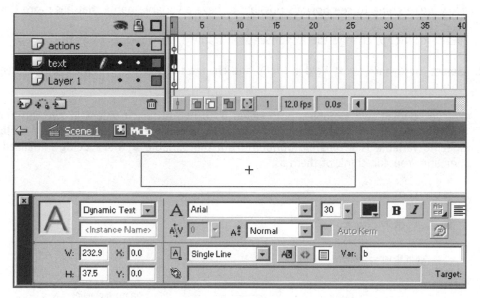

7.   To help us remember that this text field shows a variable that's *inside* **Mclip,** we're going to label it. Draw a static text field next to the dynamic one and type This is inside Mclip into it (select a different text color from the text in the dynamic text field):

This is inside Mclip

8.   In frame 1 of the **Mclip** movie clip's **actions** layer, use the Actions window and set b=10;

9.   Place an instance of the finished **Mclip** on the **clips** layer in the root timeline, and give it the instance name **Mclip** using the Property inspector.

10.   Test the movie:

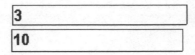

This is inside Mclip

So now you have a variable in the root called **a**, which is equal to **3**, and a variable in the movie clip **Mclip** called **b**, which is equal to **10**. Here's the current variable/text field relationship:

Main timeline: ActionScript

variable 'a' = 3 ⟶ 3   dynamic text box on main timeline

variable 'b' = 10 ⟶ 10   dynamic text box on Mclip timeline

Now we're going to see how it's possible to have a variable name that has more than one value...

11.   Inside of **Mclip**, change the ActionScript in frame 1 from b=10; to **a=10**;

12.   Select the dynamic text field in **Mclip** and change the **Var** field on the Property inspector from **b** to a.

You've now set two variables, both called **a**, to two different values in two different places. The a=10; ActionScript inside of **Mclip** is initializing a *new* variable called **a**, *inside* **Mclip**. This **Mclip**-specific variable is a *different variable* from the variable **a** that's being initialized on the main timeline. You can think of them as:

■   **_root.a**

■   **_root.Mclip.a**

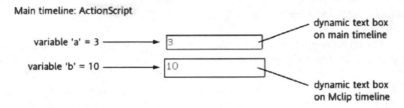

Main timeline: ActionScript

variable 'a' = 3 ⟶ 3   dynamic text box on main timeline
variable 'b' = 10

Mclip timeline: ActionScript

variable 'a' = 10 ⟶ 10   dynamic text box on Mclip timeline

Each variable is associated with the timeline that it was initialized on.

13. Test the movie to see how Flash implements this:

> 3
>
> 10

Both text fields will show the same values as they did before. Although both text areas are displaying an **a** variable, one is showing 10 and the other is showing 3, because the two different variables have different *scope*. The **a** variable spawned from the main timeline applies to the main timeline, and the **a** variable spawned inside **Mclip** applies to the movie clip only.

14. Try running the movie again, but this time select the **Control > Debug Movie** menu option instead of **Control > Test Movie** and take a look in the **Debugger** window:

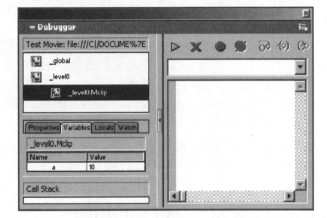

Once again, Flash is showing us the path to each of our movie components: the path for the main stage/timeline is `_level0`, and the path to the movie clip is `_level0.Mclip` – showing us that **Mclip** is inside **_level0**.

As the icons suggest, the main or root timeline is *really* just another movie clip: **_level** is represented by the same kind of icon as **Mclip**. This is something worth remembering as you advance further into Flash, because all of the things that you learn to do with movie clips can also be applied to the root movie itself.

15. If you click on the **Variables** tab on the left-hand side of the Debugger window, with one of the paths selected, Flash will display the values we've assigned to our variables.

With **_level0.Mclip** selected we'll see that the value of **a** is **10**, and if we then select **_level0** we'll see that here it has a value of **3**. Here, you'll also see a variable that represents the version of the Flash Player that is running. This can be ignored, as it doesn't affect our programming.

Although we have two variables called **a**, one is called **_root.a** and the other is called **_root.mclip.a**. Each variable is defined on a separate timeline, and exists in only one place. The version of **a** inside **Mclip** only applies to that movie clip. It is *local* to **Mclip**.

Local variables are exceptionally useful because they allow us to re-use a movie clip. For example, imagine we built a movie clip that controlled a single space invader using the internal, movie clip-specific, variables we mentioned earlier – **invader_pos**, **invaderdead,** and **fire_photon_torpedo**. If we then put another ten alien movie clips onto the stage, we would have ten space invaders with ten sets of discrete, internal, *local* variables, *all* being individually controlled.

> *The use of global/local variables and dot notation is important as it's an extremely powerful technique. We'll talk about it in more detail when we look at the third area of Flash mastery – object-oriented programming (OOP). OOP is one of the things separating supreme Flash Masters from mortal Flash designers. It's difficult to learn, so we've set aside the whole of the next chapter to cover it.*

The techniques we've introduced here are the raw materials of the really advanced and slick looking Flash web site interfaces you may have seen, and you have now taken the second step on your road towards mastering Flash.

Armed as we are with our new found knowledge of input text fields, dot notation and sprite animation, we're now ready to implement the changes we planned for our Smiler movie.

Making Smiler age-sensitive

If you don't have your fully functional version of Smiler saved from Chapter 10, you can download a ready-made Smiler in the downloadable files for this book on our web site.

Guess Smiler's age

Let's remind ourselves what our requirements specification was:

- 1.1 – Define a variable, *age*, with values between 1 and 99.

- 2.1 – Input a numeric text entry from the user.

- 2.2 – Assign this text entry to a variable called *guess*.

- 2.3 – If *guess* is not between 1 and 99, then repeat from 2.1.

- 3.1 – Create a new variable, *difference*, which is equal to *age - guess*.

- 3.2 – If *difference* is negative, make it positive.

- 3.3 – Go to a frame number that's equal to *difference* in the Smiler animated movie clip.

- 4.1 – If *difference* is zero, then stop. Otherwise repeat from 2.1.

Let's walk through this step by step.

The first thing we need to do is get Flash to come up with an age for Smiler that it can compare the user's guess against. It would be a good idea to make this a *random* value, so that it's different for every run of the game. We can do this easily using Flash's `Math.random` function.

`Math.random` returns a number between 0 and 1. Because we require a number between 1 and 99, we'll multiply Math.random by the maximum required number:

```
age=Math.random()*99;
```

This will return a number between 1 and 99 with decimal points. To force this to be a whole number, we use `Math.floor`, which returns a rounded-down number:

```
age=Math.floor(Math.random()*99);
```

We want to generate the random number right at the start of our game, during *initialization*, so that the age variable is populated, ready and waiting for the user's guess.

1. In frame 1 of the **control** layer in the existing **smiler** movie (as it was at the end of Chapter 10) we already have this ActionScript:

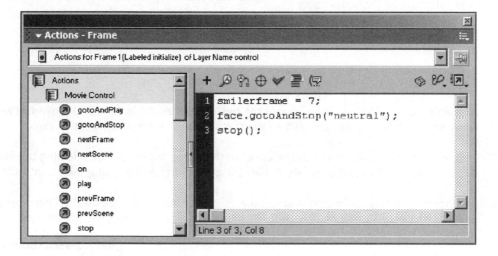

We want to assign a new variable, **age**.

2. Delete the **smilerframe = 7;** action, and replace it with the following code:

```
age = Math.floor (Math.random ()*99);
```

```
1 age = Math.floor (Math.random
2 face.gotoAndStop("neutral");
3 stop()
```

3.   Delete the **stop** action, on the last line in the Script pane.

Testing the movie will not make **Smiler** do anything at the moment, so let's work on the rest of our specification.

■   2.1   Input a text entry from the user that is numeric.

■   2.2   Assign it to a variable, *guess*.

■   2.3   If *guess* is not between 1 and 99, then repeat from step 2.1.

4.   Add frames to all the root timeline layers up to frame 20. Add a keyframe at frame 10 in the **control** layer.

5.   Label this frame loop.

6.   Your timeline will look like this:

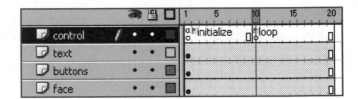

6.   Add this code to the **loop** frame:

```
guess = "";
stop ();
```

7.   By setting **guess** to '' it will set the text field to show nothing.

8.   At frame 1 of the **buttons** layer, delete the **better** button and its text, and move the **worse** button down so it's in the lower right part of the stage. Change the text inside it to Enter.

9.   Create an *input text* field next to the **enter** button. Give it a border by selecting the **Show Border Around Text** button and associate it with the **guess** variable by typing guess into the **Var** field.

10. Set the maximum number of characters the user can enter to 2, click on the Character button, and limit the characters to **Numerals (0-9)**. By doing this we are limiting the possible input to numbers up to 99:

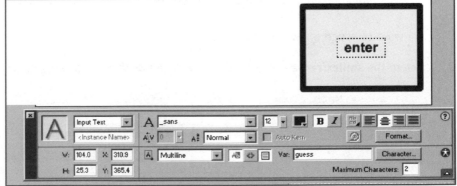

We've set **guess** to nothing initially, and it'll change to the value the user enters once they press the **enter** button.

11. Click on the **enter** button (being careful not to select the text over it), and bring up its Actions window. The current ActionScript is not required, so go ahead and delete it all.

12. Insert the following code:

```
on (release) {
        play ();
}
```

13. You can now test the movie. It will wait for an input until you enter a value that is between 0 and 99. Try to see if you can enter anything else.

Now for the next requirements:

- **3.1** Create a new variable, *difference*, which is equal to *age - guess*.

- **3.2** If *difference* is negative, make it positive.

- **3.3** Go to a frame number that is equal to *difference* in **smiler** movie clip.

We want the **smiler** movie clip to have 98 frames, because that's the maximum amount we can be wrong by when we guess its age.

14. Inside the **smiler** movie clip, add frames (using F5) to the *left* of the **neutral** keyframe to shift it up to frame 49. Then extend the layer to frame 98 as shown here by adding frames to the *right* of **neutral**. Finally, extend the **eyes** and **face** layers up to frame 98:

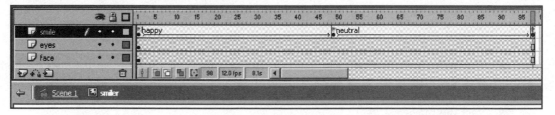

We now need to create the variable that represents the *difference* between the guess and the actual age, and create the ActionScript that'll make the **face** instance go to the frame number that matches that difference.

15. In the root timeline, add a new keyframe at frame 15 of the **control** layer and enter the following actions in the **Actions** window:

```
difference = age-guess;
if (difference < 0) {
    difference = Math.abs(difference)
}
face.gotoAndStop(difference);
```

This script tells Flash how to calculate the **difference** variable (line 1). If the calculation produces a negative number (less than zero), we convert it to make the value positive with **Math.abs** (lines 2 and 3).

> *Math.abs, in which abs is short for absolute, takes any number and converts it into a positive number.*

Next, whatever number **difference** is, we want Flash to go to that number frame on the **smiler** timeline inside the **face** instance and stop (line 5).
And the next requirement, please...

- **4.1** If difference is zero, then stop. Otherwise repeat from 2.1.

16. Directly beneath the actions you've just added to frame 15 of the **control** layer add this ActionScript:

```
if (difference != 0) {
        gotoAndPlay ("loop");
}
```

This is telling Flash that if the difference is greater than or less than 0 (which would mean that the user's guess was incorrect) then it must go back to the frame labeled **loop** where it will await another guess.

Finally, we need to alter the text at the top of the stage, which is still asking us 'How do you feel?'

17. In frame 1 of the **text** layer, change the text at the top to Guess my age! and, in frame 20 of the **control** layer, add a keyframe and add the following:

```
face.gotoAndStop("happy");
stop ();
```

18. In frame 20 of the **text** layer, add a keyframe and change the text in this new keyframe to read You got it!

19. Test the movie.

And that's it. We've followed our top down requirements specification, solved our problem, and finished our game.

You might want to give Smiler a bit more personality. For example, you could have a dynamic text box that displays a statement showing how Smiler feels about your last guess. If difference is greater than 30 it could say 'Miles away!'

Or if the difference is less than 30 it could say 'Getting warmer!'

And when the user guesses within 10 of the age it could say 'Red hot!'

All this can be done by adding if and else actions that relate to the variable you've assigned to the text field. There are many other things that you can add to this program to make Smiler more intelligent, just using the commands and techniques you've now learnt.

You've now reached the top of the intermediate learning slope. We haven't told you *everything* you need to know, but you now know all the basic principles and have had enough practice to allow you to quickly learn other structures that will increase your ability.

Case study

In this section of the case study we're going to build the remaining page for our portfolio web site – the *resume* section.

We'll write our resume in an external .txt file and then get Flash to call it into this section. Once we've done this we'll program the scroll buttons in the interface to enable the user to scroll through the resume. Flash MX also has its own print command that we'll utilize to print a hard copy of the resume.

Importing a text file

1. Open up your preferred text editor program (such as Notepad or SimpleText) and create a new text file called text_resume.txt. Save it in the same folder as all your other case study files.

2. On the first line of this new file enter:

   &varresume=

   resume will be the name of your variable that Flash will call.

3. Underneath this line, go ahead and type in any details you would like to include in your resume:

```
text_resume - Notepad                              _ □ ×
File  Edit  Format  Help
&varresume=
Work Experience ==========================

May 1996 – April 2000
Multimedia Developer – Red and Yellow Clothing Co. – Watford City, DK
- #1 job duty consisted of etc... etc... etc...
- #2 job duty consisted of etc... etc... etc...
- #3 job duty consisted of etc... etc... etc...
```

4. Once you've finished this, save the text_resume.txt file and close it.

5. Open up your main case study movie and double-click on the **content** movie clip to edit it. Go to the **resume** label in the timeline and open up the **resume** layer folder:

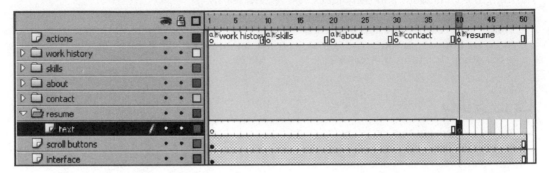

6. On the **text** layer at frame 40, use a static text field to give the page a suitable title in the top left corner of the interface:

7. Still on the **text** layer, use the Text tool to create a **Dynamic Text** field in the interface big enough to hold the imported text file. With *only* this text field selected, make the following modifications in the Properties inspector:

8. Select **Multiline** in the **Line type** drop-down menu:

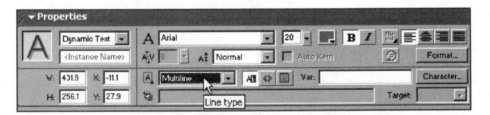

9. Type varresume in the **Var:** field. (Remember, this is the text file that you created at the beginning of this chapter's case study):

10. Set the character font, size, and color that you want the resume text to appear in when it displays in the text field.

11. Click on the **Character...** button to open the Character Options window. Check the **Embed Font Outlines For: All Characters** radio button:

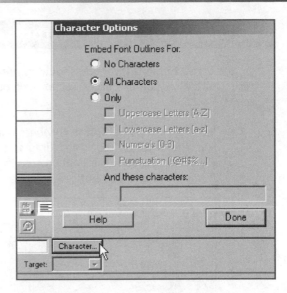

12. Now select frame 40 in the **actions** layer and open up the Actions panel. Add a **loadVariables** command using **Actions > Browser/Network > loadVariables**:

```
1   stop();
2   unloadMovieNum(1);
3   loadVariablesNum("", 0);
```

13. With the loadVariablesNum action selected in the script pane, type the name of the text file you created earlier (text_resume.txt) into the **URL** field. Set the **Location** to **Target** and then target the **content** movie clip so that the resume text file loads up exactly where we want it. You can type in _root.content or use the **Insert a target path** button to do this:

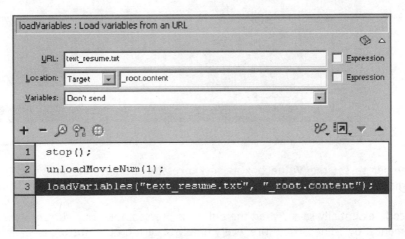

If you test the movie now, you'll see your resume text file imported into the **resume** section. Unfortunately, it's too long to completely fit in the text field so we need to activate the scroll buttons on the right-hand side of the interface. Here's how...

Wiring up the scroll buttons

On the **scroll buttons** layer you should have two arrow buttons that you imported in an earlier chapter's case study. None of the other sections of our web site require the scrolling function except for the **resume** section.

1. Insert a keyframe at frame 40 where our **resume** section starts and delete all the frames preceding it in the timeline. (Click and drag so that the frames are highlighted, right-click and then select Clear Frames from the context-sensitive menu.) Next, insert a blank keyframe directly after it in frame 41 so that the buttons are only visible in this section:

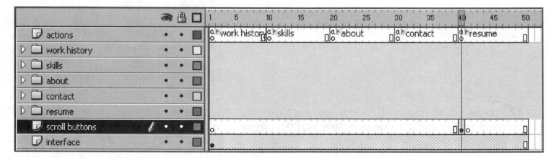

2. On the stage, select the down arrow and open up the Actions panel. Add a **set variable** action located under **Actions > Variables > set variable**. We already have a variable called **varresume** associated with our dynamic text field. If we want the down arrow to scroll down one line of our resume text, we need to add the following ActionScript to our intended down button:

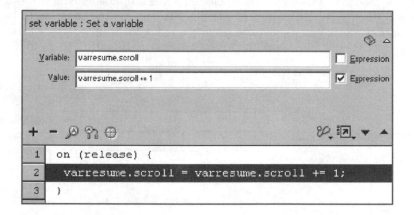

Remember to set the **Value** box as an **Expression** because we *do* want Flash to evaluate our statement and not just read it as text.

This code essentially says, 'when the button is pressed, take our current variable **varresume** and increment it by 1 line'. Therefore, every time you click on the button, it reads where it is currently located and then adds 1 line to itself – the text moves upwards by one line making the scroll effect.

3. To produce the same effect, but scrolling upwards, select the up arrow and attach the exact same actions, but decrement the variable **varresume** by 1. In the **Value** field type:

    ```
    varresume.scroll -=1
    ```

4. Test your movie. When you go the **resume** section you'll be able to scroll your imported text resume up and down a line at a time.

    You may want to tweak your text file a bit to remove any excess space. If you feel more daring, you could even change the file to read in HTML and have a nicely formatted HTML file in your Flash movie.

> *If you want your text file to scroll by more than one line at a time, change the increment/decrement value from 1 to 3, 8, or even 20. The number you type in will reflect how many lines the text will scroll per click.*

Making the resume printable

1. Create a new layer called **print button** in the **resume** layer folder. Insert a keyframe at frame 40.

2. Draw a suitable button shape and convert it to a button symbol called **print button**.

3. On the **actions** layer, remove the **stop** action from 40. Insert a new keyframe at frame 41 with the **stop** action attached there instead. Also label this frame **#p** so that it can be targeted for printing. Make the **print button** and text for the **resume** section extend through frames 40 to 41, removing any other frames on this layer:

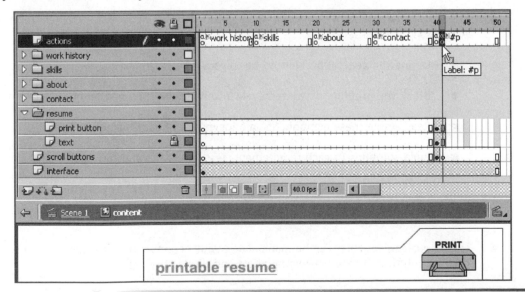

4. Select your **print button** and in the Actions panel add a **print** command located under **Actions > Printing > Print.** Select **As vectors** from the **Print** drop-down menu, set the **Location** to target _root.content, and select **Movie** from the **Bounding** drop-down:

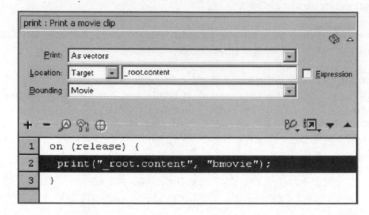

5. Test your file. You will now be able to click on your button and print off a hard copy of the resume in your resume section. Finally, in the Library, drag the print button into the printable resume folder and then save your movie.

Summary

In this chapter, we've been exploring the ActionScripting features that make Flash a powerhouse for sophisticated and powerful web applications. Once you're familiar with these principles and have applied them using the full array of actions and options, you can build the kind of web sites you've dreamed of making. We hope you started to see that, with ActionScript, the possibilities in Flash are infinite.

Specifically, we saw that:

- The **top down design** approach is a great way to approach complex programming and ActionScripting tasks:

    - Define the general problem to be solved.

    - Break the problem down iteratively into its smallest components.

    - Reassemble these components in a logical list of **requirements**.

    - Build solutions to each requirement. Test, integrate, and test again!

- Rudimentary **user input** can be captured using a simple **input text field**.

- Input text can be assigned to a variable and redisplayed in a **dynamic text field**.

- User input and variables can be manipulated with ActionScript: for instance, we used a big **+** sign on a button to add together two numbers and display the result.

- **Dot notation** gives us a secure and flexible way of targeting named movie clip instances inside our movies.

- Dot notation gives us access to the **hierarchy** of movie clip timelines implicit in every Flash movie.

- Movie clips have **properties** which we can target and modify using ActionScript, allowing us to alter a movie clip's appearance, behavior, and animation characteristics.

- We can modify movie clip properties and behavior based on user input and other movie events.

- Variables can be **scoped** and targeted using movie clip timelines and dot notation.

We're now ready to move on and tackle the remaining area of Flash knowledge you need to round off your Flash initiation – **object-oriented programming**. All the hard work and theory will seem worth it as we use these principles to build something we *nearly* built twice in this chapter: a proper game.

Intermediate ActionScript, Part 2

What we'll cover in this chapter:

- Fundamental concepts of **object-oriented design**.

- How Flash can use objects.

- Building a simple Flash game.

The real power of Macromedia Flash MX over previous versions of Flash is hidden in its code. Flash allows proper coding techniques to be applied to ActionScript, but you have to be far enough up the ladder to appreciate it. Luckily for you, you're high enough to appreciate the differences – it's just the full application that's yet to become clear.

In this chapter, we'll try to show you what all the fuss is about. It's now easier than ever to create animations and effects that are controlled directly from Flash using the dynamic animation techniques discussed in the last chapter, but it's also the ease of specifying paths and objects that gives Flash its extra power, as you'll soon see.

Part of the reason for the quantum leap in ActionScript functionality is that it allows us to implement the principles of **object-oriented design**. Object-oriented design and programming is too vast a topic to cover definitively in a single chapter like this. For a richer coverage of the theory and practice of object-oriented analysis, design, and programming, you should consult a book dedicated to the subject. If you look at **www.friendsofed.com**, you'll see there are several books dedicated to this subject.

What we'll do here is give you a taste of the *principles* of the object-oriented approach, and see how they can be applied in the Flash context, and how they might make you think differently about your Flash movies.

Object-oriented design

Object-oriented programming and design has become a standard approach in the computing industry. The reason for this is that it allows you to build computer systems that are robust enough to do their job. At the same time, they are flexible enough to be easily maintained and altered as the nature of the problem that they were set out to solve changes. How is that? Well, the essential truth of the object-oriented approach is that it models the problems it sets out to solve in the most abstract possible way: that is, it's always trying to distill a problem down to an essence that's unencumbered with surface detail. By *abstracting* the problem, you create a series of solutions that can easily be reorganized to deal with a different problem.

As an example of this, consider the task of making a cup of your favorite instant coffee.

Making coffee

First, let's think about how you'd analyze this in terms of the top down approach that we considered in the previous chapter.

In the top down design you take the problem and break it down into sub-problems. As you keep breaking it down, you're making the individual functional items smaller and more compact until you can start to see the solution in the sub-problems, because the sub-problems become more and more manageable and easier to understand. Take this problem definition:

To make a cup of coffee, with milk and one sugar

First iteration:

1.   Create some hot water
2.   Have a cup ready with coffee in it and some sugar
3.   When the water has boiled, pour the water into the cup
4.   Stir mixture for twenty seconds and add milk

Second iteration:

1.1　Fill kettle full of water
1.2　Connect kettle to power, and switch on

2.1　Get one teaspoon of sugar from sugar bowl and transfer to cup
2.2　Get one teaspoon of coffee from jar and transfer to cup

3.1　Wait until kettle has boiled
3.2　Pour water from kettle into cup
3.3　etc.....

Here, you're breaking things down until the problem is so basic that its components can be coded. The result of building a system based on this kind of analysis would be a combination of steps that carried out each stage of the task. A computer system developed in this way will usually consist of a series of carefully targeted, tightly constrained code elements – procedures – which each perform a small piece of the overall task. This approach is fine, until you want the system to do something different – say, make a cup of lemon tea, or an iced coffee. To reprogram the system to do this, you'd need to re-engineer multiple elements in the system to allow them to perform a different task. The top down method of decomposing the problem tends to 'hard-wire' the solution to the problem and make it less adaptable when your needs change.

An object-oriented cup of coffee

In object-oriented design, you try and look *beyond* the specific problem and analyze the nature of the *things* that make up that problem. That sounds a bit woolly – what does that mean? Well, if we were looking at the 'making a cup of coffee' process in an object-oriented way, we'd ignore the brand of coffee, and how hot the water needed to be, and how long you were supposed to stir the beverage. Instead, we'd think about the *general* processes involved, and try and conceptualize them.

The process of object-oriented design is a little like being in an episode of one of those drama series where fantastically wealthy, stylish and attractive thirty-somethings agonize over their inner torment, questioning the meaning and content of every aspect of their existence. OK, it's not *that* bad, but you *do* have to philosophize on 'what is making coffee all about?'

The generalized, philosophical answers to this question would be things like: 'well, there's liquid and powder involved, switching things on and seeing when they're done, moving things from one container to another, and finishing':

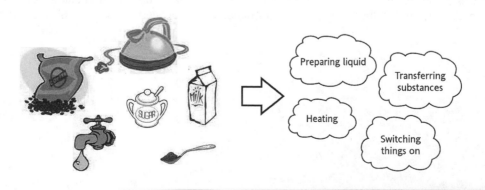

You're abstracting the problem down into building blocks, but into building blocks that are more 'loosely tied' to the actual components involved in the physical act of making a cup of coffee. You're not thinking about specific functionally any more, but are thinking about general principles like 'moving things from one container to another', 'liquid flowing', 'turning things on' and 'detecting when things have finished'.

Once you can express the process in these generalized terms, you can start creating *generic* routines that embody these general principles in code. You might create, for example, a routine that catered for the process called 'prepare the liquid'. This routine would embody the general function of preparing liquid, but it wouldn't be tied to preparing a particular *type* of liquid. Instead, this routine would be able to carry out the basic process using values that we supplied to it when we started that process. For instance, we might tell it the kind of liquid to use, and give it a temperature to heat (or chill) the liquid to:

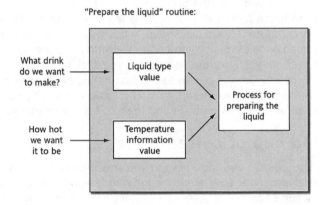

The generic routines are flexible, and, because we've distilled them down to the very essence of their functionality, they can be applied to a number of different tasks – making tea, making an iced drink, making a milkshake and so on. The 'prepare the liquid' routine is the same, but the details of an individual implementation of this process – making *this* cup of coffee or *this* iced tea – can be specified in each particular instance.

The 'prepare the liquid' routine is one part of the solution for the overall 'making a beverage' problem, and it would act in choreographed collaboration with the other generalized routines to achieve the overall aim.

The generalized routines are 'templates' for carrying out each aspect of the task, created to serve us, and waiting to do so. When we come to perform a beverage-making task, we'll initialize *instances* of each of these templates, feeding them the *specific* information that they need to perform this *specific* task properly:

Prepare the liquid class (template)

In object-oriented design terms, the templates are a **class**. The class describes the essentials of a process or an item, specifying the characteristics of the process that make it uniquely different from any other kind of process. The definition of the 'prepare the liquid' class might include: the capacity to specify a type of liquid; a variable that describes the amount of liquid, and a variable that controls the prepared liquid's temperature. The functionality for carrying out the task, and for coordinating activity with other routines, is encapsulated by the class.

To make an **object** to carry out the task, we instantiate – bring into existence – an object based on the class definition. So, if our class is called **Prepare Liquid**, we'll issue an instantiation that says:

```
Object Get Coffee Water Ready = Prepare Liquid (water, 1 cup, 200 degrees
fahrenheit)
```

The part on the left of the equals sign is just saying 'create me an object called `Get Coffee Water Ready`'.

The part on the right of the equals sign specifies the *class* you want this object to be based on – `Prepare Liquid` – and the values that you want to set for this particular object/process – the liquid type, the quantity, and the temperature. You have to feed these values in because the class defines them as being part of this general process. A class will also define the way that this class can interact with other classes, and it'll define interfaces for communicating with other classes.

Once the object is instantiated, it will run through the task it's been built to perform, using the definitions embodied in the class plus the specific attributes that we've assigned to this object.

A class is like a 'black box' that embodies a general process that solves part of a larger problem, and an object is an instance of that class that you create to perform a specific function – making *this* cup of coffee.

So what's the point of this? Why would you want to go through all this extra thinking and dip your toes into the world of object-oriented design (which is all we've done here)? The answer is that object-oriented solutions are more robust and flexible, and they're easier to maintain and upgrade. Because you've designed the solution in terms of generalized and self-sufficient components, you can reuse these components in other tasks that have a similar element in them – maybe a 'preparing a bath' task could reuse our 'prepare the liquid' component. Furthermore, as each class communicates with other entities using interfaces, you can completely change the instructions inside a class and not affect the overall solution – provided that you keep the same interfaces: each class – and the objects that are derived from it – can be reworked in isolation. Here, in essence are the benefits of the object-oriented approach:

- Reusability.

- Encapsulation – functionality embedded in a self-contained object.

- Maintainability.

- Extensibility.

- Flexibility.

The object-oriented approach helps you build solutions that can change as the world that they're modeling changes, and the strength of OO design lies in its ability to generalize: generalized solutions based on these design principles are not 'locked in' to the problem you initially set out to solve, because elements can be used elsewhere and changed when different problems arise.

What's this got to do with Flash?

That's a good question.

Flash and objects

The simple answer is:

- Reusability.

- Encapsulation – functionality embedded in a self-contained object.

- Maintainability.

- Extensibility.

- Flexibility.

ActionScript has been restructured to allow you to implement the object-oriented approach more easily, and that's one of its major internal differences from previous versions of Flash. Flash 5 ActionScript capabilities changed dramatically from Flash 4, and Flash MX has enhanced the capabilities of Flash 5. In fact, ActionScript now actually gives you the ability to define classes and instantiate objects from them, although that level of complexity is (sadly) beyond the scope of this book.

Until now, our exposure to objects has been pretty limited, right? Wrong. Flash MX is fully OO-based, so a great deal of the elements that we have already used in this book are, without you even knowing it, objects. Typical objects in the Flash environment include video, sound, components, text, buttons, and, of course, movie clips.

> You can view a full list of Flash's predefined objects by opening the Reference panel (Window > Reference) and opening the Objects book. Try not to be too intimidated by the list right now because the amount of these that you will use at the moment will be minimal.

It will help you a great deal in the long run if you remember that ActionScript is object-oriented, and if you begin to think of elements such as video, sound, text, buttons, etc., as objects.

Let's explore the concept with a basic object that you're already really familiar with: the **movie clip**.

A movie clip instance on the stage is essentially a specific named object based on the movie clip *class* embodied in a symbol in the Library:

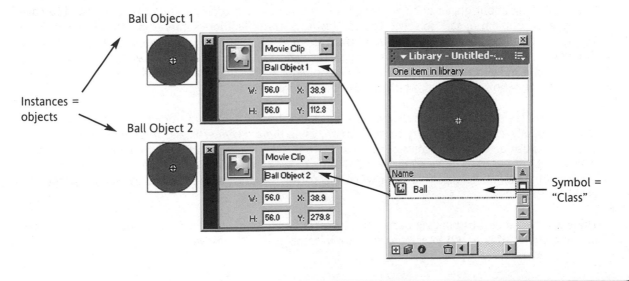

A movie clip object has standard, basic properties like 'size' and 'number of frames', and once you've built up the individual instance by adding a few actions and frames of content to it, it can start to do things.

An object has a standard general structure. At its simplest level, it calculates a certain, small but well-defined chunk of a solution (or movie), and it has well-defined interfaces that allow it to communicate with the other objects that deal with the other parts of the problem (movie). Remember that to follow the object-oriented route you have to:

- Identify the basic elements of your problem in terms of what you can see happening (or what you *want* to happen in your movie).

- Identify what these basic elements actually *are* (conceptualize) and see whether you can generalize them into basic groups (classes).

- Create movie clips in the Library that map to these basic groups and perform the functions associated with the group.

- Instantiate (drag out of the Library) individual movie clips (objects) on the stage and, if necessary, give them instance names so that you can target them with ActionScript.

The important point here is that the movie clips must be *self-contained*. They must be able to solve their part of the problem by themselves, and they must be able to do this independently of whatever else is also going on in the movie.

Objects work best in situations where there are multiple instances of a few very similar processes to be performed. We can illustrate this with a graphical effect in a Flash movie. A lot of computer graphic effects use a few basic rules that are applied many times over to give the illusion of complex behavior. Here, we'll see how a very simple movie clip object with a single simple behavior can be replicated many times on the screen to create a much more complex looking effect.

A simple mouse trail

The great thing about object-oriented design is that it allows you to *play* – you don't even need to have a high-level problem or task to solve. You can just say, 'This effect looks interesting, let's break it down into its objects and see what we can build from them'. Like child's play, you can use this as a creative thought process, and not necessarily as a logical, analytical problem solving process. The reason for this is very simple: in Flash your objects are not long-winded and obscure data elements – they're visual movie clips with animation and sound, which can be much more fun.

A mouse trail is a little group of characters or text that follows the mouse pointer. An effective mouse trail will usually contain some very complex math, using things like inertia and trigonometry to calculate the cursor position and the relative position of the trail. By stopping and thinking about it though, you'll realize that instead of using heavy math and shifting movie clips around behind the cursor, you could just use lots of static movie clips that *react* when the cursor moves over them. Basically, you're turning the problem on its head.

There are two stages to building our mouse trail: (1) building the basic movie clip object that we'll use multiple copies of later; (2) integrating the multiple copies into the movie.

Creating the basic movie clip

The first thing to realize is that all of those fancy mouse trails have one thing in common: the character furthest away from the cursor is *least* affected by what the mouse is doing now, and the closest is *most* affected.

In essence, we've abstracted the problem down to a generalization of the type of animation that's required to create the desired effect: the animation on any particular character should get weaker based on: (1) increasing distance from the mouse; (2) how long ago the mouse was near it – longer ago means a weaker animation effect.

The only thing we've encountered so far that's affected by the mouse is a button symbol, so maybe if you had loads of buttons all over the screen, you could make Flash do all the hard work for you. That's all you need to know. It seems pretty vague, but that's OK, it allows you more room to experiment...

1. Start a new movie, and change the background color to black using the Property inspector. Also make sure that **View > Grid > Show Grid** and **Snap to Grid** menu options are both selected.

2. Create a new graphic symbol and call it **sy.circle**: give the circle a blue stroke and fill. Give the circle a diameter of about **90** pixels, and center it at **0,0**:

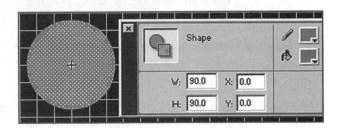

3. Now create a movie clip and call it **mc.circle**. Change the name of the movie clip's default layer to **circle**.

4. Leave frame 1 of this movie clip empty, but add a keyframe in frame 2. Drag a copy of **sy.circle** into this keyframe, and center it on the stage at **0,0**.

5. Next, using the Property inspector, select **Alpha** from the **Color** drop-down menu and give the circle a value of **70%**:

6.   Add another keyframe at frame 20. In this frame, use the **Color** drop-down again, but this time, select **Advanced** and click on the **Settings** button that appears to the right.

The **Alpha** will already be set to **70%** from before, but give the circle a red hue by moving the second **Red** slider (the one that's a *number* rather than a percentage) all the way up to **255**:

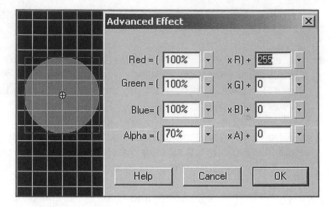

7.   Using the Property inspector, set the width and height to **1**. Finally, create a motion tween from frame 2 to frame 20.

8.   If you drag this movie clip onto the stage and test your movie you'll see a blue circle that starts off big and blue and then gets smaller and redder until it finally disappears.

You've now created your simple 'diminishing' effect. The next thing that you need to do is change the clip so that it'll only play when the mouse goes over it, when it will run through once and stop until the mouse goes over it again. The more recently the mouse was near it, the bigger the circle. This carries on for 20 frames, by which time the circle is so small it disappears. You also have to somehow persuade your object to acquire the mouse input that will control its appearance and behavior. You *could* get it to look at how close the mouse is to it, but there is a simpler option to try first.

9.   Duplicate **sy.circle** by selecting it in the Library window, clicking on the white triangle icon on the top right of the Library, and selecting **Duplicate** from the drop-down menu. Now make the new symbol into a button via the **Duplicate Symbol** dialog box and call the button **bu.circle**.

10. The button needs to be transparent, and the same size as the movie clip. In **bu.circle** insert a keyframe in the **Hit** state, and delete the circle from the **Up** state. Finally, copy the button in the Hit state, select its Over state and choose the **Edit > Paste in Place** menu option. You now have a circular button that has no Up or Down state, but *does* have an Over and Hit state, making it invisible but selectable:

11. We want to add this button, plus some simple actions, into **mc.circle**, so go into **mc.circle** and add two new layers called `actions` and `button`:

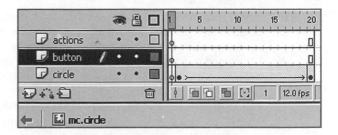

12. In the **button** layer, add the **bu.circle** symbol and center it. Then remove all of the other frames from this layer so that the button only exists on frame 1. With the **bu.circle** button still selected, give it an instance name `bucircle` in the Property inspector:

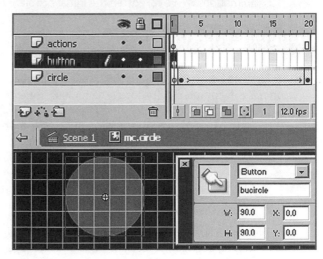

13. Next, type the following in frame 1 of the **actions** layer:

```
stop ();
bucircle.onRollOver = function() {
    play();
}
```

We don't need to include a **root** reference on the second line because we're already on the **mc.circle** timeline, and that's where we placed **bu.circle**.

14. Finally, insert a keyframe in frame 20 of the **actions** layer and simply add `gotoAndPlay (1);`

And that's it. You've created a movie clip that does the following:

- Waits at a blank first frame until it's rolled over.

- When it's rolled over by the mouse, it plays.

- When it has played once, it goes back to the blank first frame.

15. If you now drag an instance of **mc.circle** onto the stage and test your movie, you'll see a blank screen until your mouse happens to move over the button. As soon as this happens, a circle will appear, getting smaller as time goes by, until it disappears completely. That was the basic object we started out trying to create: an effect that diminishes based on either 'time since it was started' or 'distance the mouse is away from it'.

Notice that up until now we haven't even thought how we're going to use this object. We just wanted to create an object that waited until the mouse was near, and then displayed a diminishing animation. We've forgotten the initial problem completely, and concentrated on creating this object.

Building the movie

The next step is to test the object to see if this simple animation repeated many times could be used to produce the complex behavior we're looking for.

1. Start by dragging instances of **mc.circle** onto the stage until you have built up a single row of your movie clips. Use the grid to help you create a regular overlapping pattern:

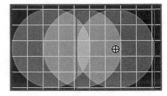

2. Keep dragging new clips from the Library until you have a complete row across the stage. To ensure they're aligned correctly with each other, use the Align panel's **Align top edge** button:

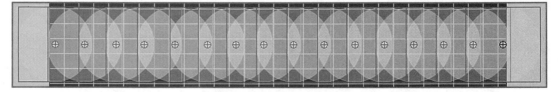

3. When you have a full row, select them all and then press F8 to convert the whole row into a new movie clip symbol, and call it **mc.circle.row**.

4. Finally, keep adding rows above and below your starting row until you've filled the screen with a neat grid:

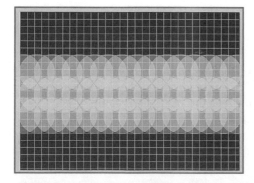
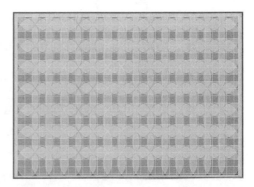

And now comes the moment of truth. Remember, we set ourselves the task of creating a trail that would start from wherever the mouse was and gradually fade as the mouse moved away, or as time passed. Did we do it? There's only one way to find out – test that movie:

It seems to have worked perfectly. Cool. You could tweak it to have smaller circles and closer gaps if you wanted, and have your animations last half as long to tie them closer to the cursor. In fact, why use circles at all? You can change the animation to be whatever you want – sparkling stars, jumping sheep – the possibilities are endless. The next step is to play and create!

Notice that in making this movie, all you've done is thought about an effect, decided what its most basic behavior was, and created an object with that behavior. Then you've made a more complex looking overall effect by making lots of copies of the simple effect. Although this movie isn't truly object-oriented, the thinking behind it *is*. The visual effect we've created is based on one button in one movie clip. One of the fundamental advantages of objects is that they're self-contained, and therefore reusable. What's more, because they are generalized solutions, they can be rearranged to fit new problems.

We'll now show you how objects and the theories behind them can be reapplied to different tasks: we're going to create a fully playable, albeit basic, Flash game.

Putting it all together

We're going to be looking at a simple memory game sometimes called 'pairs'. The first thing we'll do is define the basic rules:

- The player is presented with an even number of face down tiles with symbols on their face down side. For each tile there is at least one other identical tile.

- The player has to match each tile with another matching tile by turning a pair of tiles over per turn. If the tiles are an identical pair, the tiles are left face up. If the tiles don't match, the tiles are returned back to their face down state.

- The game has finished when all tiles are face up.

This game can be implemented using either a top down or an object-oriented approach. If you want, you can try it using the top down approach, but you're guaranteed to end up with a bunch of if-then-else statements as long as your arm, and more variables than you would believe!

Instead, let's look at it from an object-oriented point of view.

Your first thoughts should be about what the fundamental objects of the game are. In this case it's quite obvious – the only things being manipulated in this game are the *tiles*. So if we can create a generalized tile object with an appropriate range of behaviors, then we've cracked the whole game. What do we want the tile to be able to do?

At a guess, we'd want it to be able to do the following:

- Be face down when it's unselected.

- Turn face up when it's selected, and tell the user and Flash what symbol it has on it.

- Be able to ask Flash when the current turn has finished, and if it's not one of a pair, to turn back to its initial state, or stay face up if it *is* one of a pair.

Notice that there are a few things we *haven't* defined as necessary to know. Things like:

- How many tiles there are.

- How many different tile symbols there will be.

- How many tiles are already face up.

- How many tiles are already face down.

We don't need to know these things because the object we're looking at creating will represent only *one* tile. All these bits of information don't apply to *one* tile, they apply to *many* tiles working alongside each other. So, using our object-oriented design method, we'll first create the object, and then when that's working fine we'll go on to the next step up and build the object into the game – it's the game structure that provides the *context* for the tile's behavior, whereas the behavior is all built into the tile itself.

But wait a minute...

Part of this definition sounds strangely familiar. The mouse trail we just created stays still when it's not selected, and then does something when it *has* been selected. This is a subset of the same sort of behavior we want for our tile. The only difference is that the mouse trail circles were all identical, but the tiles we want to create will be different. Can we re-use part of the previous exercise? It might be a good starting point.

Creating the tile

1. Start a new movie. Using the Property inspector change the movie background to purple, and the dimensions to **800x800**.

    In the last tutorial we created a circle to start off with, then created a button that was the same size and shape to 'trigger' the movie into action. We're going to do the same thing here.

2. Create a new graphic symbol and call it `sy.tile`.

3. Next, create a tile shape by drawing a blue rectangle with rounded edges, the same as you did for your playing cards earlier in the book – you could even use them, but remember to take the character off the front, as we want them to be blank for now. Make your tile 80 pixels wide and 120 pixels high, and center it on the stage:

4. Use the **Option** menu from the Library to duplicate the symbol as a button, the same way as you did in the last example. Call this symbol `bu.transparent` – the reason for this name will become clear in a moment.

5. Add a keyframe in the button's **Hit** state and clear its Up state to create a button that's invisible, but still hittable.

6. Now we need some pictures to go on the tiles. We've provided a set of pictures of fruit on our web site that you can download and use, otherwise feel free to come up with whatever you want. For this example we'll be using four different pictures: a tomato, an orange, a lemon, and a pear:

   Once imported, you will have four new graphic symbols in your Library: **sy.fruit.tomato**, **sy.fruit.orange**, **sy.fruit.lemon** and **sy.fruit.pear**.

7. Now you need to put all of these together to make your tile. First of all, create a new movie clip symbol and call it `mc.tile`.

   We know that we'll need to have a button and an animation in this object, so we'll put them in now.

8. Rename the first layer `tile`, then create a new layer and name it `button`.

   In the **tile** layer, we'll create an animation of the tile turning over, and to create this effect we'll use the same kind of illusion we implemented for the 'flipping face' tween in Chapter 7.

9. In frame 1 of the **tile** layer, drag in a copy of **sy.tile** from the Library and center it. Now add keyframes at frames 5 and 10.

10. The next thing is to create an animation of the tile flipping over. To do this, we'll make the tile get progressively shorter as it moves between frames 1 to 5, and then grow again until it's back up to its normal size in frame 10. This will give the illusion that the tile is flipping over. Click on frame 5 and use the Property inspector to set the height (**H**) value to 1:

    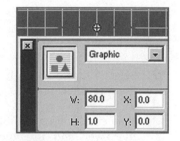

11. Now add two separate motion tweens between frames 1 and 5, and frames 5 and 10:

    At the moment your flipping tile won't really seem very convincing as both sides look the same, but when the picture is on one side the illusion will be complete.

    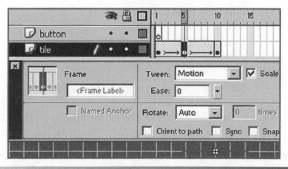

12. Add a new layer between the two current layers and call it **fruit**. What we want to do is make the fruit start to appear from frame 5 onwards, and grow in size until it's full size in frame 10.

13. Insert a keyframe in frame 10 of your **fruit** layer and drag a copy of one of your graphic symbols onto the stage – we're using the tomato symbol. Center your symbol and resize it until it fits nicely onto your tile:

14. Add a new keyframe at frame 5, then copy the fruit from frame 10 and paste it in place into frame 5. Now, here's the trick: we want the tomato to be as thin as the tile at frame 5, so using the Property inspector, change the tomato's **H** value to 1, the same value as the tile. At frame 5 you should now have a 'squashed' tile and a 'squashed' tomato over the top of it.

15. Finally, create a motion tween from frame 5 to 10. Your animation should now give a convincing impression of a tile flipping over:

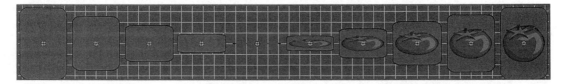

The tile should start off blank and shrink to nothing, before growing back to full size again with the tomato image on it.

16. Once the tile has flipped over face up, the next thing we'll want it to do is flip back over to its initial face down position. This motion would simply look like the animation we've created so far in frames 1 to 10, but in reverse. Create a new keyframe in frame 20 of your **fruit** and **tile** layers.

17. Select frames 1 through 10 on the **tile** layer and use the **Edit > Copy Frames** menu option to copy them to the clipboard.

18. Now click in frame 20 of the layer and use the **Edit > Paste Frames** menu option to paste the frames into the timeline:

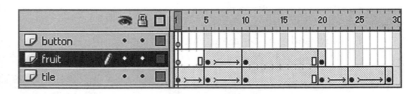

You don't need to reverse these frames – as you'll see, it looks fine if you play the movie clip.

19. If you were to do the same thing with the tomato animation though, it would be the wrong way round. Click in frame 5 on the **fruit** layer and again, use the **Edit > Copy Frames** menu option to copy it to the clipboard.

20. Now click in frame 24 on the same layer and paste the frame there. Finally, set up a motion tween between frames 20 and 24:

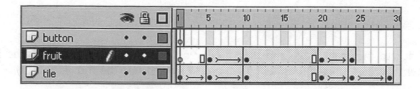

Now when you play back your movie clip, it should run through with no trouble.

So you now have a tile that starts face down, flips face up, and then flips back to face down again. The next things you need are the actions...

Making the tile work

The tile should only flip when it's selected, so you need to incorporate a button into the movie clip to trigger this behavior.

The button will go into frame 1 of the **button** layer. This layer should only have a single frame in it: once the tile has started flipping we don't want the user to be able to select it again as this could create problems later on in the game.

1. Drag the **bu.transparent** symbol onto the stage from your Library and center it on your existing tile. If you find it easier, you may want to hide and lock the other two layers by clicking on the eye and lock icons on the timeline.

The first thing we want the button to do when we click on it is to start playing the movie clip, which we can achieve with some simple ActionScript.

2. Select your **bu.transparent** symbol and in the Actions – Button panel, insert the following code:

```
on (press) {
    play ();
}
```

3. We'll be adding a lot of actions to the tile object, so to keep things neat, create a new layer at the top of the stack and name it `actions`.

4. Next, select frame 1 of the **actions** layer and using the Property inspector, label it `facedown`.

5. Still on frame 1 of the **actions** layer, open the Actions panel. We want the tile to pause in the first frame until the button is clicked, so put a `stop();` action on the first line of the script pane and press ENTER

6. The other simple thing we want the tile to do is return to the first frame when it finishes running through the animation. We can do this by putting a keyframe with a **goto** action into frame 30. Enter the following code:

```
gotoAndStop ("facedown");
```

7. Go back to the main stage and drag a copy of your movie clip out from the Library. It doesn't matter where you place it as it's only there so we can test the movie.

8. Now play your movie. The tile should stay blank until you click on it, then it will cycle through its animation and return to the facedown state. You should only be able to click on it in its fully facedown state.

The next thing you need to do is have the tile stop when it's fully face up.

Unfortunately, you'll need a little more than a **stop** action in this frame – we also want the tile to tell the user, and Flash, what symbol it has on it. The user bit is easy, as they can see the picture on top of the tile, but telling Flash is a little more complicated. The questions that you should be asking are:

- Who or what do we tell?

- How do we tell it, and what does it need to know?

One of the fundamental things to realize when creating object-oriented programs is that you have to know which parts of the program fit inside of one object, and which parts fit into another object or into external code. This is a difficult concept to grasp at first, but if you think *'What's the game doing? What can a tile do, and should it be able to do that?'* it quickly becomes obvious that the pieces of a game – the tiles – should not be the *controllers* of the action. So what *should* be controlling the game? The rules should control the game, or a referee who knows the rules.

The referee for this game will be the main timeline, and it's that which will be in control. The tiles are just saying things like 'OK, I am a tile object, and I have just flipped over', and nothing more. This is because we need to be able to add as many tile objects to the final game as we like. This is the beauty of object-oriented design: the tiles are just objects that we can plug in to the program any number of times without having to recode them. They are *self-contained* and *reusable*.

As you know from the last chapter, the main timeline is called **_root**. While using the root would be fine for our movie, it would stop it from being truly object-oriented. Remember what we said earlier about objects being reusable? Well, to keep this reusability as open as possible, we don't want to always tie things to the main timeline. The way we can get round this is to instead give control of the movie clip to the next level up: by doing this, we'll be able to move the code around within the levels of a movie and still have it work. The name for the next level up in Flash is the **_parent**. By telling the movie clip to talk to the parent level, we're keeping it as a separate portable object – wherever you place a tile in a movie hierarchy, this notation will ensure that it always talks to the next level up, irrespective of the name of that level's timeline.

That answers the first question, but now we know we should be talking to the parent, what do we want to tell it? The parent needs to know what's on the tile, and in this case it's a *tomato*.

9. In the Actions panel for your **bu.transparent** symbol, add the following highlighted code, so the ActionScript for your button looks like this:

```
1  on (press) {
2      _parent.buttonpress += 1;
3      _parent.fruit = "tomato";
4      play();
5  }
```

The next thing to do is test to see if Flash can now tell which fruit is on the tile.

10. Go back to the main movie timeline and draw a text field below the tile. Make the text field dynamic and non-selectable, and press the **Show Border Around Text** button to make Flash draw a box around your text. Make sure the text color is different to your movie color's background and, finally, assign it the variable **fruit** by typing fruit in the **Var** field.

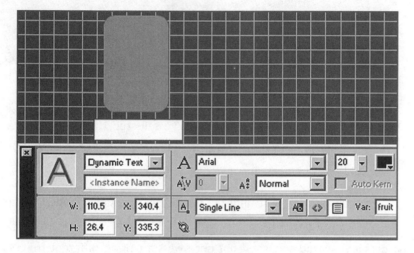

11. Now test the movie.

This time just you click on the tile, you'll see the tile communicating with the **_parent**, telling it what the variable **fruit** now is:

You've now got one tile working pretty well, but the game won't be much fun with only one tile! The next thing to do is test it with *multiple* tiles, and see what sort of problems arise.

Using multiple tiles

You now need to start thinking how you want each tile to work when there is more than one tile on the stage.

1. Add another three tiles to your main stage to make a row of four in all. You can tidy up the row by using the Align panel:

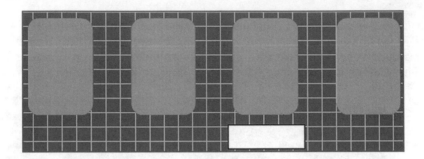

2. Now test the movie. There are a few things to notice here:

    ■   Your text field won't change after you've selected the first tile because *all* of the tiles are tomatoes.

    ■   It's possible to flip more than two tiles at the same time.

    ■   The first tile doesn't wait until the second tile has been flipped before it flips itself back round, so you'd have to be pretty quick to match a pair.

The first problem should sort itself out once we start using different fruit, so we don't need to worry about that.

For the second problem, we need to count the number of tiles that are now face up: if it's two or more, we shouldn't allow any other tiles to flip. To do this, we'll need a variable to count the number of tiles that have been flipped.

To fix the third problem, we need the first tile to wait until one other tile is face-up before it flips itself back over.

3. Go back and open up the Actions panel for the **bu.transparent** symbol. We've already told the parent that the fruit on this symbol is a tomato, and created the ActionScript that lets Flash know when the button has been pressed.

Now add the following line of highlighted code and another curly closing bracket under the **play** action, so that your ActionScript for the button symbol looks like this:

```
1  on (press) {
2      _parent.buttonpress += 1;
3      _parent.fruit = "tomato";
4      if (_parent.buttonpress<=2) {
5          play();
6      }
7  }
```

We now know how many times a button has been pressed, and have also told Flash to stop more than two tiles being flipped at the same time.

The last line of code that we attached to the **bu.transparent** symbol checks if we've already pressed any two other buttons and if so, says 'don't respond to any more button presses'. The beauty of tying **buttonpress** to the parent and not to each tile is that all of the tile objects will look at the same variable. They don't need to know *which* other buttons have been pressed, they will respond as soon as any two buttons are pressed.

4.   Test the movie to confirm this.

The third problem is a bit more involved. What we want to do is:

- Make the parent count how many times *any* button has been pressed.

- Keep the first tile flipped until a second is face up.

- Make some decisions on whether the tiles match or not.

Hang on, the first part of that sounds a bit familiar: **buttonpress** already does that – it tells the main timeline how many buttons have been pressed so far, and when this number is equal to two we know that the player has picked a pair, and that the current turn is over whether they match or not.

The next part of our task is to make the tile stay face up until our referee tells it that the current turn is over. We'll create a new variable called **hadgo** to help us with that.

5.   Create a new layer in the main timeline and name it `actions`. Name the existing layer `tiles`.

The first frame of the **actions** layer will set up the variables that apply to the whole game, and we'll insert a second keyframe that will hold those that deal with each turn.

6.   Insert a keyframe into frame 2 of the **actions** layer. There are three things that we want to happen at the beginning of every go: (1) we want the **fruit** variable to be reset; (2) we want the **buttonpress** variable to be put back to 0; (3) we want our new variable **hadgo** to be implemented.

7.   Enter the following ActionScript to frame 2 of the main timeline's **actions** layer, so that the Script pane of the Actions panel looks like this:

```
1  fruit = "";
2  buttonpress = 0;
3  hadgo = false;
```

That's our initializations done; now it's time to set up our turn loop using **hadgo**.

8. Open the **actions** layer of your movie clip and create keyframes at frames 10 and 11.

9. Put a label in frame 10 and call it `buttonloop`.

10. Now open the Actions panel and add the following ActionScript to frame 11, so that your Script pane look like this:

```
1  if (_parent.hadgo == false) {
2      gotoAndPlay ("buttonloop");
```

This bit of code looks to see if the player has had their turn, and keeps the tile face up until the turn has finished by constantly looping back to the previous frame labeled buttonloop. At the moment, this will be an infinite loop as **hadgo** is *always* false. Don't worry; this'll all be working after we get a bit more code in.

11. Go back to the **actions** layer on the main timeline and insert keyframes in frames 4 and 5. In these frames we want to wait until two tiles have been turned over, and we know that this will be when **buttonpress** is equal to **2**. So, we want a similar loop to the one that we've just used, but with **buttonpress** as the condition rather than **hadgo**. We also need to set up a new label for the loop.

12. Click in frame 4 and label it `pressloop`.

13. Now we need to add our code in frame 5. The **if** action is straightforward — enter the following code so your Script pane looks like this:

```
1  if (buttonpress == 2) {
2      hadgo = true;
3  }
4  gotoAndPlay("pressloop");
```

Notice that this time, if the condition is true (the user has flipped two tiles over), we have set **hadgo** to *true*. We've finished the loop by putting a **goto** action at the end to send it back to our **pressloop** label.

14. Use F5 to insert a frame at frame 5 of the **tiles** layer. We need to do this to make sure the tiles are visible throughout the movie. Now you can test your game...

There are now two separate loops running at the same time, one waiting for **buttonpress** to equal **2**, and one waiting for **hadgo** to be *true*. Flash will stay within frames 4 and 5 on the main timeline until two tiles have been turned face up. When this happens it will set **hadgo** to true. As soon as **hadgo** is true, the loop in frame 11 of the two face up tiles will open and the animation will run through to the end and flip the tiles back over.

Notice that there is no need to control the tiles that have not been touched in this turn. This means that you could add as many tiles as you wanted now, and Flash wouldn't care because it's only looking for two face up tiles and isn't counting the face down ones. The reason you've been able to design in this way is because you've used an object-oriented approach — the problem was abstracted down to its minimum variables and conditions. Things that you might have thought the referee and the tiles would have needed to know turn out to be irrelevant. How do you know they are irrelevant? Well, you don't really — you just know that it seems to work without them, and if it isn't broken, why fix it? It may seem a bit simpleminded to not even consider any other things, but simplicity is the key to object-oriented design, and being simpleminded takes a lot of practice.

We've almost completed the game now: the only things left to do are to run through what happens at the end of each turn, and then tell it to start the next one.

Sorting out the main timeline

The things we want to happen at the end of each turn are:

- When a matching pair has been uncovered we need to tell the tiles to stay face up.

- When a matching pair has been uncovered we need to note that there is one less pair to find.

- When all the pairs have been found, Flash must be able to detect this and finish the game.

Notice again that we're not actually interested in things that you might think we should be, like the number of tiles and the number of different symbols there are on the tiles. They are not part of the problem even though they are part of the game. The important thing in this game is to find pairs, and it's this that determines our definition of the referee.

We'll start with a 4 x 4 playing board, which will include 8 pairs – we'll eventually have four pairs of our four different fruits. This will be constant for every game, so this value will go in frame 1 of the actions layer on the main timeline. This frame is blank at the moment, but remember that we decided this frame would contain the variables that would be initialized only once for each game.

1. On the main timeline, click in frame 1 of the **actions** layer, and enter:

    ```
    pairs = 8;
    ```

    This variable will tell Flash how many pairs there are, so it will know that when it has flipped over this many pairs, the game is over. Your main timeline should now look like this:

2. In frame 2, we've already initialized **fruit**, **buttonpress**, and **hadgo**. Now we also want to initialize variables that allow us to decide if there was a match or not. We need to know which fruit was on the first tile and which fruit was on the second tile, and we can then work out if they match. So, we need to set another three **variables** on this frame.

    One to say what's on the first tile:

    ```
    fruit1 = "";
    ```

    One to say what's on the second tile:

    ```
    fruit2 = "";
    ```

    And a final one to say if they match:

    ```
    match = false;
    ```

The ActionScript for this frame will now look like this:

```
1  fruit = "";
2  buttonpress = 0;
3  hadgo = false;
4  fruit1 = "";
5  fruit2 = "";
6  match = false;
```

We now need to alter our loop in frame 5 to include these new values. There are three possible conditions our referee will have to look at in this loop:

- No tiles have been flipped.

- One tile has been flipped – Flash will need to know what the revealed fruit was and put it in **fruit1**.

- Two tiles have been flipped – Flash will need to know what the second revealed fruit was and put it in **fruit2**.

If two tiles have been pressed then the turn has finished, so we need to do a couple more things. We need to see if **fruit1** and **fruit2** are the same and, if they are, we need to set **match** to true. Then, when **match** is true, we need to reduce the number of pairs by 1 so Flash will know when the game is over.

3. Open the actions for frame 5. At the moment we just have a **buttonpress** loop running here, but we need to modify this quite heavily. So that we can see clearly what we're doing in this frame, delete all of the actions that are in it.

4. Now replace the ActionScript you just deleted with the following code:

```
if (buttonpress==0) {
   gotoAndPlay("pressloop");
} else if (buttonpress==1) {
   fruit1 = fruit;
   gotoAndPlay("pressloop");
} else if (buttonpress==2) {
   fruit2 = fruit;
   hadgo = true;
```

We now need to put in the final code that'll test to see if the tiles match. The first thing you need to be able to do is to compare **fruit1** and **fruit2**. This can be done using the same == that we've been using because we're comparing variables. If we had been comparing strings, Flash would have just compared the number of characters in each string.

5. Add an **if** action to check if both tiles are the same:

```
if (fruit1==fruit2) {
```

6. Finally, we need to put in what we want to happen if the tiles *do* match. We need to set a few variables. The first should decrease **pairs** by 1, and the second needs to tell Flash that we've found a **match**. Add this code:

```
        pairs = --pairs;
        match = true;
    }
}
```

7. Your completed code for this frame should now look like this:

```
1  if (buttonpress==0) {
2      gotoAndPlay("pressloop");
3  } else if (buttonpress==1) {
4      fruit1 = fruit;
5      gotoAndPlay("pressloop");
6  } else if (buttonpress==2) {
7      fruit2 = fruit;
8      hadgo = true;
9      if (fruit1 eq fruit2) {
10         pairs = --pairs;
11         match = true;
12     }
13 }
```

8. Test your movie.

You'll be able to flip over a tile, and then Flash will wait for you to flip over another tile before carrying on. When you've flipped over two tiles, Flash will start back at the beginning of the game. At the moment, when two tiles have been flipped over, Flash is going all the way back to frame 1 and starting again. This is a problem: we only wanted frame 1 to be played once at the very beginning of every game, whereas after two tiles are turned over we only want Flash to go back as far as frame 2.

9. Click on frame 2 in the **actions** layer of the main movie, and label it `mainloop`.

The next thing we need to do is set up a loop to make Flash go back to **mainloop** at the end of each turn. We want to give the player the chance to have another go unless they have already found all of the pairs. So, we only want to take another turn if **pairs** has not yet been reduced to zero.

After frame 5, the tiles will be flipping back to their face down state, so we'll allow a bit of time for this before we start adding more actions to the main timeline.

10. Add a keyframe in frame 20. Additionally, put a normal frame in frame 20 of the **tiles** layer to keep them displayed on the screen throughout the game:

11. Add the following actions to frame 20, so that your Script pane looks like this:

```
1  if (pairs>0) {
2      gotoAndPlay("mainloop");
3  }
```

There's one more thing to do before you test your movie: when the user's found all of the pairs, we want them to get a reward. For simplicity, we're just going to have a screen saying 'You did it!!', but we'll put it on another layer to give you room to go to town with it.

12. Add a new layer to the bottom of the main timeline and name it finished. Next, put a keyframe in frame 35. Add a keyframe to frame 35 of the **actions** layer as well, but only put a normal frame in frame 34 of the **tiles** layer. This is because we don't want the tiles to be visible on the victory screen. Of course, if you want the user to be able to carry on admiring their handiwork, you can keep the tiles in all the way to frame 35.

13. Put a **stop** action in frame 35 in the **actions** layer.

14. Now draw your victory screen in frame 35 of the **finished** layer. We've just put 'You did it!!' in big green letters across the stage. Handsome.

That completes the main timeline – you can now test your game, as the whole thing should be working perfectly. However, we've currently only got one fruit on the stage, so you'll have to select eight pairs of the same thing, but you can see how spectacular it will be when we have the full range of fruit in there.

Adding the final touches

The only thing left to do is tell our tiles to stay faceup when they are a pair, and we'll also put in a little animation to make them look different when they're matched.

Back in the **movie clip**, the crucial frame is frame 11. This frame is the brains behind the whole object because it decides what the tile is going to do next once it has flipped face up. At the moment, it's just looking for the root to tell it whether the current turn has finished via **hadgo**. Once **hadgo** is true, either one or the other of two conditions will exist:

● This tile is one of a matching pair, and **_parent.match** is *true*.

● This tile is not one of a matching pair, and **_parent.match** is *false*.

1. At the end of the current **if** statement on frame 11, add the following highlighted code so that your Script pane looks like this:

```
1  if (_parent.hadgo == false) {
2      gotoAndPlay("buttonloop");
3  }
4  else if (_parent.match == true) {
5      gotoAndPlay("done");
6  }
```

You *could* just put a **stop** action in next to keep the card face up if it's part of a pair, but we're going to go one step further and put in a little animation. There's no need to check if **_parent.match** is false because if it isn't true, then it can clearly only be false. In our code, if it's false the timeline just carries on to the 'flip back over' animation, which is what we want to happen for a turn that ends in no match anyway.

We've also included a **gotoAndPlay** action for the frame labeled **done**, but at the moment there is no frame with this label, so we'll have to make one.

2. Put a keyframe into frame 41 of the **actions** layer and label it done. Then put another keyframe into frame 49 and put a **stop** action in it:

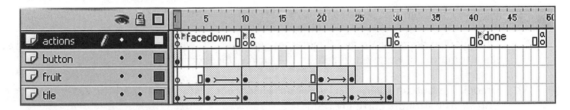

3. Put a blank keyframe into frame 25 of the fruit layer, and then put a keyframe in frame 41. Highlight frames 24 to 41and select **None** from the **Tween** drop-down menu in the Property inspector. Next, add a normal frame in frame 49 and, finally, copy the tomato from frame 20 and paste it in place in frame 41.

4. On the **tile** layer, put a keyframe in frames 41 and 49. Your timeline should now be complete:

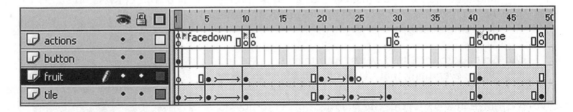

5. Still on the **tile** layer, use the **Color** drop-down from the Property Inspector to set the **Brightness** of the tile in frame 49 to **100%**, and then put a motion tween between frames 41 and 49 to make it glow when a pair is found.

You can test this glow effect now by playing the movie and turning over two tiles. Unfortunately, now that we've put in this last piece of code, the game is no longer 'completable'. We've told it that there are eight pairs to be found, but we've only got two pairs on the stage. It's time to add the rest of our fruit and get the game working fully.

6. We need a new tile object for each of our four fruits – the one that we've been using so far has got a tomato on it, so rename it mc.tile.tomato.

7. Duplicate this object three times in the Library, and name the copies mc.tile.lemon, mc.tile.orange and mc.tile.pear.

We'll change the lemon movie clip now, and then you can go back and do the same to the orange and the pear clips. There are two things that we need to do to make our transformation complete: change all of the pictures of tomatoes into lemons, and change the ActionScript that tells the timeline which fruit it is.

8. Start by locking all of the layers except for **fruit**. We know that all of the keyframes on this layer currently contain a tomato, and we need to change them even when they're squashed so much that you can't see them.

9. Click on the first keyframe in frame 5, and use the **Swap** button on the Property inspector to change the tomato for **sy.fruit.lemon**.

10. Now run through the rest of the keyframes and perform the same operation on each.

   Once you've done this to all 5 keyframes, your tomato will look like a lemon, but it will still *think* it's a tomato. So, we need to retrain it – luckily this isn't as hard as it sounds.

11. Unlock the **button** layer, select the **bu.transparent** symbol and open the Actions window for the button. The variable currently reads:

   ```
   _parent.fruit = "tomato";
   ```

   So this needs to be changed to read:

   ```
   _parent.fruit = "lemon";
   ```

   And that's it. Now you just need to go back through the two fruit conversion stages for your pear and orange movie clips, and you're ready to make the game board.

12. Go back to the **tiles** layer of your main timeline and delete everything that's currently on the stage. Now randomly place four of each movie clip into the stage in a 4 x 4 grid. Use the Align panel to tidy up the tiles and get them into neat rows:

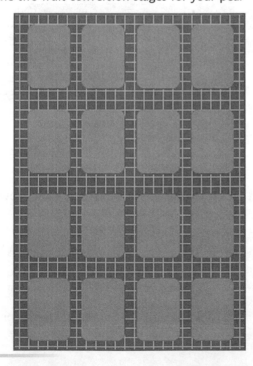

   And that's it. You're now ready to show off your first complete Flash game. Congratulations.

Possible improvements and modifications to your game

You're probably staring in disbelief at this title: it's taken you long enough to get the game working, and there's *no way* you're going to change it now. At the back of your mind though, there's a niggling little voice saying, 'it would be nice if there were a few more fruits so I only needed *one* pair of each, and maybe if there were a few more tiles, and while I'm at it the victory screen could really do with improving...' This section has been dictated by that voice.

- You can add as many as you want, creating a 16x16 or even a 32x32 grid if your eyes are up to seeing tiles that small. All you have to do is change the initial value of **pairs** (in frame 1 of the main timeline's **actions** layer) to how many pairs there are to find.

- You could make a timer, or a turn counter to score each game.

- You could make a scoring system where the player scores 5 points for each correct tile, but loses 2 for each wrong tile.

- For those feeling really confident, you could figure out how to make the game deal a random set of tiles every time a new game is started.

This game is more advanced than the simple mouse trail it's derived from. You can use it as the basis of other, even more advanced games. You could, for example, take the basic **mc.tile** and, realizing that it allows you to model a generalized 'playing card' object, go ahead and make some rather cool card games.

But what has this to do with web site design? Well, web sites and games are two branches of a tree called *interactivity*. There is an offshoot from the web site branch that's very close to the game branch, and that offshoot is called *advanced web site design*. Both make use of lots of clever bits of ActionScript to create their animations, interfaces, and effects. By learning simple games, you're priming yourself for the design and coding of *complex* sites.

The next chapter will start to look at web site design and point you on your way. You've reached base camp one on the ActionScript Everest, and, armed with what you've learned so far, combined with that little niggling voice that keeps on asking questions and telling you to try new things, the only way is up. Never lose sight of the main goal, and have fun – it'll be worth it.

Case study

While the basic structure and content of our case study is indeed finished, you can always customize and experiment with the movie as you learn more advanced techniques. As a final flourish to this case study, we're going to apply a bit of creative ActionScript to create a zoom-in magnifying glass effect over the text in our **about** section:

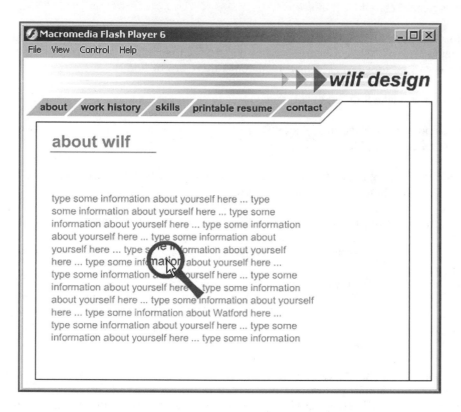

1.   Open up the case study movie and double-click on your **content** movie clip for editing.

2.   As we're only editing the **about** page, let's protect all the other layers so we don't accidentally alter anything on them. Click on the upper-most eye and padlock icons in the timeline so that all the layers are hidden and locked:

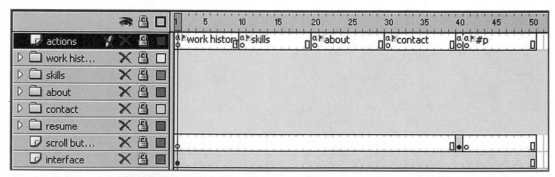

3. Now click on the red cross and lock icons on the **about** layer folder to allow us to see inside and edit it. Open the **about** layer folder – we'll see the familiar three layers:

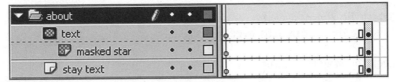

We're going to change the current masking and use one movie clip to mask another. This is done using ActionScript.

4. Double-click on the **text** layer icon to open the **Layer Properties** window and set it back to **Normal**. The **masked star** layer will automatically revert to a normal layer too:

5. Make sure the playhead is on frame 20, so that we can edit the **about** content. Select the **text** layer and delete the text field.

6. Rename the **text** layer `zoomed text`.

7. Select the star shape on the **masked star** layer and delete it. We will replace it with our magnifying glass. Rename this layer `mask`.

8. Create a new layer in this folder called `magnifying glass` and remove any additional frames so that this layer has 20 frames – the same as our other layers in the **about** folder. Move the layers around so that they're now in this order:

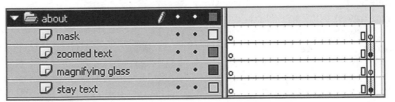

To make our magnifying illusion work, we need to place a larger version of the original text on the stage.

9. Select the main text box on the **stay text** layer and drag it down the stage a little:

> about wilf
>
> type some information about yourself here ... type some information about yourself here ... type some information about yourself here ... type some information about yourself here ... type some information about yourself here ... type some information about yourself here ... type some information about yourself here ...
> type some information about yourself here ... type some information about yourself here ... type some information about yourself here ... type some information about yourself

10. Copy it using CTRL+C or **Edit > Copy**.

11. Select the **zoomed text** layer and place a blank keyframe at frame 20. Use **Edit > Paste in Place** to paste the text directly over the original text.

12. Lock the **stay text** layer.

13. Back on the **zoomed text** layer, select the pasted text and open the Transform panel. Change the text size to **120%**. Make sure the **Constrain** box is checked so the text scales in proportion both horizontally and vertically:

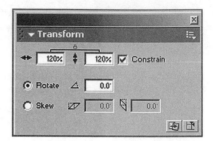

14. Convert the enlarged text into a movie clip with a central registration point and call it **enlarged text**.

15. With this new movie clip still selected, give it the instance name of largeText in the Property inspector.

   That's all the preparation done for our zoomed text. We've converted it to a movie clip because we want to use another movie clip to mask it.

16. Lock the **zoomed text** layer.

17. Select the **mask** layer at frame 20 and delete the star shape from the stage if you haven't already. Next, draw a red circle with the Oval tool. Ours is 43 pixels in diameter:

18. Convert the circle into a movie clip with a central registration point called **circle mask**. With the circle still selected, give it an instance name of circleMask in the Property inspector.

   Now we have both our movie clips – the mask and the masked. Let's add a little code to apply the masking.

19. With the circle still selected, open up the Actions panel. Add the following code:

```
onClipEvent (load){
    startDrag (this, true);
}
```

This code sets the circle to be dragged as soon as the **about** section is accessed.

20. Create a new layer called `actions` and place it above the **mask** layer (all still within the **about** layer folder). Insert a blank keyframe at frame 20 and add the following code to it:

```
circleMask.setMask (largeText);
```

As you can probably guess, **setMask** works by being applied to the intended mask object, and the parameter passed to it (in parentheses) is the movie clip to be masked.

21. Test the movie as it is now and click on the **about** page. Move the mouse around over the text and you'll begin to see that something is happening. It's not exactly quite what we want because the small text is still visible through the magnifier:

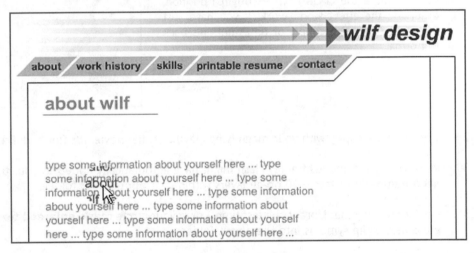

Because of this, we need to cover up the small original text somehow and also draw a magnifying glass graphic to enhance the illusion of the zoom effect.

22. Open up the **circle** movie clip and copy the current circle.

23. Return to the **content** movie clip and insert a blank keyframe on frame 20 of the **magnifying glass** layer. Paste the copy of the circle here, just above where the red circle is.

24. Change the fill color of the circle to white.

25. Select the (now white) circle and convert it into a movie clip with a central registration point. Name it `magnifying glass`.

26. With the circle still selected open the Actions panel and add the following code:

```
onClipEvent (enterFrame) {
    this._x = _parent.circleMask._x;
    this._y = _parent.circleMask._y;
}
```

By setting its **x** and **y** positions to that of the **circleMask** instance, this ActionScript is making the magnifying glass movie clip shadow the **circleMask** wherever it moves to.

27. Test the movie. This time our magnification is a little better. If it didn't work, check the order of your layers. The **magnifying glass** layer is above the **stay text** layer because it needs to obscure the original text.

Let's finish this.

28. Open the **magnifying glass** movie clip, draw a handle and make the stroke outline thicker on the original circle. Make sure when you do this that you don't displace the circle from its original position, otherwise the effect won't work. If you have, just use undo (CTRL+2) a couple of times until it's back to normal.

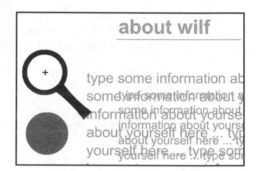

29. Once you are happy with your magnifying glass, test the movie. It's finished. Pretty cool huh?

30. Remove any extraneous frames Flash might have automatically added to your timeline – you only need frames up to frame 20 on all layers within your **about** layer folder.

31. Finally, let's tidy that Library one last time – drag your **circle mask**, **enlarged text** and **magnifying glass** movie clip symbols into the **about** folder.

That's it for the case study! Well done: you've built a complete portfolio web site to display all your Flash and ActionScripting skills, and you can keep on going if you want with any other new designs or techniques you master in the future.

Summary

In this chapter, we've dipped our toe into the vast ocean that is object-oriented design and programming. We've looked at the basic principles of the OO approach, and seen how we can map this onto the movie clip objects we use in Flash.

We saw that:

- Object-oriented design and programming delivers solutions that are:

    - Reusable.

    - Extensible.

    - Flexible.

- The key to OO design and programming is the ability to abstract yourself away from the surface detail of a problem until you can define its absolutely essential components.

- A **class** defines the characteristics of one of those components – what it is, what it can do, what its characteristics are, and how it communicates with other components. The class is a **template**.

- An **object** is an individual **instance** built using the class template.

- In Flash, you can think of a named movie clip instance on the stage as an object. This object is derived from the original Library movie clip symbol. All instances of the symbol on the stage will share the same essential properties, but we can customize them so that their behavior and properties 'individualize' them.

- Simple movie clip objects can be combined to produce complex effects.

In the next chapter, we're going to look at the considerations you need to take into account when you're **designing** your Flash site.

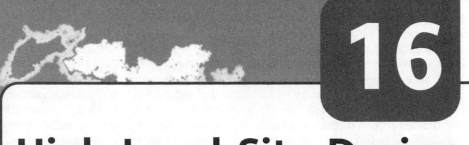

High-Level Site Design

What we'll cover in this chapter:

- *The principles of good design.*

- *Introduction to site structure.*

- *A look at dynamic site design.*

- *The authors' recommended web sites.*

At this point in the book you can afford to congratulate yourself on your new status as an intermediate Flash programmer/designer. It's been a hard road, but it was worth it. Before you rush off into the crowded world of web design though, there are a couple more things to think about. So far, this book has been about the actual technical implementation of your ideas inside Macromedia Flash, but this chapter will run through some tips on what to do when you first have that spark of inspiration, and how to make sure it will work on the web. It's here to give you a rough guide to some of the 'do's and don'ts' of designing for the web, both by reminding you of some of the considerations we've discussed earlier in the book, and by drawing new ones to your attention. At the end of the chapter there's a list of sites recommended by two of the authors, Kris and Amanda, to fire your imagination into action and get those designs flowing. Before that though, Sham, the third member of our team, is going to discuss some of the principles he follows when creating his designs.

The principles of good design

When I was in my early twenties, I worked in a design team that was creating VDU display screens for use in a nuclear power plant. The screens were going to be used by the operators as their primary point of reference to see what was going on in the plant. In an emergency, the reactor engineers had to be able to access the information they needed as quickly as possible, and it had to be shown in a form they could understand immediately. If the engineers had to move to another location to find more detailed information, the path they needed to follow had to be clearly laid out. It was important that the screens never showed too much information – just the relevant information that the engineer had asked to see.

The rules I followed to resolve this project are just as important to the work I do today because now, as then, my projects have the same basic requirements: **usability and clarity**. Of course, web sites have to be engaging, interesting, and entertaining as well, but that's really down to the choice of *content* you display. To be engaged, interested, and entertained, the user has to be able to *find* the content first. There are sites out there that intentionally break the rules, and are entertaining because of it. But the people who are able to get away with this are always *aware* of the rules they're breaking.

These principles, important as they are for the usability of your site, will not bring you success on their own: *originality* is another defining feature of good web design. Sites that don't catch the eye and draw in the mind with good ideas and solid graphic design will get fewer visitors.

Flash is a cost *and* bandwidth-effective design tool with bucket loads of features that enable you to capture your visitors with compelling visuals and sound. One of the reasons that Flash has taken over the net is its high number of creative options compared to HTML – all of them viewable with the small and simple Flash Player. However, over-indulgence will make viewers leave your site if they've already 'seen it all before' or are fed up with the two minute download time. There's a fine line between multimedia and 'junkmedia', and the designer must always be aware of which side they're on. In your design career, you're going to have to learn to balance creativity with practicality – in this chapter I'm going to talk about both.

File structure and file sizes

Whenever you do anything on the web, you have to be aware – even if it's only at the back of your mind – of what the web *is* and what it will do to your presentation as your files are downloaded or streamed across the web. We talked about these issues in the **Optimization** and **Publishing** chapters, but we'll reiterate some of the main points again here:

- Be aware of download times and optimize as much as possible to lower them.

- Differentiate between what's *central* to the message you're trying to get across, and what's just eye (or ear) candy. If download times are an issue, you should know which parts of your movie can be the first to end up on the cutting room floor.

- Consider a multiple **loadMovie** download strategy (as shown in the **Publishing** chapter) to avoid a large initial download.

- Take special care with bitmaps and sound. Optimize them all individually and don't rely on the global export settings to do the job for you.

- When you are using video, consider making a number of differently sized Flash files created for different user bandwidths. Load these in with **loadMovie**.

- Choose your symbols carefully and use a 'one symbol often' approach in preference to 'lots of symbols used once each'.

- Remember that ActionScript-based 'sprite' animation is particularly bandwidth friendly: it requires far fewer frames than the corresponding tween-based animations.

The chapters on optimizing and publishing told us all about structuring our movies correctly, but I'm going to reiterate the main points again because your increased understanding of ActionScript will help you to understand the basis of more advanced solutions.

Preloaders

One of the things we looked at earlier was the **preloader**. I work with three levels of preloader so I'll give you a brief description of their varying degrees of complexity:

Basic: timeline-based loader

The most basic preloader has been introduced in the **Optimization** chapter, and I would recommend anyone who doesn't want to get their hands dirty with ActionScript, or has a relatively simple and small SWF, to go for this option.

Intermediate: ActionScript-based loader

You can build a very efficient ActionScript preloader by looking at the **_framesloaded** and **_totalframes** properties of your movie. These are two properties of the main timeline that you can view just like any other variable – for example, using the **Properties** tab in the Debugger window (overleaf):

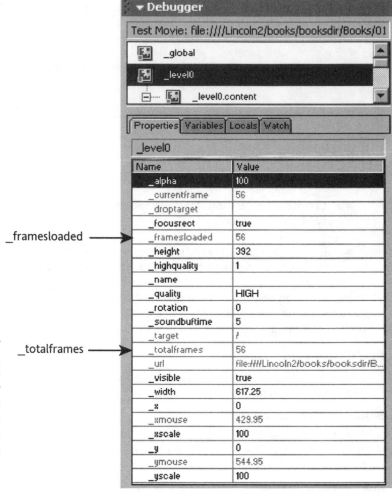

_framesloaded

_totalframes

When these two values are equal, you know that the whole of your SWF has been loaded. Essentially, what you would do here is create a simple animation to keep the user interested while the main site loads up, and use ActionScript to tell it to stop playing and go to the main site once the movie properties **_totalframes** and **_framesloaded** are equal to each other.

Intermediate/Advanced: bandwidth manager object

The most sophisticated preloader I have is a 'loading manager' object that I coded. It constantly looks at what's currently being loaded, and if nothing is, it looks to see if there are any other SWF levels to load via **loadMovie** and sets them off loading in the background. All the additional loaded SWFs have a blank frame 1 with a **stop** action in it: they just sit there, hidden (because the first frame is empty), until the lowest level sets them off with a **play** action. You can tell that 'nothing is being loaded' if **_totalframes** and **_framesloaded** are equal for the last level of SWF that you set off loading.

If you decide to embark on this project, remember **never to unload an already loaded SWF level** – instead, you can just send it back to its first (blank) frame, where it will remain invisible to watching eyes. A problem arises here if the user requests a SWF other than the one that the manager is currently loading, but explaining that is beyond the scope of this chapter. When your knowledge is sufficient to solve this problem you'll be ready to code the loading manager, and you'll have an extremely efficient method of loading your web sites – which, as we've said, is one of the main practical concerns of any web designer.

Intros

What you show during your preload is another major concern. A good intro (the animation that hides your preload) will draw the viewer into the main web site, whereas a poor one will resemble a cheesy rock band's guitar solo – it'll go on for *far* too long.

As a general rule, always have something interesting going on while the main site is loading. As we've said, the average Internet surfer will not stay long if you've put a 'please wait, loading...' screen up, and it's in this context that an intro really becomes useful. In my view, your intro must:

- Show the user what'll be missed if they click away.

- Give an indication of the quality of the actual main web site.

- Give the viewer the option to skip past it if they want to.

Different types of web site require different intros. If you were creating a web site advertising yourself as a web site designer, you'd want to show off your technical ability and give the potential client a showcase of your advanced understanding of complex animation and graphic design ability. This would not be the case if you were designing an information service for a bank. In this case, the viewer wants to see the information they came to look at, and they want it *fast and clear*. They need to be attracted to the site by a cool and slick Flash design, but once they decide to open an account the route to the 'sign me up' web page must just be a click away and free of over-indulgent Flash animation and tricks. Making your design *appropriate* to your client and audience is a vital consideration.

Tailoring your designs

Summarizing the large number of constraints and features that make up a good web site in a single paragraph is an impossible task. However, there are a number of checklist items that you should at least be aware of when you come to sit down and build your main site:

Timescales

We all want to build the coolest Flash sites possible, but if you are doing this for a living, you need to think about how soon the site is required. A good, delivered-on-time site will always get you a satisfied customer, whereas a brilliant cutting edge site delivered three weeks late *won't*. Remember, it's very difficult to change a site once it's up (people tend to become accustomed to the navigation and style) so be careful – unless, of course, the change is the *client's* idea and they're paying by the hour!

Site style

The style you choose for the site is defined in part by the content and the impression that the client wants to get across to the viewer. When defining a style, be careful to choose one that's actually suited to the message, not because it's easy to create in Flash. A lot of the time, the client already has a brief or advertising campaign that the site will be part of, so you should be flexible enough to take on their ideas and jump between styles.

Content

Unless you're creating a site based on a very specific brief, where the client has provided all the site graphics and type, you'll have to find a way to hold the audience's attention long enough to put the site's message across. The coolest visual Flash interface will be ignored if it's not properly integrated with something *interesting*.

Navigation

The content of your site will greatly influence the navigation you create for it. In some (especially commercial) sites there's a 'route that you'd prefer the visitor to take' – meaning the one that'll most likely result in a sale or a 'click-through' to your sponsor. Your navigation must make this route clear. Other sites are based around a central 'hub', with numerous links going out to sub-topics. In these sites, it's important that the user can quickly access *any* area of the site, and, as a general rule, they should be able to do it *within two clicks*.

In all of these things, there's no substitute for practical experience. To this end, I've included walk-throughs of some site designs I've been involved in, to illustrate the different methods of visualizing and creating a web site.

Case study 1: online showcase

A few years ago (which equates to several decades in Flash years), I found a really old-looking poetry book that contained a lot of verse dating back to Victorian England. Reading it, I was particularly taken by how different their thinking was to that of the twenty-first century: whereas we live in an age where everything is out in the open (especially on the web), they had a much more closed and hidden society.

I decided to update this book and put a fully interactive version onto the web using all the new technology available to me. I had to create a web site that had the same sort of feel as the book, because I wanted to use the language of the book to present this bygone world and give a sense of the cultural and behavioral beliefs implicit in the book. But I wanted to present it via Flash animations.

Before I went into the Flash implementation I had to have a very clear idea of what I wanted to create, because I could see this being a very large project. I'd have to do two things:

- Create a set of storyboards and sketches that gave me a graphical direction and template.

- Create the text, making sure that it matched the graphical style.

Storyboarding

I had to define the look of the final web site before I could continue and I knew that to work, the whole site would have to be true to the original concept. I decided that the original book would have to play a part in the final look.

However, I had a problem: to navigate within a book you turn pages, sometimes lots of pages. This sounded like something that wouldn't work on the web. To go to a particular page is easy when you're holding the book because you have an idea of the paper's *thickness*, so you know if you want to go a point a third of the way into the book, you just open the book at a third of its thickness. You can't do that with a 2D representation on a monitor. Here's the rough sketch that solved the problem:

By looking at the way address books use 'tabs' to allow you to quickly find a particular section of names – the Newmans and the Newton-Johns under 'N' for example – I was able to create a 2D representation of a book that was still easy to navigate. Each tab represents a chapter of the book.

On a whim, I used a cheap flatbed scanner to scan in an image of a small notebook I'd carried with me in my coat pocket for close on a year. Then I got some newspaper that had faded to yellow in the sun and scanned that in too, to get the effect of old book pages. I cobbled it all together in Photoshop so that it looked like this:

I now had an idea of what my open book would look like. The idea was that the animated poems would appear in the page area as SWF files. I still needed to create my navigation tabs though...

As well as the chapter tabs, I needed something to allow the user to move between the individual pages of each chapter. I needed **last page** and **next page** buttons. I also needed a **help** button somewhere, so I sketched that in as well:

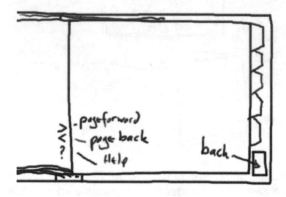

These sketches were created using a Wacom pen tablet. It's as quick a way of doing initial sketches as drawing on paper, and it helps workflow because you can import the image directly into Flash (or whatever program you're using), rather than having to scan them in and then fiddle with image resolution, color depth, and so on.

With my basic site structure worked out, I needed to make sure I could create a convincing set of tabs for navigation before I started devoting time to Flash programming. I went back into Photoshop to mock it all up:

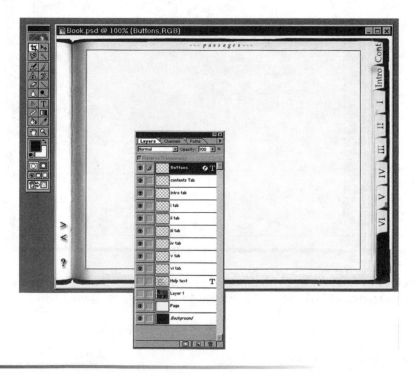

By putting each tab in a separate layer and simulating the effect of each tabbed page being turned over, I was able to check that my digital creation still looked like a book. This was obviously essential for the effect I was trying to create. I also used Adobe ImageReady, a web page preparation tool, and some JavaScript to create a simple HTML version of the book to see if the navigation was workable – and thankfully it was:

As you can see, removing tabs gives the impression that we have moved further into the book. Luckily, the fact that our virtual book still has the same number of pages left, no matter how far into the book you are, doesn't seem to kill the illusion.

By mocking up my ideas in Photoshop first, I proved to myself that the concept of a virtual book was a viable one without wasting my time trying to get it working in Flash straight away. As an added advantage, I now also had some bitmap images I could trace into Flash.

Content

The book was to be called *Passages,* and was to be about the one journey we all make – the one through life. Victorian society was full of double standards, with a very rich upper class segment and a chronically poor underclass (so, things haven't changed *that* much, then...). Using this as a starting point, I wanted the book to liken existence to the life of a young child who is forced to break into a rich man's mansion, to see what's there on offer, and take whatever they can.

Here are two initial storyboards done in Photoshop:

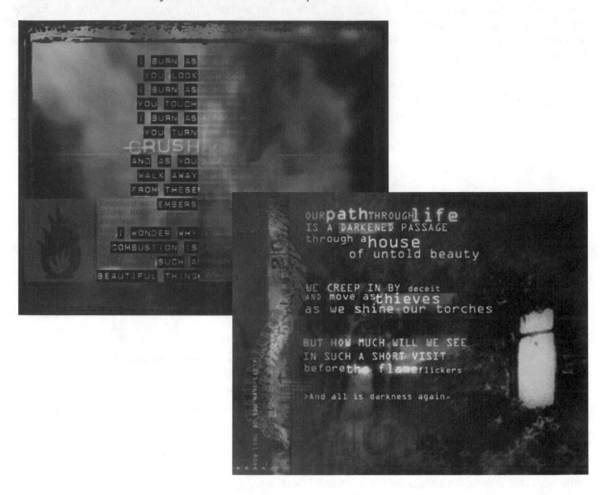

The first one is an introduction to the whole book, and the second is called *crush*. Both of these compositions are multi-layer Photoshop files. By moving the individual layers around in real time, I gave myself a good idea of how the text should appear and how the individual elements should move. These shots represent the last frame in each animation. There are approximately 40 animations for the whole *Passages* sequence, following our young thief through an entire lifetime on their trip through the mansion. By now I had lots of images, sketches, and text, and I was ready to mould it into a site. Time to start looking at Flash.

Integration

The first thing was that the book had to look *real*. It had to have pages that turned. Contemporary native Photoshop files can be imported into Flash, but with such large file sizes, you are better off splitting the layers up and exporting them as separate GIFs or JPEGs, as I did here. The separated Photoshop images were first converted to vectors and rebuilt as fully animated movie clips. Here's the final Flash symbol of the front of the *Passages* book, which is fairly faithful to the book that started all this off:

The pages were also made to turn with a simple tween animation, which you can see in this 'under construction' shot:

Here's the finished, open book in Flash. The whole book and associated animations comes in at a little over 20K:

I now built a simple intro to play as the book animations and graphics loaded in (the separate poems would come in as **onLoad** movie levels, using the loading manager I mentioned earlier).

I wanted to introduce definite symbols to represent the themes of *Passages*: the Victorian ideas of *life* and *mortality*. For *life*, I chose a butterfly, and for *mortality* I scanned in an image from *Gray's Anatomy*. There were two advantages of this second choice: it was written in the Victorian period, and its engravings are **royalty free** – providing you don't copy the whole book. Neat.

> *New designers need to pay careful attention to issues of copyright and royalties to avoid getting themselves into unwanted, and perhaps costly, trouble.*

The butterfly appears in the introduction, and flits through the book as you turn certain pages. The image of a human spine is shown as a recurring theme throughout the book, representing the Victorian fascination with mortality.

figure 1a
Existence

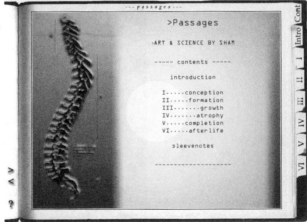

Summary

This walk-through will have shown you how Flash can be used in a creative way to make web sites that are unlike anything else on the Internet. At its lowest level, *Passages* is nothing more than an online showcase of related Flash movies: however, by creating an overall *style* and *ambience* the site will hopefully become much more than its individual components, and the user will forget that they're viewing a Flash web site and become drawn into its imaginary world – in the very way I was when I first found that old book.

The best thing about something like *Passages* is that it has no heavy ActionScripting: it's all about basic artistic skills and ideas. Those of you who are coming into Flash from a Photoshop or graphic design background could create something like this *now* because you already have the basic Flash skills required to pull it off.

Mocking up the site and prototyping it in Photoshop and ImageReady was one of the most important parts of this site's creation. Flash doesn't have the tools to take in bitmaps and other scanned data in the same way Photoshop does, and for this reason a lot of professional designers use Photoshop for the initial design and storyboarding. Even when used in the simple ways shown here, Photoshop and Flash form the basis of a very powerful set of *visualization tools* for the designer – whatever he or she is designing.

Case study 2: my Flash home site interface

Designing your own home site is where you get to *play*. Some designers use it to show off and compete with other designers, but I think that's just asking for trouble: whenever another designer uses a new technique you'll have to go one better. That kind of 'technological arms race' is not my idea of fun – I prefer to be creative.

The last example was all about design, and how to get those vague ideas in your head down onto a digital canvas, how to tie the ideas down, create a plan, and then take the elements and animate them in Flash.

This second example looks at the sites you make without ever really setting out to: what happens is that you have a folder full of half ideas and part-finished FLA files that you don't know what to do with – and then something in your head links them all together and an idea hits you out of nowhere.

Random idea #1

As I was driving down a busy highway a few months ago, I noticed some large billboards by the side of the road. It put the idea in my head that sometimes size really 'makes' a picture – wouldn't it be nice to have a browser that was as big as a billboard?

So that's what I tried to do. But if you had a really *big* site, how would you see it all? The browser is *way* too small. Then I remembered reading a book called *Fahrenheit 451* by Ray Bradbury, which had cars that were so fast that the only way people could read the adverts as they drove past was to have huge billboards with stretched images on them. This way, the enormous billboard would zip past but all the images would be stretched out so that they looked normal to you. So I decided to try and do the same with my site design by stretching it out horizontally to give me a really long billboard-type site.

I created a new movie and modified it to make it 2880 pixels x 600 pixels and then set the publish width to 300% by 95%, just to see what would happen. It looks nice as a design concept, because if you had a logo (I've used one of mine as an example below) the user would have to scroll from left to right to get to the actual web site at the end, where they'd get an eye full of oversized logo. Because this is a novel format (or will be until you all try it yourselves), the average web user will remember the first site they saw that used it. As we said at the outset of this chapter, originality is an important component of your sites.

Random idea #2

Another thought was buzzing around my head at around the same time as I was forming idea #1: my VCR was broken, and whenever you played anything on it, you got a horrible picture that was totally unviewable. It was the kind of snowy, fuzzed, picture you get when you play a video that's a copy of a copy of a copy. In a funny way, though, I liked the mangled image on the VCR. It worked really well whenever I'd accidentally recorded the test transmission pattern on the screen, making all the colors fade in and out of each other and showing ghost images or random noise within the picture. I imagined, somewhat dramatically, technology breaking out of our control and refusing to be mastered.

With this on my mind I happened to walk past a shop that had a lot of TVs all on at the same time in a 4 x 4 matrix, with no two screens ever showing exactly the same picture: one was brighter than the others, one was more red, and one had a lower saturation.

I imagined the same effect on my browser window – separate 'TVs' all doing their own thing, and I decided to create this effect.

I used an array of little movies that sit over the top of the SWF that I'm trying to see, sort of like the matrix below. If you read the chapter on masking you'll no doubt have a good understanding of how this is done:

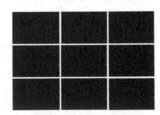

All I needed now was my broken VCR effect in each segment:

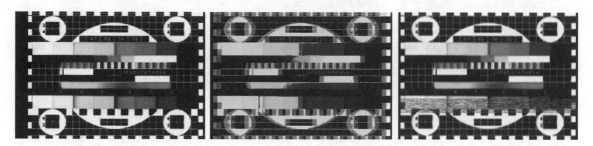

I built a set of little objects that randomly applied noise effects (distorting them) to the underlying image or SWF. Remarkably, the whole thing works! It looks a little bit like the video walls you still see in some bars or clubs that show one picture on a matrix of TVs – each TV showing a separate square portion of the image.

I now needed something to tie my two media related ideas, billboards, and broadcast, together.

Integration

I don't know what made me put the television matrix on the end of my billboard, but I did, and it worked. I was just playing around, putting this matrix idea over other SWFs and looking to see how it mangled everything up. I was just having fun. Even when the underlying SWF is motionless, there's plenty of movement going on.

I needed a menu bar to really tie it all together, and I was still in love with the test transmissions I spoke of earlier, so I created a row of rectangles that approximated the test-card color chart. It's shown in grayscale here, but it is in fact the color progression you see on a color TV – white, yellow, cyan, green, magenta, red and blue:

This menu bar is made up of little button objects that the user can press to navigate the site. The buttons 'wobble'. By this, I mean that when you press one, it performs an oscillation to look as if it's extending and contracting as if it were made of Jello. These 'wobblers' are wrapped within a parent object called 'menu'. When one 'wobbler' gets bigger the others get smaller – and vice versa – to preserve the overall length of the menu bar:

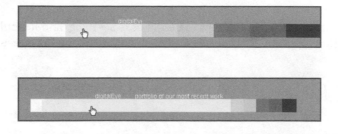

It all wobbles with a delay, so it looks a bit like a big elastic band, producing a bouncing effect that's fascinating and disorienting at the same time...

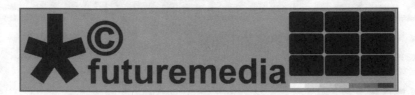

So here's my idea for my new Flash home site. You have to scroll in from left to right, going over the big oversized billboard logo. Once you get to the far right end of the movie and the mouse passes over the TV screens they spring to life and play their little test cards and video noise until you ask to see something. If you ask to jump to another web site, you don't see it in a new window...it appears in the TV screens! Every now and again one of the screens gets a little brighter or loses synch or something, and the longer you leave the mouse still, the more pronounced the effect becomes.

Sometimes the screens flick to new stuff you never asked to see: little MTV-type animations or Japanese Manga cartoons – or the grainy type of video footage that was taken from the cameras in missile nosecones during *Desert Storm*. I want to add things in those screens that are possibly *better* than the things you've come to see, so you'll say to yourself 'never mind looking at the web sites...missile command has just shown up in the top left corner! Quick...figure out the keys before it disappears!'

Summary

I hope that, from walking through these two examples, you all feel enthused to create your own innovative sites. And I also hope you realize that most of the knowledge you need to achieve something like this was given to you in the ActionScript chapters. The 'wobbler' menu uses quite a lot of ActionScript: I simplified my description above, as the objects are in fact nested about five deep – but you could simply use a 'solid' menu instead.

The use of Flash as a tool for just trying out ideas, like any design program, shouldn't be ignored. Sometimes, you find an effect that you like in a Flash tutorial site, but which has been 'done to death' by repeated use. When you've collected enough ideas like these you can take the best aspects of each and create something unique to use on your own site.

Most designers have a little box of collected effects, but unfortunately, some never change what they keep in it. The best designers are always on the lookout for new coding ideas. When they offer a client the chance to be the first to use a particular effect, they can ensure they'll have a better chance of getting the job.

Looking ahead, dynamic Flash sites look set to be the next big thing, and it would be a good idea for you, as a designer and developer, to be as proficient in working with them as possible.

Case study 3: a dynamic visual guestbook

I was just playing with Flash one night and I had an idea to build a guestbook for a site, where it would constantly build an archive of the visitors' names. But, unlike standard guestbooks, this archive was going to provide a visual representation of the visitors' names.

A dynamic site in Flash works by pulling in information (such as variables) from a data store, called a database, and displaying or processing the information in Flash. Usually, when fetching or sending information to or from the database, a server-side scripting language is used:

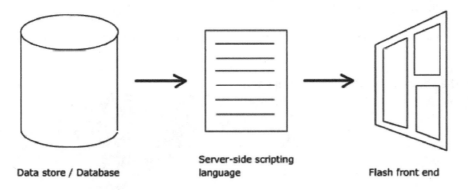

Data store / Database   Server-side scripting
                               language   Flash front end

You might have already heard of a few server-side scripting languages such as PHP, Perl, ASP, or Macromedia's ColdFusion software. Going into these areas is beyond the scope of this book, and there are many different paths you can take to develop your knowledge in this area. However, I'd advise that you get to grips with ActionScript first before attempting to integrate these languages with Flash.

Anyway. Back to the guestbook...

In devising a format for the visual representation, I decided upon a complex line to line structure, a little like a constellation of stars. Each letter of the name would have a point and two lines would connect one letter with the next. The first letter would start off the lines, the last letter would be the ending, with each letter randomly placed:

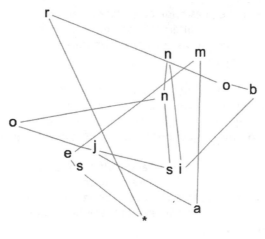

Rather than stick to a dull black and white canvas, I decided to incorporate a little color and different stroke widths. I came up with a set of simple rules to create some diversity:

1.   The color of each line is determined by the position of each letter of the user's name in the alphabet.

2.   The number of lines drawn is proportionate to the number of letters in the user's name.

3.   The stroke size and positioning of each letter is random, meaning that no two names have the same visual representation.

All of these factors are set using ActionScript in Flash, stored as variables, and are then sent to the database for storage.

So, given the above rules, Stephen looks like this:

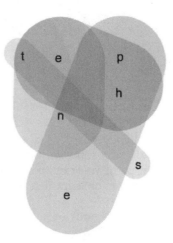

Once the user has seen their name in shapes, it is randomly placed with all the other – um – 'nameshapes' of previous visitors. The more people that sign the guestbook, the bigger the collective image will be, until all the layers are so thick that the stage is a mass of color and the guestbook needs to be cleared.

However, if I chose to clear the guestbook every month, an archive of all the previous months could be placed on display, forming a totally different image for each month. So, when a visitor comes to view the guestbook, all of the names, and the visual information for each one, are pulled in from the database and the composition is drawn in Flash.

If all this dynamic stuff sounds a little complicated, don't be put off. It's not an essential learning component for a designer...phew! However, as you advance with ActionScript, you might also find yourself interested in learning other technologies. You are not the first to do so, so there is plenty of documentation available on the subject on the web and in numerous books.

If you really don't fancy learning all this back-end stuff, then fortunately there are programmers dedicated to making all this stuff happen. In this case, the communication between you and the back-end programmer is crucial, making sure that you both decide on naming conventions for variables and so on, and you are both clear about how the two elements will tie together (this is without mentioning that you both meet deadlines of course).

Either way, dynamic sites are the next big thing and Flash MX has a lot of added functionality specifically designed for building dynamic web applications, so it pays to be familiar with some of the concepts involved.

Suggested sites

Now that you have a better appreciation of how they can be created, perhaps the best place to start looking at Flash sites is the web itself. As promised at the start of the chapter, here are some suggestions:

www.presstube.com
This site is packed with loads of amazing linear and interactive animations. You might notice that most of the Flash files are published with the quality set to low, giving them an altogether different kind of texture.

www.yugop.com
Yugop's creator, Yugo Nakamura, is always one step ahead of the pack, and his current pickings are better than ever. The creations on this site are truly amazing, and set the standard for other Flashers.

www.threecolor.com
This site has a number of sweet animations that will make you think differently about ways to work with the basic shape and motion tween tools in Flash.

www.levitated.net
A massive archive of beautiful Flash experiments showcasing the power of ActionScript combined with logic. This site has all kinds of advanced elements from basic interactivity to behavioral OOP. Many of the Flash files shown on this site are also available to download (be warned – this is advanced scripting).

www.modifyme.com
Modifyme has some amazing sounds and interaction which, when combined, make it a kind of futuristic sound mixer. You'll doubtless spend an age here, trying different combinations of settings to see what you can make those pesky nodes do. Sometimes curiosity can keep the user on your web page for much longer.

www.vectorama.org
This multiuser design pad allows a number of players to create a digital composition – working on the same canvas! Whereas the premise is to encourage collaboration with the other designers, this usually turns sour and the **kill** command comes in handy for destroying other people's hard work. For those of you that want to go out and imitate this site, be aware that it is built in both Flash and Director and has a pretty hefty back-end too.

www.friendsofed.com/fmc
Not a friends of ED plug at all, but a demonstration of how ActionScript can be used creatively to design some beautiful compositions. All of the experiments featured in the book are on display here for you to try to decipher – or just marvel at.

http://www.mtv2.co.uk/
This site shows excellent use of Flash, ColdFusion, and 3D. It makes great use of objects with a low file size and the site has appropriate sound use that doesn't get annoying – and it's always fun to play with 3D blocks in cyberspace.

http://www.derbauer.de/
This site is just amazing. These people really know how to put their images to use. The programmers and designers have together created a well-designed site. Even though the file sizes are large, the site is easy to navigate and is extremely interactive.

http://www.praystation.com/
Any site where more than 45 minutes passes by unnoticed while you're playing with all the interactive Flash toys has *got* to be a good one. Even though the toys on this site are simple shapes, lines, and effects, the results are extremely engaging.

http://www.banja.com
Great animations and a great game. Islands, treasures, pirates – the whole bit. Excellent interactivity and well thought out design with fast loading for such a large game.

Flash is ideally suited to web sites that include animated content, and here are a few favorites:

http://www.iwantmyflashtv.com

http://www.heavy.com

http://www.bulbo.com/

Summary

The summary for this chapter is short and sweet:

- Learn

- Work

- Explore

- Plan

- Play

Great Flash design comes from continually honing your design and Flash skills, from innovation, and from trying things out as you go. Remember that time spent monkeying around with little movie clips and effects can pay dividends later.

In our final chapter, we're going to look at some other Flash areas that are ripe for exploration as you build your Flash future.

Futurescape

Where next?

Flash has come a long way from being just a superb animation package. Macromedia Flash MX is capable of producing fully functional web applications that are rich in graphics, sound, video, and interactivity. As a complete web application in its own right, Flash is rapidly becoming the web developer's tool of choice for creating the whole range of e-commerce, entertainment, and community sites. Flash can talk to web servers in a highly sophisticated way, meaning that dynamic content is within everyone's reach using ActionScript, and Flash has become integrated with other web-standard technologies such as XML.

You've now learnt the basic skills required for Flash competence. In the space of a few hundred pages you've gone from a ground level beginner making a mushroom grow, to an intermediate programmer coding an interactive game.

Mastering these new skills completely will keep you content and occupied for many months to come as you explore the full range of your powers. But before too long you're going to want to do more. You'll be hungry for new knowledge and new skills, and will want to wring every possible design opportunity from Flash, and from the Internet as a whole.

Using and improving your Flash skills

There are numerous Flash tutorial sites out on the web, and most have beginners' sections. Most new Flash effects and interfaces seem to end up being deconstructed and presented as a 'how to' tutorial within a very short time, so if there's a particular design effect you want to know more about, check out the web first. Be sure to try the Macromedia newsgroups as well; these tend to be a good way of picking up the knowledge of some of the older hands. Our advice, though, is to check out the FAQs of these groups before asking questions of your own as most beginner questions will have been covered.

Here are some good starting points for Flash resources on the web:

> http://www.macromedia.com/support/flash
> http://www.werehere.com
> http://www.flashkit.com
> http://www.flashmove.com
> http://www.flashplanet.com
> http://www.screamdesign.com
> http://www.flashmagazine.com
> http://www.enetserve.com/tutorials

Flash web design presents the user with a large number of different fields to look at. You only have to look at a few sites out there created by the Flash Masters to realize that the variation in Flash sites is larger than that exhibited by any other web technology currently on view. From cartoon sites to futuristic looking 3D, Flash has a large amount of the web covered. To give you an idea of some of the areas you may want to find out more about we're going to briefly introduce them to you now.

Flash games and toys

As this chapter will go on to tell you, getting noticed as a designer is hard work, and you need to find a way to get your skills recognized. One way to attract attention is by designing quality games for people to play, as games and toys can be a good way to hold a viewer's attention. You could add them to an existing site that's in need of new blood, or make them into a site in their own right, where people can witness your Flash experimentation. If this is the area you're interested in, then perhaps existing sites that need 'perking up' with some Flash interaction would be willing to incorporate your work – if you give them enough of a nudge.

Check out **http://www.orisinal.com** as a top example of the kind of interactive games you can create in Flash.

Flashed cartoons

As a pure animation tool, Flash should not be underestimated. Managing the timeline with the skills you've learnt in this book can produce highly professional looking animations. You can generate drawings within Flash itself, scan in photos or drawings you've generated by hand to give a less 'computerized' appearance to your work, or import work from other applications that give you more flexibility when creating your images (as we saw in the walk-throughs in the previous chapter).

The animation features of Flash are used in preliminary work for TV production, for mocking up commercials, and are also now being exploited to produce content for the Sony PlayStation 2. Take a look at the Flash 'webisodes' at **http://www.s4studios.com**, one of which is a Flash animated trailer for Sony's *Twisted Metal Black* game.

Using Flash with other software

As well as using Flash in isolation, many designers use Flash everyday in conjunction with other software, such as Macromedia's Multiuser Server included with Director. Using this application, designers can set up interactive sites – for example, enabling real-time multiuser online gaming and interaction – without having to learn new server-side scripting languages. Combinations such as this allow you to extend the use of Flash even beyond whole web applications and into stand-alone programs.

Although Flash has its own drawing tools, there's a lot to be said for using programs such as FreeHand, Photoshop, and others to enhance the available options of Flash presentations. Many designers take this initial approach when designing their web projects. However, always make sure to optimize anything you bring into Flash, because some of these image manipulation applications are not quite as web-savvy as Flash can be.

Using sound effectively in Flash is another exciting area to investigate. Although creating sound can become very expensive, there are many entry-level options available by using a good soundcard as the main device, and shareware or freeware tracker and sequencer software (there's a list of sound shareware web resources in the Sound Appendix at the back of the book).

3D in Flash

As some of the examples in this book have shown – as well as many of our recommended sites – adding a 3D element to your work can achieve impressive results, giving your sites an extra edge over conventional Flash work. The applications available are well worth getting involved with; if a client wants a 3D version of their logo on their site, you want to make sure you're in the running for the job.

As the demands placed on web sites increase, and become more varied and realistic, 3D rendering skills are highly desirable. Adding this ability to your impressive Flash résumé will do you no harm at all. Flash is well suited to the use of 3D images and whether you're trying to make your name as a designer, or are merely using Flash for fun, you'll find that using 3D objects will add to your enjoyment. Check out **Swift3D** as a Flash-friendly 3D tool that can output SWF files which you can then load in your movies:

http://www.swift3D.com

Advanced ActionScript-based Flash interface designs

ActionScript is now a major force in web programming, and now that you know the basics – more than just the basics in fact – thanks to this book, you will no doubt be bursting to know what other possibilities are offered by this web-wonder. ActionScripting is a skill in itself and knowledge of it will be a tremendous benefit to your designing. We saw in the later stages of the book what effects can be achieved , but you've only seen the tip of the ActionScript iceberg. When you really flesh out your ability, the Flash designs you create will be sure to please and astound you.

Dynamic content

With a good knowledge of ActionScript, you can go on to combine server-side architectures with Flash front-ends to create dynamic web sites. You can pass data between the browser and web server using ActionScript in conjunction with a whole range of server-side scripting languages such as PHP and ASP. You can also use a middleware package such as Macromedia ColdFusion. This is their server back-end of choice for combining with Flash and we're expecting even closer integration of these products in the future.

XML

Flash MX includes support for the eXtensible Markup Language (**XML**), which is already a web standard for disseminating data in a form that can be interpreted anywhere, on any device, and rendered according to the abilities of that device and the needs of the user.

Because XML tags can be used to actually tell a browser something *about* the included information rather than just *how to display it*, XML is taking the place of HTML in a number of areas, including e-commerce, intelligent search engines, and wireless devices. Flash's ability to deal in XML data in ActionScript, coupled with the rich multimedia features that Flash is famous for, mean that Flash can be a powerful player in a world where XML and data-driven web applications are becoming evermore popular.

Flash is branching out into a whole new set of contexts: for all kinds of wireless and non-PC web devices, such as PDAs and cellular phones.

Starting a career in Flash

Flash has now become the standard for dynamic animation and sound on the web. It follows, therefore, that it's also a discipline that can be used to form part of a career in web design. The question many people tend to ask is *how do you get your foot in the door?*

If you are so taken with Flash that you're considering attempting to earn a living as a Flash designer, you'll have to stop a moment and consider the following issues:

HTML

Most employers and agencies expect you to know something about HTML. This is something that's becoming less of a constraint as time passes and the majority of operations adopt site/HTML creation packages like Macromedia Dreamweaver. However, a lot of Flash web design positions still require you to be able to *hand code* HTML. Even if this is not the case, we'd be very surprised to find Flash positions that did *not* require an understanding of Dreamweaver. Some understanding of JavaScript is usually an advantage too, as ActionScript is based on JavaScript – good news for you as it means there's much less to learn to achieve competency.

Graphic design

Web design is an offshoot of a much wider discipline called graphic design. As a web designer, you'll not be expected to get your pencils and paints out, but a knowledge of computer based graphic design and layout packages is usually a distinct advantage – Adobe Photoshop is usually stipulated as a competency. It's also worth your while considering a point that the earlier chapters alluded to: with the ever-increasing competition for web surfers, your potential clients are going to take it for granted that you can produce a functional site. They're going to want something that's visually appealing *as well* – so your artistic skills need to be up to the job.

Getting in

Having an impressive home site is one of the best ways to get noticed on the web. There are a number of well-known Flash designers who started out by building themselves a killer home site. Having a cutting edge site does not necessarily mean that you have to be an ActionScript or 3D guru: there are plenty of other site styles that will appeal to users – humor, animation, innovation and a distinctive style spring immediately to mind.

There are of course other, more stealthy, ways into Flash design and these seem to be the routes that most of us tend to end up following.

One of the things we'd recommend is that you look at what is already up on the web in your locale. A good starting point when looking for your very first site job (after your own of course) is charities. They tend to be run and organized by volunteers, and many won't turn away a volunteer Flash expert who asks to re-engineer the existing HTML site to full Flashed status, with the promise of a much more entertaining site and therefore more visitors. This is the way many designers start out, doing odd web site jobs in their spare time and keeping up the day job, slowly increasing their portfolio and gaining a good reputation.

Although your first few Flash sites may be more in the 'solid-but-dependable' ballpark, it won't be long before you have a few sites that you're actually proud of. That's the time to start looking at full time **freelancing**. This is much easier to do now that the web has really taken off, and there are a number of web sites in America and Europe that will e-mail you with weekly lists of contract positions.

A good tip is to add Flash, Dreamweaver, Photoshop, and JavaScript to your resume's list of keywords. Be aware that most freelance contracts specify that you work at the client's office, and working from home is much less of an option. Flash web design seems to be attracting more and more of this type of contract work, particularly around October as Christmas nears and hourly rates really start to rise. If you choose this route, our advice would be to find a few web sites that allow online portfolios, and add links to your three best sites. You'll find that a lot of traditional employment agencies now scour such entries, and you sometimes find e-mails from agencies you have never worked with imploring you to get in touch about a contract!

Applying directly to web design houses is another option. However, unless you've already created a stir on the web with your home site or other work, be prepared for a disappointing starting salary. There's a lot of money to be made from the Internet, but junior web designers seem to be seeing a minimal part of it. A lot of people may choose this option despite lack of initial pay, because it can create a very good portfolio of work very quickly. Working with the right company, the work can be very satisfying and you can move up to more senior positions, or into freelance work, after a couple of years. There's much less uncertainty when starting out on this route than there is with freelancing, where you may not be employed all year round.

Flash farewell – for now

So, the end of this book is very much the beginning of your Flash career – whatever you choose to do with your new skills. You now have a platform of knowledge that'll allow you to branch out into a variety of areas – all with their own pitfalls and possibilities. Flash is already a major force on the web, and is destined to increase its power and influence. There's an opportunity now to ride in on the crest of Flash's wave and all make your mark in the world of web design. Don't rest on your laurels: practice the skills you have and search out new ones and new ways to apply them.

See you on the beach.

Sound Sampling

The first time you glance at this appendix will probably be to locate some sound resources on the web for use in conjunction with the exercises in Chapters 9 and 11. Here they are:

MIDI sequencers

http://www.cubase.net
http://www.cakewalk.com
http://www.webmassiva.com

Sound editing and looping

http://www.sonicfoundry.com

Free sample sounds

http://www.soundshopper.com
http://www.deusx.com
http://www.flashkit.com/soundfx

Fun sound effects

http://www.wavcentral.com

The rest of this appendix will give you a more detailed understanding of how sound works, and of the things that you need to bear in mind when creating your own sounds for use on the Internet.

Sound

Sound travels through the air in waves. The bigger the wave is, the louder the sound. To help you visualize sound waves and how they move, think about the ripples that are created when you throw a pebble into a pond.

The ripples move outwards from the point of impact at a constant speed (frequency) that's independent of the size of the pebble, but at a height that is determined by the size of the pebble. The water is displaced and pushed along by the pressure that the pebble's impact creates.

A sound wave works in much the same way: pressure caused by objects vibrating displaces air particles and creates a 'ripple' in the air. This ripple of pressure strikes your eardrum, causing it to vibrate, and this vibration is what we hear as sound. The ripple of air particles forms a sound wave:

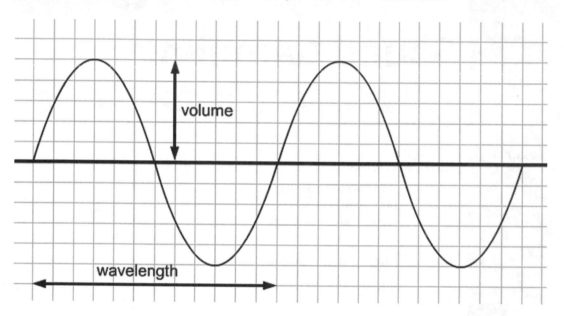

The height of the wave represents its **volume** and is determined by the power of the sound source, or the strength of the initial vibration that created the pressure wave. (Using our pond analogy, the bigger the pebble, the higher the ripples in the water.)

The length of one complete wave is called the **wavelength**, and the number of completed waves that pass a fixed point in a fixed unit of time is the **frequency** of the wave, which is measured in Hertz (Hz or KHz).

Digital sound

Before we can bring any sound into Flash, we have to **digitize** it. The digitizer will most likely be your soundcard connected to a microphone. The digitizing process involves recording the current height of the sound wave at regular intervals. The length of the interval is called the **sampling rate**: the higher the rate, the more frequently the samples are taken. This process is sometimes called **quantizing** or just **sampling**. Each level is called a sample, and when you put them all together in order they form a digital representation of the sound wave:

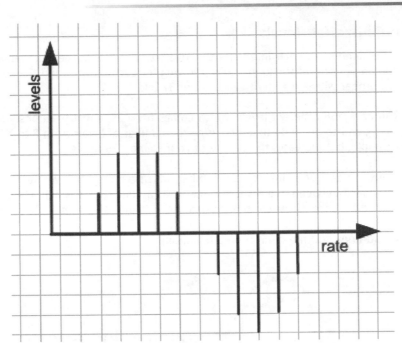

Defining the sampling rate

The **sampling rate** is expressed in either samples per second or, like frequency, in Hertz. The sampling rate defines the highest frequency, or sound range, your sampler will capture. There's a sound sampling law (discovered by Nyquist), which states that if your sample rate is twice the highest frequency that your sound contains, you can actually sample the audio with no loss of quality. For example, the highest frequency we can hear is about 20Khz (for a newborn baby), and about 10 – 16Khz for adults. This means that if a sound is sampled at 40Khz, no one will be able to tell the difference between the real sound and the sampled sound. For this reason, compact discs contain sound sampled at just over 40Khz. In practical terms, you can define your maximum sampling rate (which equates to a perfect digital copy) by the type of sound you are trying to capture. A violin sound contains harmonics that extend beyond the audible range and so would have to be captured with a sampling rate of 40Khz. Normal speech tends not to go much beyond 10Khz so you could sample it with a rate of 20Khz. Finally, a telephone only records sounds up to approximately 2.5 KHz, so you could reproduce vocals at that quality with a sampling rate of just 5Khz.

Many beginners in sampling tend to assume that if, for example, you're sampling a guitar string at 500Hz, then the sample rate should be 1000Hz (1KHz) to reproduce it correctly, but this isn't true. The guitar string has a main frequency (or fundamental frequency) of 500Hz, but has many harmonics superimposed upon it. These may extend for quite a distance up the frequency scale, and it is the harmonics that define the difference between a guitar sound at 500Hz, and a trombone playing the same frequency. To get a good musical sample you must therefore use a high sampling rate if you want to get the detailed ambience of the sound that the harmonics will create.

When sampling sound for the Internet, you can get away with quite a lot by making your sounds deep and bassy. Drum and bass beats tend to sample very well at low sampling rates so can be used to overcome the bandwidth limitations you'll inevitably face on the Internet.

Defining the quantization levels

As we've seen, the samples at each interval are converted to a level. The number of available levels depends upon the amount of information you're allowing for each sample, and the soundcard will store them as a binary number with a length of 8, 16, 24, or 32 bits.

For 8 bits you can have 256 different levels, which comes from 2^8, and for 16 bits you can have 65536 different levels (2^{16}), and so on. Note that increasing the number of levels from 8 to 16 bits only doubles the size of your sample, but increases the quality of your sound 256 times.

Because the samples are encoded into a binary number, which can only be a whole number, the sampling process can only choose between one level and the next. If your sound is actually between two levels, then there'll be a difference between the original sound and its sample. This error is called the **quantization error**, and will be heard as a background buzzing and popping. It's this distortion that makes speech sound tinny and mechanical on a telephone:

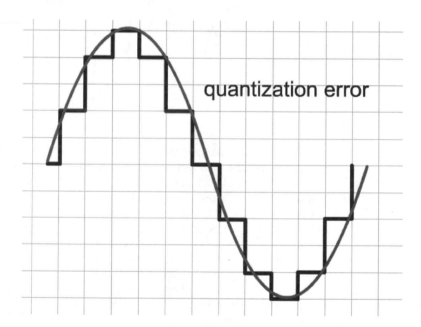

As you can see, the sampled signal frequently misses the actual wave, and if you select 8 bit sound as your export bit rate you'll hear it very loudly as it manifests itself as background interference. Remember, the export bit rate you choose will determine the background noise in your final sample. Samples that have high noise content anyway (such as explosions, doors slamming etc) can be sampled at very low bit rates because, although they'll sound different from the original, they won't sound any worse.

If you're particularly sneaky and allow for quantization noise in your compositions, you can actually mask out the noise in the higher pitched voices by hiding them behind louder and lower pitched drum and bass beats (which, as noted above, tend to sample well). MP3 compression actually uses this to intelligently hide quantization noise completely. When it detects a loud bass sound, it will look to see which higher pitched sounds are being drowned out, and will start to sample them much less frequently, using the extra free bandwidth to sample sounds the listener is more likely to hear.

As a general rule, you can optimize your bandwidth use by assigning high bit export rates to sounds that are more prominent, or loud, in your composition, and get away with lower rates for background sounds. However, take care when sampling quiet passages of sound: they'll result in the largest, and most noticeable, quantization error of all. You can combat this by setting an appropriate **record level**.

Record levels

The sound levels you sample at have a large effect on the sound quality. Unlike normal sound recording, the quantization error in digital sound is always constant because it's a function of the sampling process itself, rather than a function of the sound. As your sound gets lower in volume, you're using less of the available quantization levels, and the signal to noise level will get worse at a quicker rate than it would if you were recording using analog only. The best way to get round this is to always set up your record level so that you're using as many of the quantization levels as possible. This is achieved by making the sound input as loud as possible without distorting the recorded sound:

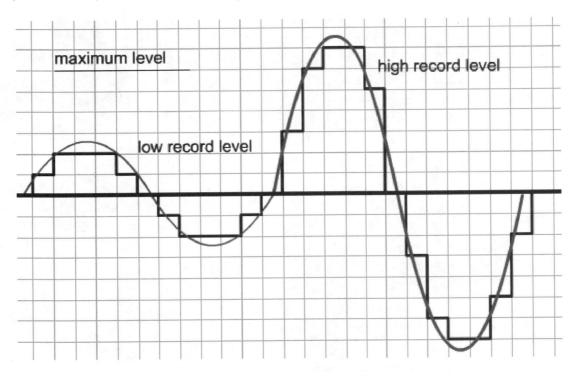

When you come to play the sound back in Flash, use the sound envelope to set the volume back to its original level within the composition. This way, you're drowning out the constant quantization noise with a louder sound, and may well be able to move down to a lower bit export rate, thus optimizing your sound for Internet use.

HTML and Flash

For those readers with a knowledge of HTML, or those who might be thinking of looking into it in the near future, here are a couple of examples of more advanced HTML and Flash integration.

Embedding your SWF file in an HTML page

In order to view your SWF file properly on the Internet, it's a good idea to embed the file into an HTML page. This gives you more control over the layout of the file, and also gives you the ability to use HTML on the Flash page as well. There are many ways you can embed your SWF file into an HTML page – these are just a couple of the easiest.

Embedding with Dreamweaver

Macromedia Dreamweaver is a 'what you see is what you get' web design application. Its user-friendly visual interface allows you to insert and format objects on the screen while Dreamweaver generates the necessary HTML. Using Dreamweaver, you can embed a Flash file simply by opening the **Window > Objects** panel and using the Common objects.

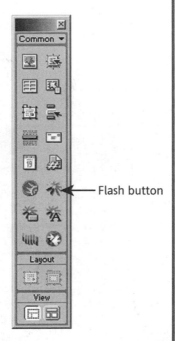

As you'll see in the screenshot here, this panel contains a Flash icon:

When you press this button, a dialog icon will appear asking you where your SWF file is. Browse to the file, click **OK**, and your SWF file is automatically embedded into the HTML page.

Flash button

Of course, the file might not be exactly the way you want it. Dreamweaver will set the SWF file to its original size and background color by default. If you want to change any of this, you can click on the SWF file in Dreamweaver and it will bring up a familiar looking Property inspector:

You can also open the Property inspector in Dreamweaver by selecting the **Window > Properties** menu option. Using the Property inspector, you can change, amongst other things, the size, file, background color, quality, alignment, vertical and horizontal spacing, and whether the movie will loop or not.

Manually embedding a Flash movie

Dreamweaver provides by far the quickest and easiest way to integrate your Flash movies into HTML files. However, if you don't have Dreamweaver, you can always embed the code into your HTML page manually.

This next screenshot shows the code for a HTML page with a movie embedded into it. The highlighted snippet is what you need to type in order to embed your movie into your HTML page. All you need to do is replace the width, height, and file name details used here (inside the quotation marks) with those from your own file. These are the areas in the highlighted snippet that are surrounded by a small box:

```
<html>
<head>
<title>Untitled Document</title>
<meta http-equiv="Content-Type" content="text/html; charset=iso-8859-1">
</head>

<body bgcolor="#FFFFFF" text="#000000">
<object classid="clsid:D27CDB6E-AE6D-11cf-96B8-444553540000"
    codebase="http://download.macromedia.com/pub/shockwave/cabs/flash/
    swflash.cab#version=5,0,0,0" width="32" height="32">
<param name=movie value="YOUR FILE NAME HERE.swf">
<param name=quality value=high>
<embed src="YOUR FILE NAME HERE.swf" quality=high
    pluginspage="http://www.macromedia.com/shockwave/download/
    index.cgi?P1_Prod_Version=ShockwaveFlash" type="application/
    x-shockwave-flash" width="32" height="32">
</embed>
</object>
</body>
</html>
```

There is not really that much information to change from the code given above, so embedding the code is quite easy.

If you don't know the width and height dimensions of your movie, just open the FLA in Flash and check the dimensions in the Property inspector. The width and height are important: if you don't enter the correct values, your Flash movie will stretch or shrink itself accordingly.

You can also use a percentage instead of pixel width, so instead of **width="32"**, you could use **width="100%"**. Overall, you have a lot of control over how your SWF file is displayed in your HTML page.

Titling and Meta tags for your Flash page

Titling your Flash page is exactly the same process that you would undertake to title an HTML page. Since your Flash file is 'embedded' into the HTML page, then technically you still have all the HTML code to work with. This also applies to Meta tags as well.

Both titles and Meta tags (if you haven't studied HTML), are inserted in between the <head> </head> tags in your HTML. For example, if you wanted to title your Flash page 'My Flash Portfolio On-Line', then you would type this in between your <head> </head> tags:

<title>My Flash Portfolio On-Line</title>

If you look back at the third line of the last screenshot, you'll see where <title> </title> tags fit within your HTML page. Whatever you place inside will then be displayed on the title bar of the browser window:

The two most popular Meta tags for search purposes are description and keywords. Between your <head> </head> tags in your HTML, you'd place the two Meta tags as listed here:

<meta name="description" content="The description of your web page would go here">
<meta name="keywords" content="Your keywords would go here, such as: Flash, web, design, etc">

All you need to do is change the **content="whatever..."** part. This will ensure that the pages on your web site are searched correctly.

Removing the white page border

Many times when you embed your SWF file to take up the full HTML page, there'll be a small margin between the edge of the SWF file and the browser window.

These are the default margins that browsers have, and you have to manually specify their removal. A quick way to do this is with Dreamweaver, which can fix the margins in both Internet Explorer and Netscape.

To do this in Dreamweaver, select the **Modify > Page Properties** menu option to open the **Page Properties** dialog window:

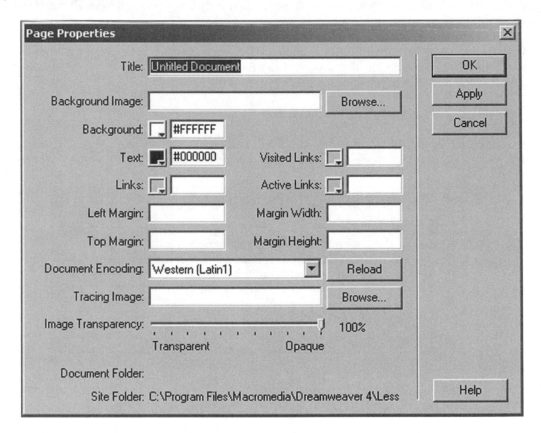

You can specify your page margins for Internet Explorer browsers in the **Left Margin** and **Top Margin** fields, and in the **Margin Width** and **Margin Height** fields for Netscape browsers.

If you set all of these fields to zero, it will force the SWF file to butt directly up next to the browser window, meaning that you'll no longer have that annoying gap around the edge of your movies.

Publishing your Flash site with Dreamweaver

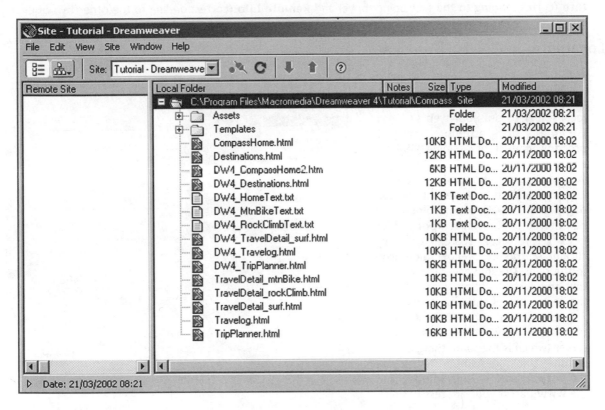

Macromedia Dreamweaver has probably the biggest following amongst web designers compared to other applications. As a budding Flash web professional, Dreamweaver will suit you because of its ease in handling Flash files.

The site management is performed via Dreamweaver's **Site Files** window, accessed using **Window > Site Files**.

To define a new site, you need the following information:

- The location of the site on your hard drive.

- Where the site will be on the server, and its Internet address.

- The file transfer method you'll be using.

Let's enter this in Dreamweaver.

From the Site Files window, select the **Site > New Site** menu option. The Dreamweaver **Site Definition** window will appear. To the left is a category window. You only need to provide information for the **Local Info** (corresponding to the first point above) and **Remote Info** (corresponding to the other two points).

Local info

The **Site Name** field is for Dreamweaver's (and your) benefit. On your hard drive, you must create a local folder to put your web site into. For your first attempt, this will probably consist of a single SWF file and the associated HTML file (which you should normally rename index.htm if it will be the default page). The full path of this folder must be entered in the **Local Root Folder** field, or you can search for it by clicking on the little yellow folder icon to the right. Dreamweaver can assume that this local location is actually on the server by substituting its path for whatever is in the **HTTP Address** requester. This is the address of your server (which is the same thing as your website URL). Remember to include the **http://** part of the address, and the **www** part if your address has one.

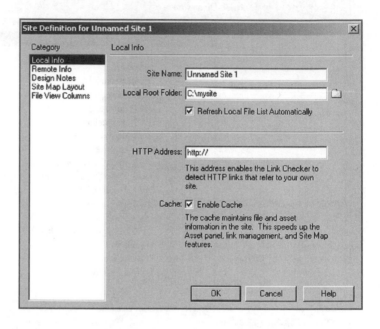

Remote Info

When you first select the **Remote Info** category, you'll see a single drop-down menu called **Access.** This will be set to **None.** If you change it to **FTP**, a set of new fields will appear as shown here:

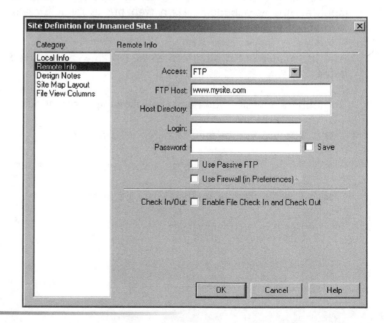

You need to enter the FTP of the server as a minimum, which will be the same as the **HTTP** Address value you just added in the last window, minus the **http://**.

If you haven't made your address point to an existing subfolder (unless you know different, chances are you haven't), you don't have to add anything in the **Host Directory** field. You can enter the **Login** and **Password** details if you wish to avoid having to enter them every time you connect.

And that's about all you need. In the **Site Files** window, click the **Connect** button. After you've connected to the server and assuming all the addresses are OK, you will be notified that you are connected. You can now simply drag your files across from the right pane (your local site) over to the left pane (the server). After Dreamweaver has sent the files over to the server via FTP, they should appear in the left-hand panel. Now open your browser and enter your chosen web address. And there you are; visitor number 1!

Some servers have a short delay before the uploaded file appears on the web, but most servers now present uploaded material immediately.

> *When you are uploading your files in Dreamweaver 4, a dialog will appear asking you if you want to upload dependent files. Dependent files are files such as your SWF, GIFs, or JPGs that are called in the HTML. Clicking* **Yes** *will ensure all dependent files are uploaded to the remote server. In previous versions of Dreamweaver, you can make sure dependent files are uploaded by selecting the Edit > Preference> FTP menu option and checking all 'dependent file' check boxes.*

FTP clients

In order to publish your finished Flash site you're going to need an FTP program. This can also help you to transfer files across the Internet and to download software and music. Here are some of the places you can get hold of an FTP program:

www.cuteftp.com
www.coffeecup.com
www.vicomsoft.com

Glossary

.FLA

The Flash authoring file. This is the file that you create initially in Flash and are able to edit while you're building your movie.

.SWF

The compressed, streamlined Flash movie that you put up on the web. Once exported, this is no longer in an editable format.

Actions

Commands that designers and programmers can use to give Flash movies added interactivity and functionality, taking them beyond the level of simple animation and linear playback into fully-developed web applications.

ActionScript

Flash's own programming/scripting language. Used to create more complex and interactive Flash movies, and can also be integrated with other server-side scripting languages to talk to servers and databases.

Alpha

This percentage value refers to the *transparency* of an object. An Alpha of 0% is fully transparent, 100% is opaque.

Anti-alias

Setting in Flash that smoothes edges on lines, text, and bitmaps.

Bandwidth profiler

The tool used to fine tune a Flash project before final publication. The Bandwidth Profiler indicates how much bandwidth a file is using and the download time required for the movie to load.

Break apart

Breaks an object down to its most basic level – *lines* and *fills*. Similar in effect to *ungrouping* an object.

Color mixer

The Color Mixer panel contains modifiers for the Paint Bucket and Ink Bottle tools. You can adjust the color and transparency of fills and lines by adjusting the RGB settings and the Alpha value, and also create your own custom gradients.

Color swatches

The panel where the colors, gradients, and your customized fills are stored and accessed.

Components

Pre-defined common interface components (such as radio buttons and scrollbars) that you can incorporate in your movies and customize. Designers can also create their own components and distribute them.

Controller

Located under the **Window > Toolbars** menu, the Controller gives you the ability to play, stop, rewind, and fast-forward through the frames of a Flash movie. The Controller will only play the frames of the given scene.

Device fonts

Device fonts are not embedded into a Flash movie: instead the Flash Player goes hunting on the local computer for the fonts to display. Because Flash is not embedding the font into the movie the file size is much smaller. Flash comes with three device fonts: _sans, _serif, and _typewriter. The '_' (underscore) before the font name in a selection box denotes a device font.

Dynamic text

Text that changes as the variable assigned to the particular text field changes during the movie.

Easing

Effect used during motion tweening to control the apparent acceleration or deceleration of an animated object.

Frames

The building blocks of your timeline. Objects placed on your stage with a particular frame selected appear in the played-back timeline at that particular moment.

Frame rate

The speed at which a Flash movie plays. The default frame rate is 12 fps (frames per second).

FreeHand

Macromedia's vector-based illustration program. This program is tightly integrated with Flash MX to allow easier image editing and importing.

Gradients

A graduated blending of two or more colors. Gradients can be *radial*, where the color change radiates from the center outwards, or *linear*, where the color transition stretches from one side to another.

Hand tool

The tool used to move the location of the entire stage. This tool is useful when working with multiple panels.

Ink Bottle tool

The tool used to change the color, thickness, and style of a line.

Input text field

Field used to enable the user to input text in a Flash front-end. Used in forms or interactive applications.

Instance

Version of a symbol on the stage. You can modify the color, size, and shape of a named instance without affecting the original symbol.

Kerning

Adjusting the space between individual text characters, moving them apart or closer together.

Layers

Used to separate objects and symbols in the timeline to give you more control and organization over your movie. Also used to arrange the stacking order of objects on the stage. Can also be used in conjunction with **layer folders** to organize material.

Library

Stores and organizes all the symbols you create and the files you import into Flash. You can create folders and organize symbols as you would in a regular file browser.

Masking

A *mask* layer selectively hides and reveals whatever is on any *masked* layers below it. The mask layer consists of a filled area that acts as a window through to the masked layers. Masks can be static or animated.

Motion guide

Guides an object's movement by defining the path that the object moves along during motion tweening. Motion guides have their own layer.

Motion tweening

Animating an object between point A and point B. Motion tweens can also rotate, scale, and change the colors of the objects during the animation.

Movie clip

A self-contained movie that's placed on the stage, but which runs independently of the main timeline. Has all the features as the main timeline does, and is a fully functional 'mini movie' in its own right. A movie clip is a symbol and is stored in your Library. It's essentially a 'movie within a movie' when being used. You can use ActionScript to control movie clips as you would any other object on the stage.

Movie Explorer

The Movie Explorer is a tool used to view all the elements, objects, and ActionScript of your Flash movie and their relative locations within it. This is a very useful tool for fault finding in large or complex movies containing many objects.

Onion skins

Displays multiple frames of an animation at the same time, showing what's on the stage in each individual frame, either in a solid or outline form.

Paint Bucket tool

The tool used to change an object's fill color.

Playhead

Rectangular red marker at the top of the timeline that signifies which frame you are currently working on.

Property inspector

Flash MX's focal resource panel for editing the attributes of selected objects on the stage. The Property inspector is context-sensitive, changing to reflect the tool or asset you are working with, giving you quick access to frequently used features.

QuickTime

A movie format established by Apple. You can export your Flash movie as a QuickTime movie file using the options in the **File > Publish Settings** window.

RGB settings

RGB stands for Red, Green, and Blue, and the range for each color value is from 0 to 255. If all three values are 0 the color created is black, and if all three are at their maximum of 255 the color created is white. By changing the RGB values in the Color Mixer, you can create your desired color.

Scenes

Individual sections of your movie, which play in the order you specify.

Shape tweening

Sometimes referred to as morphing. This takes an object (which must first be ungrouped) and changes (tweens) it into another object over a chosen timeframe.

Snapping

With snapping enabled, Flash will 'stick' an object to the grid at the object's centering point. If you grab an object at its center point, the crosshairs change to a hollow black circle called the snapping ring. The snapping ring snaps to the grid at any line but is snapped easiest at an intersection (where vertical and horizontal gridlines meet).

Soften fill edges

Used on fills to make the edges look slightly blurred to give a 'shadow' or 'blur' effect.

Stacking order

Objects in Flash, similarly to layers, function in a background/foreground relationship. Within an individual layer, Flash stacks objects based on the order in which they were created, with the oldest at the bottom.

Stage

The working area of your Flash movie. Whatever you place inside the stage will appear in your final exported movie.

Standalone projector

Refers to the ability to build a Flash project and compress it into a self-contained executable file, which can then be used on a machine that does not have the whole Flash program. Typically used to put files on CD-ROMs.

Static text

The inanimate text you place on the stage that does not change throughout the movie.

Streaming

Method used to enable the browser plug-in to start displaying the data before the entire file has been downloaded and prevent pauses in the playback of the Flash movie.

Symbols

Fundamental components of Flash movies. Objects that are converted into symbols get stored in the Library. There are three types of symbol: graphic, button, and movie clip. Symbols are used to keep file size low when using the same object more than once, as once downloaded they can be instantly re-used within the movie.

Timeline

The area above the stage showing all the frames and layers that you've created and their order. It allows you to organize the content and length of your movie.

Transform

This panel contains several modifiers, such as Rotate and Skew, that transform or manipulate the selected object.

Tweening

Flash term for animation. There are two kinds of tweens in Flash: motion and shape. See separate entries for each.

Vectors vs. rasters

Flash uses vector graphics because the size of the images can be changed (they can be scaled) without the quality deteriorating. Everything remains in proportion, irrespective of the resolution at which the viewer is seeing the vector animation. Rasters, on the other hand, only look good at the image size they were originally created at. If they are made larger, the individual pixels become visible giving a rough line, and when made smaller the image begins to look fuzzy.

Index

The index is arranged hierarchically, in alphabetical order, with symbols preceding the letter A. Many second-level entries also occur as first-level entries. This is to ensure that users will find the information they require however they choose to search for it.

Foundation Action Script for Macromedia Flash MX

One of the biggest compliments paid to a friends of ED book last year was Amazon.com's judgment that "Foundation Actionscript is perhaps one of the finest introductory programming books ever written".

With the release of Flash MX, scripting in Flash has moved from being a desirable asset to an essential skill in the world of web design. It's also become a whole lot more difficult, and the major advances with Flash MX are code based. If you're scared of the idea of code, but even more scared of missing out, this is the book for you.

This is no simple re-write - with the help of friends of ED Flash guru Sham Bhangal, Foundation ActionScript has been re-written from beginning to end, with the addition of substantial new material to reflect the major changes bought about with Flash MX.

If you've never coded in Flash, you're going to want to very soon. This book will make that desire reality, with fully worked examples and a chapter-by-chapter case study that turns into a fully fledged top ActionScript site by the end of the book.

Flash MX Studio

The principle behind this book is to advance your skills in Macromedia Flash MX and hone them for a real-world scenario. How does your work stand up in the freshly competitive environment of the Flash MX marketplace? How can you streamline your ideas to give them greater usability? Where can you take your ideas next?

This book examines all the avenues open to professional or aspiring professional Flash MX designers. It gives guidance on building whole new structures for Dynamic Content, video, animation, and other media benefiting from the latest Macromedia Flash version.

home · interviews · code

news · designer ²designer · books

videos · freshfroot · contact

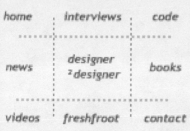

friendsof

DESIGNER TO DESIGNER™

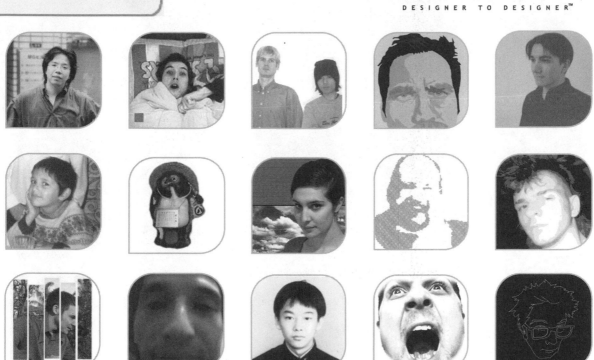

You've read the book, now enter the community.

friendsofed.com is the online heart of the designer to designer neighbourhood.

As you'd expect the site offers the latest news and support for all our current and forthcoming titles – but it doesn't stop there.

For fresh exclusive interviews and videos every month with our authors – the new and future masters like Josh Davis, Yugo Nakamura, James Paterson and many other friends of ED – enter the world of D2D.

Stuck with a design problem? Need technical assistance? Our support doesn't end on the last page of the book. Just post your query on our message board and one of our moderators or authors will make sure you get the answers you need – fast.

Welcome to friendsofed.com. This place is the place of friends of ED – designer to designer. Practical deep fast content delivered by working web designers.

Straight to your head.

www.friendsofed.com

Notes

Notes

DESIGNER TO DESIGNER™

friends of ED writes books for you. Any suggestions, or ideas about how you want information given in your ideal book will be studied by our team.

Your comments are valued by friends of ED.

For technical support please contact support@friendsofed.com.

Freephone in USA: 800.873.9769
              Fax: 312.893.8001

UK contact
              Tel: 0121.258.8858
              Fax: 0121.258.8868

Registration Code: | 01018Q10K2BV3T02 |

Foundation Flash MX – Registration Card

Name ....

Address ....

City ....State/Region ....

Country ....Postcode/Zip ....

E-mail ....

Profession: design student ☐ freelance designer ☐
             part of an agency ☐ inhouse designer ☐
             other (please specify) ....

Age: Under 20 ☐ 20-25 ☐ 25-30 ☐ 30-40 ☐ over 40 ☐

Do you use: mac ☐ pc ☐ both ☐

How did you hear about this book?......................................

Book review (name)..

Advertisement (name) ....

Recommendation ....

Catalog ....

Other ....

Where did you buy this book? ....

Bookstore (name) ....City................................

Computer Store (name)..

Mail Order...

Other...

How did you rate the overall content of this book?
   Excellent ☐   Good ☐
   Average ☐   Poor ☐

What applications/technologies do you intend to learn in the near future?...
....

What did you find most useful about this book? ....
....

What did you find the least useful about this book? ....
....

Please add any additional comments ....
....

What other subjects will you buy a computer book on soon?
....
....

What is the best computer book you have used this year?
....
....

Note: This information will only be used to keep you updated about new friends of ED titles and will not be used for any other purpose or passed to any other third party.

friendsof

DESIGNER TO DESIGNER™

NB. If you post the bounce back card below in the UK, please send it to:

friends of ED Ltd.,
30 Lincoln Road,
Olton,
Birmingham.
B27 6PA

BUSINESS REPLY MAIL

FIRST CLASS   PERMIT #64   CHICAGO, IL

POSTAGE WILL BE PAID BY ADDRESSEE

friends of ED,
29 S. La Salle St.
Suite 520
Chicago Il 60603–USA